St. Petersburg
& PINELLAS COUNTY, FLORIDA

THE GULF COAST JEWEL ON TAMPA BAY

Welcome!
to St. Petersburg & Pinellas County

Start at Oldsmar in the north and travel clockwise along the coast to Tarpon Springs and you'll span 71 miles and count 24 municipalities – all located in the County of pines, or "Pinellas" as it evolved from its Spanish name. This circumnavigation takes place on two of the nation's grandest bodies of water – Tampa Bay and the Gulf of Mexico. When the Bay and the Gulf are mixed with more than 35 miles of white sand beaches and 587 miles of coastline, the formula equals one of Earth's most enticing places to live.

I knew growing up on this peninsula that it was special. In those days, St. Petersburg's Evening Independent gave away the newspaper each 24 hour period when the sun did not shine. It was also a time of the great depression and war: a time when residents enjoyed life before air conditioning and mosquito control. Florida was less than three million people and cattle ranged a countryside without fences. Winter visitors were largely Eastern and Midwestern folk escaping harsh winters. In many ways, those were the halcyon days of the late thirties and forties.

As air conditioning and mosquito control became commonplace and GI's returned from World War II to raise a family, the county became younger demographically and a haven for new businesses.

"Quality of life" is frequently used in such a nebulous context that it fails in its meaning. To us "Pinellans" though, it means a place that God has prospered naturally: where 900,000 people make their home and enjoy unprecedented access to solid jobs, fine hospitals, public and private school systems.

A place where recreational facilities abound, where world class art and music prosper and where business and government have partnered to foster excellence. Pinellas is a place where a doctorate can be achieved and where some of the world's leading research is being done in health and marine sciences.

So, we start this millennium year with a pictorial tribute to Ponfilo de Navarez's discovery. Our path is clear – we must continue to foster responsible growth and assure that our quality of life is not diminished by disregard for our natural beauty.

To residents and visitors alike, I hope you will continue to share in this marvelous environment which we call St. Petersburg and Pinellas County.

Sincerely, Bob Ulrich

BOB ULRICH, a native of St. Petersburg and Pinellas County, brings a lifelong perspective to this introduction highlighted by his two terms of distinguished service as Mayor of St. Petersburg from 1987 to 1991.

Sandwiched between his undergraduate degree from Duke University and his law degree from Stetson University College of Law, Bob served with distinction as a U.S. Air Force pilot from 1956 to 1959.

Bob Ulrich is one of St. Petersburg's most respected civic leaders and he has unselfishly blended his legal practice with major commitments to the long term growth and development of St. Petersburg, Pinellas County and Tampa Bay.

Bob and his wife Barbara Ann have four grown children and he is also a lifelong member of First United Methodist Church.

This spectacular twilight view of St. Petersburg's beautiful downtown waterfront, as viewed from the stately Renaissance Vinoy Resort, showcases the bay, St Petersburg's well-known pier, marina, parks and downtown. St Petersburg's downtown waterfront ranks as one of the most beautiful in all of America and the City's marina is the largest municipally-owned marina in Florida.

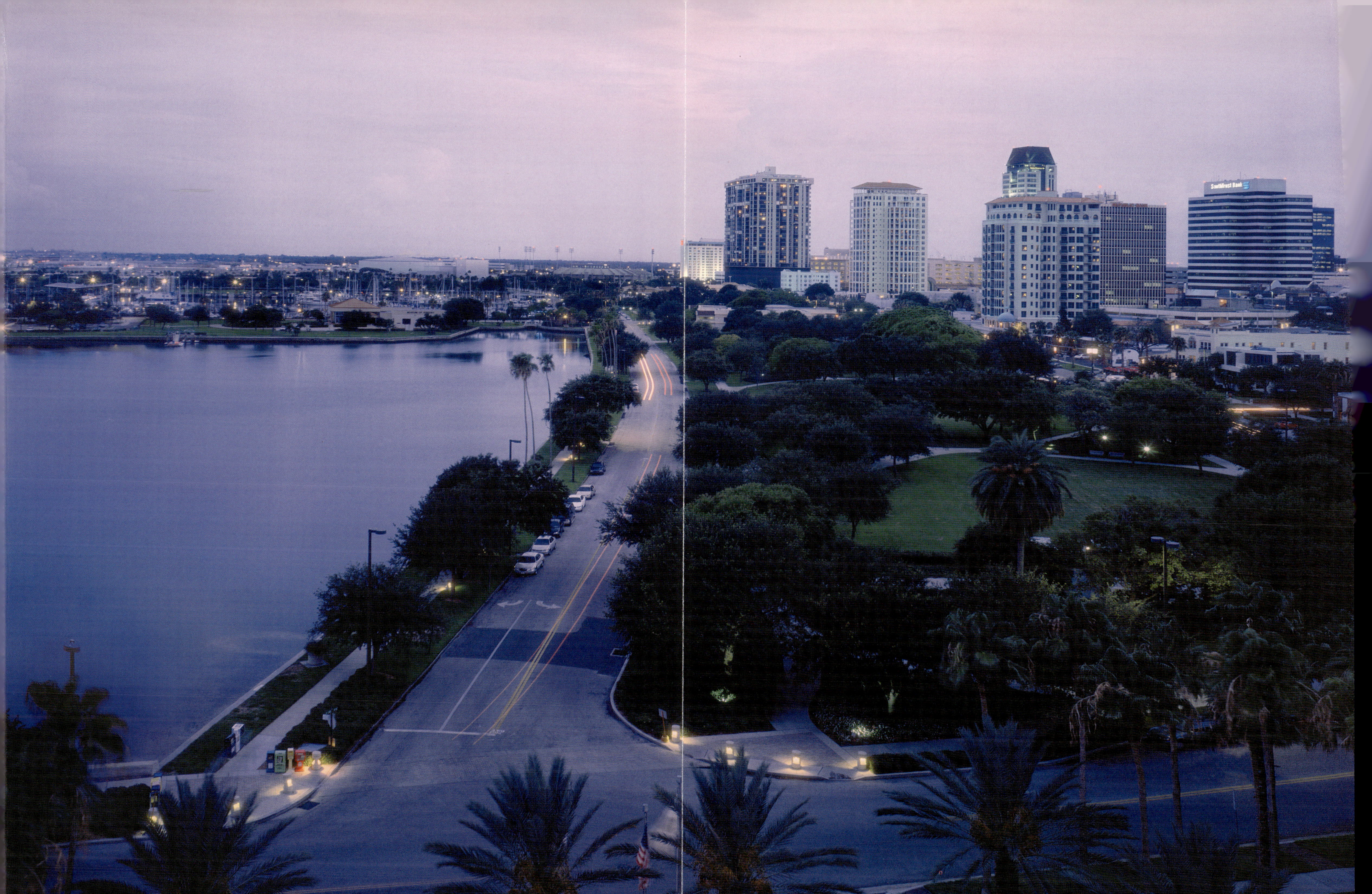
SouthTrust Bank

Together in the Sun, an oil painting by Christopher M. Still commissioned by the City of St. Petersburg for the City Council Chambers.

St Petersburg & Pinellas County

MAP KEY

MAJOR ATTRACTIONS

1. Bayfront Center - Times Bayfront Arena & Mahaffey Theater
2. Baywalk
- T Busch Gardens - Tampa Bay
3. Clearwater Marine Aquarium
4. Derby Lane - St. Petersburg Kennel Club
5. Dunedin Fine Arts Center
- T Florida Aquarium - Tampa
6. Florida International Museum
7. Great Explorations
8. Pinewood Cultural Park
9. Florida Holocaust Museum
- T Lowry Park Zoo - Tampa
10. Museum of Fine Arts
- T Museum of Science & Industry - Tampa
11. Pier 60/Pier Park - Clearwater
- T Raymond James Stadium - Tampa
12. Ruth Eckerd Hall - Clearwater
13. Salvador Dali Museum
14. Sponge Docks - Tarpon Springs
15. St. Petersburg Museum of History
16. Suncoast Seabird Sanctuary
17. Sunken Gardens
18. Sunshine Skyway Bridge
- T Tampa Bay Performing Arts Center
19. The Historic Coliseum
20. The Pier
21. Tropicana Field

PARKS

22. Anderson Park
23. Boca Ciega Park
24. Boyd Hill Nature Trail
25. Brooker Creek Preserve
26. Caladesi Island State Park
27. Fort DeSoto Park
28. Fred Howard Park
29. Honeymoon Island State Park
30. John Chestnut Sr. Park
31. John Taylor Park
32. Lake Seminole Park
33. Moccasin Lake Nature Park
34. Phillipe Park
35. Pinellas Trail
36. Sand Key Park
37. Sawgrass Lake Park
38. Walsingham Park
39. War Veterans Memorial Park
40. Weedon Island Preserve

T   Refers to Tampa Location

THE GULF COAST JEWEL ON TAMPA BAY

DISTANCE FROM ST. PETERSBURG TO OTHER MAJOR FLORIDA CITIES

Clearwater	21 miles
Ft. Lauderdale	246 miles
Fort Myers	110 miles
Gainesville	157 miles
Jacksonville	247 miles
Miami	263 miles
Naples	151 miles
Ocala	119 miles
Orlando	108 miles
Pensacola	498 miles
Sarasota	38 miles
St. Augustine	209 miles
Tallahassee	301 miles
Tampa	24 miles
W. Palm Beach	200 miles

Source: American Auto Club South

COURTESY OF THE TAMPA BAY PARTNERSHIP

Publisher – St. Petersburg Area Chamber of Commerce™
Publication Associate – Pinellas County Economic Development Department and the City of St. Petersburg
Editor-In-Chief – Russ Sloan
Writer/Editor, Narrative – Ruth M. Bross
Writer/Editor, Business – E.L. Harris
Design Director & Production – Judy Fallon
Creative Consultant, Illustrator – June Allard Berté
Photo Editor/Chief Photographer – Herb Snitzer
Corporate & Institutional Sales – Mike Littmann
Special Assignment Photographer – Ty Heston
Proof Readers – Peggy Sloan, Ruth M. Bross, E.L. Harris, Kathy Oathout and Anita Treiser
Printed by: RR Donnelly & Sons Company

©2000 by St. Petersburg Area Chamber of Commerce™
All Rights Reserved
Published in 2000
Printed in the USA
First Edition

Library of Congress Cataloging-in-Publication Data
Authors – Ruth M. Bross, E.L. Harris

References - pg. 317
Includes Index
St. Petersburg and Pinellas County - History
St. Petersburg and Pinellas County - Description
St. Petersburg and Pinellas County - Quality of Life

I. Title - St. Petersburg and Pinellas County: The Gulf Coast Jewel on Tampa Bay

ISBN 0-9659469-6-7 (Hard Cover)
ISBN 0-9659469-3-2 (Soft Cover)

St. P

THE GULF COAST JE

etersburg

WEL ON TAMPA BAY

TY HESTON

Contents

Chapter 1
A Sense of History and Community   1
A city built on vision, sunshine and enviable lifestyle.

Chapter 2
Neighborhoods and Religious Heritage   23
Diversified neighborhoods & abundant religous choices.

Chapter 3
Downtown, Waterfront, Museums & the Arts   47
St. Petersburg's renowned waterfront & cultural center.

Chapter 4
Health Care and Education   87
Comprehensive medical care and schools of excellence.

Chapter 5
Tampa Bay Sports & Recreation   119
A wealth of sporting activities for all ages & seasons.

Chapter 6
Manufacturing and Technology   145
The anchor of Florida's high-tech corridor.

Chapter 7
Business and Service Industries   167
Thriving entrepreneurship.

Chapter 8
Finance and Professions   189
A major financial & professional base.

Chapter 9
Networks and Area Shopping   213
Communications, transportation, government & retail.

Chapter 10
Spectacular Beaches and Resorts   237
Thirty-five miles of acclaimed beaches, beach communities and resorts.

Chapter 11
Around Pinellas County   261
Other distinctive cities and towns in Pinellas County.

Chapter 12
Tampa Bay Treasures   281
Leading attractions & major entities sharing Tampa Bay.

Chapter 13
Vistas of Tomorrow   301
Striving for unequalled excellence.

Index   313
Acknowledgements   316
References   317
Corporate and Institutional Patron Index   318

Fast Facts: St. Petersburg and Pinellas County

TY HESTON

POPULATION
St. Petersburg – 251,000 (Est. 2000)
Founded 1858 Incorporated 1892

Pinellas County – 900,000 (Est. 2000)
Established 1912

LAND AREA
St. Petersburg – 59.25 sq. mi.
Pinellas County – 280 sq. mi.

MEDIAN AGE
St. Petersburg – 38.6
Pinellas County – 44.4

PER CAPITA INCOME
St. Petersburg – $27,311

AVERAGE HOUSEHOLD
2.18 persons

AVERAGE HOUSE COST
$90,000 to $110,000

TOTAL RETAIL SALES
12.15 billion (Est. 2000)

EMPLOYMENT COMPOSITION
Agriculture	0.8%
Construction	4.9%
Manufacturing	11.3%
Transportation & Communication	3.4%
Wholesale	5.1%
Retail	19.4%
Finance & Insurance	7.1%
Service	37.6%
Unassigned Industry	0.4%
Government	10%

PINELLAS COUNTY SEAT
Clearwater

24 INCORPORATED CITIES
(by population)
- St. Petersburg
- Clearwater
- Largo
- Pinellas Park
- Dunedin
- Tarpon Springs
- Safety Harbor
- Gulfport
- St. Pete Beach
- Seminole
- Oldsmar
- Treasure Island
- South Pasadena
- Madeira Beach
- Kenneth City
- Belleair
- Indian Rocks Beach
- Redington Shores
- Belleair Bluffs
- Belleair Shore
- Belleair Beach
- Redington Beach
- Indian Shores
- North Redington Beach

- St. Petersburg and Pinellas County lie on the western edge of the Tampa Bay Area with the Gulf of Mexico bordering the western side of the county and Tampa Bay bordering the eastern side.

- St. Petersburg has the largest city marina in Florida.

- St. Petersburg has 234 miles of waterfront property.

- St. Petersburg and Pinellas County anchor central Florida's high-tech corridor.

- The St. Petersburg area is among the nation's top six employment centers of high-tech professionals.

- St. Petersburg and Pinellas County rank number two in the number of manufacturing employees in Florida.

- St. Petersburg has a state-designed Enterprise Zone where businesses receive state corporate income tax, sales tax and property tax credit.

- St. Petersburg's business market has attracted 20 corporate relocations and 9,000 jobs since 1995. The downtown has attracted a public/private investment over $900-million since 1982.

- St. Petersburg shares one of Florida's top public universities; has world-renowned medical facilities and a world class marine science research complex.

- St. Petersburg has the largest reclaimed water system in the U.S.

- The City of St. Petersburg and Takamatsu, Japan have been "Sister Cities" since 1961 and participate in cultural exchange programs.

Tampa Bay Area

TAMPA BAY AREA

- Encompasses Hernando, Hillsborough, Manatee, Pasco, Pinellas, Polk and Sarasota Counties

- With 3.3 million residents, the Tampa Bay area ranks number one in population in Florida, and number two in the Southeast.

- More than one-third of the people moving into the Tampa Bay area each year are 25 to 34 years old.

- As Florida's wealthiest market, Tampa Bay is number one in effective buying income and number one in retail sales. It is the second wealthiest market, following Atlanta, in the Southeast.

- According to *Southern Business and Development Magazine,* the Tampa Bay area ranks first among southern MSA's for expansion and relocation.

- In a survey of 400 American CEO's, the Tampa Bay area ranked in the top five as a business location.

- The Tampa Bay area leads Florida in the number of businesses, manufacturing employment, new business formations, effective buying power, retail sales and bank deposits.

- According to the Census Bureau, the average 21.8-minute commute here is among the lowest of any metropolitan area in the United States.

- Housing is very affordable in Tampa Bay. In 1998, the median price of an existing home in Hillsborough County was $104,477 in Pinellas County $107,772 and in Pasco County, north of Pinellas, just $74,144.

- Tampa Bay rings up the highest food sales in Florida.

- With more than 100,000 registered pleasure boats, Tampa Bay is a nautical haven.

- Cost of living is 5% below national average.

- Home to 19 colleges and universities

- University of South Florida - one of 20 largest universities in the United States

- State leader for providing and acquiring medical patents

- Over 95 million sq. ft. of office, industrial and warehouse space

- Ports and airports export over $2 billion and import $1 billion

GOOD NEWS ABOUT TAMPA BAY

- #1 in job growth of all major metro areas – U.S. Labor Statistics

- #1 in South for Job Announcements – *Southern Business & Development*

- 4th Best US Metro Area in which to live – *Places Related Almanac*

- "Florida's Only Five Star Quality of Life" – *Expansion Management Magazine*

- "7th Best Airport in The World" – *Conde Nast Traveler*

- "#8 Best Places for Small Business" – *Entrepreneur Magazine*

- "#10 Market for Projected Job Growth" – *Newsweek Magazine*

- "A Top 10 City for Small Business" – *Dun & Bradstreet*

- "15th in the Nation for Business & Careers" – *Forbes Magazine*

WEATHER

Month	Temperature Avg. Max.	Avg. Min.	Mean	Rainfall Avg. In.	Rain Days
January	70.0	49.5	59.8	2.21	6.4
February	71.0	50.4	60.8	2.79	6.8
March	76.2	56.1	66.2	3.03	6.8
April	81.9	61.1	71.6	2.00	4.6
May	87.1	67.2	77.1	3.04	6.3
June	89.5	72.3	80.9	6.82	11.7
July	90.0	74.2	82.2	7.69	15.8
August	90.3	74.2	82.2	7.95	16.7
September	88.9	72.8	80.9	6.54	12.9
October	83.7	65.1	74.5	2.62	6.8
November	76.9	56.4	66.7	1.65	5.5
December	71.6	50.9	61.3	2.04	6.2

TAMPA BAY MARKET DATA

Population:	3.3 million
Labor Force	1.7 million
Unemployment Rate:	2.96%
Per Capita Income:	$27,783
Number of Businesses:	87,871
Gross Regional Product	$76 billion
Job Growth Rate vs U.S. of 2.2%	4.8%
Number of Jobs Created Every Day:	186
New Residents Annually:	33,000

HERB SNITZER

The Sunshine State never looked better
than it does in St. Petersburg…

Centrally located on the west coast of the Florida peninsula, St. Petersburg has so many things going for it that living here has become the first and only choice of nearly a quarter-million people.

Population changes have always led to growth in our real estate and construction industries. Now the profiles of younger, more affluent and better-educated new residents have dictated an upscale trend in products and housing. There are new jobs for this new generation of high-tech workers, and active redevelopment of existing properties for new business relocating to Pinellas County. Indeed it is population growth that has reconfigured even the boundaries used for statistical studies here.

St. Petersburg is a decisive part of a larger area known throughout the world as Tampa Bay. Demographically, our metropolitan statistical area (MSA) includes seven separate counties for a total population of 3.3-million, and these regions now blend together to form the west central portion of Florida. The identifying phrase "Tampa Bay" literally comes from the name of a large body of water that once divided and now unites the two major components of the MSA – the city of Tampa in Hillsborough County, representing a county-wide population of over 900-thousand and the city of St. Petersburg in Pinellas, comprising another nearly 900-thousand countywide.

Of these two dynamic cities, St. Petersburg enjoys the closest proximity to the famous Florida beaches – a string of barrier islands fully developed with resorts, hotels, motels, condominiums and single family residences. Even before there were adequate bridges and causeways to facilitate easy travel between, to and from the main peninsula, people chose

St. Petersburg as their vacation destination for the year-round sunshine, sand and warm gentle waters of the Gulf of Mexico. Throughout our history those natural elements have been the key ingredients for one of our major industries – tourism.

Tourism has steadily helped fuel our economy (at the turn of this century that meant $2-million a day in Florida) and provided a variety of employment opportunities in the traditional job market. What's more, Florida visitors, especially here in Pinellas County, have traditionally formed strong ties with their preferred destination; a pattern that begins with a few days vacation, then a week or two, followed by one month, a three-to six-month stay and, ultimately a permanent address.

Yesterday they returned to build retirement communities and shopping malls and open manufacturing facilities for the defense and aerospace industry. Today they help transform downtowns with deluxe housing and exclusive retail centers and launch or expand businesses in electronics, medical manufacturing and information technology, including e-commerce – industries in which decision makers can select a place to relocate primarily because it has the lifestyle they want for their employees and themselves!

A contributing factor of St. Petersburg and Pinellas County's continuing success story is offering a quality of life that is second to none. As in the decades of our past, the ingredients that attract our 4.5-million visitors each year are the same factors tugging at newcomers to put down roots.

Wonderful weather and miles of sandy beaches, a relatively low cost of living, agreeable taxes and progressive employment opportunities draw people to our area from around the nation and the world. Add to these amenities an impressive public and private school system, a variety of quality colleges and universities, top-notch hospitals and outstanding recreational facilities, and it is easy to see why we are so attractive.

"St. Petersburg was conceived... with a purpose.

It was envisioned, from its very beginning,
to become one of the nation's great cities –
unrivaled in climate, unsurpassed in healthful living,
unequaled in natural splendor.
With the uprooting of the first palmetto bush
the designers and their followers dreamed and
planned a paradise stretching across the peninsula,
bathed on the east by Tampa Bay, on the west by
Boca Ciega Bay and the Gulf of Mexico.
St. Petersburg wasn't founded, it was created..."

Del Marth, *St. Petersburg: Once Upon A Time* 1976

Chapter 1
History & Community

HERB SNITZER

MAP OF THE TOWN OF St. Petersburg FLORIDA

1888

G. A. Miller, Draughtsman
A. L. Hunt, Chief Engineer

BEING THE E½ and the E½ of the NW¼ and the N½ of SW¼ and SW¼ of the SW¼ of Sec. 19 T. 31 S. R. 17 E. and E½ of SE¼ and a strip 114 ft. wide of the W½ of SE¼ of Sec. 24 T. 31 S. R. 16 E.

Filed Aug. 1st 1888
Recorded April 16th 1889

Reservoir — All Riparian Rights to this Water are reserved from the Public

Williams Grove

Tampa Bay's Bountiful Waters

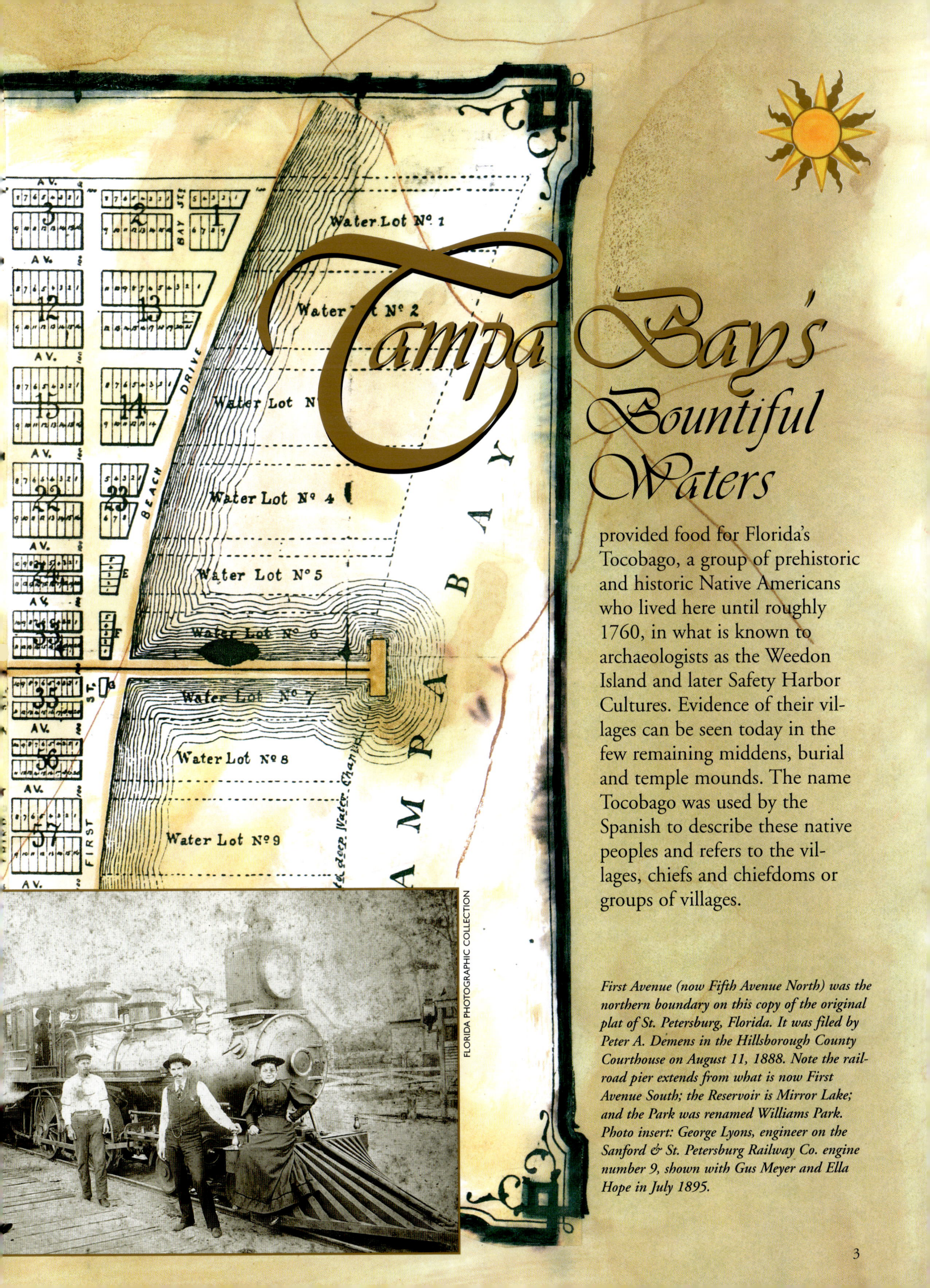

provided food for Florida's Tocobago, a group of prehistoric and historic Native Americans who lived here until roughly 1760, in what is known to archaeologists as the Weedon Island and later Safety Harbor Cultures. Evidence of their villages can be seen today in the few remaining middens, burial and temple mounds. The name Tocobago was used by the Spanish to describe these native peoples and refers to the villages, chiefs and chiefdoms or groups of villages.

First Avenue (now Fifth Avenue North) was the northern boundary on this copy of the original plat of St. Petersburg, Florida. It was filed by Peter A. Demens in the Hillsborough County Courthouse on August 11, 1888. Note the railroad pier extends from what is now First Avenue South; the Reservoir is Mirror Lake; and the Park was renamed Williams Park. Photo insert: George Lyons, engineer on the Sanford & St. Petersburg Railway Co. engine number 9, shown with Gus Meyer and Ella Hope in July 1895.

History & Community

St. Petersburg's downtown waterfront has historically been a source of pride for the city. In 1903, the year the city got its first charter, newspaper editor W. L. Straub looked at the framework of a town of only 2,200 people and drew what he expected to happen with waterfront development and city planning. With uncanny vision, he put on canvas his idea of an attractive and active downtown waterfront. F.A. Davis, owner of the power company, took the painting and another work by Straub and hung them in the Pennsylvania Railroad Station in Philadelphia to attract northerners. Later, it was displayed at the St. Petersburg Area Chamber of Commerce and eventually came back to the Times.

It was the Spanish who arrived and recorded their findings in the 1500's. Juan Ponce de Leon, legend has it, came to the land while sailing around Florida in search of a fountain of youth in 1521. He was followed by the ruthless Panfilo de Narvaez in 1528 who left a path of destruction before leaving the area on his quest for gold. Next came Hernando DeSoto in 1539 who established a base camp for over 800 Conquistadors on the land once known only to the Tocobaga.

In 1757, a Spanish naval officer named Jose Jimenez was placed in charge of an expedition to survey Tampa Bay for the King of Spain. He called the peninsula "Punta del Pinal" meaning "point of pines," giving the county the beginnings of its permanent name – Pinellas. His expedition resulted in one of the first charted maps of the area.

In 1765, two years after Florida was ceded to Britain by Spain, an English chart maker further detailed the land. During the 18th century pirates roamed the coastline, including the infamous Captain Gomez, and for centuries, Spanish and Cuban fishermen came to fill their water kegs at a fresh water spring at the mouth of the Anclote River in northern Pinellas. Eventually others followed, exploring the area by entering the harbors of Tampa Bay, as had those before them.

Settlements began in earnest in the mid-1800's after the Second Seminole War, spurred by an act of Congress that opened South Florida to private ownership through homesteading. Northern immigrants came in search of land arriving by horse and oxcart or by schooners and sloops to the seaports and trading centers of the region. Some came in search of a healthier climate.

In Dunedin, one of Pinellas County's 24 incorporated cities and towns, they came from Scotland and in Tarpon Springs, our most northern city, they arrived from Greece. And as hundreds more new settlers came, each brought a special cultural heritage to the region, which lives on today.

History & Community

Early photo portrait of Peter Demens, who brought his Orange Belt Railroad to the waterfront on land purchased from General John C. Williams. St. Petersburg was named for the Russian city of Demens place of birth, while the city's first hotel (shown on this 1906 postcard) was named for Williams' hometown of Detroit, Michigan.

The first known settler in Pinellas County that can be documented, was Antonio Maximo who, in 1843 secured a land grant from the United States Government for services he had performed during the Seminole War. He established a "fish rancho" at the lower end of the Pinellas Peninsula, now called Maximo Point. Three years later William Bunce joined him and the two men did a good business supplying fish to a Cuban market until their property was destroyed in the hurricane of 1848.

Other pioneers followed. They fenced in a few acres, mostly raised farm produce and cattle, and a few started small citrus groves. In the Pinellas peninsula's Safety Harbor area, Dr. Odet Phillipe, a French surgeon, grew the first citrus on his plantation.

The first black settlers in what is now St. Petersburg were John Donaldson, a former slave, and Anna Germain, a housekeeper, who met and married while employed by homesteader Louis Bell Jr. The Donaldson's purchased 40 acres, in 1871, on what is now Tangerine Avenue South in St. Petersburg. They became successful farmers at a time when Florida rarely allowed minorities to acquire their own land, and years before other black families settled here.

Documents from 1873 show Dr. James Hackney bought 600 acres from the State of Florida at twenty-five cents an acre. He built a home and cleared land for farming. Then in 1875 General John C. Williams of Detroit, Michigan, visited the peninsula. He lost no time in acquiring property and purchased 1,600 acres from the State at an average of one dollar an acre. He returned north for his family and in 1879 brought them by train to Gainesville then on a 250-mile journey by covered wagon to St. Petersburg. It was Williams who conceived the idea of making a town here, complete with rail facilities.

Hamilton Disston inaugurated Florida's first great real estate promotion after buying four million acres of land from the State in 1881. Disston also built the first hotel and stores in the area. Meanwhile, Peter A. Demens (Pyotr Alexievich Dementyev), who came to Florida from Tver, Russia, had built a narrow-gauge railroad from Lake Monroe to Lake Apopka, and it became the headquarters for the Orange Belt railroad. Demens wanted to extend his railroad to the Gulf, particularly to the land now owned by Disston.

While accounts vary in detail, Demens was unable to secure the property. Instead an arrangement was made with General Williams for 500 acres. Williams, a wealthy merchant, agreed to donate land to the Orange Belt providing the railroad would complete the line to his property and erect a

St. Petersburg's first black family was that of John Donaldson.

History & Community

Agricultural land eventually gave way to the demands for real estate development in St. Petersburg. The picnicers were probably visitors who arrived by steamboat from Tampa, around 1906

wharf into Tampa Bay at the line's end. Demens saw a future in the arrangement. In one of his many exhortations to financial brokers in the north, he wrote: "The southern terminus of the road is the most important feature of the whole business... we have a chance to build a city of international importance."

On June 8, 1888, the rail line reached its terminus, a deep-water port where steamers and sailing vessels could land – St. Petersburg, named after the capitol city of Russia, the homeland of the railroad's organizer, Peter Demens.

For countless communities, the route of a railroad made the difference between development and decline. In Florida, the arrival of the Orange Belt railroad, running southwest from Sanford, was inevitably followed by growth for the towns it connected – Tarpon Springs, Sutherland (Palm Harbor), Ozona, Dunedin, Clearwater, Largo and now St. Petersburg.

Following the birth of the downtown section, General Williams placed some of his property on the market and the Orange Belt Investment Company also opened for business. Both the General and the investment company offered lots for sale on liberal terms, allowing the purchaser nine years in which to pay for them.

The Federal census of 1890 showed that St. Petersburg had 273 inhabitants, most of whom lived around Ninth Street. St. Petersburg's first important growth started as a summer resort. The railroads ran low-rate excursions from other parts of the state and many people came to spend their summer vacations here because it was much cooler.

The big freeze of 1894-95 proved a tragedy to thousands of people in Florida, but resulted in good for St. Petersburg where many groves survived the low temperatures. Soon a number of growers from other parts of the state who had lost citrus came here to make

St. Petersburg women rallied for such town improvements as wooden sidewalks, an "anti-cow" ordinance that called for fences, and this 1890s bandstand for the city Park.

History & Community

1904 view of the Railroad Pier, extending 2,000 feet into Tampa Bay and popular with fishermen. The bathing pavilion shown on the right was added in 1890 as a visitor attraction.

St. Petersburg's waterfront in 1906, the year the Board of Trade (forerunner of the Chamber of Commerce) secured several key properties to hold as trustees.

a new start. They played an important part in the development of the city.

Already lauded as "the healthiest spot on earth" by Dr. W. C. Van Bibber of Baltimore at the 1885 American Medical Society Convention, St. Petersburg was poised to become the Pinellas peninsula's major city.

1900–1910

By the end of the 19th century, St. Petersburg had electricity (the St. Petersburg Lighting Co., precursor to Florida Power Corporation) and a public telephone system. St. Petersburg's tourist industry thrived from the beginning, and quickly created the need for secondary industries. A newspaper account from 1897 noted the following businesses: three general stores, a jewelry shop, a novelty store, two drug stores, a barber shop, a bicycle shop, a livery stable, an ice company, a cigar factory, a steam laundry, one tailor, two bakeries, two millinery shops, a blacksmith and wheelwright, a sawmill, several hotels and boarding houses and an opera house.

Newcomers who came by the new railroad brought along their wealth and a demand for the modern conveniences developed in this age of invention. The Peninsula Company acquired an infant telephone system, begun in 1898, in 1904. F.A. Davis, who introduced electric service to St. Petersburg in 1897, opened an electric streetcar line in 1904. In 1913, the streetcar line was extended all the way from Tampa Bay to Boca Ciega Bay to the southwest.

St. Petersburg was incorporated as a town in 1892, yet, in this first decade of the 20th century, Pinellas was a part of Hillsborough County. The most significant development was the coming of the automobile. Distance, with lack of bridges, the need for roads, tax dollars collected here and spent in Tampa, led to talks of secession.

On February 23, 1907, W.L. Straub, then editor of the *St. Petersburg Times,* published the first of a series of editorials. It came to be known as the "Pinellas Declaration of Independence" and called for a separation of the peninsula from Hillsborough County. Straub persisted, all the way to Tallahassee where it took the Florida Legislature four years to approve the separation.

History & Community

This 1908 view of a quiet Central Avenue and Fourth Street shows the real estate offices of Noel "The Sandman" Mitchell. 1908

Passenger steamers docked at the "electric" pier in St. Petersburg. A second wooden "recreation" pier," shown on the right, was added in 1913.

1910-1920

On May 23, 1911, Florida Governor Albert Gilchrist signed into law a Pinellas independence bill. Six months later the peninsula's voters overwhelmingly ratified the proposal, and on January 1, 1912, the area officially became Pinellas County. The newly formed County consisted of emerging communities and vast undeveloped areas. The settled areas were separated by distance. Among the communities that were already incorporated were Tarpon Springs (1887), Clearwater (1891), St. Petersburg (1892), Dunedin (1899), Largo (1905), Gulfport (1910), Pass-a-Grille (1911), Pinellas Park (1913), and Safety Harbor (1917). Settled, but unincorporated places included: Oldsmar, Sutherland (Palm Harbor), Ozona, the Crystal Beach/Wall Springs area, the Seminole/Oakhurst area, Indian Rocks (mainland), the Harbor Bluffs area, and the Anclote area.

From the beginning of the century to 1920, Pinellas County's communities experienced steady and often dramatic growth. St. Petersburg's population grew by 804 percent from 1,575 to 14,237. In 1913 Pinellas had 25 schools and a total enrollment of 3,263. By 1918, the number of schools had increased to 34, and total school enrollment numbered 4,781.

On January 1, 1914, St. Petersburg made aviation history when Anthony "Tony" Jannus made the first scheduled commercial airline flight. Jannus and one passenger made a 23-minute trip from St. Petersburg to Tampa in a 26-foot seaplane. By March 1914, 1,200 passengers had flown on the St. Petersburg-Tampa Airboat Line.

When World War I ended in 1918, thousands of tourists invaded the state of Florida, many of whom headed for Pinellas County. The tourists flush with spending money and a desire to travel, came for vacations, to buy new homes, and to invest their money. In addition, Henry Ford's affordable Model T enabled people of even moderate incomes to make the trip to Florida. Pinellas County finally had its first system of real paved roads when 75 miles of 9-foot brick roads were completed in 1917. The first bridge to Pass-a-Grille, on the beaches, opened on February 4, 1919 and property owner W.G. McAdoo developed his northern part of the island as a resort named St. Petersburg Beach.

History & Community

Generous gifts from E.H. Tomlinson gave a boost to St. Petersburg's education efforts including orginization of a school band.

1920-1930

With 23 million cars registered by the late 20's the automobile became America's biggest industry, as well as its most desired commodity. This was the jazz age. And Americans were in love with fun.

By 1921 St. Petersburg had a ballpark for America's favorite pastime, located near the site of the present Florida Power Park. The Boston Braves played there from 1921 through 1937. It was the same year a hurricane struck Pinellas County causing widespread damage on October 25, 1921. Two wooden bridges to the beaches were demolished, as was the Municipal Pier in St. Petersburg, two people were killed, and all communication with the outside world was knocked out.

This 1919 view of downtown St. Petersburg shows the Plaza Theatre, built by George S. Gandy, on Central Avenue and Fifth Street looking east.

History & Community

Despite the hurricane, Pinellas remained attractive to tourists and real estate speculators. The Florida real estate boom began in 1921, and reached its height in 1925. As more people migrated to Florida in the early 1920's, the housing supply became inadequate, which, in turn, touched off a building frenzy. One effect of the boom, St. Petersburg's land area grew from 1.05 square miles in 1920 to 53.22 square miles in 1926.

It was also during this period that many of Pinellas County's big hotels were built. Ten new hotels were constructed in St. Petersburg alone, adding some 2,000 rooms to the City's inventory of public accommodations. In order of completion they were: the Soreno, the Pheil, the Suwannee, the Mason, the Pennsylvania, the Dennis, the Vinoy Park, the Jungle Country Club, the Rolyat, and the Don CeSar. A number of small hotels were also built to accommodate the new automobile travelers.

167 miles of new roads, many large bridge structures, and three causeways were built to connect the mainland with the Gulf Beaches and accommodate a growing tourist industry. By 1927 the Corey Causeway, John's Pass Bridge, and a highway along the Keys (Gulf Boulevard) had been completed.

The city's nickname was used in many ways, including this early band.

The Gandy Bridge officially opened on November 20, 1924 as the longest automobile toll bridge in the world. Built by George S. Gandy, the bridge that linked St. Petersburg to Tampa shortened the traveling distance between the two cities from 43 to 19 miles.

In 1926, public transportation bus service was inaugurated in St. Petersburg. From 1923 to 1928 traffic in Pinellas had increased approximately 2,000 percent. In addition, a ferry

St. Petersburg became the birthplace of scheduled commercial aviation when pilot Tony Jannus flew a 26-foot seaplane across the bay from St. Petersburg's waterfront to Tampa on New Year's Day, 1914.

History & Community

service began operations in 1924, carrying passengers and cars between the southern tip of Pinellas County and Manatee County.

Tourists came every winter. They would dance to the music of the era at the new Coliseum built in 1924 and stage to some of the most famous names in the musical entertainment world. When the New York Yankees announced they intended to hold spring training in St. Petersburg, a new field was built at Crescent Lake and named after Yankee manager Miller Huggins. The Yankee star, Babe Ruth, played right field at the park.

Visitors loved baseball. When there wasn't a game they would congregate at the Million Dollar Pier, built in 1926 and an imposing structure that became the place to meet, dance, socialize and even fish. That same year a man called Doc Webb opened the "World's Most Unusual Drug Store", which would eventually cover seven city blocks with 77 stores. The retail wonder became celebrated all over the country.

St. Petersburg residents got their first experience with air conditioning, when the "air-cooled" Florida Theater opened in 1926. Summers in Florida would never be the same. And WFLA radio was on the air, jointly owned by the St. Petersburg and Clearwater Chambers of Commerce.

Pinellas County's population had grown 119.9 percent between 1920 and 1930. In St. Petersburg it had reached 40,425. The economy was dependent on tourists and seasonal residents. But, as rapidly as it had developed and grown, construction activity all but ceased and tourism declined dramatically in the mid twenties. And on October 24, 1929 came the event that brought the decade to a close and the Great Depression hit the nation.

The open-air post office, built in 1917, is still a downtown St. Petersburg landmark.

1930-1940

Even during the Depression years there was steady growth along the Florida Gulf beaches. Cottages, houses, apartments, bathing pavilions, stores, hot dog stands and beer parlors sprung up along once unnamed sections of beach. Treasure Island, Boca Ciega, Mitchell's Beach, Sunset Beach, Madeira Beach, Bennett Beach, Sunshine Beach, Belle Vista Beach, and Redington Beach...some names remain today.

Sunken Gardens opened in 1936 to become a legendary part of St. Petersburg's tourism industry for decades to come.

Babe Ruth poses at Crescent Lake Field with local twins Sam and Bill Bond in 1927.

James Earl "Doc" Webb created Webb's City, the "World's most unusual drug store." a St. Petersburg icon from 1925-1979.

11

History & Community

The green benches of St. Petersburg were a hallmark of the city for decades.

In addition, baseball was alive and well and the St. Louis Cardinals announced that they would move their spring training camp to St. Petersburg in 1938. The baseball craze would continue to be a driving influence on the city.

While the stock market crash took its toll on a local economy that was still reeling from a dramatic drop in real estate values, Pinellas County benefited from its share of federal money designed to spur local economies.

In St. Petersburg, funding provided by the WPA enabled the development of Albert Whitted Municipal Airport, a new campus for St. Petersburg Junior College, as well as park and sewer construction. St. Petersburg's city hall was built and a major federal project, the Bay Pines Hospital and Veterans' Administration Center was constructed.

Federal money helped further the development of the Gulf beaches, including completion in 1939 of a causeway extending Central Avenue on the mainland in St. Petersburg to the newly-incorporated city of Treasure Island.

In 1934 St. Petersburg's Albert Whitted Municipal Airport became the site of a U.S. Coast Guard Air Station, as

Winter visitors at Spa Beach near the Sunshine City's famous "million dollar" Pier.

History & Community

Left: Lawn bowling and shuffleboard were popular games played at facilities across from the Coliseum.

Below: Before the end of World War II, more than 120-thousand military personnel would be based at major resort hotels.

well as the first regularly scheduled commercial flight of National Airlines. Four years later, the U.S. Post Office authorized a daily mail service on National's St. Petersburg – Miami route via Sarasota and Fort Myers.

Toward the end of the 30's economic growth had resumed and Pinellas County's population had grown 47.8 percent, concentrated primarily in the cities of St. Petersburg and Clearwater.

1940-1950

As the 1940s began, Pinellas County's economy had begun to recover from the depression of the previous decade. Then, on December 7, 1941, the United States entered World War II. Travel restrictions and the rationing of gasoline and tires practically wiped out the major industry, tourism, in Pinellas County. The war might have devastated the local economy, but fortunately, the U.S. military began operations here.

Capitalizing on our temperate climate and abundance of empty hotel rooms, St. Petersburg became a site for basic training for the Army Air Corps. Many of the city's luxury hotels, including the Vinoy Park, the Soreno and the Princess Martha, began filling with soldiers, while the Don CeSar Hotel in Pass-a-Grille was used as a hospital.

As the flood of recruits soon filled St. Petersburg's hotels to capacity, temporary tent barracks were set up in the Jungle area for another 10,000 soldiers. Soldiers also occupied the Gray Moss Inn in Clearwater and the Belleview Biltmore Hotel in Belleair.

In 1941, construction of the Pinellas County Airport (the St. Petersburg-Clearwater International Airport) began and the Army Air Corps leased the facility for fighter pilot training. Albert Whited Municipal Airport served as a naval aviation cadet training facility, while the Marines used local beaches to test The Alligator, an amphibious vehicle invented by Clearwater resident Donald Roebling.

World War II's end in 1945 marked the start of another era of rapid growth for Pinellas and tourism resumed. Social Security payments and private retirement pensions enabled retirees to migrate here. Many of the soldiers who had trained here returned with their families. Postwar prosperity meant higher wages, more paid vacations, a desire for resort living, more leisure time, affordable cars and greater mobility, fueling the vacation industry.

Big things were beginning to happen in St. Petersburg. News from the state legislature as early as 1944 hinted at the possibility of the city securing a new state university to be called the University of South Florida. Construction of the Sunshine Skyway bridge had begun; there was talk about building a cultural and arts center on the bay; and, as always,

13

History & Community

Top: Al Lang Field, named for St. Petersburg's "ambassador of baseball," was dedicated on March 12, 1947

there was eternal hope that St. Petersburg might become more than just a spring training camp for major league baseball. In 1947, the first Al Lang Field was dedicated.

1950-1960

The 1950's witnessed the most spectacular growth in the history of Pinellas. The population increased by more than 135 percent, from 159,249 in 1950 to 374,665 in 1960. Citrus and agricultural areas gave way to new development for urban living. When demand for waterfront property began to exceed the supply, developers started dredging sand to turn portions of shallow bays into dry land. By 1970, dredge-and-fill added 4,800 acres to the county, mostly in Boca Ciega and Clearwater Bays.

The first span of the original Sunshine Skyway Bridge was completed and opened on September 6, 1954. The spectacular toll bridge rose to a height of 150 feet and replaced the long-outdated BeeLine Ferry service to Manatee County. In addition, a twin span to the Gandy Bridge was constructed across Tampa Bay.

On July 19, 1955, the last segment of the Gulf Coast Highway (U.S. 19) opened for traffic in St. Petersburg, providing a direct route between Pinellas and Tallahassee. The new road was hailed as another boon to tourism, and development began alongside it almost as soon as it was completed.

In 1952, baseball from St. Petersburg was broadcast by radio to 52 stations. The prestigious *New York Times* ran several articles featuring sporting events in the city. When WSUN (Why Stay Up North?) television went on the air in 1953, citizens watched the first live broadcast of the World Series in the area.

In 1956 Elvis appeared in person at the Florida Theater in St. Petersburg while around the country fourteen movies featuring the "Sunshine City" were flooding the nation's theaters. A locally produced film, "Sunny Skies" was shown 277 times in 96 cities located in 33 states (all within a one-month period). Even Hawaii requested the film.

During the late 1950's, a number of large electronic and aerospace companies began locating manufacturing facilities in Florida. And although the Pinellas economy continued to be dominated by the traditional employment sectors of retail trade and services, the growth of the manufacturing sector diversified the economic base.

In the immediate post-war era, Pinellas County along with the rest of the nation began to see a major change in commercial development — the shopping center. And yet another innovation that had tremendous impact on residential development here was the mobile home. By the early 1960's Pinellas County had more mobile homes than any other county in the state.

1960-1970

During the 60's, the manufacturing sector of Pinellas County continued to grow steadily. As in the past, however, the retail trade and service sectors, influenced by increasing numbers of tourists and retirees, continued their domination of the local economy.

The Howard Frankland Bridge opened in 1960 connecting St. Petersburg and Tampa with the most direct route. As a city, St. Petersburg continued to dream the dream of a major league baseball team playing in a stadium. But the city was now, for the first time in its history, connected to both Hillsborough and Manatee County. More than St. Petersburg,

continued on page 16

BRUCE WATTERS JEWELRY

First with the finest

St. Petersburg is unique in that it is a city large enough to maintain a busy, metropolitan feel, yet small enough to nurture its historic institutions. Bruce Watters Jewelry is one of those institutions, and the history of the business is almost a mirror image of the growth of St. Petersburg.

In 1905, when Roger Watters opened the doors of his small jewelry store on St. Petersburg's main street - Central Avenue – there were, as yet, no street numbers nor automobiles. St. Petersburg was a city with less than 2,000 inhabitants. But they did have watches in need of repair, and visitors, already recognizing the "therapeutic" benefits of the climate, were often disposed toward the purchase of fine jewelry.

Within a short time, Watters nephew, Bruce Weaver had taken over the business, moved the store to 326 Central Avenue and prepared to take the business to the next level. That level occurred in 1939 with another move to larger quarters at 360 Central. It was the beginning of the war years when St. Petersburg would be inundated by servicemen. Watters young son, Bruce Walter. (the current owner), has fond remembrances of those days.

"My father was constantly traveling back and forth to New York City to buy watches," Watters says. The reason was the influx of servicemen, and Watters Jewelry had eight watchmakers on duty to handle the repair of precision timepieces needed in the war effort. Success eventually led Watters to purchase his rival, Cole Jewelry, in 1944, becoming *The* jewelry store in town. Fifty years later, it still is.

As St. Petersburg's oldest retail store, Bruce Watters Jewelry has built a solid reputation as a family-owned business with impeccable integrity, the highest quality jewelry and a price structure which consistently beats its shopping mall counterparts. "What's really wonderful," Watters says, "is to sell a wedding ring to a fourth generation customer."

Three generations of Watters. Bruce Walter and wife Patricia (standing, L & R), son James Bruce (center) and patriarch Bruce Weaver Watters (seated).

Similarly, Watters takes pride in providing a special touch for his clientele. One such customer was looking for a particularly rare stone in a ring setting. At the time, none were available, but she was invited to return. When she did, five rings were available for her to chose from. Today, four remain in the showcase. Special service, indeed.

Located at 224 Beach Drive NE since 1973, Bruce Watters Jewelry's commitment of being "First with the Finest" shows no sign of slowing down. The elder Watters son, James Bruce, has already taken the business to the next level. As in the past, St. Petersburg residents and its visitors will continue to benefit from that kind of promise.

www.brucewattersjewelry.com

History & Community

more than Tampa, the words "Tampa Bay" had a new meaning. A melding of both borders and ideas.

After two disastrous winters – the big freeze of 1962 and an unprecedented snowstorm in January of 1964 – St. Petersburg had some showing off to do. Both the Bayfront Center and the Museum of Fine Arts were remodeled and open for business in 1965. Projects in excess of $20 million were underway in downtown. In 1967 the Million-Dollar Pier was razed to get ready for a new one. And as if looking for a newer, more upscale image, all the green benches in the city were replaced September 15th, 1969, with redwood benches.

Significantly, during the mid-60's, Pinellas County's population surpassed that of Hillsborough to make it the third most populous county in the state.

President John F. Kennedy received a warm Tampa Bay welcome as his motorcade arrived in Tampa in 1963. A permanent exhibit of JFK memorabilia is at the Florida International Museum in St. Petersburg.

1970-1980

The boom period of the early 1970's saw tremendous growth in residential construction in Pinellas County, with the greatest growth occurring in 1972 and 1973 when more than 30-thousand building permits were issued each year! During 1970 to 1974, construction of multi-family housing or condominiums far outpaced that of single-family structures.

In response to the rapid population growth and increased residential construction, the 1970's witnessed the development of large regional shopping malls of more than a half-million square feet. Tyrone Square Mall opened in 1972, Clearwater Mall in 1973, Countryside Mall in 1975, and Pinellas Square Mall (ParkSide Mall) opened in 1977.

A second span of the Sunshine Skyway Bridge was completed in 1971 and a new span of the Gandy Bridge replaced that original bridge built in the 1920's. Even a new Municipal Pier opened in 1973.

The Tampa Bay Buccaneers played their first game in 1976. Groundbreaking ceremonies took place in 1978 for the University of South Florida (USF) Bayboro Campus in downtown St. Petersburg, and the city's population reached 216,232.

1980-1990

St. Petersburg and Pinellas County steadily continued to attract new residents and saw a number of changes and innovations in public services and facilities as well as new attractions for its 4-million annual visitors who had recovered from the fuel crunch of the mid-70's.

Then a maritime disaster would stun all who turned on their local news the morning of May 9, 1980. A freighter had rammed a support pier of the Sunshine Skyway Bridge causing its southbound span to fall into Tampa Bay. The tragedy claimed 35 lives when seven vehicles and a Greyhound bus went over the edge with the collapsed roadway. A new bridge would be completed in 1987.

The 80's saw more interest in the arts and higher education. In 1982 the Salvador Dali Museum opened in St. Petersburg, housing the world's largest private collection of works by the famed Spanish surrealist. And the following year a new performing arts center, Ruth Eckerd Hall, opened in Clearwater.

In the late 1980's, downtown St. Petersburg's Bayfront Center underwent a $26-million renovation resulting in an 8,400-seat arena (the Times Bayfront Arena) and the 2,000-seat Mahaffey Theater. Additionally, the St. Petersburg campus of USF began a major expansion, increasing its size from 11 to 46 acres and building a new $15-million library.

St. Petersburg became an important center of marine science research with the addition of the United States Geological Survey Center for Coastal Ecology building and the Florida Marine Research Institute (FMRI) constructed by USF and the Florida Department of Natural Resources and now part of the Florida Fish and Wildlife Conservation Commission. Simultaneously, Eckerd College established the Galbraith Marine Science Laboratory teaching facility at its campus. And at Bayboro Harbor in downtown, the United States Coast Guard relocated to the city.

St. Petersburg also opened a number of new parks in the 80's, including Maximo Park, Boyd Hill Nature Park, and Demens Landing Park, named for the man who named the city. The mid-county Gateway area became one of the most active regions for new development, with the greatest emphasis on industrial, office and hotel projects. Expansions continue there today.

In 1983 a new resource recovery plant began operations, capable of producing enough electricity to service 45,000 homes a day, and became a prototype for others throughout the country.

The 1980's saw the end of Amtrak train service to Pinellas County, signifying the close of an era in passenger train travel that had begun in 1887. The St. Petersburg-Clearwater

continued on page 18

WEDDING, STEPHENSON & IBARGÜEN ARCHITECTS

The passage of 100 years can often lead a family back to its roots.

Such is the case with Wedding, Stephenson & Ibargüen Architects. Randolph T. Wedding, a transplanted Kentuckian who saw Pinellas County and St. Petersburg as a good place to "pursue business in a favorable climate", established a business as a landscape architect. His first location was at the "goose pond" – an area that would later become Central Plaza. That was in 1905.

Today, Wedding, Stephenson & Ibargüen, guided by Wedding's grandson, also named Randolph, is responsible for St. Petersburg's new YMCA, built on the same Central Plaza location. A coincidence not totally unexpected considering the extent of Wedding's stamp on the architecture of St. Petersburg and Tampa Bay.

With over 4,000 designs to their credit, projects approach $2 billion in construction value and range from boutiques to banks, marinas to manufacturing plants, single-family homes to skyscrapers. From their headquarters in St. Petersburg, Wedding's projects have spanned 14 Florida counties and 14 other states.

Together with partners Mark Stephenson and Marcos Ibargüen, Weddings list of accomplishments truly document the history of St. Petersburg and Pinellas County. In 1958, for example, Wedding began a ten-year transformation of 20 acres of sandspurs and one oak tree into Tampa's Busch Gardens. More recently, downtown St. Petersburg's waterfront skyline changed with the graceful addition of the Cloisters high-rise condominiums (see page 64).

Wedding himself has had a personal impact, acting a mayor of St. Petersburg from 1973-1975. "As an architectural firm, or as an individual," Wedding reflects, "we've never needed to look further than where we were. We've always been challenged here and would like to think our efforts have been a positive influence on the built environment."

Those efforts include All Children's Hospital, WTSP-TV, Times Publishing Co. headquarters, Mansions by the Sea condominiums, Smith & Nephew U.S. headquarters, Florida Federal (Bankers Life) Tower,

Wedding Architects has been the recipient of many awards over the years.

and renovation of both Ceridian Information Systems headquarters (see page 172), formerly Florida Power's corporate headquarters, which Wedding originally built) and the Sirata Beach Resort, to name a few.

Such projects had been greatly abetted by Wedding, Stephenson & Ibargüen's ability to develop solutions quickly. With in-house structural and civil engineering, interior design and landscaping capabilities, it's no wonder the firm has left its mark on almost every building in downtown St. Petersburg, either from original design or renovation.

Wedding was the original designer of Busch Gardens, including the Swiss house, pictured above.

Randy Wedding begins planning yet another project for the Tampa Bay Area.

www.weddingarchitects.com

History & Community

St. Petersburg's skyline changed dramatically with completion of a new domed stadium in 1989.

International Airport however was serving a growing number of planes and passengers, mostly Canadian charter flights.

Tourism continued to be important to the economy, particularly with the growth in the 1980's of international tourism. St. Petersburg and the Gulf beaches became a popular summer vacation spot for Europeans, who visited in growing numbers. By 1990, Europeans represented half of all vacationers in the county in the late summer months.

In downtown St. Petersburg, the $93-million restoration and expansion of the Vinoy Hotel (Renaissance Vinoy Resort) brought its hundred-year history full circle and the rest of the city was ready for the fulfillment of an approved master plan for redeveloping downtown called Bay Plaza.

1990-1999

By 1990, approximately 81 percent of Pinellas County's land had been developed. Of the 36.4 square miles that hadn't been built on, 20.2 square miles were planned for development and the remainder consisted of environmentally sensitive lands and preservation areas. The bulk of the county's jobs were in the trade and service sectors, respectively accounting for 29 and 43 percent of all jobs.

In St. Petersburg, however, Bay Plaza didn't happen. Ten years and millions in expenditures later, the developers gave up. But the vision remained.

In March 1995, after 18 years of trying, the Tampa Bay Area gained its Major League Baseball franchise. The new baseball team is named the Tampa Bay Devil Rays and the first pitch went out on March 31, 1998 with appropriate fanfare in the newly restored and renamed Tropicana Field in St. Petersburg.

The Florida International Museum was organized in 1992 and opened in 1995 with the first of its annual world-class exhibits. By the decade's end there would be plans for a permanent collection. Another historically significant museum, the Florida Holocaust Museum, opened in downtown St. Petersburg in 1998. It is the fourth largest Holocaust museum in the country.

St. Petersburg met its neighbors along The Pinellas Trail, a 47-mile linear park built on abandoned railroad right-of-way. It has received national publicity as one of the longest urban rails-to-trails projects in the United States, stretching from St. Petersburg to north of Tarpon Springs.

And we learned to extend a friendly nod to neighbors from Hillsborough County when another recreational path opened in December 1999 across Tampa Bay. The old span of the Gandy Bridge became the Friendship Trail Bridge, opening a new picturesque connection for bicycle riders, inline skaters and joggers between St. Petersburg and Tampa.

The City purchased Sunken Gardens which had been a privately owned tourist attraction for 64 years, but whose owners were ready to sell. It seemed destined for commercial or residential development. It is now a public park.

Ground is broken for a new $30-million, 150-thousand square foot downtown entertainment and retail center called BayWalk. It will feature a 20-screen movie theater with stadium seating, retail stores and a half-dozen restaurants. A pedestrian walkway will connect the plaza-style complex to a seven-level parking garage and additional office and retail space.

Three high-rise waterfront condominiums begin to add their silhouettes to the changing downtown skyline – The Florencia, The Cloisters and Vinoy Place – bringing more residential units to downtown.

This is a city that greeted the 21st century with energy and change all around us. The Friendship Trail, Sunken Gardens, BayWalk and the new condominiums are symbolic that there are still visionaries in St. Petersburg. Their only differences are that some work with the original foundation and others use new mortar to create business and beauty from beaches to bay.

BELLEVIEW BILTMORE RESORT & SPA

The Belleview Biltmore Resort & Spa has reigned as one of Pinellas County's *grand dames* since January 15, 1897. Still reputed to be one of the largest occupied wooden structures in the world, the resort has aged with graceful charm while yielding to the addition of state-of-the-art resort amenities expected by today's upscale traveler.

Complete with 244 guestrooms, including 16 suites (one of which – the Presidential Suite – is 3,400 square feet with three bedrooms), the Belleview Biltmore Resort & Spa caters to both individuals and conferences (the resort has 30,000 square feet of meeting and banquet space) in an unparalleled Southern style uniquely Florida.

Located on 21 acres atop Florida's highest coastal bluff, the resort is only 10 minutes away from the Gulf of Mexico's white sand beaches and features a championship golf course and red-clay tennis courts The newly renovated Spa and Fitness Club presents an array of relaxation opportunities, including indoor and outdoor swimming pools and whirlpools.

The Belleview Biltmore represents an amazing blend of old world charm, seen in its on-site restaurants and boutiques, and hi-tech dazzle available for meetings and conferences. Whether banquets for 1,000, or more intimate surroundings, such as the 78-seat Belleaire Amphitheater, the resort maintains an ambidextrous ability to satisfy the demands of both business and social gatherings.

Listed in the National Registry of Historic Places, the Belleview Biltmore remains committed to preserving the 19th century style of the resort envisioned by its builder, West Central Florida pioneer and railroad magnate Henry B. Plant. While the resort gained success in its early years as a favorite retreat for industrial magnates, company presidents and international dignitaries (including the Duke of Windsor), the passage of time has not altered the basic commitment of providing world class amenities to all its guests.

The aura of the resort's long and illustrious history permeates the modern Belleview Biltmore. While the magnitude of the resort is inspiring, it is the open spaciousness of its common areas and grounds that makes the Belleview Biltmore Resort & Spa truly unique. Unlike other resorts – traffic bound and clamoring with metropolitan mayhem - the Belleview Biltmore is a quiet refuge and definitely a crown jewel on West Coast.

The Belleview Biltmore Resort in the early 1900's.

www.belleviewbiltmore.com

FLORIDA POWER CORPORATION

A Proud Past, Powerful Future

"The latest improvement of magnitude in St. Petersburg is the completion and inauguration of the electric light system. By this enterprise, every part of the town is brilliantly illuminated. A formal inauguration of the new undertaking occurred in St. Petersburg on August 5, and was the occasion of much rejoicing among the inhabitants and invited guests. The trial illumination was a success in every particular. No pains had been spared by the company to provide themselves with the latest scientific devices, and the appliances connected with the work are of the utmost importance."

Those were the words Frank Allston Davis, founder of the company that would become Florida Power Corporation, used to describe the lighting of the first streetlights in St. Petersburg on the evening of August 5, 1897.

By today's standards the first electric system in St. Petersburg was primitive and pintsized. The entire electric system consisted of thirty 32-candle-power streetlights and two arc lights located at the corners of Central Avenue and Second and Third Streets.

A wood-burning boiler produced enough steam to power the 50-kilowatt dynamo that powered the lights. The unit was housed in a small building beside Tampa Bay at the site of the present day St. Petersburg Yacht Club. One of the earliest known photographs of the plant show three men and a boy standing in front of the building leading some to speculate that it may have taken "three men and a boy" to keep it running.

Florida Power proudly marks July 18, 1899, as the official date the company was chartered with the state of Florida. Since then the St. Petersburg-based investor-owned electric utility has grown and prospered as Florida developed into one of the most populous and wealthy states in the nation.

Florida Power's service area eventually grew to cover 20,000 square miles of west central Florida.

Electricity helped energize the economic development of Florida and Florida Power was at the forefront of this effort. The company partnered with local governments, chambers of commerce and regional economic development organizations to see that the metropolitan area around St. Petersburg stayed at the top everyone's relocation short list.

Those efforts paid off as the St. Petersburg-Pinellas County market became a prime location for a diverse group of large-scale commercial and light industrial customers as well as hundreds of thousands of residential customers who chose to make this area home.

Florida Power continues to play a key leadership role in the economic development of the region through an ongoing commitment to quality public education and community development.

Florida Power has always seen St. Petersburg as a major league city with major league potential. Company executives led the effort to bring a major league baseball franchise to St. Petersburg's community-owned Tropicana Field.

Florida Power rolled out the red carpet for the Tampa Bay Devil Rays by building a striking 900 foot-long ceramic tile sidewalk called the "Sunsation Walkway" at Tropicana Field. It gives visitors an inviting pathway into the dome for baseball and other major events.

Florida Power's first order of business is to provide customers with safe, reliable and economically priced power. The company's service reliability record continues to be a top priority. Customers know power will be restored quickly following tropical storms and the more typical late afternoon thunderstorms that produce more lightening than any other location in North America.

Florida Power used the slogan "Count On Us" as part of the company's 100th anniversary celebration in 1999. That sentiment continues to be a guiding force as the company begins a second century of service.

In late 2000, Florida Power expects to double in size at the conclusion of a combination with Raleigh, North Carolina-based Carolina Power & Light. Together these companies are destined to become one of the largest energy providers in the Southeastern United States.

www.fpc.com/flpower

21

TOURTELOT BROTHERS, INC

The Trusted Name For Real Estate Services

In 1928, John and Rita Tourtelot established their real estate office on Central Avenue in downtown St. Petersburg. The Great Depression hit St. Petersburg's housing market hard and houses were being sold for the price of their tax deeds alone. Not a market in which to start a real estate company. But, the couple survived because of their resolve and expertise in property management.

The Tourtelot's dedication and skill was ingrained in their family and 70+ years later, Bill and Rick Tourtelot have grown their grandfather's company into a multi-office, multi-service organization whose name is synonymous with quality throughout the Tampa Bay area. Today, Tourtelot Brothers, Inc., offers complete residential and commercial real estate services to an ever-increasing range of clientele.

Area residents and businesses turn to Tourtelot for their real estate needs because Tourtelot knows the market. As one of the fastest growing counties in the nation, Pinellas County continues to attract relocating individuals and companies. Bill Tourtelot, President of Tourtelot Brothers, recognized that a company's longevity alone does not equate to success. It is necessary to offer buyers and sellers the assistance of educated, professional associates and to provide the most complete range of services possible,

As the area's RELO affiliate, the nation's leading relocation network, Tourtelot's specialists provide solutions for individuals moving in and out of the Tampa Bay area. Tourtelot also offers expert Property Management Services for residential and commercial properties. And because of their experience and reputation in the marketing of luxury homes Tourtelot was chosen by Christie's Great Estates to be their exclusive affiliate in Pinellas County. This prestigious designation allows Tourtelot to extend Christie's unique marketing opportunities, including their international referral network. Tourtelot has also been chosen as the area's only representative for Who's Who in Luxury Real Estate.

Whether a modest two-bedroom home, a multi-acre estate or commercial property, Tourtelot Brothers, Inc., has the team and the marketing services to provide a successful transaction.

According to Bill Tourtelot, the best realty services are "a combination of the latest marketing methods and technology built on years of experience. Reputation is important, but so is providing the full range of personal services needed by our clients. Being attuned to the needs of this community, as well as being affiliated with the nation's leading real estate firms, is what makes us different."

This kind of dedication to quality and integrity is what has built, and continues to build Tourtelot Brothers, Inc., as one of Tampa Bay's most trusted names for real estate services.

Top: Accommodating the growth of a large, full service real estate firm necessitates new facilities. President Bill Tourtelot (center right) discusses with some of his sales and management team, the plans for Tourtelot's grand new office complex in downtown St. Petersburg.
Above: Original Tourtelot offices through the mid-80's

www.tourtelotbrothers.com

Chapter 2
Neighborhoods and Religious Heritage

TY HESTON

From any angle St. Petersburg is a beautiful waterfront city. Our downtown begins on the tranquil shores of Tampa Bay and the city unfolds to even more water vistas in all directions...

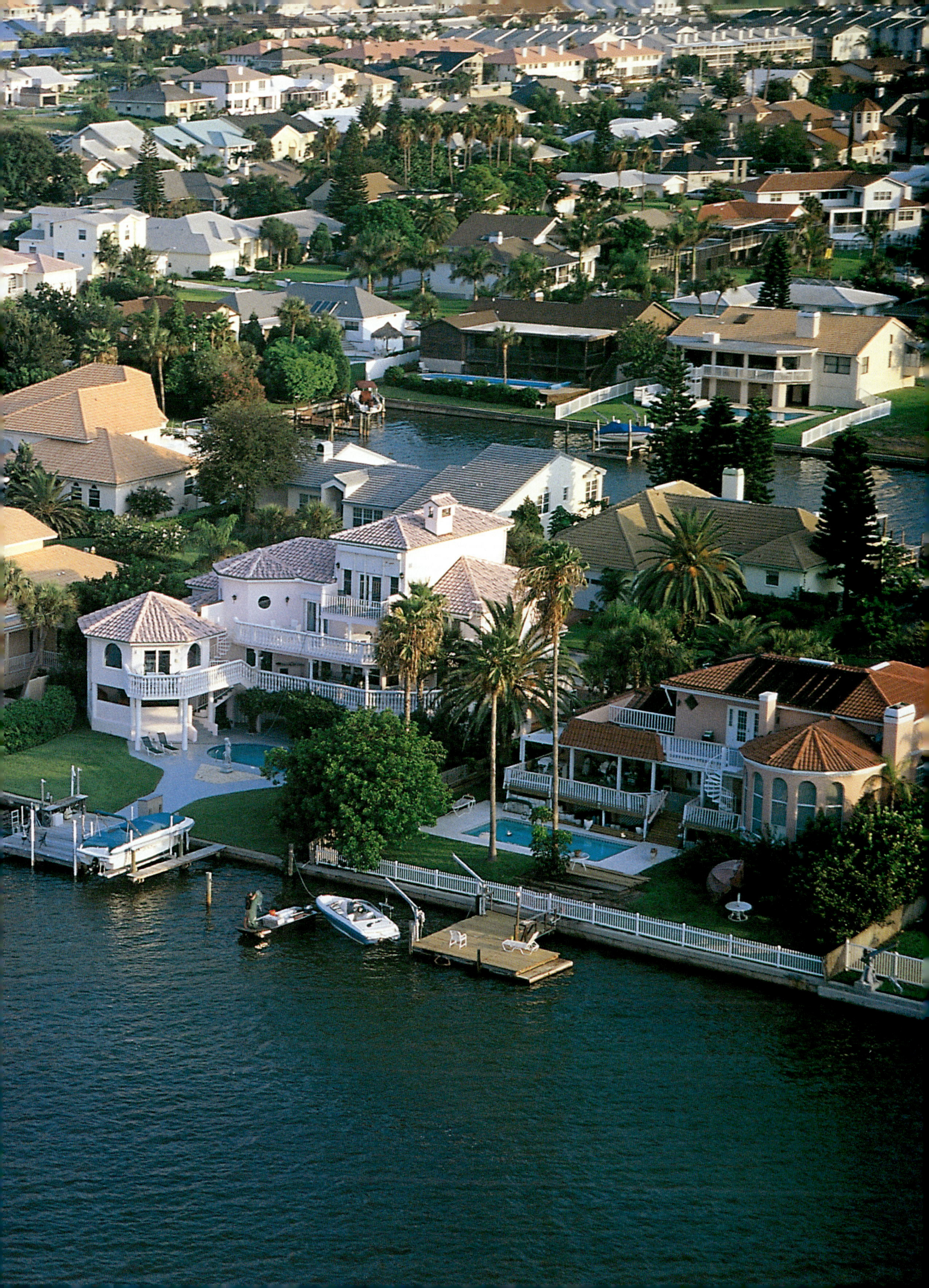

Neighborhoods & Religious Heritage

St. Petersburg has the largest reclaimed water system in the U.S., providing a cost effective essential resource for lawns and landscaping.

The quarter-million people who call St. Petersburg home are its community and live in neighborhoods that extend from the pink streets of Pinellas Point at the southernmost tip, to the new residential developments of the Gateway area toward the Howard Frankland Bridge and the city's northern boundaries – continuous neighborhoods that also follow the sun from downtown St. Petersburg's eastern shores, reaching westward to the nearby beach communities of the Gulf of Mexico.

St. Petersburg is a city where you can live, work and play in the same general vicinity; in fact, our average 21.8-minute commute time, from home to job, is one of the shortest of any metropolitan area in the nation.

The city operates under a strong mayor form of government. This system combines the strong political leadership of a mayor, who is responsible for running the affairs of the city, with an elected city council, representing its geographical districts.

The St. Petersburg Police Department is housed in one main building located near downtown and employs more than 500 sworn law enforcement officers and 200 other employees. Under the direction of a Chief of Police, the department provides a full range of services within a 60 square mile area and also covers 142 square miles of surrounding waterways. In addition to the main police building, residents are served at several Community Resource Centers that are staffed by police officers and volunteers.

A City of Trees

In 1993 the City of St. Petersburg launched Operation Greenscape to beautify its roadways and neighborhoods with rows of tropical palm trees and oaks, flaming Oleanders and other landscaping. All of the I-275 on and off ramps leading to St. Petersburg have sabel palms and sea grapes, while flowering white Indian hawthorne can be seen along the city's medians. In five years the city had planted 15,000 trees and over 100,000 shrubs!

The program soon expanded to include homeowners. Young oak trees shade neighborhood sidewalks and pine trees transform retention ponds into mini parks. Under Operation Treescape, the City offers oak trees at reduced prices, and entire neighborhoods can participate through their neighborhood associations.

Neighborhoods & Religious Heritage

St. Petersburg Fire & Rescue has several divisions with specific responsibilities including a prevention division that reviews architectural plans and inspection of occupancies, and also provides public education services to the public. Today 13 fire stations provide fire suppression and emergency medical services to St. Petersburg residents, along with a number of specialty teams including: Hazardous Materials Response, Technical Rescue, and a Marine Unit. The department has over 300 personnel and responds to over 40,000 emergency calls per year.

In recent years many residents have opted to have their neighborhoods included in the Council of Neighborhood Associations (CONA) which partners with the City of St. Petersburg for support. There are over 100 of these associations throughout the city and they are true networking groups that hold festivals, block parties and an annual open house that includes tours of homes.

While certainly no one loses their individuality, there is a sense of pride connected with being in a neighborhood association, and many improvements have resulted from the cooperative effort – from decorative signs identifying neighborhoods to newly planted trees along the streets and avenues. It has also proven to be good motivation for residents to research the history of the area in which they live.

During the "big Florida boom" of the twenties, buildings of all kinds and for all purposes changed St. Petersburg's landscapes. Real estate advertising filled the local newspapers and out of town media. People arrived in St. Petersburg to see for themselves and bought land from what has been described as "an army of salesmen" waiting to greet them. Even a railroad embargo in 1925 did not stop construction; instead, shipments of building materials arrived by boat. Streets paved in Augusta bricks and sidewalks made of hexagon shaped concrete blocks can be found throughout the older neighborhoods of St. Petersburg today.

Five men in particular promoted multi-million dollar developments that forever changed the city and remain as neighborhoods today. Snell Isle was fathered by C. Perry Snell; Pasadena by Jack Taylor; Lakewood Estates by Charles R. Hall; The Jungle by Walter P. Fuller; and Shore Acres by N.J. Upham.

North

St. Petersburg's most recent new housing and apartment development has paralleled the business growth of the Gateway and Carillon areas. Residential development continues to grow in areas concentrated along Fourth Street and Ninth Street where many apartment complexes are located, and in Feather Sound where a variety of housing types are available. New residential space in the Gateway area includes more than 6,000 housing units with another 1,500 residential units expected in the future. Within Carillon itself are 1,500 units of multi-family property in keeping with its town center concept.

Bay Isle Key apartments on Ninth Street North became a first for St. Petersburg. Designed for short-term corporate tenants and long-term apartment dwellers it offers a club-

---

North Shore Park & The Gizella Kopsick Palm Arboretum

There are more than 300 palms representing 73 species from around the world at the Gizella Kopsick Palm Arboretum.

The arboretum, or tree farm, is on a two-acre park site on North Shore Drive at the foot of 10th Avenue NE, just north of the Renaissance Vinoy Resort. Development of the arboretum began in 1976 after a concerned resident and park volunteer, Mrs. Elva Rouse, proposed the idea. It was created through a generous gift of stock from Miss Gizella Kopsick, a long-time palm admirer.

Snell Isle is a luxurious waterfront community of spacious homes initially fathered by C. Perry Snell.

house, concierge service, business center, fitness and recreational facilities and security. Other choices of extended-stay lodging near Gateway can accommodate the newly-relocated business person still shopping for a permanent home address.

Townhouse condos are found in the family oriented community of Mariners Pass and executive homes are prominent in the new developments near Weedon Island, all convenient to the Gateway area and downtown St. Petersburg. Riviera Bay and Renaissance are two such desirable communities. Another is the Harbor Isle subdivision, platted in the 1970's. This waterfront community is north of the Mangrove Bay golf course.

But before there was a Gateway there was, and still is, Meadowlawn, a neighborhood of single family homes and condos that was developed mostly in the 1950's. Its early history includes that of an open range used by the cattle of two local dairies who were often at odds about straying cows!

The Feather Sound golf course area, on the north side of the Carillon business center, is adjacent to St. Petersburg and appeals to buyers concerned with mid-county location and those with a strong sense of community. It is a neighborhood of single-family homes and town homes.

Northeast

The entire northeast area of St. Petersburg has always held appeal to professionals, executives and business owners because of its location close to downtown and the distinctive styles of larger homes in its neighborhoods.

Easy access to the waters of Tampa Bay is another advantage for homeowners in the Northeast. Snell Isle, Venetian Isles, and Harbor Isle provide a boater's haven. Other prestigious waterfront communities are Patrician Point, and the gated communites of Placido Bayou and Caya Costa. Elegant homes along Coffee Pot Bayou have docks across the street on the bayou canal, while the North Shore neighborhood overlooks North Shore Park and Tampa Bay.

The North Shore subdivision was the first established neighborhood within the city limits. It was begun in 1911 by a group of men led by C. Perry Snell and J.C. Hamlett. Their goal was to establish the area as the premier residential neighborhood adjacent to the City of St. Petersburg along the shores of Tampa Bay and Coffee Pot Bayou. The resulting residential flavor of the neighborhood is one greatly influenced by its early settlers. An architectural mixture of predominately Mediterranean revival, Colonial revival, bungalow styles, Prairie, Williamsburg as well as vernacular style homes is prominent.

This Brightwaters Boulevard home has a stunning view of Tampa Bay.

Snell was an advocate of William Straub's waterfront park system and was instrumental in extending the park northward by giving the City the waterfront part of his 600 acres, from 13th Avenue North to Coffee Pot Bayou. The Bayou is known for the manatees that swim into the shallow waters during cold weather.

Snell Isle is a luxurious waterfront community of spacious homes featuring a wide spectrum of classic European and Spanish design. The distinctive Woman's Club on Snell Isle Boulevard, located on land donated by Snell in 1928, and the nearby Renaissance Vinoy Resort, present a spectacular view as you cross a historic bridge across the Bayou to the area.

The St. Petersburg Woman's Club is on the National Registry of Historic Places and has two of the many decorative statues found throughout the neighborhood. To enhance the European influence of these first homes, Snell obtained such statuary, tiles and ornaments on his extensive travels throughout Europe.

Shore Acres, Eden Isle and Snell Isle Estates are additional adjacent waterfront communities that can be reached from Snell Isle. Shore Acres has a wide range of home styles and prices, from modest masonry block construction to multi-level waterfront estates on exclusive Bay Shore Boulevard. Nathaniel J. Upham developed it in the 1950's and today's residents have remodeled many homes, a mix of first time homeowners, young families and retirees.

Nearby Venetian Isles is a small deed restricted community on deep-water canals. It is a typical example of dredge and fill land that can be found in the Tampa Bay area. One of the more significant events of Venetian Isles was obtaining the deed to the submerged waters that would become 60 percent of Venetian Isles. Its developer, George R. Davis, directed the operations of eight similar major projects simultaneously. The actual building of homes did not start until nearly ten years later, in 1968.

Barcley Estates was built from 1964 to 1974 as a deed restricted community with an active homeowner association. It is a family neighborhood noted for its stately pines and oaks. Closer to downtown, the Allendale Terrace section of St. Petersburg has many large estate homes

TY HESTON

An aerial view of the "pink streets" only hints of the beautiful blend of custom homes, lush landscaping and mature trees,

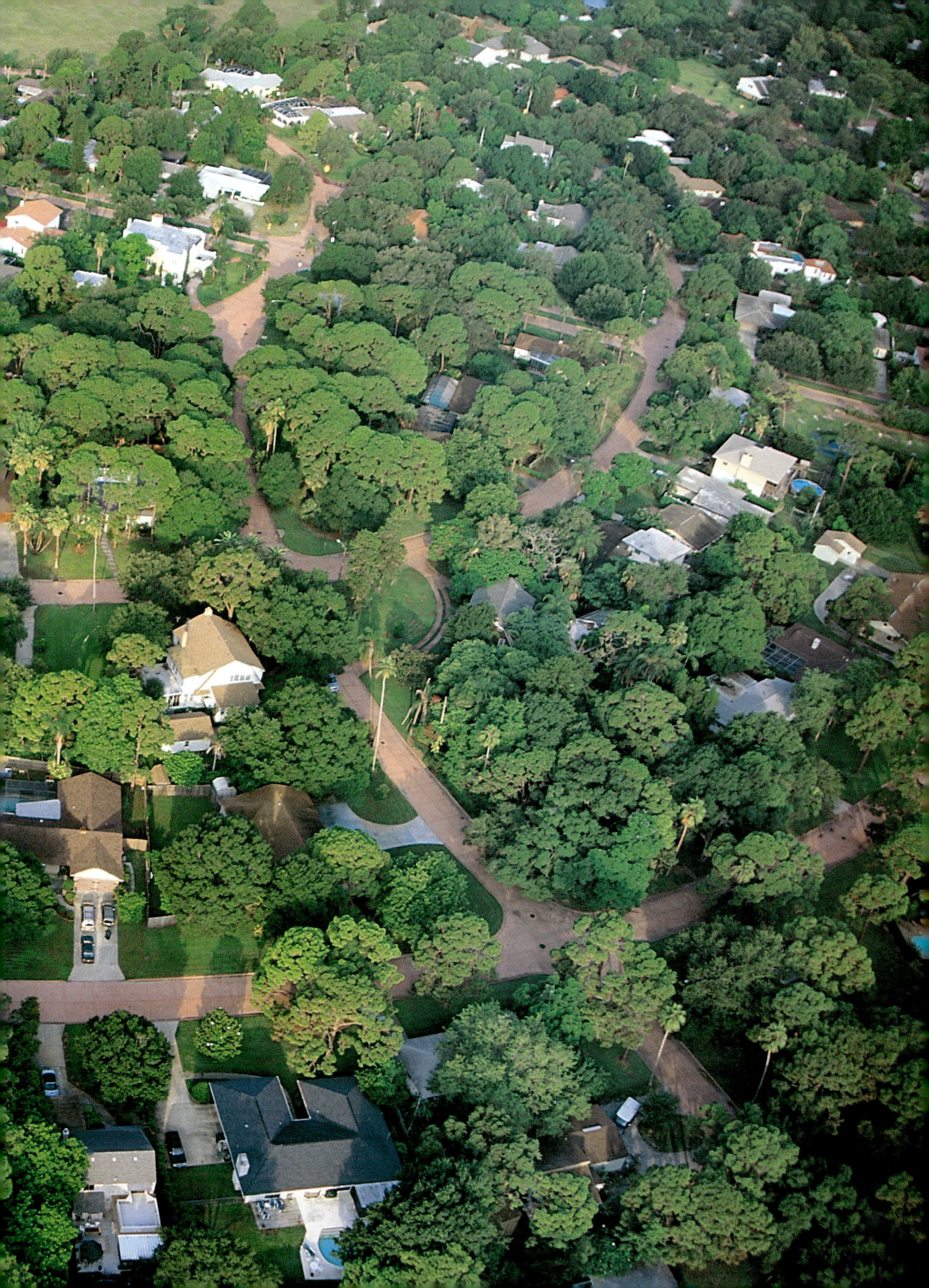

This newer Allendale home north of downtown St. Petersburg has many neighboring estate homes built in the 1920's and 1930's.

built in the 1920's and 1930's shaded by oak trees along brick streets. It was developed at a time when waterfront property temporarily lost some of its popularity, after a major hurricane, and it remains one of the city's finest areas.

Greater Woodlawn is a middle class community of homes built in the 1920's and again in the 1940's and 1950's, representing typical growth periods for St. Petersburg. Its homes of bungalow, Colonial revival, Tudor revival, and frame or masonry vernacular also represent the preferred architectural styles of those periods. The half square-mile area has a circular road layout unlike the rest of the city.

Central and North Central

In the 1870's and 1880's, settlers of European origin put much of the land that is now St. Petersburg to agricultural use, chiefly citrus groves. Other areas were simply considered a woodsy fringe, not worth farming. Of course, once the railroad arrived, the city grew and when streetcar service was extended in the newly incorporated city, groves and woods became valuable suburban property and subdividing began.

Typical of this early development, Historic Kenwood has one of the highest concentrations of 1920's craftsman-style, two-bedroom bungalows in Florida and the neighborhood is a good example of community neighborhood involvement.

Many of Historic Kenwood's residents, who work in the fields of architecture, real estate and construction, have helped their neighbors renovate their homes in keeping with the original architectural details. In the mid 1930's, approximately 170 homes from other St. Petersburg neighborhoods were moved to Historic Kenwood, which is north of Central Avenue and west of I-275. Brick streets, hexagon block sidewalks and plenty of mature trees add to its character.

As recently as the 1950's, a large part of the city, including the Disston Ridge area, west of 34th Street and north to 40th Avenue, consisted of only a few main roads with lots of sand, low shrubs, trees and many tall pines. As builders built still more subdivisions, buyers purchased homes as fast as they were completed and the need for road improvements, more utilities and services was successfully coordinated between civic associations and the City.

In the 1950's there was also Central Plaza, a shopping mecca that declined in the early 70's with the new popularity of suburban malls. Today, there is Central Avenue Tomorrow, a citizen-driven planning and design project to revive the area between I-275 and 34th Street. Economic development and revitalization of the district began to take shape with the groundbreaking for a new $11-million YMCA complex, the Jim and Heather Gills YMCA of St. Petersburg, in the fall of 2000.

Many quiet neighborhoods stretch west and north of the Central Plaza area, following St. Petersburg's typical grid pattern of streets and avenues. Concrete block homes mix with other architectural styles including many American hybrids

Above: A Park Street estate blends its architectural character amid the beauty of Florida landscaping.
Below: This Driftwood areas street and its tree lined canopy is but part of the residential charm found in south St. Petersburg.

ranging from 700 square feet to more than 3,000 square feet. Families enjoy the neighborhoods for their affordability and convenience to direct arteries leading east to downtown and northwest to the Tyrone area.

West Central

This section of St. Petersburg is popular for its proximity to the Gulf Beaches and the largest mall in Pinellas County, Simon's Tyrone Square Mall. It is also near the Gibbs campus of St. Petersburg Junior College and Admiral Farragut, a private military boarding school.

Its many neighborhoods include the Jungle area, distinguished by stately mansions on large lots that back up to Boca Ciega Bay along Park Street. It is believed that Panfilo de Naverez landed on these shores and a commemorative marker acknowleges his discovery of the peninsula in 1528. However, more frequently told are the tales of the area's colorful past during the roaring twenties.

The Mediterranean revival building, which houses the Admiral Farragut Academy, was originally the Jungle Country Club Hotel one of the finest of the boom era hotels in the area. It was built by Walter P. Fuller in 1925 and designed by Henry Taylor, the architect who built the Vinoy Park Hotel, now the Renaissance Vinoy Resort in downtown St. Petersburg.

The Jungle Hotel featured inlaid tile, Spanish patios and tropical gardens. Fuller even had his own radio station for a while, and broadcasted chats with guests along with music from the orchestra, which played daily during the dinner hour.

Fuller formed a corporation, which developed Jungle Terrace, and owned the Piper-Fuller Airport. The airport hosted bootleggers during Prohibition as well as General Claire Chenault of the Flying Tigers. Tyrone Square Mall is built on land that was once part of the airfield.

Fuller also bought out the stockholders who owned the Jungle Golf

33

Boat docks and sea walls line much of the 234 miles of St. Petersburg waterfront.

Course, which had been operating since 1915, and replaced the old clubhouse with a new one. Riding stables and the city's first night club, the Gangplank, at the Jungle Prado, were a part of his development. The Jungle Prado is now a popular Caribbean-style restaurant.

Nearby are the family areas of Azalea and Crossroads. These quiet neighborhoods are prime locations for convenience and everyday living with minimum traffic beyond the major road arteries. Architecture spans several decades beginning in the late 1930's to the early 1970's with styles that include small bungalows and larger one and two story homes.

Three recreation centers and the Science Center of Pinellas County, add to the amenities available to the public. The Science Center is equipped with workshops and laboratories, a computer center, nature trail, planetarium and Discovery Center that provide hands-on learning opportunities for youth and adults.

Holiday Park is also in the Tyrone area, on land originally settled by a group of farmers from Tyrone, Pennsylvania. They came to grow sugarcane and tap the pine trees for sap to make turpentine. The first phases of development began in 1957 by a man named Frank Stumm who recorded subdivision restrictions to maintain the quality of custom homes added later to the community.

South

While Snell was developing much of the land near and north of downtown, Charles R. Hall purchased the largest parcel in the southern portion of the city. He decided to design a golf course surrounded by a residential community on property that was so heavily wooded and filled with streams and ponds that it had to be cleared and drained before development could begin.

Lakewood Estates became a distinctive neighborhood that continues to feature the Lakewood Country Club. Its winding, quiet streets follow the fairways and greens of the 18-hole golf course, and bear the names of Spanish explorers, cities and landmarks. The Spanish influence was also seen in the first homes built there during the 1920's. As Lakewood developed, additional homes were built in the popular styles of their time – cottages, Mediterranean revival, ranch and vernacular.

As integration progressed and the demographics of Lakewood and other neighborhoods changed, this community set a positive example of how people of different origins can live in harmony as neighbors – a characteristic that Lakewood residents take pride in today.

Bahama Shores, just four miles south of downtown, is another quiet, stable waterfront area of homes built mostly in the 1940's and early 1950's. The Neighborhood Association owns a waterfront lot on Tampa Bay that serves as a park used and maintained by the residents. Renovation opportunities attract buyers to the Mediterranean style architecture and detailing of the homes, many with tile roofs. In fact, several

continued on page 36

THE ST. PETERSBURG SUNCOAST ASSOCIATION OF REALTORS®

Headquarters of the St Petersburg Suncoast Association of Realtors®

Looking for a place in paradise?

Whether gulf or bay, house or condominium, office building or storefront space, Pinellas County offers some unusual challenges to prospective buyers. Being a peninsula – a very popular peninsula – can make the search difficult, simply because of so many wonderful choices.

Simplifying the search needs professionals. That's why the St. Petersburg Suncoast Association of Realtors® is made up of more than 2,200 real estate professionals and affiliates representing almost 450 companies and offices doing business in St. Petersburg and Pinellas County.

Realtor members represent a variety of disciplines from residential and commercial specialists, leasing agents, property managers, 1031 exchangers, appraisers and general brokers. Members include Realtor licensees and offices from throughout Pinellas County, St. Petersburg, Clearwater, Largo, Seminole, Pinellas Park, and other communities, including the Gulf Beaches.

Originally organized in the fall of 1912, the Association celebrated its 85th anniversary in 1997. While furthering the professionalism of Realtors through its Code of Ethics, and ongoing educational and training programs, the Association is also actively involved in the Florida Association of Realtors, and The National Association of Realtors.

It is a part of District VI, which includes other Realtor organizations from around the Tampa Bay area, works cooperatively with other Boards, and is committed to a number of important community activities including longtime ongoing support for PARC (the Pinellas Association for Retarded Children).

Realtor members represent many years of experience in addition to a variety of professional designations, and literally billions of dollars in sales. They include practitioners who are volunteer members of numerous boards and commissions, are active in local, county and state politics, and others who give of their time and expertise in support of various pro bono activities.

With some of the most beautiful waterfront property in the world, and with hundreds of miles of coastline, this area is a place where "sold" signs appear almost overnight. Locating the right property or finding a dream home can best be accomplished by contacting the St. Petersburg Suncoast Association of Realtors.

The members live in, know and understand this area and are ready to help find that special place in paradise.

www.ssar.org

Two homes that reflect the beautiful Mediterranean style found throughout St. Petersburg and Pinellas County.

residents that lived in the neighborhood as children have moved back to bring up another generation!

Many historical homes dating from the 1920's are in Driftwood, another neighborhood popular for the remodeling potential of a home that comes on the market. Closer to downtown is Roser Park, the first local and national historic district in St. Petersburg. Its history dates to 1910 and a man named Charles Roser, who, according to local legend, pedaled milk until he made his fortune selling his Fig Newton cookie to National Biscuit Company.

Winding through the neighborhood is Booker Creek and a hilly terrain untypical of the rest of St. Petersburg. Two homes significant to the City's beginnings have been preserved and relocated near the neighborhood – the home of Perry Snell and that of General Williams.

The Tampa Bay waterfront homes at Tropical Shores and Coquina Key in the southeast sections of St. Petersburg were built in the 1950's and are often chosen because of floor plans adaptable to room additions. Florida ranch, split level and neo classic designs lend diversity to the home styles found

*Above: This stately Colonial design home, found in south St. Petersburg, shows the diversity of architectural styles available.
Below: Residents take great pride in taking full advantage of landscaping provided by both man and nature.*

here, while a large apartment complex, completed in 1979 on Coquina Key, offers short and long-term leasing. Limited access to the small peninsula of Tropical Shores, and to the island of Coquina Key, add privacy to these neighborhoods.

At the southernmost tip of Pinellas County is Pinellas Point, with its locally famous "pink streets," so named for their tinted roads, canopied by the branches of ancient live oak trees. Custom-built executive homes on large lots offer the rewards of a panoramic view of the water and the Sunshine Skyway Bridge. Smaller ranch homes, well suited for retirees and young families, are also found throughout this culturally diverse community. Several streets are named for St. Petersburg's early pioneers, including General John Constantine Williams. It is one of the few locations where there are still remains of a Tocobago temple mound from the Native Americans that once populated the area.

South Central

In the mid-1950's, US 19 was extended to connect St. Petersburg to the newly opened Skyway Bridge, providing access to parcels of undeveloped land. Within ten years, waterfront communities were created – from fill left from the dredging of deep-water canals in Boca Ciega Bay.

Broadwater, Maximo and Dolphin Cay are all located along the shores of this bay. The predominant architectural style of the neighborhoods is primarily one-story Florida style homes with stucco construction and tile roofs. There are also condominiums and apartments in the neighborhoods.

These two homes (above and below) lie in the Tierra Verde area, a natural island development south of the Bayway on the way to Ft. DeSoto Park. Top: Sands Point neighborhood. Bottom: Monte Cristo neighborhood.

The Pinellas Bayway is the connecting link from the southern tip of St. Petersburg to St. Pete Beach and the Gulf of Mexico. Just south off the Bayway is a prestigious, gated, 24-hour guarded, deed restricted island community of about 200 homes, called Bayway Isles. Architectural styles range from modern to Spanish and European. It is a community of mostly professionals and executives and consists of two main islands, giving homeowners a waterfront view of Boca Ciega Bay or across the water toward Eckerd College.

Unlike other nearby island communities, Bayway Isles lies within the city limits of St. Petersburg. It is another example of land bought from the State of Florida in the 1950's, with riparian rights to dredge and develop canals, using the fill to form the island. The first home was built on Bayway Isles in 1965.

As waterfront property became scarce, in 1984 an affluent group of buyers began building large houses and condominiums on Tierra Verde, a natural island south of the Bayway on the way to Fort DeSoto Park. They chose to keep their community independent and unincorporated as it remains today. Tierra Verde is reputed to have one of the highest per capita income levels in the Tampa Bay area. Elegant homes and impressive yachts line its shores and connecting canals.

Southwest

In the mid 1950's there were few restrictions on dredge and fill operations that produced so much of the land that developers used for building their communities. One of them, Robert E. Lee, came here from South Carolina and created Yacht Club Estates, one of the last areas to be built by that method. The Pinellas County Aquatic Preserve Act halted dredging and seawall construction in 1972.

The island community is bounded on all sides by Boca Ciega Bay. Original homes there were built from 1959 through the late 1970's and are almost exclusively ranch style, concrete block, three and four bedroom homes. Almost all have docks and most residents have boats. Many of these homes, like in other waterfront communities, have been remodeled and enlarged with an additional second story, a three-car garage, spa and swimming pool.

Neighborhoods & Religious Heritage

As people of any nationality or background settle in a new area, their religious beliefs come with them...

Top: Dawn breaks over St. Petersubrg lending additional splendor to this Easter sunrise service of Grace Bible Church.
Above: These towers of the Epiphany Of Our Lord Ukranian Catholic Church add a simple but majestic presence to the skyline of St. Petersburg.

If they find there is no place to worship, establishing a spiritual home becomes a high priority.

Such is the foundation of every religious group in St. Petersburg – from established mainline churches to non-denominational chapels to the practice of beliefs more common in other parts of the world. Each can speak of their beginnings here and the growth that followed; forming congregations that inevitably reach beyond their members and into the community.

When they have the resources, these churches and synagogues become providers for those most in need with outreach ministries. When not, they help with generous donations of facilities, time and money to local social service agencies. They run our daycare centers, retirement places, preschools and some of the finest private schools in St. Petersburg. They adapt to social change by altering the style or method in which they deliver their message.

Many predominantly African-American congregations had their origins in the neighborhoods of a once segregated city. These churches filled a need not addressed by their all-white counterparts. The first was Mount Zion AME and much of St. Petersburg's black community grew up in the neighborhood around it. From the pulpit of the Bethel Community Baptist Church, the Reverend Enoch Douglas Davis, a highly respected crusader for civil rights, ministered not only to his congregation but to the entire community. Another anchor church is that of the National Baptist Convention, the Bethel Metropolitan Baptist Church.

Above; Part of the charm of downtown St. Petersburg is the marking of each hour and quarter hour by the chiming of bells from the carillon at First United Methodist Church. Opposite page: (upper left) Northside Baptist Curch (upper right) St. Peter's Episcopal Church (lower left) First United Methodist Church (lower right) 10th Street Church Of God.

Today's St. Petersburg churches continue to strive for a better understanding of each other while finding similarities through worship. Some have even introduced pulpit exchange programs to encourage integrated congregations.

There are churches that broadcast their services on television. Many have Internet sites. Several denominations have expanded their services to include separate times for singles or additional services with more contemporary formats using drama and music.

Here are just some of their stories.

Among the first groups to establish a presence in the new town of St. Petersburg, were the Congregationalists who held services in a railroad car shortly after the arrival of the first train. A few months later they built a church that became the foundation for three other United Church of Christ churches in the area.

Another emerging church was the Clearwater Mission of the Methodist Church, established in Pinellas in the late 1800's. Its new church became known as the St. Petersburg Methodist Episcopal Church South, since the Conference was in the southern branch of a pre-Civil War partition of the denomination. According to church accounts, however, the influx of northerners into St. Petersburg had prompted the formation of a congregation of the "northern" Methodist Episcopal Church. And the similarity in names caused considerable confusion to all but the parishioners themselves.

It wasn't until 1939 that the "northern" church became First Avenue Methodist Church and, later, Christ United Methodist Church – and the "southern" one became First United Methodist Church. Both have active congregations in downtown St. Petersburg, in buildings that were constructed during the boom of the twenties.

Such urban churches have tried to meet the spiritual needs of the Monday through Friday population of their downtown neighborhood. For example, when a group of city employees wanted to conduct a mid-day bible study, Christ United Methodist offered the use of its chapel during the week. Today the Episcopal Cathedral Church of St. Peter has a daily Eucharist; and St. Mary's Roman Catholic Church a daily Mass.

From 1892 to 1895 Mass was celebrated only a few times a year, when Jesuit priests journeyed from Tampa to minister to the needs of the Catholic population across the Bay. Today, more than 365-thousand Roman Catholics reside in the Diocese of St. Petersburg, its offices at the Cathedral of St. Jude the Apostle. The diocese covers Hillsborough, Pinellas, Pasco, Hernando and Citrus counties.

St. Mary Our Lady of Grace was one of three catholic churches built in the late 1920's following the rapid growth of St. Petersburg. Definite architectural plans to make the parishes of St. Joseph's (1926) Florentine, St. Mary's (1929) Byzantine, and St. Paul's (1938) Roman were carried out under pastoral direction. Yet it is the legend of the eight-sided brick building of St. Mary's that persists.

Local architect Henry Taylor came up with the unusual octagon design and, according to church accounts, built a prototype in order to work out any unforeseeable problems in advance. The smaller scale architectural building turned out to be the public restrooms on the approach to The Pier. The "comfort station" is stilled referred to as "Little St. Mary's" along with various versions of the story.

What was to become the Cathedral Church of St. Peter owes its legacy to the Church of St. Bartholomew. St. Bartholomew's was organized by a group of English immigrants who, as members of the Anglican Church, wanted to establish Episcopal churches in their new Pinellas community. The mission was established in 1887, a year before St. Petersburg was founded, in what was then Disston City.

continued on page 44

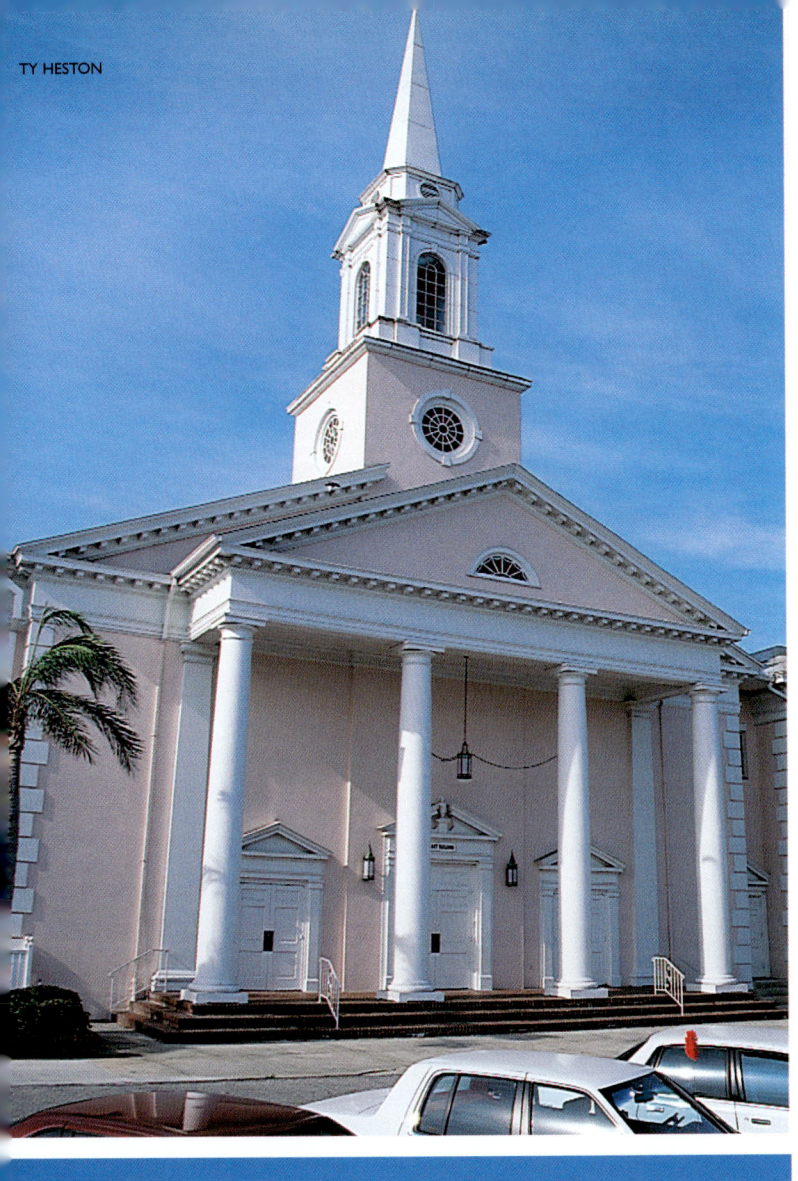

TY HESTON

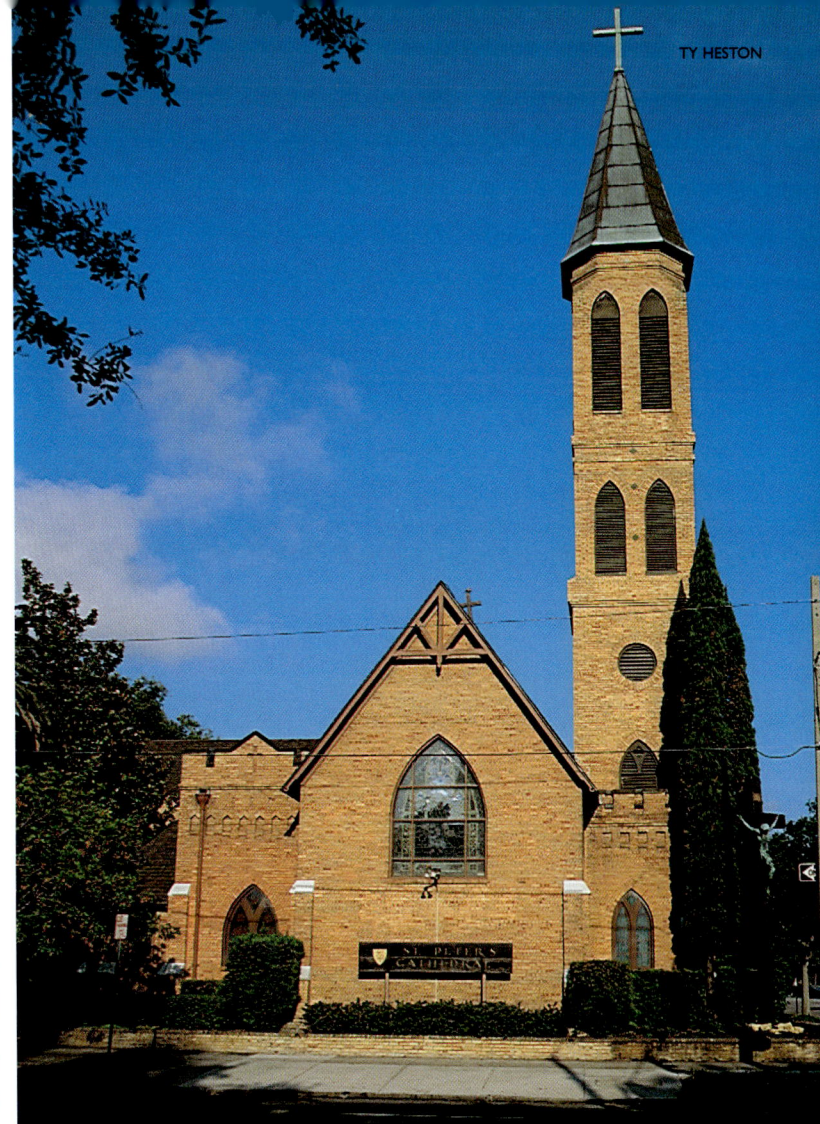

TY HESTON

TY HESTON

HERB SNITZER

FIRST PRESBYTERIAN CHURCH

A Presbyterian Presence

First Presbyterian Church, a member of the Presbyterian Church (USA), has been a spiritual cornerstone in St. Petersburg since October 1894. As part of the Reformed tradition, First Presbyterian maintains a strong emphasis on dynamic worship, innovative Christian education programs and comprehensive outreach to those in need. Members continue to be involved in the community, upholding a history of serving in varied city leadership roles.

Over the years, the church has been housed in three structures, moving to the current site alongside Tampa Bay in May 1967. "Relevant Classic" might best describe the striking architectural style of the church, designed by Harold E. Wagoner. The grand white sanctuary building marks the downtown shore of Tampa bay like a seaworthy ship in port.

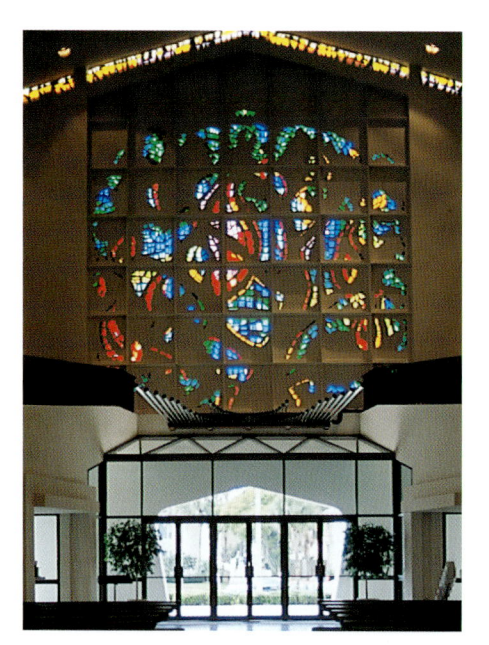

The hallmark stained glass portrayal of Moses' Burning Bush on the Beach Drive facade depicts one of the first Old Testament symbols of God's presence and sustaining power. Illuminated at night, the window beckons those outside the cathedral-like structure.

Inside, the vast nave manifests a quiet splendor. The communion table is a dominant feature of the chancel. Its central and forward position silently speaks to its accessibility. The choir is located to one side, allowing the worshipers' attention to be focused upon the central symbols (the marble cross and communion table) as the singers carry out their leadership in the service.

The empty cross is dominant on the wall behind the pulpit, which is elevated. The baptismal font is centrally located in the nave, affording proper significance to baptism as the important stepping stone into life. A ribbon of stained glass gives the effect of a "floating ceiling," seemingly diffusing the upper walls around their entire circumference. The ribbon of color restates the glory of the Burning Bush window above the narthex.

First Presbyterian Church has been long noted for inspirational leadership in worship and excellent music program. The sanctuary's exceptional acoustical clarity and outstanding Reuter pipe organ contribute to the rich, musical experience in worship and an annual concert series open to the public.

The organ, a 4-manual instrument with 58 ranks and 3,539 pipes, was renovated and updated in 1997. The new solid-state console controls both the main and antiphonal divisions, including the majestic Tropeta Imperial mounted below the Burning Bush. An outstanding choral program that includes all ages enriches the life of the church and community.

As First Presbyterian Church plans for the future, it strives to expand its mission. In this effort, the church has participated in making St. Petersburg a caring community. The church sponsors a comprehensive Day School for preschoolers on campus; it owns several group homes for children at risk, which are administered by local agencies; and it supports local helping agencies that assist the poor.

As the church prepares for ministry in the twenty-first century, it is developing programs to address the concerns of all ages, from infants to older adults, within and outside the church family. In seeking to encompass the diversity and talent of the community, First Presbyterian Church has a spiritual commitment to help others find peace as well as develop a social consciousness to share with those in need.

As a downtown church, First Presbyterian is experiencing a spiritual renewal that is attracting all ages. The beautiful facilities prominently located on St. Petersburg's waterfront avenue, Beach Drive, have the church well situated to continue its mission and ministry throughout the twenty-first century.

www.fpc-stpete.org

Neighborhoods & Religious Heritage

Temple Beth-El synagogue began in 1928 and now resides in South Pasadena.

With the new railroad to St. Petersburg and the increase in winter visitors, St. Bartholomew's built The Church of the Holy Spirit mission. In 1893 preparation to unite the congregation of south St. Petersburg with the one near the railroad terminus was begun and St. Peter's Episcopal Church was established. It moved to its present location, downtown, on land donated by Peter Tomlinson the following year.

Trinity Lutheran Church in St. Petersburg was the first Lutheran church on the West Coast of Florida, established in 1911 and moved to its present downtown location in 1924. In the 1950's Trinity was responsible for the establishment of three additional Lutheran churches in the area. From 1941 through 1943, its pastor also served a group of Lutherans in Bradenton and traveled by ferry across Tampa Bay every other Sunday afternoon to conduct an afternoon service between the morning and evening services in St. Petersburg.

It only took two women to start The Unitarian-Universalist Church of St. Petersburg in the early 1900's, and one was its minister. It is the second oldest UU Church in Pinellas County and occupies a charming Spanish-style building, on Mirror Lake Drive, downtown. One of its early members, a contractor who built the Don CeSar, donated leftover tile from the beach resort for use in construction of the church. Today the Unitarian-Universalist Church is committed to be an urban church and opens its doors to other groups who meet there.

The Orthodox community of St. Andrew Russian Orthodox Church was founded in 1948 by a small group of Russians who bought and moved a small garage to create a chapel. They chose St. Andrew Stratelat as their patron saint and rebuilt the chapel into a church. Today St. Andrew's Russian Orthodox Church, in south St. Petersburg, is the largest parish of its kind in the southern part of the United States. It follows the age-old Orthodox traditions of its pre-revolutionary Russian roots.

Several Reform temples, Conservative synagogues, and one Orthodox synagogue (in Palm Harbor) serve Jewish life in Pinellas County. From its 1928 beginings in downtown St. Petersburg, Temple Beth-El (Reform) moved to its present home in 1955 where it has grown to more than 600 families. Founded in 1923, Congregation B'nai Israel of St. Petersburg (Conservative) evolved from a nucleus of 12 families to a congregation of more than 400 families spanning at least four generations. In April 2000, its members ceremoniously walked three city blocks to their large, new synagogue in the Tyrone area of St. Petersburg.

Nearby is one of the largest protestant congregations in St. Petersburg – that of Pasadena Community Church, which, in addition to its 2,000-seat sanctuary, has introduced radio broadcasts to those parked in their cars outside. The church has been at the same location since 1925 and offers four Sunday services. Before the present building was constructed in 1960, Pasadena, a United Methodist church, used outdoor loudspeakers to reach its overflow winter crowd.

Crowds of worshipers once filled the sanctuary of the First Congregational United Church of Christ as well. But in 1994 the church stood empty at its downtown location of over 100 years. Now it is a part of new chapter being written about several historic church buildings in St. Petersburg. Having served as catalysts for other churches throughout the city, the buildings themselves are enjoying a second life.

Six years after closing its doors, the Gothic stone sanctuary and adjacent theater and parish hall of First Congregational found a buyer in one of Pinellas County's leading developers of business parks. His plans for the building include a restaurant, private living quarters and art studio.

The Disciples of Christ congregation sponsored two churches in other locations, before moving out of its original location. Now the former Mirror Lake Christian Church, at 100 years and on the National Register of Historic Places, is the Mirror Lake Lyceum, restored by four partners who saw its potential as a reception and meeting facility.

The First Church of Christ Scientist, built in 1925, was converted to a medium-sized performance hall in 1999. Now called The Palladium Theater, the downtown building serves local artists and organizations. A Christian Science Reading

continued on page 46

PASADENA COMMUNITY CHURCH

Faith for the Future

When Pasadena Community Church celebrated its 75th Anniversary at the turn of the millennium, there was little doubt that this United Methodist congregation and church leadership had progressive eyes focused as clearly on the future as the past. Located in St. Petersburg at 112 70th St. South, the church is a powerful spiritual magnet for residents of southern Pinellas County and the visitors to nearby beach communities.

The secret of Pasadena Community Church's significance in the community is a combination of contemporary style and religious substance, packaged in an accommodating blend of programs and services aimed at spreading the gospel to as large an audience as possible. As the church which broadcast services on loudspeakers to overflow crowds in the parking lot during the 1950s, beach goers can today tune car radios to a designated frequency to become a part of the fellowship inside.

While the Christian message has remained the same, the church's delivery has become a mixed media event, combining video productions, live contemporary music and drama. Labeled the Direct Connection, the church's 9:30 a.m. upbeat service is followed by a more traditional service at 10:45 a.m. Both are in fulfillment of a vision in which the church's 8,000-worshiper capacity will be realized.

In support of this goal, other, more personal programs continue to reach out to specific groups. Pasadena Community Church has offered a school from preschool through kindergarten for more than 40 years, and five years ago added a full elementary curriculum. PCC is also launching a Christian Academy geared to all ages. Similar to a Christian mentor program, classes for spiritual growth will be offered to novices and adepts alike.

The church's children and youth programs each are guided by a minister with sole responsibility for the group, whether teen or pre-school. The high-energy teen programs include mission trips, choir and a band, as well as a variety of sports teams. There's even a "mother's morning out" program which provides limited nursery day care, allowing mothers two to three hours of free time during the day.

This dynamic church has been a pioneer in offering Christian counseling to the community with two counselors on staff for over 20 years. The outreach to people in pain is also a hallmark of the church with years of support for community and international relief agencies.

Beyond Pasadena Community Church's futuristic offerings, the rich trappings of tradition include a 4,000 pipe Moller organ and a 100-member choir as part of the central focus to the sanctuaries 2,000-worshipper capacity. Outside there is parking space for 3,500 cars. Considering church records show that on Easter morning in 1951, 10,500 people were in attendance, the modern Pasadena Community Church is prepared to better that mark and continue to grow as the spiritual leader of the beach communities and southern Pinellas County.

www.pcumc.org

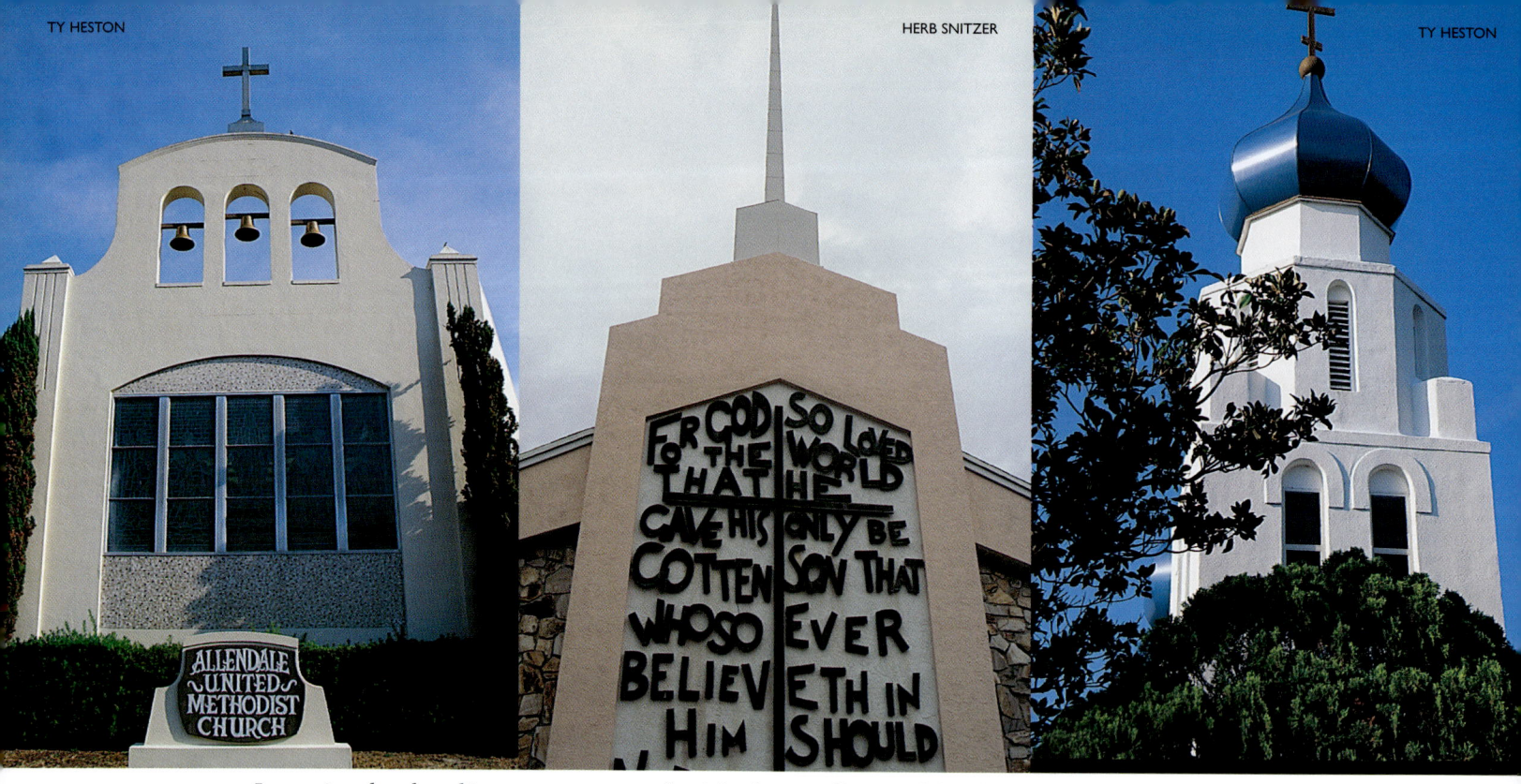

Interesting church architecture accentuates the rich religious offerings of the Allendale United Methodist Church, Northeast Park Baptist Church and St. Andrew Russian Orthodox Church in St. Petersburg..

Room remains open near Williams Park on First Avenue North in downtown.

Here in Florida, because there are so many seasonal residents, congregations are constantly challenged by fluctuating attendance between the winter tourists' months and the rest of the year. Another reality is that congregations sometimes decline in membership as people move from one neighborhood to another. One solution is to accept the statistics, close the building and try to sell it. Another is to move the church, which was the path taken by the parish members of Saint Bartholomew's.

In the late 1960's, with integration of its neighborhood and a loss of members, the historic church, the oldest in St. Petersburg, moved its building section by section to another location, 20 blocks south along 34th Street where it remains today.

At the same time, another stayed. Lakeview Presbyterian Church was founded as an all-white church affected by desegregation in the mid 1960's. As its neighborhood changed, Lakeview's focus became one of civil rights and social services. It began the first Head Start pre-school program in Pinellas County and established other outreach ministries.

On a more global scale, St. Petersburg congregations have consistently extended a helping hand and offered fresh starts, including the sponsorship of refugee families. Today there are many cultures within St. Petersburg's Asian community, a growing population estimated at about 15,000, including Cambodian, Chinese, Filipino, Hmong, Japanese, Korean, Laotian, Thai and Vietnamese.

Our Extended Family

Since 1994, the Asian Family and Community Empowerment Center has served more than 4,000 people with Asian origins in St. Petersburg. This neighborhood family center offers every type of assistance from driver's license preparation to employment referrals. Using funding agencies' guidelines, the center allows the Asian communities to interact in educational, cultural, social service and community activities while helping to empower participants to become self-sufficient.

The St. Petersburg International Folk Fair Society (SPIFFS) functions on a social level only. With its over 40 ethnic member groups, SPIFFS is one of the largest organizations of its kind in the United States. The highlight of the year is the folk fair itself, featuring continuous entertainment center stage, surrounded by displays that reflect the heritage, culture and traditions of each group.

Chapter 3
Downtown, Waterfront, Museums & The Arts

TY HESTON

With each new sunrise, the showy sparkle on the waters of Tampa Bay reflects a St. Petersburg skyline that is undeniably looking more and more like the significant city it was destined to become…

Downtown, Waterfront, Museums & The Arts

We believe St. Petersburg's downtown waterfront is the most picturesque in Florida – seven miles of natural beauty and public parkland, with a backdrop of businesses and residences, historic and new – here for all to enjoy, thanks in part to the foresight of the St. Petersburg Area Chamber of Commerce.

In 1906, members of the Board of Trade, predecessor to the Chamber, acquired several key waterfront properties to hold as trustees until such time that the city could take them over. City Council approved and requested that the Board's Waterfront Committee secure options on as much waterfront as possible.

Others agreed. "The People's waterfront is coming, and when here it will be unequalled anywhere else in all Florida, and excelled by few places in the whole world," said *St. Petersburg Times* editor William L. Straub, a strong supporter of the idea. The City of St. Petersburg eventually acquired the entire downtown waterfront.

Nearly a century later, after the building boom of the 20's, the lull of the 50's and the incomplete efforts of the 80's, downtown St. Petersburg and its waterfront are today, more than ever, a source of pride. The seven-mile stretch of public

Preceding pages: Aerial view from above the Pier shows St. Petersburg's beautiful waterfront.
Opposite: St. Petersburg's waterfront Yacht Club (foreground) borders the heart of downtown.

TY HESTON

Downtown, Waterfront, Museums & The Arts

The "Looper" serves the downtown residents and tourists.

land extends as far north as 18th Avenue NE on Coffee Pot Bayou near North Shore Park. It follows the coastline south, with few interruptions, beyond the Coast Guard station and Bayboro Harbor to Lassing Park.

Set your sails for longitude 82° 38.00' W, latitude 27° 46.15' N. If it is early you will catch the sunrise showering its morning glow across the downtown skyline, and maybe see a bottle-nose dolphin leap from Tampa Bay and some brown pelicans dive into the water for a meal. If there's a good breeze you will be able to hear one of the gentle sounds of St. Petersburg – the rhythmic chime of rigging against masts. You will be headed for the downtown waterfront marina in the nearest yacht basin to The Pier.

Since the early days of the city, The Pier has been a gathering spot where people could enjoy the waterfront, its marine life and its moods, along with the exceptional view. There have been three different pier buildings at the same location — the Municipal Recreation Pier built in 1913, the Million Dollar Pier of the 1920s and the present structure built in 1973 and reopened in 1988 after renovation. The Pier, extending 1,400 feet into the bay, is one of the most photographed landmarks of St. Petersburg and is symbolic of the tourism industry here.

The Pier attracts an average of half the area's annual 4.5-million visitors. The building itself has its own style of entertainment with three restaurants and a food court, an array of interesting shops, and a small aquarium museum. On the third floor of this five-story structure is Great Explorations the children's hands-on museum with its variety of science-theme exhibits. The Pier Aquarium and Great Explorations are two of seven downtown museums.

The panoramic view from the top of The Pier encompasses the central and south yacht basins of the St. Petersburg Municipal Marina, the St. Petersburg Yacht Club (80 slips), and to the north, the Vinoy Yacht Basin. There are 610 permanent wet slips at the City Marina, the largest municipal marina in Florida. All are occupied with approximately 150 live-aboard families year round. There is a 500-foot transient dock for vessels up to 110 feet.

Look to the south towards Albert Whitted Airport, one the nations few executive airparks located in a downtown. This city-owned waterfront airport caters to corporate planes, helicopters, and private pilots and instructors. There are over 140 aircraft based at Albert Whitted which records approximately 89,000 aircraft operations annually.

The modern, curved architecture of the next building facing the waterfront is the Bayfront Center complex. It houses the Mahaffey Theater for the performing arts and a separate 23,500-square foot arena, The Times Bayfront Arena, used for concerts, sporting events, conferences and trade shows and the famous Ringling Bros. and Barnum & Bailey Circus.

Continue to follow the shoreline and notice the lights of Florida Power Park, home of Al Lang Field and an integral part of the city's spring training baseball history. Listen carefully and you can imagine the sound of Stan Musial hitting the first home run of that first game — onto Beach Drive — when the Cardinals beat the Yankees in 1947.

With the arrival of the Tampa Bay Devil Rays in 1998,

continued on page 56

*Above: Numerous masts fill the largest municipal marina in Florida.
Below: The Pier – the single most visited attraction in St. Petersburg and Pinellas County.*

BAYWALK

The Soul of St. Pete

No project in downtown St. Petersburg typifies the heart of the community or the soul of the city more than BayWalk. As a vital and dynamic city reaches to achieve the services and amenities for its citizens so typical in major metropolitan areas, the core of downtown St. Petersburg has long sought an anchor for entertainment and retail excellence. BayWalk is that anchor.

Opened in 2000, BayWalk represents a 150,000 plus square foot open-air, themed plaza filled with top-notch retailers, innovative and fun restaurants and the plaza's anchor tenant, Muvico, a 20 screen, all stadium seating theater complex. Occupying one square block in the heart of downtown, BayWalk is connected to a 1,380-space parking garage by a half-block long colorful pedestrian promenade.

As unique as the city itself, BayWalk's Mediterranean Revival architecture and lush tropical landscaping blends in with the natural beauty of St. Petersburg's waterfront while offering a plaza with features both casual and distinctive. No ordinary retailers call this home. The blend of restaurants, cafes, clothing, the bookstore and service shops provides a new concept in upscale retail excitement for residents and visitors alike.

The Muvico complex, as an example, not only features stadium-style seating in each of the 20 theaters, but also digital sound systems, wall-to-wall curved screens and specially designed plush seats created exclusively for Muvico Theaters and automatic customer self-serve ticket dispensing machines. Additionally, the BayWalk 20 brings some exciting exclusives: an in-theater child care facility which offers parents a fun and entertaining solution to the babysitting dilemma; and concession stands that feature much more than just popcorn and sodas. Extended menu items include

Anchoring BayWalk is Muvico's 20 screen state-of-the-art theater complex.

54

freshly prepared pizza, an array of appealing gourmet appetizers, delicious desserts and gourmet coffee.

The development as a whole is more than just a themed plaza. BayWalk's existence represents a dynamic consortium of local businesses whose vision of downtown St. Petersburg was incomplete without BayWalk. The driving forces behind this vision were The Sembler Company, a St. Petersburg company responsible for the development and management of many of the Southeast's shopping center successes for the past 40 years, and Redevelopment Partners. Inc.

Joining The Sembler Company's Chairman, Mel Sembler, were Fred Bullard, CEO of Clearwater's The Bullard Group and Van McNeel, Chairman of McNeel International, Inc, both Tampa Bay area businessmen, who merged their resources into the creation of Redevelopment Partners as co-developers of the project. BayWalk's exclusive leasing agent, Retail Estate, Inc. of Miami, is responsible for such retail successes as Miami's CoCoWalk, Streets of MayFair, Peabody Place in Memphis, and Centro Ybor located in the historic district of Tampa. Development Design Group, an international architecture, planning and design firm, performed conceptual and architectural development for BayWalk. Development Design Group is a world leader in the creation of high profile, award-winning specialty retail environments. Working in conjunction with Development Design Group, our locally based CSJM Architects completed the collective design vision unique to BayWalk. Completing the design team was the locally based landscape architect firm of Phil Graham & Associates. The physical construction of the project was successfully performed by Bay Area Site Improvement Company and Sound Construction Group.

In addition to BayWalk's themed plaza, the City of St. Petersburg was responsible for the design and construction of the nearby six level parking garage. Portions of the first floor of the garage also contain an additional 80,000 square feet of retail space.

Located between 1st and 2nd Streets North and 2nd and 3rd Avenues, BayWalk is just steps away from downtown museums, the St. Petersburg Pier, sports complexes, a four-star resort, numerous hotels and high-rise condominiums, and just 15 minutes away from the Gulf beaches. With more than 7 million annual visitors and 2 million area residents in the Tampa Bay area, BayWalk, as the soul of St. Petersburg, is the new, lively destination.

www.sembler.com

Downtown, Waterfront, Museums & The Arts

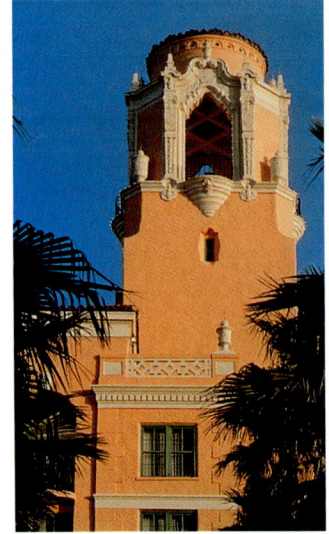

St. Petersburg became more that a spring training city; the major league team has a year-round home in St. Petersburg. The Devil Ray's spring training games are played at Florida Power Park and regular season home games are played at Tropicana Field, about ten blocks west in what is the city's sports fan-friendly Dome District.

On the approach to the Pier is St. Petersburg's own Museum of History. This facility was completely remodeled and reopened in 1993 with three galleries. The Flight One Gallery celebrates the birth of the world's first scheduled airline service and features a replica of the Benoist airboat flown across Tampa Bay in 1914. The Timeline Gallery features a collection of local artifacts and interactive displays, while the Rotating Gallery presents changing exhibitions. The Museum of History is home to the St. Petersburg Historical Society whose members maintain an extensive archive of city history.

Among the pages of that history is the story of the Vinoy, another of St. Petersburg's most recognized downtown landmarks. Originally built in 1924, the regal 360-room hotel reopened as a world-class resort in 1992 after a $93-million historic renovation. The restored building, now the Renaissance Vinoy Resort, is nostalgically grand, inside and out. It features its original hand-painted wood beam ceilings and Mediterranean arches and tile mosaics.

It is one of three major downtown hotels in a tourist destination that boasts the world's finest accommodations

continued on page 60

Above: The 8,000-seat Times Bayfront Center Arena hosts a variety of activities from basketball to the circus. Right: The North Yacht Basin fronting the majestic Renaissance Vinoy Resort.

CITY OF ST. PETERSBURG

VINOY PLACE

While many residences are elegant, only one resorts to such indulgence. Vinoy Place on the downtown waterfront.

The majestic residences of Vinoy Place overlook the downtown St. Petersburg waterfront and are served by the indulgent amenities of the opulent Renaissance Vinoy Resort and Golf Club, which has been named to the National Register of Historic Places. The gated Vinoy Place community encompasses four condominium towers and ten villa-style Cityhomes, and is positioned perfectly in the heart of the downtown community.

The residences are located within a short distance of the area's many cultural and entertainment attractions, including the Fine Arts Museum, Salvador Dali Museum, the Mahaffey Theater, Florida International Museum, BayWalk, the "Pier," Tropicana Field and two bayside beaches. Many fine shops, boutiques and cafes are a short stroll away along the beautiful palm-lined Beach Drive.

The four mid-rise towers offer only two residences per floor, each with sweeping views of the St. Petersburg waterfront. Individual elevator lobbies ensure privacy, while 24-hour security provides owners with peace of mind. Selected amenities of the historic hotel, such as room service, laundry and dry cleaning service, concierge service are made available to every privileged resident. In addition, the golf, tennis, spa and other four-star resort facilities of The Vinoy Club are only steps away for resident members.

Old-world elegance is renewed in the finest sense in this world-class community. Each residence features a full gourmet kitchen equipped with granite countertops, custom cabinets and top-of-the-line appliances. As well, the residences are equipped with the most advanced wiring to accommodate computers, fax machines and other technological devices commonly found in homes today. Only the exquisite beauty and elaborate furnishings outweigh the functionality of these residences.

As the showplace of St. Petersburg's scenic waterfront, Vinoy Place recalls the style and glamour of another era; one that for decades has been a haven for moguls, socialites and celebrities and today is reborn in these captivating residences.

www.vinoyplace.com

RENAISSANCE VINOY RESORT AND GOLF CLUB

Similar to Camelot's castle, the modern Renaissance Vinoy Resort and Golf Club has a transcendental quality that defies time and space. Opened on New Year's Eve, 1925, the original Vinoy Park Hotel became an extraordinary fantasyland for the world's most rich and famous. The passing decades have not diminished the quality nor the stature of downtown St. Petersburg's crown jewel.

While it may be hard to believe that the Vinoy Park was slated for demolition in the early 1990's after remaining vacant for 18 years, revival efforts were began by Stouffer Hotels and Resorts. After a painstaking $93 million renovation, the *Grand Dame* of the waterfront was back better than ever. In 1993, one year after the grand reopening, Renaissance Hotels International purchased Stouffer.

Today's Renaissance Vinoy Resort boasts a total of 360 guest rooms, 258 in the original building and 102 in a new connected tower. All of the seven story tower's first-floor rooms feature outdoor patio spas. Twenty suites offer the ultimate in executive amenities. Most of the resort's suites and guest rooms feature spectacular water views.

Some of the Renaissance Vinoy's enhancements include outstanding recreational amenities, such as an 18-hole championship golf course and clubhouse, a 12-court tennis complex, two heated outdoor swimming pools, three spas and a fully-equipped fitness center. A 74-slip marina is located opposite the resort allowing immediate access to Tampa Bay and the Gulf of Mexico.

With five superior restaurants, each offering a unique ambiance and cuisine, the Renaissance Vinoy Resort also boasts 35,000 square feet of indoor function space and an additional 21,000 square feet of artfully landscaped outdoor function space. The Vinoy Grand, Plaza, Sunset and Palm Court Ballrooms are perfectly suited for any business or social occasion.

What the Renaissance Vinoy Resort has to offer is only superceded by the way in which it is offered. True to the hotel's heritage, opulence is around every corner, superb service is a cut above the best and unique, intimate events ranging from musical to theatrical are always underway. Whether meeting for conventions or afternoon tea, the Vinoy's eclectic bill of fare is ever fresh and always surprising.

Named to the National Register of Historic Places and a member of the exclusive Historic Hotels of America, the Renaissance Vinoy Resort and Golf Club is both a landmark in time and in human imagination. Like Camelot, the hotel represents a reality found few in other places, and the majority of those are entirely fictional.

www.renaissancehotels.com

Downtown, Waterfront, Museums & The Arts

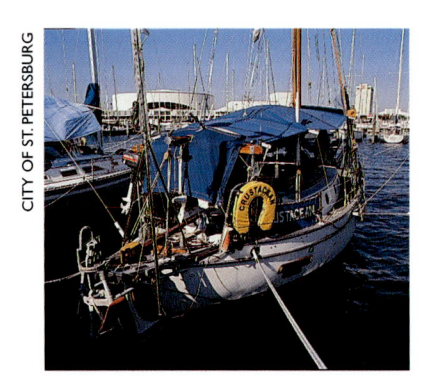

including many wonderful bed and breakfasts. The convenient Hilton-St. Petersburg, across from Florida Power Park, and the Holiday Inn Heritage with a recent 80-room addition, are also located within a few blocks.

You could begin a walking tour of St. Petersburg's downtown from the city-owned waterfront Vinoy Park the site of many of St. Petersburg special outdoor concerts and events, to Beach Drive, a winding waterfront promenade of awning-covered shops, restaurants, galleries and more parkland.

You would soon reach Straub Park, one of 125 city parks and another site for outdoor activities such as the three-day Taste of Pinellas when our most popular restaurants participate in this summertime sampling of fine food set to music. In November, at Vinoy Park, it's Ribfest, more music and some highly competitive best ribs-best sauce entries.

Such events and a myriad of others – like offshore powerboat races, a world class triathlon, running festival, two annual boat shows a year, extreme sports competitions, and a Festival of States with two parades and a jazz festival – are very

continued on page 62

Grand view of the South Yacht Basin encompassing Albert Whitted Airport, Bayfront Center and Mahaffey Theater, and Florida Power Park.

MUSEUM OF FINE ARTS

The Museum of Fine Arts was founded by art collector and philanthropist Margaret Acheson Stuart (1896-1980), who wanted people in the area to have direct contact with world masterpieces. She gave magnanimously to this project and recruited the assistance of others in pursuing her dream. The City of St. Petersburg donated the four-acre site of choice waterfront property. The Museum opened to the public in 1965, the first art museum in the city.

The Museum has been guided by three distinguished directors – Rexford Stead (1963-1967), Lee Malone (1967-1980), and Michael Milkovich (1982-present) – and for many years, by the founder's nephew, Charles W. Mackey, now the President Emeritus of the Board of Trustees. Mr. Mackey, his fellow trustees, and Mr. Milkovich raised substantial funds to double the galleries from ten to twenty and to add a second floor for administrative offices, classrooms, and a library by 1989. The Museum was accredited by the American Association of Museums in 1973 and reaccredited in 1983 and 1998. Civic leader and art collector Carol A. Upham, the current President of the Board, is energetically leading the Museum into the new millennium.

The permanent collection has grown from 500 works to more than 4,000 today and is the only comprehensive art collection, extending from antiquity to the present day, on the Florida west coast. Among the major French artists represented in the collection are Fragonard, Vigée-Lebrun, Daumier, Corot, Cézanne, Monet, Rodin, Morisot, Gauguin, Renoir, and Picabia. American artists with work in the collection include Thomas Moran, Whistler, Homer, Inness, Prendergast, Bellows, Henri, Luks, O'Keeffe, Warhol, Rauschenberg, and Rosenquist.

The photography holdings feature works by Fox Talbot, Steichen, Weston, Adams, Cartier-Bresson, Siskind, Strand, Avedon, and Arbus. Also on view are ancient Greek and Roman, pre-Columbian, Asian, African, Native American, and decorative arts, including a dramatic gallery of Steuben glass.

The elegant Palladian-style building, designed by John Volk, is a Florida landmark combining the style of a classic art museum with a Mediterranean villa. The vast majority of the galleries are room-size and carpeted, and decorative arts are combined with paintings and sculpture of the period. The Museum also has splendid Membership and Sculpture Gardens, which encourage reflection, and the striking Marly Room, a lecture and performing arts hall and the setting for a highly respected chamber music series.

Georgia O'Keeffe's *Poppy,* **1927**
Gift of Charles C. and Margaret Stevenson Henderson in memory of Jeanne Crawford Henderson

www.fine-arts.org

The SPIFFS folk fair annually showcases a rich history of the cultures that make up Pinellas.

Since 1917, the Festival of States is one of St. Petersburg's most popular annual events.

inviting for people to come downtown and have fun. In fact there are 800 events and festivals held in St. Petersburg every year, attracting an annual attendance of 9-million people, according to city figures. On quieter days there is enough cultural and artistic expression for a city twice the size of St. Petersburg.

Across from the banyan trees of North Straub Park, is the St. Petersburg Museum of Fine Arts. This museum, with its intimate setting of a Mediterranean villa, is accredited by the American Association of Museums and has the only comprehensive art collection on the Florida west coast. Included in the museum's significant holdings are collections of European, American, pre-Columbian and Far Eastern art; works by such major artists as Cézanne, Monet, Gauguin, Renoir, Rodin and O'Keeffe. Special exhibits are present throughout the year in painting, sculpture, the decorative and even the performing arts.

Three blocks to the west is the Florida International Museum. Opened in 1995, the museum has seen over two million visitors making it one of Florida's most popular cultural attractions. The museum is now a Smithsonian Institution Affiliate and has its own collection of Kennedy family artifacts and presents changing exhibits in addition to its permanent galleries.

Beyond the Florida International Museum is the fourth largest museum of its kind in the United States. The Florida Holocaust Museum gives visitors the opportunity to view the unparalleled permanent exhibit "History, Heritage and Hope." Changing special art and historical exhibitions are always on view at this repository for photographs, memorabilia, books, films, video tapes and other materials from and about the Holocaust, World War II and the events leading up to it. An expansive second floor gallery focuses on Holocaust art.

At the south end of downtown is the Salvador Dali Museum, permanent home of the most comprehensive collection of this significant artist's works. Dali's longtime friends, Eleanor R. and A. Reynolds Morse of Cleveland, Ohio, assembled the museum's vast collection over a 45-year period.

First Night has become a tradition for welcoming in the new year.

Taste of Pinellas is a food lovers delight.

A New Year's Eve tradition – First Night labyrinth of lighted candles.

Mainsail art festival in St. Petersburg's waterfront park.

Bayboro Harbor's Port of St. Petersburg and Albert Whitted Airport both are convenient to downtown.

Lighted Boat Parade

The annual SCLC Martin Luther King Jr. Drum Major for Justice Parade.

Downtown, Waterfront, Museums & The Arts

A nationwide search for a permanent home for the art culminated with the Morse's selection of St. Petersburg, Florida. The Salvador Dali Museum opened in 1982 with major renovations in 1995. The scope of the collection, spanning the years 1914 to 1980, presents a panorama of Dali's diverse and evolving art. Periodic rotation and changing special exhibitions allow visitors to view varying works on repeat visits.

In addition to the museums, at least 20 art galleries can be found throughout downtown. Renowned artist P. Buckley Moss, a resident of St. Petersburg, occasionally works from the adjoining studio of her landmark gallery near Straub Park. The P. Buckley Moss Gallery houses the largest collection of her works in the southern states.

Across the street The Glass Canvas Gallery is the region's largest and most extensive studio quality, art glass gallery. It has works by over 300 glass artists from around the world in a constantly changing panorama of form and color. And along Beach Drive, Pinellas County's first Thomas Kinkade Signature Gallery features a comprehensive collection of works by the "painter of light."

Meanwhile, local established and emerging artists have dozens of galleries in which to show their works, including downtown restaurants that encourage the arts with receptions and exhibit space. Salt Creek Artworks houses two galleries for contemporary art and has working artist's studio space. Artist's studios and arts related office suites are also available at a place called Artspace in downtown.

Classes in jewelry, pottery, painting and sculpture are offered year round at The Arts Center, which has gallery exhibitions of local and nationally know contemporary artists, while Creative Clay Cultural Art Center has arts related courses for persons with developmental disabilities.

In addition to its rotating national exhibitions, Florida Craftsmen Gallery is a statewide organization featuring contemporary craft art by over 100 Florida artists. The gallery is in St. Petersburg and, along with two-dozen others, is a member of the Downtown Arts Association. This organization actively coordinates several art-awareness events in St. Petersburg, including a monthly Gallery Walk of the downtown galleries.

Art festivals are not only good for the arts, but serve as visitor attractions in Pinellas County. Mainsail is one of the biggest. The annual outdoor art festival, so appropriately named for its St. Petersburg downtown waterfront location, has become one of the major events of its kind in the United

continued on page 66

Part of St. Petersburg's seven miles of public waterfront parks and activities is the playground at Demen's Landing.

GLASS CANVAS GALLERY

Art is defined by its medium but seldom is the medium, in itself, considered art. Glass is one of the exceptions, and one of St. Petersburg's exceptional galleries takes this art to its highest form. The nationally renowned Glass Canvas Gallery is a gallery like no other and a dazzling, exciting place to visit.

Imagine being an artist using only sand, soda, heat and magic to create the canvas upon which to present art so beautiful the viewer must pause to admire it. Art so sensuous and silky the hand must reach out to caress the object to confirm what the eye sees. Imagine this art presented in a beautiful gallery along St. Petersburg's downtown waterfront.

The gallery presents an ever-changing palette of breathtakingly beautiful art. It offers a treasure chest of ideas for weddings, holidays, and more. The serious collector will find a wealth of exquisite collectibles.

The Glass Canvas Gallery, which is just off Beach Drive, was founded in 1991 to bring the world's finest studio quality, glass art to St. Petersburg and the Tampa Bay area. The Gallery works with more than 350 artists from around the world. All the pieces presented are one-of-a-kind and are signed by the artist. All forms of art glass are presented to the Gallery's clientele, along with biographical information on the artist and specific techniques used in its creation.

The Gallery is one of the largest art glass galleries in the country. Clients from all 50 states and many foreign countries come to the Gallery because of its unmatched service, selection and value.

The Gallery's owners, Rosalee and Dick Fortune discovered St. Petersburg while living in California amid careers with large multinational corporations. The Fortunes quickly fell in love with Florida's Sun Coast and commuted coast-to-coast as often as possible. Now full-time residents, the Fortunes and their Glass Canvas Gallery bring a unique perspective to St. Petersburg's vibrant and growing art and cultural community.

www.GlassCanvasGallery.com

Above: The beloved Historic Coliseum still actively serves a wide array of events and activities.
Below: The Florida Orchestra is an outstanding regional orchestra and the Mahaffey Theater acts as its host venue in St. Petersburg.

States. It is on the April calendars of major artists everywhere who hope to be included among the 250 participants selected to show their works.

Another Spring event occurs when American Stage, Tampa Bay's oldest professional theater company, moves out of its intimate, 130-seat theater and builds an outdoor stage at Demen's Landing, the downtown waterfront park at the south yacht basin. Here, under the stars, the company delights sell-out audiences by putting music and staging to one of Shakespeare's works for its annual American Stage in the Park performances. The innovative productions draw more than 20,000 people each year.

For more traditional theater in St. Petersburg, the 2,000-seat Mahaffey Theater is a magnificent performing arts center, considered one of the most beautiful rooms in central Florida. It is part of the waterfront Bayfront Center. The Mahaffey is host to the Florida Orchestra, recognized as a major cultural institution, one of the leading professional symphony orchestras in Florida, and one of the best regional orchestras in America. A local tradition has become the orchestra's annual, free, outdoor concert in North Straub Park. The orchestra, under the direction of Jahja Ling from 1988 through 1999, became the first symphony orchestra to play at a Super Bowl. It was 1991.

One of St. Petersburg's most celebrated pieces of public art is the Security Lizard perched atop the city's fleet maintenance building on the approach to I-275. The huge metal sculpture is so named because the lizard's prey is actually a working security light that shines down on the grounds below. It is one of many pieces of public art funded through a percent for the arts ordinance.

For even more evidence that the arts thrive in St. Petersburg, in 1998 an historic church building was transformed into a 903-seat, non-profit performing arts hall. The First Church of Christ Scientist, built in 1925, is now the

continued on page 68

THE ST. PETERSBURG MUSEUM OF HISTORY

Sometimes the best place to see history is to visit the site where it all began.

St. Petersburg's Museum of History, because of its close proximity to the Pier, is located in the heart of what certainly is one of the city's most historic areas. Founded in 1920 as the St. Petersburg Historical Society, the city of St. Petersburg provided the use of an old aquarium building (located on the same site as today's Museum) for the public display of its collections.

In 1950, the aquarium building was razed and a new larger facility served as the Museum until December 1991. In 1990, the city began an expansion of the Museum to house both the growing collections of the Society (today numbering a remarkable 32,000 objects) and the collections of the Florida Aviation Historical Society. This collection includes a life-size working replica of the Benoist Airboat, which flew the first scheduled passenger air service in the world not far from the Museum's current location!

In January 1993 the new Museum opened with four exhibit galleries. The Timeline Gallery offers a chronological walk through time from the area's prehistory to today's social and cultural stories. Visitors will see, hear, touch and learn the area's history through exhibits, displays, videos and interactive computers.

The Flight One Gallery tells the story of the birth of scheduled passenger aviation through artifact displays, models and videos. The Rotating Gallery houses two major exhibitions each year highlighting the rich and unique histories of the Pinellas Peninsula. These exhibitions include items from the Museum's incredible collections and archive materials, combined with research and loans from scholars, collectors and the general public.

Finally, the Hall of History presents traveling displays, an eclectic assortment of artifacts from the collections, and a special focus display with changing themes of historical significance. The Museum's Archival Library contains over 5,000 resource materials in the forms of books, documents, photographs, films, records, drawings and maps. Many of these materials are original and one-of-a-kind items.

The Benoist Learning Center provides space for meetings and training sessions, as well as many of the over 35 public education programs hosted by the Museum each year. The Museum gift shop has a very unique assortment of gifts, reproductions, books, jewelry, art, and historic memorabilia that cannot be found elsewhere.

www.ij.net/spmh

Palladium Theatre, brought back to life with private funds and a state grant enabling local dancers, musicians and actors to present public performances at affordable ticket prices.

It is located near the landmark Coliseum. Built in 1924, the Historic Coliseum was purchased by the City of St. Petersburg in 1989. The "south's finest ballroom," as it is known, opens it's oak dance floor for everything from ballroom dancing to corporate functions with seating for up to 2,000. It is one of the Tampa Bay area's most unique multi-use facilities.

Studies show that downtowns are back and buyers are interested in a bustling urban environment with cultural amenities. They want to be able to work near where they live and live near where they can enjoy the conveniences of a progressive city. If it has a gorgeous waterfront view, all the better! St. Petersburg can now fulfill such preferences.

Overshadowing the unfulfilled hopes of the 1980's, land once acquired by Bay Plaza, has now yielded to two luxurious waterfront condominium developments and yet another near the Vinoy. Together, these three new additions have added nearly 200 new residential addresses in St Petersburg. What has always been the first choice in Florida real estate – waterfront – is now available downtown.

The well-appointed homes of the Cloisters on Beach Drive range from 1,800 to 2,800 square feet and occupy three homes per floor of the 14-story condominium. The private second floor includes pool, business center, guest quarters and gym.

Florencia, across from the St. Petersburg Yacht Club, has 21 stories and homes range from 2,630 to 3,000 square feet.

continued on page 70

Above: The celebrated public art sculpture "Security Lizard" snaps its prey.
Below: Three of the beautiful downtown condos that overlook the parks and waterfront.

BANKERS INSURANCE GROUP

Choose To Lead

Headquartered in St. Petersburg, Bankers Insurance Group has long played an important role in the development of the downtown area and the economic strength of the community. From its beginnings as a small property and casualty company, Bankers has grown steadily during the past 25 years into a recognized industry leader. Today, the Group does business in all 50 states through its three property and casualty insurance companies, its life and health insurer, and a variety of related enterprises.

Bankers has been a national leader in flood insurance since 1984, and today ranks as the country's second largest provider. In both 1999 and 2000, the company was recognized by the National Flood Insurance Program for having the highest growth in policies. Bankers also maintains an active consumer information program designed to educate property owners about the risks of flooding. The program includes an interactive web site, a coloring book for children, and media interviews with Bankers' flood insurance experts.

Building on its early success in flood insurance, the company has gone on to excel in other product lines including homeowners, auto, and commercial insurance.

"Customer Service Has No Boundaries" is the theme of the annual Customer Service Week and ongoing training programs. This theme reflects Bankers' philosophy of responsiveness and total service to policyholders, agents and other customers. Associates are committed to looking beyond immediate solutions and quick answers, constantly seeking better, faster, more efficient ways to meet customers' needs.

Bankers' corporate culture is geared to the development of leadership qualities and skills. The corporate training program, Bankers University, provides extensive career advancement and professional growth resources for all associates. By identifying and focusing on core competencies that apply to every position across the company, Bankers creates a clear path to job success. The result is a work environment that cultivates leadership, fosters creativity and rewards initiative. Individually and collectively, Bankers' nearly 400 associates support a wide variety of local non-profit organizations. From sponsoring a charity golf tournament to collecting toys and food for needy families, Bankers continually reaches out to the St. Petersburg community.

www.bankersinsurance.com

Central Avenue, near Tropicana Field, is undergoing a stunning transformation.

This condominium also features three homes per floor, each with direct water views. Florencia's third floor amenities include a lap pool and fitness center.

Vinoy Place is a luxury condominium and town home project built in the Mediterranean Revival style of the adjacent Renaissance Vinoy Resort. It consists of four mid-rise condominium towers and ten two- and three-story town homes. There are two condominium residences per floor, ranging from 2,633 to 3,653 square feet. The city homes have 2,932 to 4,407 square feet.

In keeping with these lifestyle preferences is BayWalk a $30-million downtown entertainment and retail center developed by the Sembler Company. The 1999 groundbreaking for BayWalk was symbolic for St. Petersburg. After earlier disappointments for retail development, we had something we could see and touch – here and now. We were reminded that this is not a city to settle for what could have been. This is St. Petersburg, where visions become reality.

BayWalk is a 150-thousand square foot open-air retail plaza anchored by an 84-thousand square foot, 20-screen Muvico Theater with stadium-style seating and wall-to-wall curved screens. A pedestrian promenade with more shop-

continued on page 72

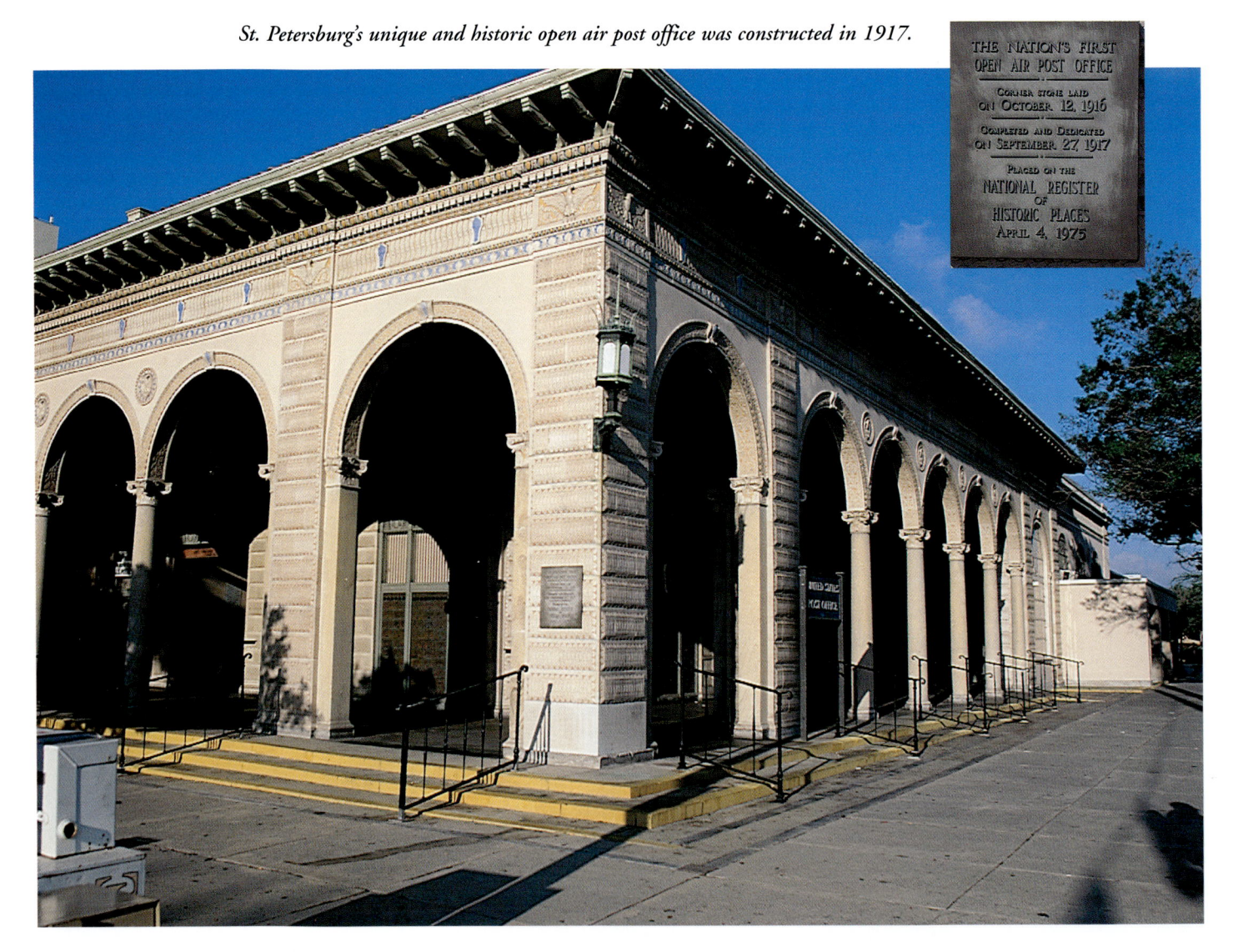

St. Petersburg's unique and historic open air post office was constructed in 1917.

70

FLORENCIA

Both the history and the future of downtown St. Petersburg have met at one location on Beach Drive. Long-time residents have fond memories of the Soreno Hotel, but time and changing conditions brought the hotels demolition in 1992. In the Soreno's place has risen Florencia, a 50-condominium residence in a singularly spectacular 21-story building.

The Florencia's Mediterranean style architecture pays respect to the Soreno by incorporating some of the architectural details in its design. But from there the differences are distinctive and definitely modern. Florencia features large three-bedroom homes with only three residences per floor, each with walls of glass allowing owners panoramic direct open water views of Straub Park and Tampa Bay to the east and city views and sunsets to the west. The sweeping views are bracketed by spacious verandahs.

Built by JMC Communities, the leading developer of condominiums in the St. Petersburg area for over 20 years, Florencia features quality construction throughout, including laminated glass windows, variable-speed air conditioning, cast iron drainage piping, sound proofing, and a structured wiring system for the future including CAT5. Each floor is supported by post-tension construction and has reinforced concrete masonry on the exterior walls. JMC also invested a half-million dollars to enhance the streetscape around the building.

The Florencia's two-story entry lobby offers 24-hour concierge service and specialty boutiques are located on Beach Drive. A covered colonnade with an understated memorial, the Soreno Plaza Fountain, honors the historic hotel that once stood on this location.

The "Park Room," named for one of the gathering places in the Soreno Hotel, is Florencia's 3rd floor social room overlooking Straub Park and the harbor. Two walls in the Park Room are used as displays for Soreno Hotel memorabilia.

Florencia stands proudly along St. Petersburg's waterfront.

Florencia's elegant 2-story entrance lobby.

www.jmccommunities.com

Downtown, Waterfront, Museums & The Arts

ping kiosks will leads from BayWalk to a new parking garage directly across from the Florida International Museum. The project also has meant additional jobs downtown.

St. Petersburg's estimated 25,000-plus downtown work force represents the largest concentration of businesses in Pinellas County. Echelon International Corporation developed St. Petersburg's tallest building, the Bank of America Tower, and has plans to build additional office space on other downtown property it owns.

When the Veterans Administration moved federal employees from downtown to its Bay Pines facility it allowed for still more office space. The building, renamed Bay View Tower, got a new owner and $3.5-million in renovations, including fiber optic telecommunications lines, making it St. Petersburg's first downtown SmartCenter®. It will give its next tenants, small companies, access to high-speed services usually only afforded to large corporations.

St. Petersburg's downtown has a unique blend of businesses, small and large. Bankers Insurance Group, Florida Power Corporation, Andersen Consulting Solution Works and Republic Bank are some of the companies with enough employees to have significantly changed the Monday through Friday makeup of downtown in recent years. Other large employers include the Times Publishing Company, Wm. Hough Company, SunTrust Bank, All Children's Hospital, and Bayfront-St. Anthony's Health Care System – all located downtown.

Instrumental to much of the change has been the business-based St. Petersburg Downtown Partnership, under the leadership of its executive vice president, Martin "Marty" Normile. This not-for-profit organization, comprised of area business leaders, is focused on the redevelopment and business growth of St. Petersburg's downtown. It has been in place since 1962 – always at the forefront – involved in overall planning, office development, and business recruitment, including the expansion of the U.S. Geological Survey's Center for Coastal Geology which moved here in 1988.

The USGS Center and the Florida Marine Research Institute (part of the Florida Fish and Wildlife Conservation Commission) work closely with faculty and students at the University of South Florida's (USF) Department of Marine Science and are among some of the finest names in marine science in the southeast. Joining them in St. Petersburg is the Florida Institute of Oceanography, also located at the USF-St. Petersburg campus.

continued on page 76

South Straub Park is but a part of a waterfront park system first discussed in 1902 by the Board of Trade (now the St. Petersburg Area Chamber of Commerce).

FLORIDA INTERNATIONAL MUSEUM

Above: 13 Days of October Calendar designed by President Kennedy and Presidential doodle made during the Cuban Missle Crisis.
Below: President John F. Kennedy's rocking chair.

The Florida International Museum, opened in 1995, has helped transform downtown St. Petersburg into the cultural hub of the West Coast of Florida. With well over 2 million visitors since it opened, the museum has presented exhibitions such as "Treasures of the Czars," "Splendors of Ancient Egypt" and "Titanic: The Exhibition." Over 250,000 school children have toured the museum to date.

The museum acquired a collection of Kennedy family artifacts in 1999, and features a permanent exhibition around the collection that has proven popular with residents and tourists alike. In the spring of 2000, the Florida International Museum was designated a part of the Affiliates Program of the Smithsonian Institution and has brought collections of the Smithsonian to Florida as a result of this prestigious affiliation.

The museum also has added new exhibitions to compliment its Kennedy collection and intends to operate permanent galleries that will house collections from the Smithsonian and other museums from around the world.

There's always something new and exciting happening at the Florida International Museum. Located at 100 Second Street North, adjacent to the retail and entertainment complex BayWalk, and within walking distance to dozens of downtown restaurants, the Pier and St. Petersburg's waterfront, the museum offers the perfect day trip for individuals and families.

www.floridamuseum.org

THE CLOISTERS ON BEACH DRIVE

Of all St. Petersburg's prestigious addresses, none are more distinctive than Beach Drive. The city's famous waterfront drive that follows the broad sweep of Tampa Bay has attracted local, national and international paparazzi for decades. And now there's a new, premier address. The Cloisters on Beach Drive.

This unique 14-story residential tower offers 32 individual custom-designed homes with spectacular views, true luxury and gracious living. With only two or three residences per floor ranging in size from 1,800 to 6,000 square feet, each home features a panorama of the city skyline and the Vinoy Yacht Basin.

The Cloisters architecture draws on a Florida history of Mediterranean Revival: the amenities in the tradition of the area's grand hotels. Ten-foot ceilings with soundproof construction. Three-foot-wide doors and ample storage space. At ground level, privacy and security are assured by a porte cochere with 24-hour security office, mail room, staffed concierge desk, and individually keyed elevators. Exclusive boutiques fill the ground level area along Beach Drive.

The Cloisters second level holds an intimate swimming pool and private hot tub, discretely hidden beneath an elegant cupola. Also on this level are a card room, fitness gym, lounge, entertainment area and tastefully appointed guest quarters reserved exclusively for visitors. Two covered garage spaces are also provided per residence.

Individual homes feature a host of absolute state-of-the art amenities. Multiple phone lines for fax and modem are in each residence. Designer tile graces each foyer, kitchen and bath. A gourmet gas cook-top is in each kitchen. And, because of Florida's unpredictable weather, a centrally located emergency generator provides power for lighting, elevators and refrigerators.

As the centerpiece of St. Petersburg's beautiful downtown waterfront, the Cloisters assures residents of a vista that lasts from sunrise to sunset. In between are urban pleasures close at hand, including private golf, tennis, yachting and fitness centers. Even a municipal airport is within blocks. Professional spectator sports and St. Petersburg's burgeoning arts district are also nearby.

The Cloisters at Beach Drive has come to represent a new era for both gracious living in downtown St. Petersburg and for the fortunate residents whose address is as much a part of today as yesterday.

http://cloistersonbeachdrive.com

P. BUCKLEY MOSS GALLERY

The P. Buckley Moss Gallery of St. Petersburg was opened in 1984 in a spacious setting overlooking the St. Pete Harbor. The Gallery, which was conceived as a museum of the artist's work, houses one of the most extensive collections of her work.

P. Buckley Moss, known for her portrayal of the Amish and Mennonite people, grew up dyslexic at a time when little was known of this perceptional disorder. Nonetheless, her budding artistic talent was discovered early and encouraged through high school. Ms. Moss' early artistic success more than compensated for her learning difficulties and became the foundation for today's reputation as a highly prized and collectible artist. In 1951 Pat Moss received a scholarship to New York's Cooper Union for the Advancement of Science and Art where she specialized in fine art and graphic design.

However, Pat Moss' career as an artist had to wait until 1979, after twenty-three years of marriage and bringing up six children, (one of her first awards was "Mother Artist of the Year"). Living in the Shenandoah Valley of Virginia, Pat came to know the Amish and Mennonite families in the area. In the lives of these people, Pat found a secular expression of the religious subjects she had painted throughout her early career. Pat was attracted to them and incorporated them into her art because the Amish and the Mennonites "live" the doctrines of faith: love of family and nature, simple living, and respect for one's elders.

Today, Pat Moss has become a role model to the learning impaired and frequently is asked to speak to special education classes. Donations of her original works and prints have raised more than $1.5 million for children's education and health. Assisting Ms. Moss in her charitable endeavors is the 20,000 member strong P. Buckley Moss Society and the P. Buckley Moss Foundation for Children's Education, which seeks to promote the use of art in teaching those who learn differently.

The P. Buckley Moss Gallery serves to illustrate the artist's career and her charitable goals through the exhibition and sale of her art. The artist maintains a home above the gallery and is often to be seen there. Twice a year she appears at the gallery for special signing events.

www.p-buckley-moss.com

The stately and ornate Snell Arcade building is captured in the window reflection of the Bankers Insurance building.

USF-St Petersburg's curriculum was expanded to a four-year undergraduate program in 2000. The school is part of the state university system and the entire USF-St. Petersburg campus is located on the city's downtown waterfront. In addition, USF and All Children's Hospital have joined together to build a 50-thousand square foot, $12-million pediatric research center downtown.

Downtown is also the address of the Poynter Institute for Media Studies non-profit journalism school, the Women's Tennis Association, and the National Association of Professional Baseball Leagues. And once a month, everyone is invited to the city's Get Down Town musical block parties. On the first Friday of the month traffic is barricaded and a one-block area in the heart of downtown becomes center

continued on page 82

HILTON ST. PETERSBURG

Since 1971, the landmark Hilton overlooking Tampa Bay has been downtown St. Petersburg's hotel. The Hilton's proximity to offices, the Bayfront Center, museums, Florida Power Park and the Pier have made it a longtime favorite for visitors as both a vacation and business destination.

With 333 rooms, including 28 guest suites, the Hilton St. Petersburg features the Café 333, a lobby bar, deli, heated swimming pool, oversized Jacuzzi, health club and 33,000 square feet of meeting and banquet facilities. Newly renovated in 1998, the Hilton offers the finest in amenities as well as high-tech touches for businesses.

The Hilton's Executive Training Center is comprised of four rooms, each capable of seating 25 in a classroom setting. Wider than normal tables accommodate laptop or work station computers that can be networked directly into the hotel's secured server. Totally customizable, the system provides individuals with easy access to the Internet. Each classroom is also equipped with ceiling mounts for LCD projectors. Swivel armchairs add to the comfort necessary for a successful training meeting.

After work, the Hilton St. Petersburg puts guests in the center of the action. With Gulf beaches less than ten miles away, the hotel features "The Looper", a complimentary trolley system that services the hotel and all major attractions within the waterfront area, including Tropicana Field.

Whether for banquets of up to 600 or a quiet, waterfront getaway weekend, the Hilton's professional, multi-lingual staff is prepared to pamper: just why visitors continue to consider this as downtown St. Petersburg's hotel.

www.stpetehilton.com

*Left: History of Florida bas relief on the city parking garage.
Right: North Straub Park. Below: Mirror Lake and a resident duck captures a small boy's attention.*

SALVADOR DALI MUSEUM

Surreal Events

The events leading to the location of the Salvador Dali Museum in downtown St. Petersburg in 1982 are as surreal as the paintings that today grace the Museum's walls. The story begins in the 1940s in Cleveland, Ohio, with industrialist A. Reynolds Morse and his wife, Eleanor Reese Morse, establishing a close friendship with Dali and his wife, Gala.

For the ensuing four decades, the Morse collection of Dali works would grow to become the most comprehensive collection of Dali's art in the world. So extensive was the collection that the Morses began a nationwide search for a permanent home for the prized works. Recognizing the collection spanned Dali's entire career, the Morses stipulated that the artwork and all the supplementary descriptive material be kept intact.

Enter St. Petersburg attorney James A. Martin, who, after reading about the Morses' search for a home in a "tourist-oriented community in order to enhance exposure of the works," immediately organized a dynamic group of community leaders to undertake the task of capturing the collection. The resulting Dali Task Force included Florida's governor, legislature, the City of St. Petersburg and private citizens. Impressed by this solidarity of support, the Morses agreed to the selection of St. Petersburg.

After the formation of two independent foundations to receive and manage the collection, $3 million was earmarked for acquisition of a building and operating support. Renovations of an existing marine storage warehouse alongside Bayboro Harbor began immediately. Since that time, growth has been almost continuous.

Officially opened in 1982, today's Dali Museum contains a retrospective collection of 95 original oils, over 100 watercolors and drawings, and nearly 1,300 graphics – plus sculptures, *objets d'art,* photographs, and an extensive archival library on Dali and Surrealism. Four out of 10 visitors to the museum come from outside the United States.

More than just a museum, the Dali, as it is affectionately known, features changing exhibitions of other works in the collection as well as temporary shows allowing visitors to view more outstanding works by Dali, other artists and specific aspects of Surrealism.

www.salvadordalimuseum.org

SOHO SOUTH GALLERY AND CUSTOM FRAMING

The cultural and artistic Mecca sprouting along St. Petersburg's main thoroughfare – Central Avenue - is not by accident, but rather by the design of entrepreneurs that continue to make the impossible possible. Soho South Gallery and Custom Framing represents one of those artistic possibilities that prove like does attract like.

Once a two-story vacant building, Soho South has transformed 18,000 square feet into a viable art space that many museums would envy – complete with galleries, a frame shop, 12 upstairs studios for artists and an Internet Café. As a central fixture to St. Petersburg's new Grand Central District (just west of Tropicana Field), Soho South has become a magnet attracting not only throngs of art lovers, but other businesses and galleries as well.

The vision for Soho South belongs to Marylyn and Bob Lowe, long time St. Petersburg residents who play an active role in both the communities cultural and business endeavors. Because of the size of the gallery, both the Grand Central Council and Dome District Business Council hold monthly meetings at Soho South. In keeping with their belief of the continuing rejuvenation of Central Avenue, Marylyn Lowe is also a member of the Central Avenue Tomorrow task force.

Art, however, is the primary focus for Marylyn Lowe, who has, for a number of years, been in the gallery and framing business, although in more modestly sized accommodations. Soho South opened in 1997 after a half-million dollar renovation and has continued to undergo a metamorphosis integrating art in all its many forms.

The principal gallery, for example, is dedicated to local artists offering a wide selection of affordable art for the beginning collector, or one-of a kind artwork for the serious art aficionado. Soho South also carries serigraphs, limited edition reproductions and open edition prints.

As part of Marylyn Lowe's continuing commitment to the community, Soho South's expansive space is often used by charitable groups for art shows and auctions. Definitely an integral part of St. Petersburg's growing art community, Soho South Gallery and Frame Shop has become a must-see stop for both local and visiting art lovers.

www.soho-gallery.net

FLORIDA HOLOCAUST MUSEUM

As the fourth largest museum of its kind in the United States, the Florida Holocaust Museum plays an integral role raising the consciousness of visitor's knowledge about the Holocaust. Located in downtown St. Petersburg, the Museum, established in 1992, is recognized as a national resource and recognized for internationally renowned educational programs, exhibits and outreach programs.

Originally conceived by St. Petersburg businessman and philanthropist, Walter P. Loebenberg, the Museum, with support from local businesses and community leaders, is dedicated to advancing public awareness and understanding of the Holocaust while honoring the memory of those who suffered and died.

Beyond the permanent and many special exhibits, The Florida Holocaust Museum reaches hundreds of public, private and parochial schools each year with lessons of tolerance and the effect of indifference. The Museum played a critical role in shaping legislation making Florida the nation's first state to mandate Holocaust education in the public schools from kindergarten through twelfth grade.

In a collaborative effort between the Museum and the Pinellas County School System, guidelines were developed for teachers of those grades. This includes grade-appropriate instructional goals, resource materials and cirriculum connections to infuse the lessons of the Holocaust.

The Museum continually hosts acclaimed exhibits on loan from leading artists, photographers, museum and Holocaust institutions around the world. Prominent authors are invited to share thoughts and ideas at the Author-Discussion series. Award winning films are offered for dialogue and interpretation.

The Museum continually plays an important role fostering advanced research and study on Holocaust and related subjects through the Teachers' Summer Institute, education conferences and the Murray Tolerance Learning Center, housing the largest collection of books and materials in the Southeast.

The Museum is a repository for the recorded eyewitness testimonies of Holocaust survivors, Liberators and Rescuers.

Challenging hate and bigotry while lighting the flames of hope, the vision of the Florida Holocaust Museum is a future in which peace and harmony are a reality throughout the world.

www.flholocaustmuseum.org

Downtown, Waterfront, Museums & The Arts

stage for live bands, food and fun after five.

Set your sails for longitude 82° 38.00' W, latitude 27° 46.15' N.

If it is December join the parade of boats for our annual Lighted Boat Parade, something only a Florida waterfront city could enjoy. Small dinghies to major yachts decorate their decks and masts with lights and holiday decor and wind their way from the Harborage Marina, past the Bayfront, Florida Power Park and The Pier, over to the Vinoy Basin and back again.

If it is midnight on December 31st you can be dazzled by the vibrant and colorful bursts of fireworks in the sky and reflected on the waters of Tampa Bay. Fireworks that welcome another new year by showering their light over the downtown skyline of St. Petersburg.

Top right: Museum of Fine Arts sculpture gardens. Above: St. Petersburg's City Hall has undergone significant interior improvements and is home to the impressive art works of Christopher M. Still.

STERLING RESEARCH GROUP, INC.

The Information Age has made an imense amount of information available at the click of a button. Getting the information has become easy: determining how to interpret and use it in its proper perspective have become the new challenges. Sterling Research Group, Inc., a St. Petersburg-based market research company, is experienced in providing companies with innovative solutions to information gathering, analysis and interpretation.

Sterling was founded in 1987 and chose St. Petersburg as its corporate headquarters. Sterling provides high-value, quality market research that yields timely and actionable results. Sterling's success has been built upon the ability to develop operating efficiencies that allow the company to conduct multiple large-scale research studies, while still providing a personalized commitment to doing "whatever it takes" to meet client needs through flexible, responsive service. Sterling Research Group's services include both "traditional" research capabilities (focus groups, mail and phone surveys, one-on-one interviews etc.) and proprietary, state of the art services. The latest document scanning capabilities, automated telephone and Internet technologies have kept Sterling on the leading edge of market research techniques.

The application of technology, however, does not necessarily ensure a successful research project. Sterling starts each research project by fully defining the clients needs. Next, a project team is formed from the Sterling staff of seasoned research veterans to apply their hands-on management approach. Once the data is gathered and tabulated the Sterling project team compiles the results which are then interpreted and presented to clients in the form of actionable answers. Sterling's team of experienced, dedicated market research professionals consistently produces results that will "Wow" clients with each and every contact.

At the heart of all of Sterling's work is the company's commitment to quality. This unwavering dedication to quality is exemplified in Sterling being one of the few market research firms in the US to be ISO 9001 certified. This means Sterling's quality management system meets the quality standards as set by the International Organization for Standardization.

It's no wonder that Sterling's client list reads like a Who's Who in American business – AT&T, J. Walter Thompson, DePaul University, Hilton Hotels, the U.S. Marine Corps, Chase Manhattan Bank, US Airways, Publix, Walt Disney World and Chevron, just to name a few. The company currently employs 55 individuals in St. Petersburg and also maintains sales offices in Dallas, TX, and San Diego, CA.

www.srgtampa.com

TY HESTON

If it is midnight on December 31st you can be dazzled by the vibrant and colorful bursts of fireworks in the sky and reflected on the waters of Tampa Bay. Fireworks that welcome another new year by showering their light over the downtown skyline of St. Petersburg.

THE MAHAFFEY THEATER FOR THE PERFORMING ARTS

Robert Goulet in Camelot

Matching the sparkling waterfront bay that it sits on, the Mahaffey Theater has been called by many the most beautiful and intimate theater on the west coast of Florida.

As part of the 231,000 square-foot Bayfront Center, the Mahaffey Theater has been the performing venue for some of the world's most famous entertainers. In 1965, Ted Mack's Original Amateur Hour filmed four shows in the theater, and since then stars such as Pavarotti, Liza Minelli, Louis Armstrong, Leontyne Price, Wynton Marsalis are but a few of the great entertainers who have performed at the Mahaffey Theater. The 1996 Vice Presidential Debates were hosted in the Mahaffey Theater and were covered by four major television networks. The wide range of activities taking place at the Mahaffey Theater run from the Class Acts Performing Arts Educational Series, which hosted over 28,000 school-age children in 1999-2000 to a diverse series of national and world-renowned performing artists.

Undergoing major renovation in 1986, the Mahaffey Theater seats 1,996 guests in European-style elegance with impeccable acoustics. The lobby of the Mahaffey Theater boasts a beautiful grand staircase, marble floors and an elegant skylight that floods the lobby with St. Petersburg's natural sunlight. The second floor of the lobby serves as a gallery for Bay Area artists to exhibit selected artworks in a rotating exhibit throughout the season. In addition to the vast array of entertainment featured at the Mahaffey Theater, the facility also serves as an impressive back-drop for receptions and special private or corporate events.

The Sun Pavilion occupies the second floor of the theater lobby and commands a breathtaking view of the waterfront and has the capacity to handle up to 500 guests. The Backstage Lounge can accommodate 250 people and with its beautiful wrap-around bar and casual cocktail seating, it is a popular place for small receptions, meetings and parties.

The Mahaffey Theater is certainly one of St. Petersburg's downtown waterfront jewels, and along with its listing as a venue for world class performances, it also has the flexibility to host a multitude of other events and activities.

www.mahaffeytheater.com

THE ARTS CENTER

Be A Part of the Art!

The renaissance of downtown St. Petersburg, like many metropolitan areas, is being driven by a combination of business and cultural engines. Primary to a part of this effort is The Arts Center – the contemporary visual arts axis of the community.

In existence for more than 80 years, The Arts Center has become a dynamic central focus to a renewed dedication to the arts. Recent renovations have expanded the Central Avenue facility to over 33,000 square feet. It is a major anchor among nearby museums and galleries in the growing downtown arts and cultural district.

The passion for enjoying art flourishes in four professional galleries where work from local, regional, national and even international working artist's debut to opening night crowds every two months. A fifth gallery rotates the work of area school children and serves as a focal point for quarterly Family Days.

Art instruction accommodates beginners to professionals, children to seniors. Approximately half the faculty has master's degrees. Nine studio classrooms include recently renovated spaces for clay, painting and drawing, digital imaging, photography, printmaking, and jewelry/metalsmithing. The new children's studio provides a fun, safe and appropriate atmosphere for the youngest artists year round as well as for the booming summer Art Camp.

With the support of individuals, community leaders and area businesses, being "a part of the art" has made The Arts Center integral to the continuing development of the unique character of downtown St. Petersburg.

www.theartscenter.org

Chapter 4
Health Care & Education

HERB SNITZER

If you feel you have misplaced the keys to happiness, try looking in Pinellas County where health care and education have a history of excellence and impact our economic and professional resources...

Health Care & Education

Hospital and physician networks are well established in St. Petersburg and all of Pinellas County. They can address every medical symptom and mental health problem – from neonatal to geriatric care, from chemical dependency and substance abuse rehabilitation to cancer treatment – using the most advanced medical techniques and equipment.

As managed care organizations continue to promote preventative healthcare and the use of outpatient surgeries and clinics, our hospitals have conformed and expanded their systems of service. For example, Bayfront Medical Hospital now includes six Convenient Care Clinics for primary care in neighborhoods settings. It has "call doc," an old-fashioned physician house call program, plus three outpatient rehabilitation centers and several primary care physician groups.

Recognizing the fact that families are more pressed for time and convenience, there is a growing, cooperative effort between large emergency rooms and dozens of associated or private ambulatory care clinics. Whether hospital-based or off-site, such clinics, located throughout our communities, provide patient care in non-emergency situations; urgent care as opposed to emergency care.

In recent years the community boards of Tampa Bay area's leading hospitals, including Bayfront Medical Center, signed a joint operating agreement that created the region's only full-service community owned health care system, BayCare Health System. The system provides managed care companies and their members convenient access to health care services in a broad geographical area reaching from south Pinellas through Pasco and Hillsborough.

With 16 hospitals, employing nearly 14,000, and over 130 medical manufacturers in Pinellas County alone, the health care industry is also a vital component

continued on page 92

Preceding pages: Commencement ceremonies at Stetson University College of Law.
Below: BayCare Health System's three partnerships serve the Tampa Bay area.

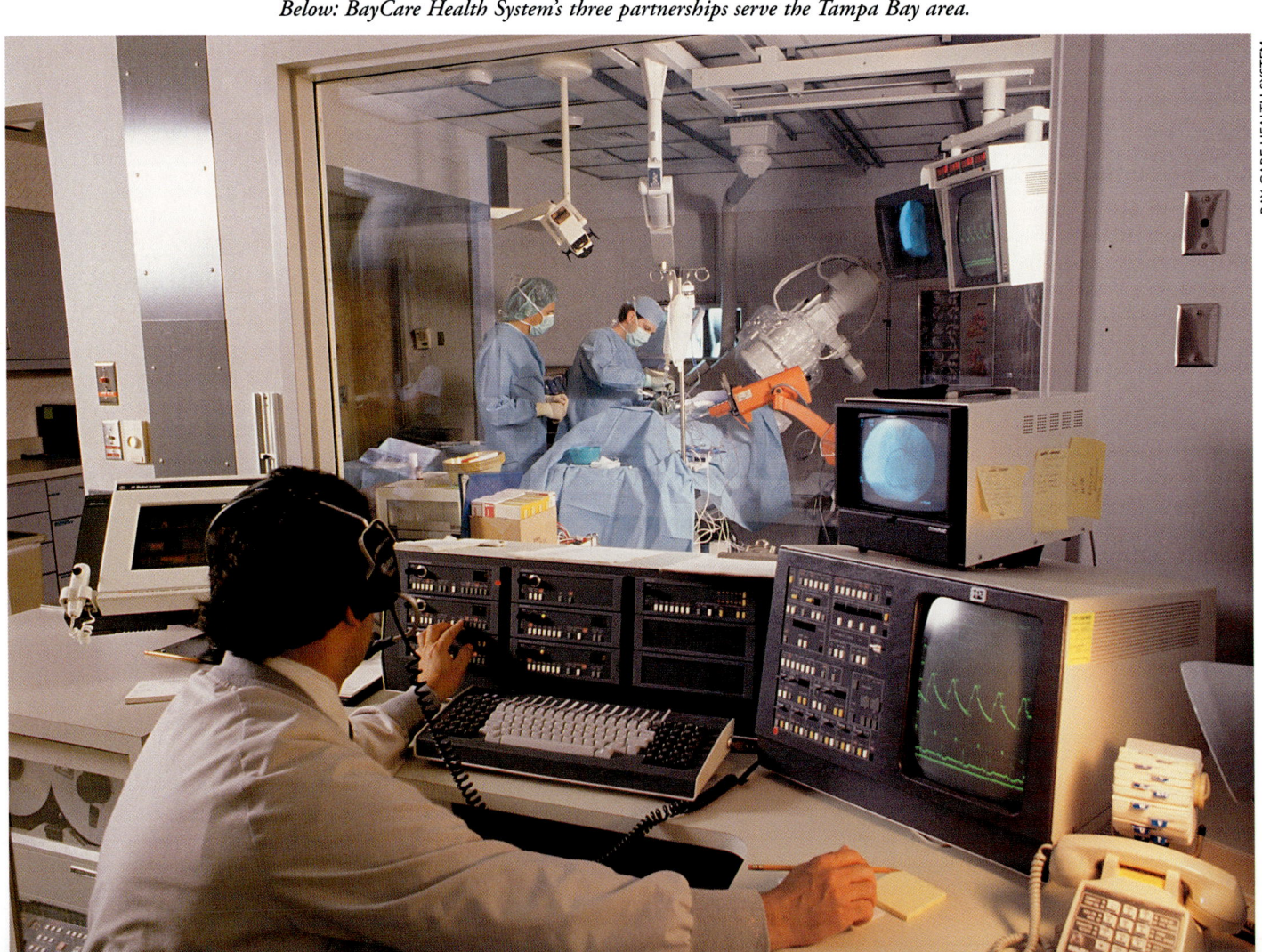

PALMS OF PASADENA HOSPITAL

The availability of quality medical care in southern Pinellas County and the beach communities is capably provided by Palms of Pasadena Hospital, located on Boca Ciega Bay in South Pasadena. Serving both a large resident and tourist population, Palms of Pasadena provides full service acute care, as well as a number of medical specialties.

The facility has 307 licensed beds, including 13 skilled nursing beds, a 24-hour emergency room and a full and part time staff of over 900 health care professionals. In addition to the hospital itself, the 13-acre campus includes an Outpatient Diagnostic Center and a Comprehensive Outpatient Rehabilitation Center.

The Diagnostic Center is equipped to provide a wide range of outpatient testing procedures. Services include a full laboratory, cardiology, CAT scan, respiratory therapy, mammography, nuclear medicine, ultrasound, MRI and X-ray.
Palms of Pasadena Hospital's medical staff includes over 300 physicians offering care and treatment in a wide range of medical specialties, including orthopedics, cardiology, general surgery, oncology, gynecology, ostomy surgery, pulmonary medicine and sleep disorders.

The hospital also provides a number of unique services. The Florida Joint Replacement Center and Continent Ostomy Center have gained a national reputation for specialized procedures. Similarly, the St. Petersburg Sleep Disorders Center is equipped with a sleep lab for the diagnosis of a wide range of sleep disorders ranging from snoring, insomnia and sleep apnea.

Palms of Pasadena also offer specialized treatment for wounds that resist healing. The Wound Healing Center's "team approach" develops individualized treatment plans for individuals with wounds that may not heal due to circulatory problems, diabetes or the use of certain medications.

The hospital is also equipped with a hyperbaric chamber for the treatment of wounds.

Although originally opened in 1963 as an 80-bed nursing home and convalescent center, the facility was licensed as an acute care hospital within a matter of months. The hospital's continued growth has matched that of South Pasadena, Gulfport, St. Petersburg Beach, Treasure Island and surrounding areas. As an integral part of these communities, the hospital also provides comprehensive home health services.

Currently owned by Iasis Healthcare, Palms of Pasadena Hospital has become southern Pinellas County's premier health care facility.

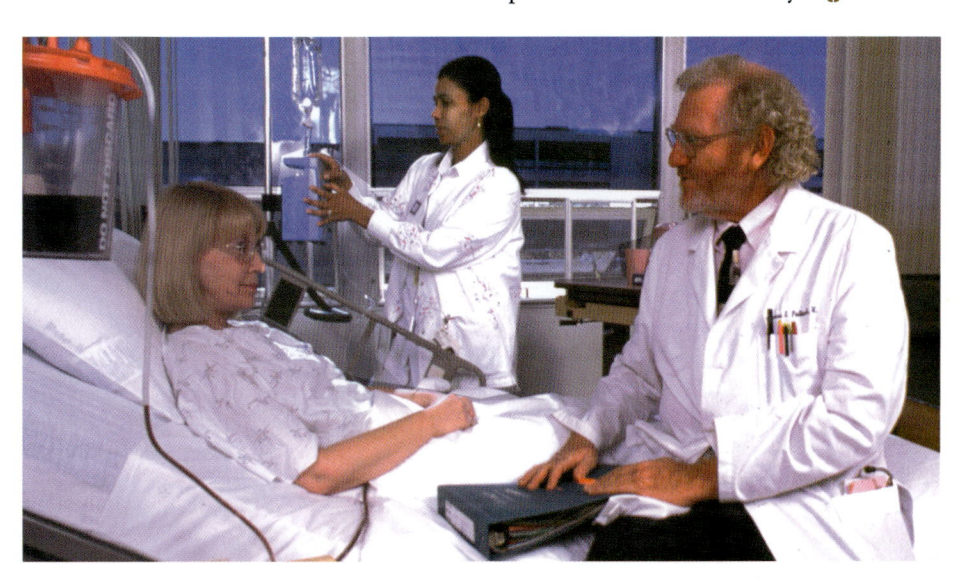

Health care & Education

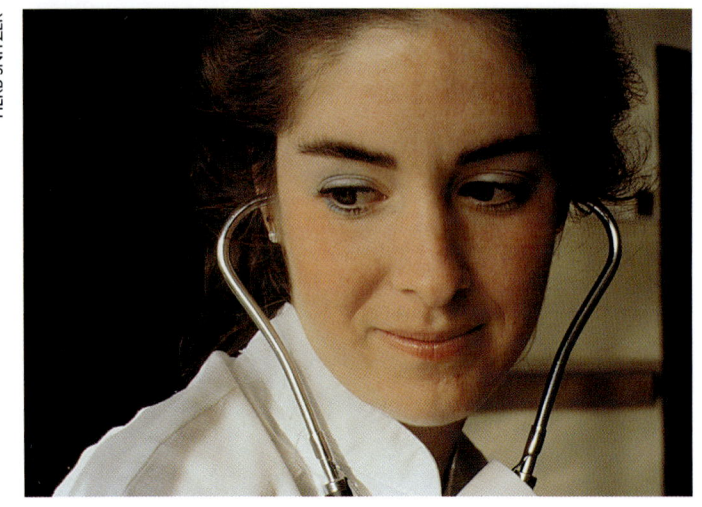

of the St. Petersburg infrastructure. The average annual employment in health services here is expected to exceed 63-thousand by the year 2005 with home health aide occupations among the top ten fastest-growing occupations in the state.

More that a century earlier, in 1885, at the 36th annual meeting of the American Medical Society, a noted physician proclaimed the St. Petersburg area as the ideal place to build a "health city." His paper read, in part, "Where should a health city be built? Overlooking the deep Gulf of Mexico, with the broad waters of a beautiful bay nearly surrounding it, but with little upon its soil but primal forest, there is a large sub-peninsular, Point Pinellas, waiting the hand of improvement."

"It lies in latitude 27 degrees and 42 minutes, and contains, with its adjoining keys about 160,000 acres of land. No marsh surrounds its shores or rests upon its surface; the sweep of its beach is broad and graceful, stretching many miles, and may be improved to an imposing extent. Its average winter temperature is 72 degrees. Those who have carefully surveyed the entire state think it offers the best climate in Florida."

It was this kind of professional opinion that influenced others to move to St. Petersburg and led to our early development. Climate isn't everything, of course and by 1906 St. Petersburg had its first hospital; it had 15 beds. It was soon replaced by the St. Petersburg Emergency Hospital in 1910, which with changes in population, expanded to a 35-bed facility three years later. A wing was added in 1923 and eventually that original building was replaced by a four-story hospital that had 150 beds. It was the beginning for what is now Bayfront-St. Anthony's Health Care, the largest health care provider in St. Petersburg.

BayCare Health System consists of three partnerships serving residents throughout the Bay area. The partnerships being Bayfront-St. Anthony's Health Care (Bayfront Medical Center and St. Anthony's Hospital), Morton Plant Mease Health Care (Morton Plant Hospital, Mease Dunedin Hospital and Mease Countryside Hospital), and in Tampa, St. Joseph's Baptist Health Care (St. Joseph's Hospital, St. Joseph's Women's Hospital, Tampa Children's Hospital and South Florida Baptist Hospital).

continued on page 94

ALL CHILDREN'S HOSPITAL

Behind Every Face is a Story

The faces are those of children, and they tell the story. It's a story of hope, dedication and resolve. And St. Petersburg's All Children's Hospital has the unique ability to write a happy "beginning" for as many young lives as is possible.

For more than 70 years, All Children's Hospital has been the only freestanding children's hospital on Florida's west coast. As a regional referral center for children with challenging medical problems, All Children's Hospital has more than 140 pediatric specialists and subspecialists dedicated to treatment, education and research.

The hospital draws patients from far and wide, with half coming from outside Pinellas County. In fact, families from all 50 states and 36 foreign countries have chosen All Children's Hospital. The institution's pediatric cancer program is one of the largest in the Southeast, and the hospital is a referral center for pediatric heart, bone marrow and renal transplantation. All Children's provides outstanding programs for treatment of pediatric heart disease, cystic fibrosis, cleft palate, sickle cell disease, and many other chronic and congenital disorders. All Children's is a teaching hospital for the University of South Florida College of Medicine, with approximately 250 ongoing research studies.

Nearly half of the hospital's 219 beds are devoted to intensive care patients, and research shows that the patient acuity level at All Children's is over three times the average level for community hospital pediatric units. To provide such sophisticated care, physicians and nurses call on a full spectrum of state-of-the-art clinical services, supported by professionals with years of special training to meet the needs of children and teens at each stage of development.

Quality care for children goes beyond advanced technology. All Children's never forgets the special touches that can help an anxious child – or worried parent. These touches include fold-out beds in patient rooms for parents, daily activities and recreation therapy in three cheerful playrooms and a host of colorful kid-friendly extras aimed at brightening a patient's stay.

All Children's St. Petersburg campus features a Pediatric Emergency Center, a Center for Child Development, an Education & Conference Center, and the world's largest Ronald McDonald House serving a single medical center. The new All Children's Hospital/University of South Florida Pediatric Research Institute is home to cutting-edge research seeking new understanding and treatment of children's diseases. Five regional outreach centers and three All Children's Therapy Centers bring many of the Hospital's outpatient services closer to home for children and their families.

Jarred was among the first group of children in the country to receive a bone marrow transplant for sickle cell anemia. Chaz, Jarred's brother, supplied the marrow, All Children's provided the expertise.

David is one of more than 35 patients who have received a new heart. All Children's pediatric heart transplant program is recognized as one of the most successful such programs in the country.

www.allkids.org

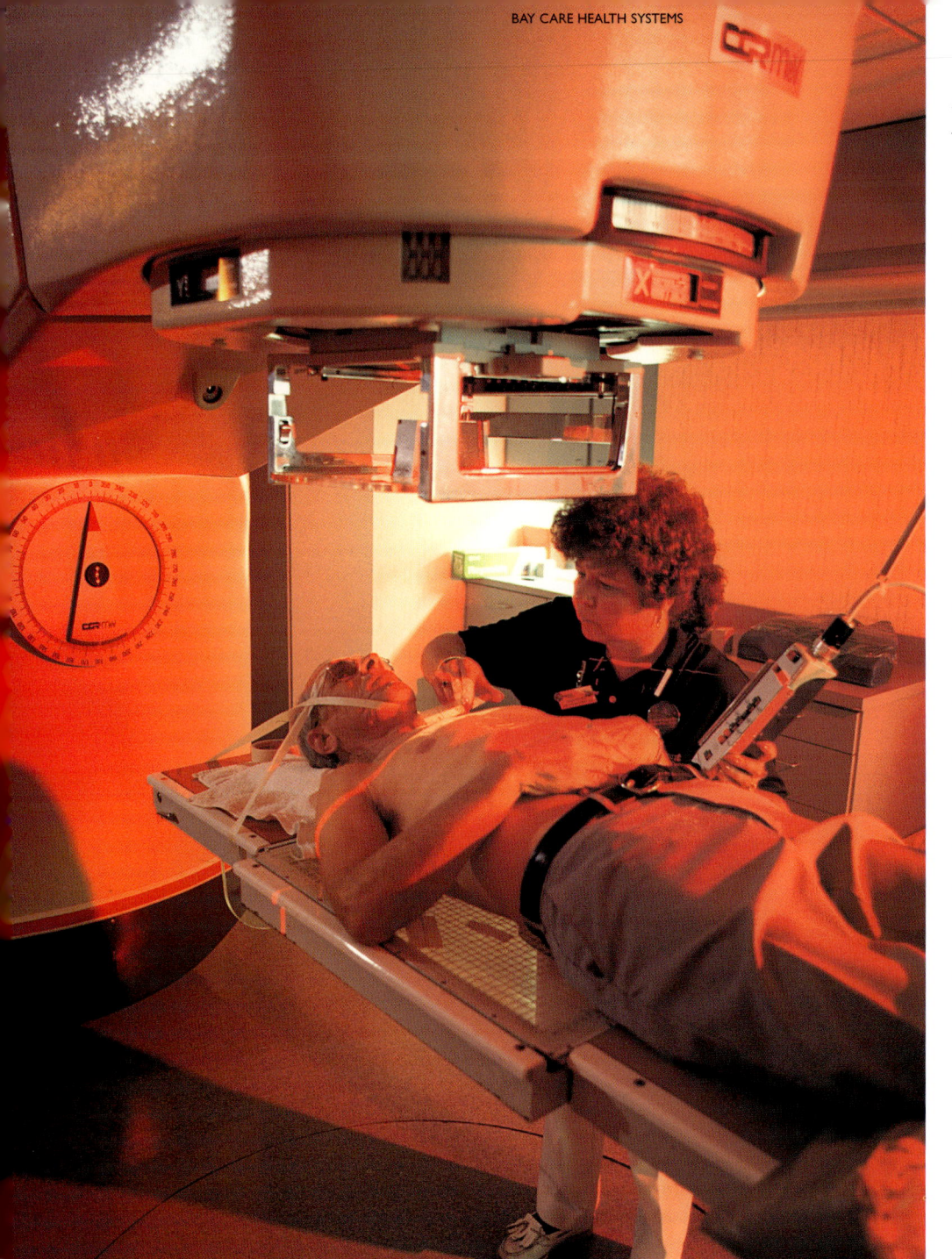

Diagnostic imaging is part of Bayfront Medical Center's health care services.

In addition to cost efficiencies, the BayCare hospitals are able to standardize and improve care by sharing the knowledge of what they do best, while each hospital retains its own individual identity and heritage.

Bayfront Medical Center is a non-profit multi-specialty teaching facility and serves as the area's only Level II Trauma Center with advanced emergency care resources, including the Bayflite helicopter program. The medical center encompasses 16 city blocks in downtown St. Petersburg and includes a 502-bed hospital, a modern glass five-story complex for physician offices and centers for same day surgery and diagnostic imaging.

St. Anthony's Hospital specializes in behavioral medicine, diabetes and cardiology. The Franciscan Sisters of Allegany, New York, founded the 415-bed, non-profit general/acute care facility in St. Petersburg in 1931 and today it is one of the most technologically advanced facilities in Florida.

In addition to these downtown hospitals St. Petersburg is the location of one of only 49 tertiary care pediatric hospitals in the United States – All Children's Hospital. Since 1930, the now 168-bed facility has been the regional referral center for children with some of the most challenging medical problems. Its pediatric cancer program is the largest in the Southeast and the hospital is a referral center for infant and pediatric heart transplantation, bone marrow transplantation and renal transplantation.

The Ronald McDonald House at All Children's is the world's largest RMH that serves a single medical center. Opened in 1980, it was the first Ronald McDonald House in the state of Florida, and now provides lodging for more than 2,000 families a year.

There are four affiliates of HCA (the former Columbia/HCA Healthcare Corporation) in St. Petersburg including Columbia Center for Special Surgery, Edward White Hospital, Northside Hospital, and St. Petersburg General Hospital.

Tenet Health System, another nationwide provider of healthcare services, owns the 307-bed Palms of Pasadena Hospital, located in nearby South Pasadena. Founded in 1963 as a general acute care facility, the hospital offers care and treatment in a wide range of medical specialties.

To the immediate northwest of St. Petersburg is the sprawling campus of Bay Pines VA Medical Center, a 591-bed complex situated on 337 acres overlooking Boca Ciega Bay. In addition to providing acute medical, surgical, and psychiatric care, the center supervises a community nursing home care program, which is one of the largest in the VA system.

On March 10, 1997, Vencor Hospital-St. Petersburg became the first long-term acute care hospital in Pinellas

Florida's first Ronald McDonald House is at All Children's Hospital, St. Petersburg.

continued on page 98

MOFFITT CANCER CENTER

A Unique Approach to Patient Care

Two out of five people will get cancer in their lifetime. If it happens to you or someone you love, the Tampa Bay area is home to one of the finest cancer care centers found in the United States – the H. Lee Moffitt Cancer Center & Research Institute at the University of South Florida in Tampa.

As the only cancer center in Florida designated by the National Cancer Institute, Moffitt team members work tirelessly in the areas of patient care, research, education and screening to advance their fight against this devastating disease. Moffitt's unsurpassed success in Florida is not by chance, but by a unique approach that includes patient care delivered by teams of medical specialists, research scientists offering the latest investigational treatments, and a partnership with the University of South Florida to train medical professionals in all aspects of cancer treatment.

The Cancer Center, a non-profit facility, is named for H. Lee Moffitt, former speaker of the Florida House of Representatives. Moffitt spearheaded a nine-year Legislative effort that resulted in a $70-million appropriation, largely from Florida's cigarette tax, to build the facility. Its doors opened in 1986.

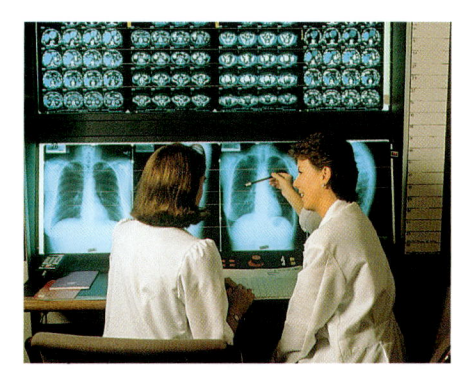

The Cancer Center has greatly expanded through the years, and by the year 2003, the existing research and outpatient clinical space will be dramatically increased by the addition of the new Tower Project. Moffitt currently serves more than 4,500 inpatients and 110,000 outpatients yearly.

Moffitt's physicians, nurses and staff have specialized and nationally-recognized training in cancer research and treatment. More than 60 Moffitt physicians, nearly 25 percent of the staff, are listed among the Best Doctors in America. This prestigious national publication features only two percent of the practicing physicians in the country.

The Cancer Center offers a team approach to treating cancer, which means patients do not have to travel between various specialists or wait for weeks before learning their diagnosis and treatment options. Team services also include psychosocial support for patients and families - vital care that can impact a patient's recovery and the ability of a family to cope with the disease.

Behind the scenes, scientists work to translate laboratory successes to patient bedsides, offering them the latest investigational treatments. More than 200 clinical research studies are active at the Cancer Center, allowing patients access to treatment options that are simply not available at a majority of hospitals.

www.moffitt.usf.edu

BAYFRONT-ST. ANTHONY'S HEALTH CARE

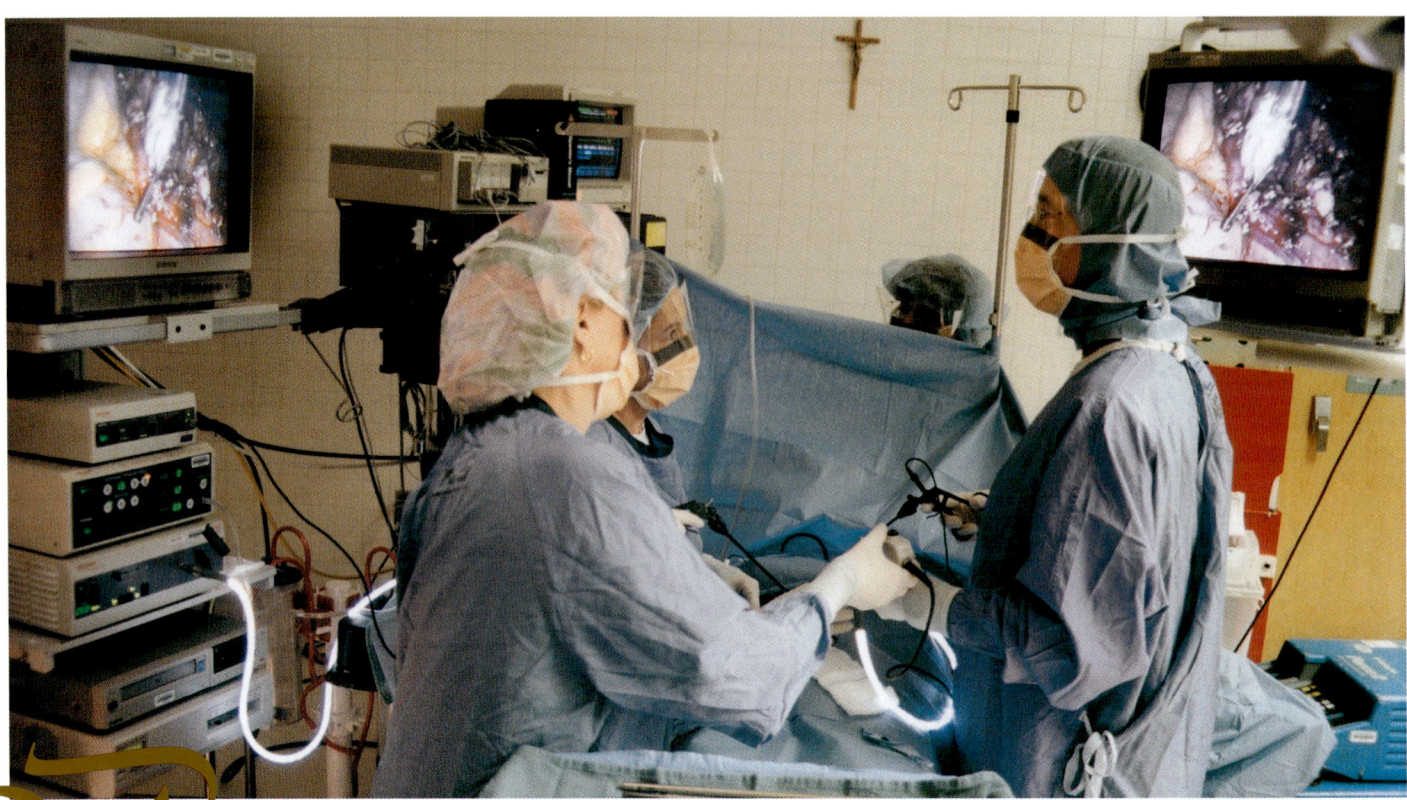

Bayfront-St. Anthony's Health Care is a unique community partnership between Bayfront Medical Center and St. Anthony's Hospital. Bayfront-St. Anthony's, part of the BayCare Health System that formed in 1997, serves St. Petersburg and southern Pinellas County, an area rich in diversity, community resources and natural beauty.

The mission of Bayfront-St. Anthony's Health Care is to improve the health of all we serve through community-owned health care services that set the standard for high-quality, compassionate care.

Bayfront-St. Anthony's Health Care includes over 1,000 physicians across all specialties. The two hospitals, with a combined total of 907 beds, offer a comprehensive range of services. Bayfront Medical Center, named one of the nation's top 100 hospitals by HCIA-Sachs Institute, features a Level II trauma center, Bayflite emergency helicopter program, rehabilitation services, women's and children's services and neurological services. St. Anthony's Hospital specializes in behavioral health services, cancer care, vascular procedures and older adult services. Both institutions offer wellness programs, health clinics, community outreach programs, medical education, outpatient services and medical research.

Community outreach is a sign of Bayfront-St. Anthony's commitment to the people it serves. Seven Convenient Care Centers are located throughout southern Pinellas County, offering physician exams and treatment of minor emergencies. St. Anthony's Hospital offers an innovative Adult Day Health Center, providing care and supervision to older adults who cannot be left alone during the day. Bayfront-St. Anthony's affiliations with the Center Against Spousal Abuse (CASA), the YMCA, the Pinellas School System and the University of South Florida offer additional programs that support families, children and adults of all ages throughout the community. The annual St. Anthony's Triathlon draws 1,500 athletes from around the world and has been named "Best Race" by USA Triathlon.

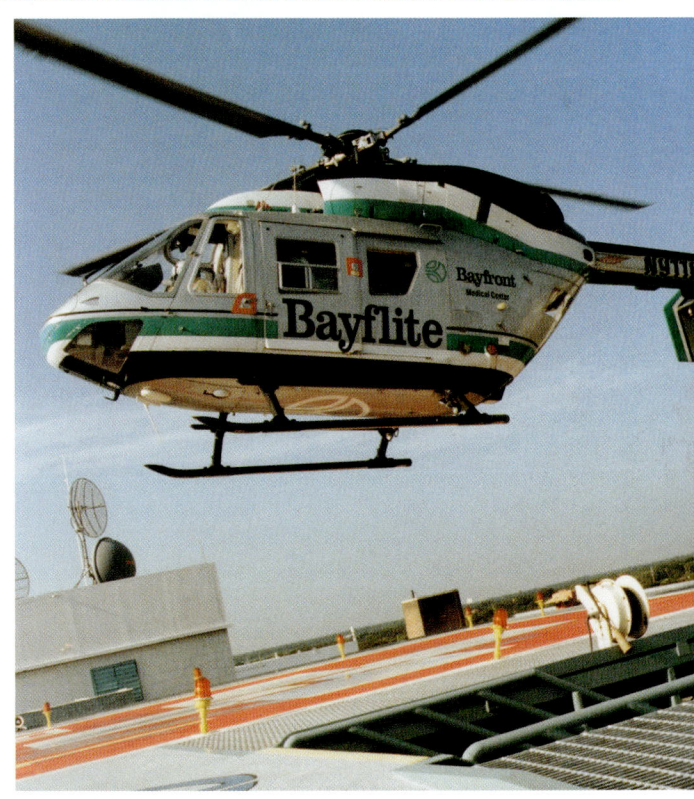

Top: The surgical center at St Anthony's Hospital
Above: Bayflite lands at Bayfront Hospital Medical Center

www.bsahealth.org

MORTON PLANT HOSPITAL MEASE HEALTH CARE

Morton Plant Hospital

Morton Plant Hospital, a 687-bed community-owned hospital in Clearwater, has been serving the health care needs of northern Pinellas County for more than 80 years. During this time, Morton Plant Hospital has earned a reputation for being one of the most effective, well-managed hospitals in America.

For the past two years, Morton Plant Hospital has been named one of the nation's top 100 cardiovascular hospitals by HCIA-Sachs Institute. The hospital is also one of the premier cancer treatment centers in the state. Among Morton Plant Hospital's resources for cancer care is PET imaging, state-of-the-art technology that represents a major advance in our capability to diagnose, stage and follow many types of malignancy.

In addition to cardiology and oncology, Morton Plant Hospital offers a full range of medical and surgical services led by physicians who are board certified in their fields. These include emergency care, outpatient services, health education and prevention, rehabilitation, women's and children's services, and diabetes care.

Morton Plant Hospital is a nationally renowned health care provider that remains dedicated to the health of the local community. Its commitment to excellence continues to bring the most advanced health care resources to the residents of Pinellas County and the Tampa Bay area.

MEASE DUNEDIN HOSPITAL

Located in the heart of historic Dunedin, Mease Dunedin Hospital has been serving the health care needs of the community for more than 60 years. The 234-bed medical facility is committed to providing the best health care possible.

Among its services, Mease Dunedin Hospital offers complete medical, surgical and obstetrical care. It was also named one of the nation's top 100 hospitals in orthopedic care. In addition, the hospital offers a Sleep Disorders Center, Transitional Care Unit and a newly renovated Emergency Center.

Mease Dunedin Hospital has accomplished a great deal in the past half-century. It has established itself as a leading provider of health care both locally and nationally, to the benefit of the residents of northern Pinellas County.

MEASE COUNTRYSIDE HOSPITAL

Opened in 1985, Mease Countryside Hospital is the fastest-growing hospital in Pinellas County. This 144-bed hospital is a recognized leader in making exceptional health care readily available to local residents. Mease Countryside Hospital was named to the list of the nation's top 100 hospitals by HCIA-Sachs.

At Mease Countryside Hospital, residents of northern Pinellas County have access to the services of more than 600 physicians and specialists. Services include a state-of-the-art outpatient surgery center, specialized pediatric care and a newly renovated Emergency Center.

Mease Countryside Hospital's staff is dedicated to improving the community's health with the facilities, technology, skilled professionals and resources needed to deliver an exceptional level of care.

Mease Countryside emergency

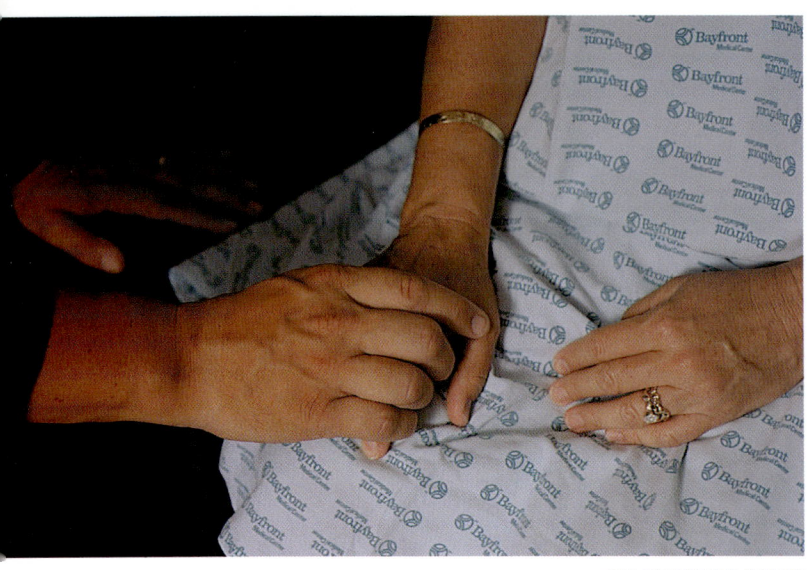

Health Care & Education

BAY CARE HEALTH SYSTEMS

County. The licensed 60-bed facility, located on a tranquil waterfront campus, has 140 physicians and includes pediatric services for acute intermediate intensive care patients as young as one month old. Vencor manages more ventilators and employs more respiratory therapists than any other healthcare provider in America.

Across Tampa Bay, in Hillsborough County is a National Cancer Institute-designated comprehensive cancer center, the Moffitt Cancer Center. Moffitt serves as a statewide research institute; a national resource for basic research, clinical research, and multi-disciplinary approaches to patient treatment; and a community resource through outreach and communications efforts.

The Center opened in 1986 as a private, not-for-profit facility and is named for H. Lee Moffitt, former Speaker of the Florida House of Representatives, who was instrumental in creating the Cancer Center. Construction of the facility was funded largely by proceeds from Florida's cigarette tax. It is located at the University of South Florida in Tampa and constitutes a growing component of the teaching and research activities of the USF College of Medicine.

While the St. Petersburg area has perfected and enhanced its health care services it also has a strong base of medical device manufacturers and serves as one of the western anchors of the Florida High Tech Corridor. For example, the nation's largest producer of battery-operated cauterizing devices is located here; it is one of only three manufacturers of new electro surgical devices that are now in demand in operating rooms around the world. It is this type of industry that is responsible for an annual payroll of $109.5 million in Pinellas County for the manufacture of medical instruments and supplies.

continued on page 102

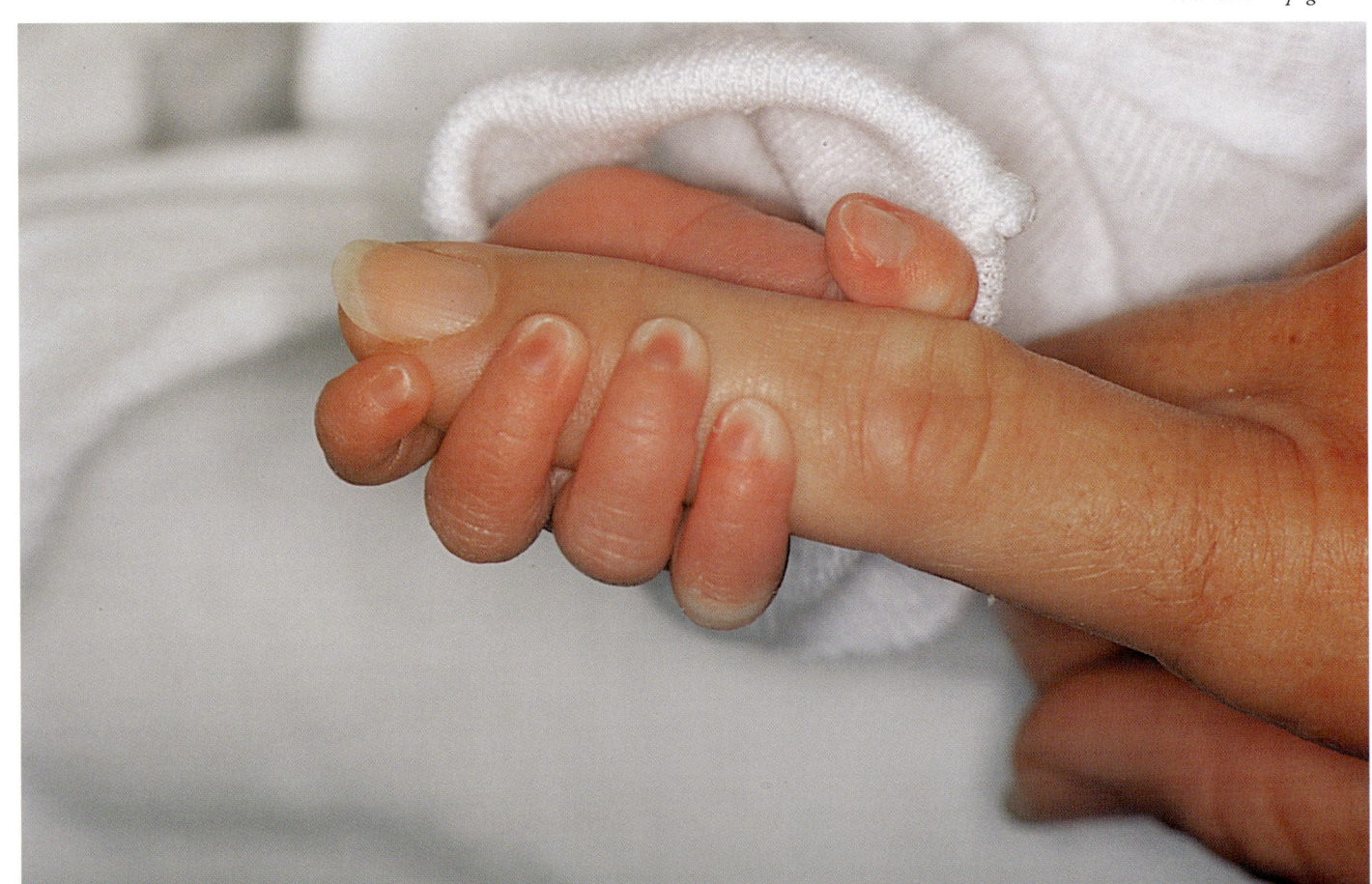

VENCOR HOSPITAL

When faced with a catastrophic illness, individuals and families face difficult decisions, lengthy treatments and uncertainty about eventual outcomes. Vencor Hospital – St. Petersburg is a place where state-of-the-art technology and human caring combine to overcome the uncertainty of an individual's future.

Vencor is dedicated to helping patients and families work through this long-term medically complicated process by focusing on a team-oriented and patient-centered approach to the healing needs of the patient.

Vencor Inc. has grown since its beginnings in Rockcastle County, Kentucky in 1985. A network of 57 hospitals nationwide are now the premier, low-cost providers of long-term, intensive care services to the acutely ill patient. On March 10, 1997, Vencor Hospital - St. Petersburg became the first long-term acute care hospital in Pinellas County. The licensed 60-bed facility, located on a tranquil waterfront campus, has 140 physicians and includes pediatric services for acute intermediate intensive care patients as young as one month old.

The majority of patients are referred directly from intensive care units of other hospitals. Typically they are stable enough to move out of an ICU, but not yet ready for a skilled nursing center – for example, an open-heart surgery patient who has experienced trouble getting off a ventilator. In fact, Vencor manages more ventilators and employs more respiratory therapists than any other healthcare provider in America.

Coordination of the patient's care is possible because of the arrangement and operation of the hospital's many parts. Care is directed by an interdisciplinary team of highly trained specialist supported by the latest advances in electronic medical record keeping.

Patient Care Conferences are held on a regular basis. Coordinated by the patient's physician, a conference includes all care-providers for that patient. Goals for the patient are established, progress is evaluated, and changes are noted for the plan of care.

Family members are considered essential to a patient's progress and are encouraged to participate in these conferences. Vencor understands that illnesses, like all other life processes, go through stages. Recognition of what is happening, why and when, can often make the difference in successful outcomes.

At Vencor Hospital – St. Petersburg everything and everyone is focused on meeting the needs of the long-term, "medically complex" patient. The hospital combines three elements to assure comfort and confidence in the face of uncertainty: wise use of resources, competent care from a specialized staff, and the time necessary for the process to work. It is the combination of experience, education and equipment, as well as the appropriate setting for its use, that enables Vencor Hospital – St. Petersburg to provide quality services.

www.vencor.com

UPDEGRAFF LASIK VISION

See the Difference

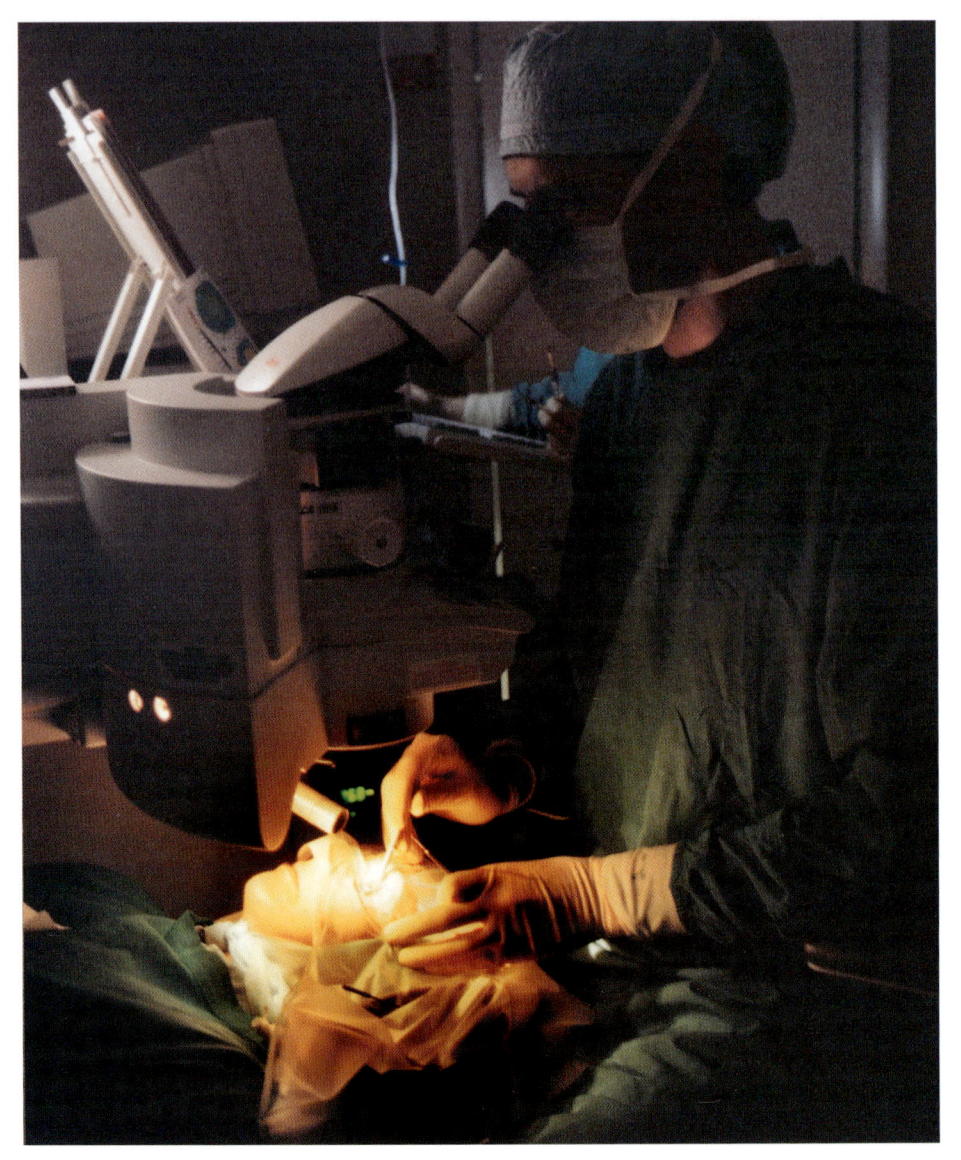

For more than 40 years, Drs. Ambrose G. and Stephen A. Updegraff have been committed to reshaping the vision of residents in the St. Petersburg area. With an international reputation of excellence in corneal and refractive surgery, Dr. Stephen Updegraff, the owner and Medical Director of Updegraff Lasik Vision, has continued to invest in the community by not only using new technologies, but helping to develop them, as well.

A St. Petersburg native, Dr. Updegraff is a Board Certified Ophthalmologist, a Fellow in the American College of Surgeons and, at the turn of the millennium, was the only Lasik Fellowship trained doctor in Florida. One of a select number of surgeons in the United States who owns and has exclusive use of two permanently installed lasers, Dr. Updegraff also holds six patents in Lasik techniques and technology.

With Steve having performed more than 7,000 LASIK procedures through early 2000, both Drs. Updegraff have demonstrated their personal confidence and commitment to the LASIK procedure by having undergone the surgery in both eyes, Steve in 1995 and Ambrose in 1999 at the age of 72.

Striving for perfection, Updegraff Lasik Vision maintains stringent regulations in the St. Petersburg office. Precision instruments and lasers are used only by Dr. Updegraff. Additionally, disposable instruments are single use and documented to each patient's chart.

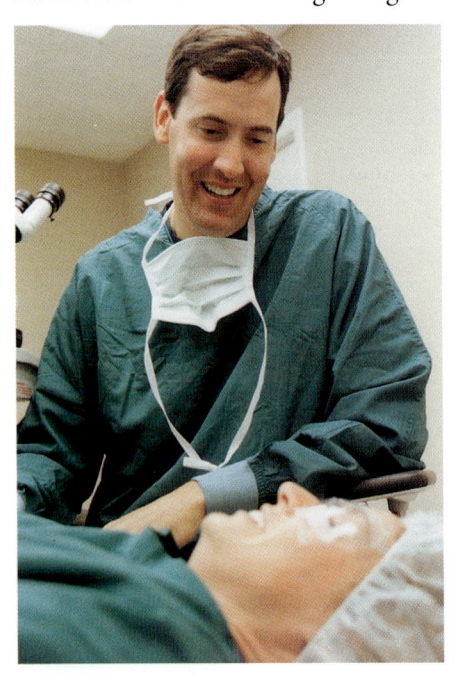

Updegraff Lasik Vision triple checks each patient's prescription and utilizes computerized eye mapping. Laser calibrations are performed for each patient and each eye. Surgery is accomplished in a climate-controlled, dust-free environment. Highly trained and knowledgeable LASIK counselors are on hand to assist in both the surgical process and during the aftercare period. Recovery is extremely brief.

LASIK surgery is utilized to correct nearsightedness, farsightedness and astigmatism. Patients have both eyes done in a single session of less than one hour. After the initial testing, total time away from work can be as brief as the afternoon of surgery and the next morning.

Dr. Updegraff evaluates and treats patients who have experienced complications of past surgery, including radial keratotomy, PRK and LASIK at other facilities, or who have been advised that no satisfactory treatment exists for their problem. Updegraff has helped people whose occupational duties are hampered by glasses and contact lenses, such as doctors, pilots, divers, police and professional athletes.

When not involved in helping Tampa Bay residents "See the Difference", Dr. Updegraff continues to lecture about LASIK procedures or perform LASIK surgery in Canada, Europe, Asia and Africa. Closer to home, Dr. Updegraff can often be found pursuing another passion – fishing the area's waters.

www.lasik4me.com

OPERATION PAR, INC.

Addiction & Mental Health Services

If the heart of a community is best tested by adversity, then the size of the response is an equally telling indicator. Sometimes it only takes a single, inspired person to begin the process. In 1970, such was the case with one mother whose teenager faced a drug problem. With no available recourse for counseling, Operation PAR was born - Parental Awareness and Responsibility.

Today, staffed with more than 600 employees, PAR provides integrated addiction and mental health services at numerous sites in Hernando, Pinellas, Pasco and Manatee counties. The organization's mission is to improve the health and well being of individuals, families and communities impacted by drug abuse, mental disorders and other social related problems.

PAR achieves this by providing a "continuum of care" that is cost-effective, culturally competent and includes research, prevention, intervention, treatment and evaluation. The not-for-profit corporation has established its presence throughout the four county region by founding programs and facilities wherever the need arises.

Certainly more than just a drug prevention and counseling organization, PAR's continuum of care encompasses intervention programs, neighborhood and residential treatment centers, employee assistance, transitional housing, homelessness prevention and therapeutic development services. Innovative programs include mobile counseling units, juvenile and adult offender's services, psychiatric evaluation and on-site residential treatment programs for adolescents.

What PAR is really about, in the final analysis, is to provide hope in an often-chaotic world. Meeting that challenge has brought PAR critical acclaim from local, state and national leaders. The best praise, however, comes from those individuals whose lives have been positively altered because of PAR's prevention and intervention efforts.

Dr. Shirley Coletti, PAR's Founder & President

After more than 30 years of finding success one life at a time, PAR's journey has been accomplished by the work of dedicated professionals and volunteers alike. The organization's board is composed of 19 volunteers representing a cross section of professionals, many of whom are active in other community issues.

PAR's President, Dr. Shirley Coletti, is recognized internationally as a leader in the field of substance abuse prevention and treatment. She sits on several national and state advisory councils. She is also the mother who, some 30 years ago, began the process of proving that the heart, as part of the community's collective consciousness, can indeed move mountains. Operation PAR is proof positive.

www.parnext.org

Health Care & Education

At the same time, St. Petersburg and Pinellas County are committed to provide the types of job-related education and training necessary to meet the high standards and international challenges of a global economy. Our own work force depends on qualified, educated and trained personnel, not only in the medical fields, but also in all aspects of business and industry.

Students and educators come together in the classrooms of 143 schools in the Pinellas County Schools district, involving parents, business leaders and community representatives as new programs are developed each year. Adding to a wide range of public educational programs, there are 86 state-registered private elementary and secondary schools from religious-based institutions to special academic education facilities to college preparatory schools. Pinellas is a diverse county and each school has its own strengths. For example, some elementary schools require uniforms and others stress the use of technology in the classroom.

The first Pinellas schools, in 1885, were two typically small one-room buildings with one teacher for each. With the arrival of the railroad, and the founding and rapid growth of St. Petersburg, even those teachers left to open the first general stores in this new frontier. However in 1888, under the direction of the Congregational Church, a school building was constructed in this new community and classes were held for 29 students.

After St. Petersburg was incorporated as a town, bond money paid for a larger, wood, two-story school complete with seven classrooms, a library, and assembly hall. A high school was established in the same building, with courses in mathematics, science, history, English and Latin. And it was the financial generosity of E. H. Tomlinson that gave the schools a boost in those early years. His gifts helped organize a school orchestra, the school cadet company and the fife and drum corps.

In 1901 Tomlinson paid for and deeded to St. Petersburg a second school building built specifically as The Manual Training School, for instruction in "manual training, physical culture and military science." It was the first of its kind in Florida and opened with great ceremony. A manual training annex was also built by Tomlinson and opened in 1902.

Establishing schools was a challenge for the rapidly growing city, which authorized bonds for new school construction until all schools in Florida came under county jurisdiction. The City continued to try and meet the needs of its growing student population until Pinellas County was created with its own school board.

Today, Pinellas County Schools is the 21st largest school district in the United States and the seventh largest in Florida. The elected seven-member Pinellas County School Board appoints the superintendent who serves as the chief administrative officer. It is also the largest employer with nearly 14,000 full-time employees, and operates with an annual budget of more than $1-billion. As of the 1999-2000 school year, more than 109,400 students were enrolled in kindergarten through grade 12 and nearly 36-thousand adults were enrolled in postsecondary, career, technical and adult education programs.

HERB SNITZER

Health Care & Education

Magnet schools are one of Pinellas County Schools greatest success stories. They offer extra courses and resources including foreign languages at the elementary level, special science labs in middle school, and rigorous college-prep classes in high school. All programs have specific admission requirements and many are highly competitive, attracting so many applicants that final selection is done by lottery.

Among Pinellas County's 82 elementary schools, three in St. Petersburg are magnet schools. Melrose Elementary opened the Center for Communication and Mass Media in 1998, a program that emphasizes global studies, literary arts, foreign language and mass media technology. Bay Point Elementary houses the Center for Advancement of the Sciences and Technology – a math, science, foreign language and technology magnet featuring an integrated curriculum focused within these areas. The Center for the Arts & International Studies is at Perkins Elementary, where kindergarten through third grade students take classes in all areas and by the fourth and fifth grades choose one area of art, foreign languages and humanities for concentration.

Ridgecrest Elementary in Largo, houses The Center for Gifted Studies. The general education and magnet programs at this school operate together, allowing increased academic success for all students. However, the full-time gifted magnet program curriculum helps prepare its students in first through fifth grade for academically challenging programs in middle and high school.

Pinellas County has 23 middle schools. Two are magnet schools located in St. Petersburg. Bay Point Middle houses the Center for Advancement of the Sciences and Technology, a magnet that is independent of the traditional grades 6-8 program at the school. Its integrated curriculum is based on math and science themes. John Hopkins Middle – Center for the Arts & Communication Studies, is also a total magnet school serving students through the study of global studies, literary arts or the fine arts.

Added to the 16 regular high schools in Pinellas, there are twelve magnet programs, one choice program and three career academies at various campuses throughout the county.

The Center for Wellness and Medical Professions opened at Boca Ciega High School in Gulfport, adjacent to St. Petersburg, in 1994. The center offers programs to students in the rapidly expanding fields of medicine and health care with three options. One is for employment immediately fol-

Pinellas County fifth graders learn the value of economics first hand at Enterprise Village.

Health Care & Education

lowing high school, another prepares students for postsecondary education; and the premedical program provides the academic foundation for students planning further education in occupations such as physician or pharmacist.

The Pinellas County Center for the Arts (PCCA) at Gibbs High in St. Petersburg provides a pre-professional arts training program for qualified high school students. All students in PCCA are taught by practicing professional artists and the academic instruction is college preparatory. Each day, students attend four regular academic classes and spend three periods concentrating on their arts discipline – dance, music, theatre and visual arts.

Gibbs also is home to the Pinellas Academy for the Technical Arts, a career academy that opened in 1999. This program provides students with four years of instruction with electives on finance, business management, web design and Internet services, networking and digital publishing. Students and teachers work closely with business partners who provide consultation, career shadowing and internship opportunities.

The Center for Advanced Technologies (CAT) at Lakewood High in St. Petersburg offers a rigorous four-year academic program that emphasizes advanced mathematics, science, computer applications/programming, multimedia/television production and scientific research. Pinellas Park High has the Criminal Justice Academy magnet program, a four-year course of study designed to introduce students to career opportunities in law, law enforcement and related fields. Partnerships with several community agencies provide students with the resources necessary to gain a working knowledge of all aspects of their chosen careers.

St. Petersburg High School has one of Pinellas County's two International Baccalaureate (IB) programs. Requirements for the IB diploma are structured to meet the entrance requirements of the finest universities. The two-phase program includes classes equivalent to college freshman-level courses as well as 150 hours of community service. The county's other IB program is at Palm Harbor University High, the county's newest high school. In addition, that high school houses a second magnet program – The Center for Wellness and Medical Professions similar to the one at Boca Ciega High in Gulfport.

The 21st Century Learning Center & Teaching Arts Academy at Largo High School is an innovative school model with emphasis placed on preparing students for college. Dual enrollment, advanced placement and SAT/ACT prep courses are included in the magnet program so that students will have opportunities to earn college credit and increase their college entrance test scores. Students at Largo High also may become better prepared for a vocational career while participating in programs such as cosmetology and health occupations as well as a variety of options at the Seminole Vocational Education Center and Pinellas Technical Education Centers.

Early Graduation Options (EGO) at Osceola High is designed for students who wish to accelerate completion of high school. Students who complete advanced placement or dual enrollment classes with St. Petersburg Junior College have the option of completing their senior year of high school and first year of college simultaneously.

The Program for International Culture and Commerce (PICC) at Clearwater High opened in August 1994. PICC emphasizes international studies with a strong vocational concentration and expertise in foreign language. The four-

Computer skills are part of the early education curriculum taught in Pinellas classrooms such as these at Maximo Elementary School in St. Petersburg.

continued on page 106

PINELLAS COUNTY EDUCATION FOUNDATION

Since its creation in 1986, the Pinellas County Education Foundation has become the catalyst for community investment in public education. Beyond being an advocate for children, the organization provides focused, effective and accountable avenues of involvement, achieving unprecedented success in developing 23 innovative educational initiatives benefiting school children and educators throughout Pinellas County. The Gus A. Stavros Institute, for example, houses four separate programs. Enterprise Village is a thriving mini-mall for fifth-graders, educating students about the principles of the free enterprise system. Since opening in 1989, every fifth-grade student in the Pinellas County Public School System - as well as students from private and parochial schools and students from surrounding counties - has visited Enterprise Village. An estimated 15,000 students benefit from the endeavor annually.

Building on this program, Finance Park gives students a firsthand understanding of economic issues confronted upon graduation from high school. In a reality-based simulation, students learn asset allocation and gain an understanding of the decision-making process involved in planning a personal budget.

The Stavros Institute also has established the AEGON Communications Center and the Dan Doyle Ethics Center. The Communications Center is a prototype program for school districts across the nation in promoting readiness for post-secondary education and the workplace. The Ethics Center provides instruction in the understanding of business and personal ethics. The program is utilized by students at all levels and ultimately by businesses and members of the extended community.

Other Pinellas County Education Foundation initiatives include Doorways, a comprehensive, early intervention and dropout prevention program established in 1992. Doorways offers low-income school-children post-secondary education scholarships, mentorship support and opportunities to participate in an array of cultural and recreational activities. Partner support has enabled the Foundation to sponsor scholarships in 120 schools.

Another initiative, SAVE (Scholarships for Adult Vocational Education), has been nationally recognized for achieving remarkable success in providing high school dropouts with life and career options necessary to become productive members of the community. By enrolling at one of the Pinellas Technical Education Centers (PTEC), students earn a General Education Diploma (GED) and learn marketable skills ensuring future employment. In its first 12 years, the SAVE program graduated 1,541 students. Over 99 percent of these students earn a GED. An impressive 89 percent are currently working in their field of study.

Teacher Mini-Grants, Outstanding Educators & Teacher of the Year Awards, Science and Economic Fairs, and the Quality Academy are just a few of the other outcome-based initiatives of the organization.

www.pinellaseducation.org

Health Care & Education

Pinellas Technical Education Centers, with two campuses, focus on career, technical and adult education.

Pinellas County Center for the Arts at Gibbs is one of 12 high school magnet programs.

year curriculum, part of Pinellas County's choice programs, prepares students for careers in the international business community.

Three high school career academies are also available to students in Pinellas County. They are the Agriscience Academy at Tarpon Springs High School, designed for students taking career paths in veterinary technology, horticultural science and environmental technology; the Architectural Design and Construction Academy at Dunedin High, intended for students who are considering a career in the fields of architectural design and construction; and the Transportation Academy at Northeast High in St. Petersburg which offers training in automotive body repair and refinishing and automotive technology.

Pinellas County Schools has five fundamental elementary and two fundamental middle schools that offer a back-to-basics environment. In St. Petersburg these schools are Bay Vista Fundamental, Lakeview Fundamental and Pasadena Fundamental. The other two at the elementary grade level are Curtis Fundamental in Clearwater and Tarpon Springs Fundamental in Tarpon Springs. The fundamental middle schools are Southside Fundamental in St. Petersburg and Coachman Fundamental in Clearwater.

Middle school programs are available for students gifted in math through the three-year MEGSS program – the Mathematics Education for Gifted Secondary School Students. Another program is designed for seventh and eighth graders gifted in science and math. It is the IMAST or Integrated Mathematics and Science Technology program.

Underachieving students, who need extra support, may qualify to attend a challenge or discovery school. St. Petersburg Challenge and Robinson Challenge in Clearwater

continued on page 110

Pinellas County Schools District Administration Building in Largo. The Pinellas County School system ranks 21st in size (110,000 students K-12) of the more than 16,000 school districts in the United States. With more than 140 schools, the district offers a full range of programs. Pinellas County students continually rank among the top in state standardized tests and the district has forged a significant partnership with the business community and over 21,000 registered volunteers.

SHORECREST PREPARATORY SCHOOL

As the school's name implies, Shorecrest has been preparing Pinellas County youngsters for the rigors of college since 1923. Located in northeast St. Petersburg, Shorecrest Preparatory combines challenging course work, personal guidance and extracurricular activities to produce students who are intellectually curious, socially responsible, creative and independent thinkers.

The school's broad range of curriculum extends from early childhood through 12th grade, and includes courses which encourage students to demonstrate a competency in literature, writing, foreign language, history, mathematics, science and the arts. But beyond the academic curriculum, Shorecrest instills its students with positive habits of thought and study, intellectual curiosity, all within an atmosphere of encouragement and nurturing.

Beginning at the earliest grades, children are introduced to Spanish, computers, music, art and physical education, coupled with core subjects. Classroom instruction is interactive, and "hands-on" project learning complements traditional lectures.

Shorecrest's Science & Technology Center houses biology, chemistry and physics laboratories, and two computer classrooms. Every classroom on the Shorecrest campus is linked by computer and – through the Internet – to the world as well. Students are also encouraged to explore their creativity with the power of imagination. Visual and performing arts courses are a requirement for all students and include theater, playwriting, instrumental and vocal music, studio art, graphic design, photography and videography.

Shorecrest's athletic programs balance academic pursuits by helping students develop self-confidence, good sportsmanship, appreciation for teamwork and discipline. Lower School students participate in physical education classes at least three times a week. Over 80 percent of the Middle and Upper School students compete for at least one interscholastic team.

The total learning experience provided to students has resulted in Shorecrest's nationwide reputation for excellence. The quality of academic work, a proven work ethic and a belief in individuality have earned Shorecrest graduates the respect of college admissions officers across the United States. Shorecrest's College Counseling Office encourages students to begin the search and application process during the junior year.

Working in partnership with parents and students, the College Counseling Office views this process as part of a student's total Shorecrest education, involving personal reflection, independent thinking, and informed decision-making.

Throughout the educational process, parents, teachers, students and administrators form a team whose goals are competence, confidence and unity. It is this teamwork and the rich tradition which assures the enduring strength of Shorecrest Preparatory School, making it St. Petersburg's premier private learning institution.

www.shorecrest.org

ADMIRAL FARRAGUT ACADEMY

Success Is Never Accidental

One of St. Petersburg's most unique institutions of learning is the Admiral Farragut Academy. Located on Boca Ciega Bay, Admiral Farragut Academy has been an honor naval school since 1946 and today is a coed boarding and day school with grades K – second (adding third and fourth grades in 2001 and 2002 consecutively) and fifth through twelfth.

While not the school for every child, students who seek academic excellence will find the Academy a fitting challenge. Farragut students also participate in a wide variety of sports and extra curricular activities. The Academy's rigorous mental and physical programs are designed to prepare young men and women for the demands of the colleges for which they are best qualified.

Twenty-four credits are required for graduation. They must include a minimum of 19 major credits, including one naval science and four electives. Upper Division students have the opportunity to earn college credits through a wide range of dual-credit electives. Middle Division students take math, social studies, science, English and physical education, as well as foreign language, computer science, music, speech, and health. The newly incepted Lower Division boasts a non-military atmosphere with a focus on individuality and students working at their own pace in a nurturing environment conducive to maximizing potential.

Interscholastic sports include: cross-country, football, swimming and diving, basketball, soccer, golf, tennis, track and field, baseball, volleyball, wrestling, softball and cheerleading. Extracurricular activities at Farragut include flight training, scuba, sailing, riflery, theatre arts, band and choir. Other activities include providing community service, a requirement for graduation.

The Academy has the distinct honor of nominating cadets who qualify to any one of the United States Service Academies. Fourteen nominations per year are available. Farragut has placed more graduates into colleges on full Naval ROTC scholarships than any similar school in the nation. Almost 100 percent of each graduating class have consistently been admitted to colleges and universities. In 1999 over $800,000 in scholarships were awarded to Admiral Farragut graduates.

When space became the new frontier, two Farragut graduates joined the Space Program. Admiral Alan Shepard '41, the first American in space, and General Charles M. Duke, Jr., '53, Apollo 16, were two of the 12 men who walked on the moon.

The key to Farragut's success lies in small classes and close personal attention. Faculty members know their fields well and are dedicated to teaching. Students are encouraged to develop individuality, self-discipline, leadership and initiative.

www.farragut.org

THE CANTERBURY SCHOOL OF FLORIDA

The Canterbury School of Florida was founded in 1968 by a group of civic leaders who felt the strong need to sponsor a school in St. Petersburg dedicated to academic excellence. Canterbury is a coeducational, college-preparatory day school beginning with early pre-kindergarten through 12th grade. While affiliated with the Episcopal Church, Canterbury admits students of all races, creeds, and religious origins to all activities and programs, encouraging a diverse student body representative of the St. Petersburg community.

The Canterbury School is situated on two campuses just minutes apart in northeast St. Petersburg: Hough Campus for pre-kindergarten through grade 5 and Knowlton Campus for grades 6 through 12. The philosophy of instruction and reputation are rooted in the best of traditional styles of learning with emphasis on strong fundamental academic skills. A student/teacher ratio of 11:1 and an enrollment of just under 450 students provide an educational environment with individual attention given to every student, whether in lower, middle or upper school divisions.

The Canterbury School strives to foster creativity by developing and enriching the curriculum to challenge each student. Canterbury's faculty is committed to helping students discover their unique talents and abilities to aid in the development of high level skills, values and self-esteem. Through academic, athletic and extracurricular programs, students build confidence, learn teamwork and demonstrate leadership abilities. The skills and values become durable and lasting contributions to success in college and life beyond.

The Canterbury School of Florida is accredited by the Florida Council of Independent Schools and holds memberships in the following educational organizations: National Association of Independent Schools, Southern Association of independent Schools, Bay Area Association of Independent Schools, Educational Records Bureau, National Association of College Admission Counselors, Southern Association of College Admission Counselors, Florida Kindergarten Council and Florida High School Activities Association.

Canterbury is a school for students, teachers and parents, all of whom have a voice and make a difference. At The Canterbury School of Florida, education can become the gift of a lifetime.

www.canterbury-fla.com

Health Care & Education

serve students in fourth and fifth grades. Lealman Discovery in St. Petersburg and Clearwater Discovery are for students in sixth through ninth grades. The schools offer at-risk students small group and individual instruction and have programs coordinated with community agencies and business partnerships. Students' self-esteem is improved through strengthening their basic skills and personal development.

In addition to the many choice schools mentioned, Pinellas County Schools has five partnership schools. These are cooperative efforts between the district and employees at Bayfront Medical Center, Honeywell, Morton Plant Mease Health Care Systems, Pinellas County government and the City of Clearwater.

Career, technical and adult education is available through Pinellas County Schools CTAE Centers where basic skills and GED preparation is offered as well as continuing education. Career and technical programs are also offered full time and part-time at the Pinellas Technical Education Centers (PTEC) and apprenticeship training is available through two campuses, one in mid Pinellas County and one in St. Petersburg.

Because of our orientation towards light industry and high-tech businesses, there is a need for specialized job training and higher education. High school and college graduates find an outstanding selection of institutions offering a wide array of degree and non-degree study choices. Within the immediate area there are 13 college and university campuses with an enrollment exceeding 80,000 students.

St. Petersburg Junior College (SPJC) is recognized as one of America's best community colleges. From its founding in 1927 until 1942, SPJC was a private, non-profit institution operating in downtown St. Petersburg. Today it has four traditional campuses in St. Petersburg, Clearwater, Tarpon Springs, and Seminole, a health education center in Pinellas Park, and a corporate training facility and criminal justice/law enforcement training center also in St. Petersburg. In addition, SPJC offers classes at various off-site locations as well as via television and computer.

Students can select from 26 distinctive Associate in Science (A.S.) degrees that prepare them for careers immediately upon graduation, as well as six shorter-term certificates. Or they can pursue an Associate in Arts (A.A.) degree, which grants the holder admission as a junior to one of Florida's 10 public universities. The AA degree transfers outside the state as well.

Florida's state universities include the University of Florida in Gainesville; Florida State University, Tallahassee; Florida Agricultural and Mechanical University, Tallahassee; the University of South Florida, Tampa and St. Petersburg; Florida Atlantic University, Boca Raton; the University of West Florida, Pensacola; the University of Central Florida, Orlando; the University of North Florida, Jacksonville; Florida International University, Miami; and Florida Gulf Coast University, Fort Myers. These universities offer more than 250 different bachelor degrees.

USF St. Petersburg is the only public university in Pinellas County. The 33-year-old campus is the University of South Florida's largest regional branch and hosts colleges of arts and sciences, business, education, and nursing. It is nationally recognized for its graduate program in marine science. The U.S. Geological Survey's Center for Coastal Geology, the Florida Institute of Oceanography and a branch of the Department of Environmental Protection are located at the downtown St. Petersburg waterfront campus on Bayboro Harbor.

Stetson University College of Law, founded in 1900, is

continued on page 114

Experienced-based learning opportunities are part of the focus of John Hopkins Middle School Center for the Arts and Communication Studies.

KESWICK CHRISTIAN SCHOOL

Higher Standards. Eternal Value.

Keswick Christian School is not only distinctively Christian; it also endeavors to provide a superior education academically as well. Conveniently located near the beaches in western St. Petersburg, the school has been serving families throughout Pinellas County since 1953. Classes begin at Junior Kindergarten and continue on through high school.

Keswick's standards have contributed to the school's exceptional academic outcomes, with students scoring substantially above the national average in every field of study, and nearly 100 percent of all graduates continue on to college. Keswick is continually broadening the school's curriculum, offering a truly superlative educational experience.

The school's Computer Technology Program is constantly evolving, offering online research for students, the integration of computer software into the various academic curriculum areas and providing distance learning for faculty members. Keswick also offers a Dual Enrollment Program and Advanced Placement courses, which allows academically advanced students the opportunity to earn college credit. Home school students are also offered classes on campus and may participate in extracurricular activities.

These activities include highly competitive athletics for both boys and girls, widely recognized as some of the finest athletic programs in the state. The Keswick Fine Arts department offers vocal, instrumental, drama and art opportunities. These groups compete in district, state and international competitions and consistently receive superior ratings.

From an academic standpoint, Keswick provides a phonetic reading program in primary grades, a special education program for children with learning difficulties, foreign language instruction and well-equipped science labs. Spiritually, biblical training is an essential part of a child's education. Keswick offers both Bible classes and weekly chapels.

Keswick Christian School educates children from the perspective that they are spiritual beings as well as physical and mental beings. Therefore, by combining academic and spiritual disciplines, Keswick helps develop the entire child. This is true Christian education. Keswick has been designed to be an extension of the Christian home by partnering with parents and their churches.

Accredited by the Association of Christian Schools and the Southern Association of Colleges and Schools, Keswick's faculty is fully state certified or eligible with an average of 13 years of educational experience. High school classes meet or exceed all state graduation requirements and the school's strong academic program is verified by achievement tests and college entrance exams.

Guided by a self-perpetuating board, Keswick has a growing capacity and plans are in place for continued expansion. Planning for the future, Keswick is today, what many other area schools are striving to become tomorrow.

www.keswickchristian.org

ST. PETERSBURG JUNIOR COLLEGE

Certificate programs at SPJC: answers to employers' needs

Stories about employers who complain they can't find skilled workers don't go unnoticed at St. Petersburg Junior College. In fact, they're a call to action.

In the past two years, the college has increased its number of certificate programs more than sevenfold. Today, those programs – which require 18 to 28 credit hours for completion – number between 40 and 50 and provide credentials for jobs in half-a-dozen fields where employer laments have been the most voluminous.

The certificate programs are grouped under six headings: Computer and Network Technology, Environmental Resource Management, Health Care, Industrial Development, Business Development and Administrative Services, and Public Service. The latter includes programs as diverse as Crime Scene Technology, Basic Corrections and Fitness Professional. Scattered among the other categories are programs ranging from Perioperative Nursing to Irrigation Technician, from Advanced Plastics Engineering Technician to Food and Beverage to Windows Programing.

These are just the ticket(s) for individuals who wish to upgrade their professional skills without investing the time, effort and expense necessary to earn a degree. (But at the same time, most of the credit hours earned are applicable toward an SPJC Associate in Science or A.S. degree later if the certificate holder decides to pursue further academics.)

In some cases, by attending classes full time, a student can complete a certificate program in a year. Completion of work toward a degree can take more than twice that long. Right now, 2,000-2,500 students annually are receiving training in SPJC certificate programs.

What's hot? Information Technology.

"Currently," said SPJC Associate Vice President Kay Adkins, "our strongest focus is on our programs that train individuals for industry standard certification tests: Oracle, Microsoft, Cisco, A+ and E-Commerce. These have been really able to take off since we received a $250,000 grant from the Microsoft Corporation."

E-Commerce programs

E-Commerce arguably is the hottest new field of job development in the country, and St. Petersburg Junior College is rising to the challenge. Thanks to a quarter-million-dollar grant from Microsoft Corp. – one of only eight awarded nationwide – SPJC is assembling the goods for a new Associate in Science (A.S.) degree in E-Commerce, plus five new, related certificate programs.

Some of the classes began in Session I (fall term) of the 2000-2001 school year, which started Aug. 21. By Session II (January 2001), all systems are expected to be go.

"It is a tremendous honor for the college to be chosen to participate with Microsoft in this program," said Carol Copenhaver, SPJC's vice president of Educational and Student Services. "Earlier, we had a summit of the top 100 business leaders in the Tampa Bay area and they all identified E-Commerce as the top priority. We want to answer the needs of the area business community, and this grant will enable us to make giant strides."

Associate Vice President Kay Adkins pointed out that by offering a degree program and separate certificate programs concurrently, SPJC provides students with flexible options. "For those who don't feel they have the time to pursue a degree now, they can complete a certificate program in less time and greatly enhance their hireability," Adkins said. "Then later, if they choose, they can re-enroll at the college and apply their certificate credit hours to pursuit of an A.S. degree in E-Commerce."

The five certificate options are Web Server Administration, Web Applications Development, Web Enterprise Development, E-Commerce Design, and Web and Information Technology Project Management.

"These are very comprehensive offerings," Adkins said. "The certificates encompass all aspects of E-Commerce: development of Web sites, operations and management, designing, programming, project management, and also security issues related to E-Commerce."

SPJC's Clearwater Campus will be the main site for the programs. The Web Design and E-Commerce certificates also will be offered at Seminole Campus, and some courses in the programs will be offered at other college sites.

More than 140 institutions throughout the U.S. applied for the grants from Microsoft. In addition to SPJC, the other winners were Bristol (Mass.) Community College, New York's Fashion Institute of Technology, Ilisajuik (Ark.) College, San Diego Community College, Kentucky Community and Technical College District, Southwest Virginia Community College and Southwestern Oregon Community College.

Health Care & Education

Florida's first law school and the only one in the Tampa Bay metropolitan area. The College moved to St. Petersburg in 1954, and is set on a 21-acre Spanish Revival campus. It is an integral part of Stetson University in DeLand, Florida, its original location.

Ranked number one in Trial Advocacy among the nations 180 ABA-approved law schools, it is one of the first law schools to establish a pro-bono graduation requirement. It is also the only law school in the nation to win five national level law school trial championships in one academic year (1993-1994).

Eckerd College is an independent, coeducational, liberal arts college founded in 1958 as Florida Presbyterian College. Its 167-acre campus includes a mile of waterfront and is located near the Pinellas Bayway that connects St. Petersburg to St. Pete Beach. The school offers a full range of bachelors degrees in thirty-five majors, including strong interdisciplinary majors in environmental studies, marine science, international business, and international relations and global affairs.

The college also has a series of special programs including a degree completion program for adults called the Program for Experienced Learners (PEL), the Academy of Senior Professionals at Eckerd College (ASPEC), the Management Development Institute (MDI), the Leadership Development Institute (LDP), the Human Resources Institute (HRI), and is the area's host site for Elderhostel programs and for ELS Language Centers.

ASPEC is a membership organization that supports Eckerd College and its programs through the contribution of time and talent. Members come from all professional areas to share their wisdom and experience with the students, each other, and the community. They are individuals recognized and elected for distinguished achievement in business, professional, scientific, technical, political, or cultural and academic areas. Most reside within a 50-mile radius of St. Petersburg. The program is unique in the nation.

Information Commons at SPJC Seminole campus. The school now offers access to junior and senior level courses at its College University Center.

The Science Center of Pinellas County goes beyond the classroom with interactive exhibits that explore physics, archaeology and inventions. It is open the entire year.

ECKERD COLLEGE

A Florida College of National Distinction

Overlooking beautiful Boca Ciega Bay in St. Petersburg, Eckerd is a private, coeducational college of liberal arts and sciences related by covenant to the Presbyterian Church (U.S.A.). Founded in 1958, Eckerd is a pioneer of responsible innovation - developing programs that have been adopted nationwide and earning the College an international reputation for academic excellence.

With a traditional student body of more than 1,535, the College attracts outstanding young people from 49 states and 62 foreign countries. More than 54 percent of this year's freshman class ranked in the top 20 percent of their high school class. Our student body includes 50 National Merit Scholar finalists and semifinalists. And College Board (SAT) scores for incoming freshmen have been on an upward trend since 1983: the Eckerd average is now more than 150 points above the national average.

Eckerd is also meeting the needs of adults through the Program for Experienced Learners (PEL), a bachelor's degree program designed specifically for those who have the motivation and maturity to succeed, yet need the flexibility and personalized attention the program provides. Today more than 1,200 adults are enrolled in the Program for Experienced Learners.

Students at Eckerd College also enjoy a unique opportunity provided by the Academy of Senior Professionals (ASPEC), a transgenerational program where senior professionals share their thoughts, insights and experiences with students both inside and outside the classroom. Volunteering their time as mentors, career advisers, lecturers and friends, ASPEC members provide students with a special perspective gained from a lifetime of experiences. The pioneering concept of ASPEC was one of the reasons Eckerd College was cited by *U.S. News & World Report* as one of the five most innovative colleges in America.

In keeping with the vision of its founders, Eckerd College offers value-centered general education programs that form the framework for a wide selection of majors. These range from the traditional liberal arts to marine science, international business, international relations and global affairs, environmental studies, computer science, and opportunities for study in Europe, Asia, Central America and many other locations throughout the world.

Along with an exceptionally strong academic program, the cocurricular program adds a valuable dimension to the student's education outside the classroom. Through participation in voluntary service projects, career exploration and extracurricular activities, students become competent givers, people whose future lives will be characterized by leadership and service.

www.eckerd.edu

UNIVERSITY OF SOUTH FLORIDA

The University of South Florida's St. Petersburg campus is the first regional campus established in Florida, and the only public four-year university in Pinellas, a county of nearly one million people.

Nestled along the waterfront of Bayboro Harbor, it is considered one of the loveliest urban campuses in the nation. It is located in the heart of the Bayboro district, a serene setting on the edge of downtown St. Petersburg that borders hospitals, museums and performing arts arenas.

USF St. Petersburg is one of four USF campuses, which is the first public university created in the 20th century and now is among the 20 largest in the nation. Academic excellence is one of the University's hallmarks, and it has won national acclaim for its research and instruction efforts in the fine arts, teacher education, accounting, marine science, psychology and medicine. The university fully prepares Tampa Bay's future leaders for the demands of a rapidly changing world.

The St. Petersburg campus offers programs at the undergraduate, master's and doctoral levels that are notable for their small class sizes and individual faculty attention. Flexible scheduling and affordable tuition allows students of all ages to accommodate family, work and school in a balanced fashion. USF St. Petersburg places value on each and every individual it serves, making it a welcoming and nurturing environment for all who come on campus.

Students can receive degrees in business, education, nursing and the arts and sciences. The highly regarded Teacher for All Children program, which prepares students for certification in both elementary and special education, is considered one of the best of its kind in the United States.

USF's College of Business Administration carries the highest academic accreditation available for schools of business, and accounting graduates are consistently among the highest scorers in the nation on the CPA exam. The College also offers a special MBA program on Saturdays geared to working professionals.

The University's honors program challenges and enhances the quality

ST. PETERSBURG CAMPUS

education normally generated by the campus. Exciting programs are offered through the Science Journalism Center, which merges both disciplines to convey the latest scientific breakthroughs to the public.

The campus also is known for its ethics programs. The Program for Ethics in Education and Community infuses the teaching of ethics throughout the curriculum and beyond through a popular public lecture series. It also actively engages with the school system and the Stavros Institute in providing character education to all Pinellas students. Through its service learning program, the campus creates many community service opportunities that build character as well as resumes.

The Poynter Memorial Library provides superior reference and resource materials through technical advances in library science and is a leader in distance-learning education. A thriving special collections section contains the finest Mark Twain collection in the state, and the signed documents of U.S. presidents ranging from George Washington to Harry Truman.

As a research university, USF is a catalyst for economic development and in applying new knowledge to industry. The College of Marine Science is recognized nationally and is one of the top research and grant award recipients in the entire State University System. The Center for Ocean Technology is creating microinstruments with a technology called micro-electromechanical systems (MEMS) that eventually will provide critically needed advances in the fields of medicine, marine science, water quality and the military.

Affiliated agencies, such as the U.S. Geological Survey's Center for Coastal Geology, Florida Institute of Oceanography and Florida Marine Research Institute, also are located on campus. The Children's Research Institute is a collaboration between the University and All Children's Hospital. The Institute, which hosts seven endowed chairs, investigates cures for childhood disease. Expectations are high that it will be a major force in pediatric research internationally.

USF St. Petersburg has developed many fruitful partnerships with the community including the YWCA/USF Family Village and Florida Humanities Council. The latter organization directs the campus's Florida Center for Teachers, which holds seminars for the state's best teachers to enrich our education system as a whole.

The campus is deeply involved in the community through its Urban Initiative. The Urban Initiative aims to improve life in St. Petersburg's poorest neighborhoods by facilitating economic and social programs. The Urban Initiative works with various community agencies, grassroots groups and city government. Top priorities are literacy and education, public safety and workforce and small business development.

With its affiliates, USF St. Petersburg has a $66 million annual budget and employs more than 700 employees. Its estimated economic impact on the area is more than $165 million annually. The campus is poised for future growth but respects the past as well. USF St. Petersburg's two historic houses, circa 1900, were the private domains of Gen. John C. Williams, one of the city's founders, and C. Perry Snell, an early developer. The campus has refurbished the homes, which are open to the public.

USF St. Petersburg is an invaluable asset for the city and Pinellas County, providing educational access, critical research and community partnerships that better the quality of life for all in the region.

www.stpt.usf.edu

STETSON UNIVERSITY COLLEGE OF LAW

100 Years of Excellence in Legal Education

Stetson University College of Law is Florida's first law school. Founded in 1900, the College was originally located in DeLand on the main campus of Stetson University. In 1954, the College relocated to Gulfport to a larger facility that could accommodate the growing post-war enrollment.

With a current enrollment of only 650, the College provides an intimate environment for learning and personal growth in a beautiful campus setting. The College is located on the site of the former Rolyat Hotel resort, built in 1925 and designed to resemble a medieval Spanish village. The hotel was considered a luxurious oasis for society's elite. The tower building, a landmark for the College of Law, was patterned after the Torre de Oro in Seville. The College of Law continues to maintain the architectural splendor of the original hotel.

Through the years, Stetson has evolved from a small local institution to one of national prominence. The *U.S.News and World Report* annual national survey of law schools consistently ranks Stetson's trial advocacy program as one of the best in the nation. In 2000, the *U.S. News* general ranking placed Stetson in the top half among all law schools nationwide. The College's growing graduate and international programs prepare students for the global legal marketplace. Students may enroll in a joint J.D./M.B.A. program, and attend a Summer Abroad Program in Tallinn, Estonia. A new Master of Laws (LL.M.) degree program in International Law and Business attracts lawyers from all over the globe.

Other Centers of Excellence provide specialized training, including the Elder Law Center, the Center for Dispute Resolution, the Institute of Litigation Ethics, and the Health Law Consortium with the University of South Florida College of Medicine. Students may enroll in selected "concentration programs" to better prepare for emerging areas of practice.

The new 58,000 square foot Law Library and Information Center houses more than 350,000 volumes and study carrels are wired for access to the Internet and legal research systems. Every student is expected to arrive on campus with a laptop computer and is linked via e-mail and voice mail.

As Stetson continues to develop new programs to meet the demands of the Twenty-First Century, the College remains committed to excellence and professionalism in a close community environment emphasizing individual attention to student needs.

www.law.stetson.edu

Chapter 5
Sports Leisure & Recreation

Tampa Bay fans are loyal to their hometown teams, no matter which side of the bay has the scoreboards...

ROBERT ROGERS / TAMPA BAY DEVIL RAYS

Sports, Leisure & Recreation

TY HESTON

For starters, we have some of the finest major league facilities in Florida. The silhouettes of Tropicana Field in St. Petersburg and Raymond James Stadium and the Ice Palace in Tampa are recognizable landmarks on Tampa Bay skylines.

Tropicana Field opened as the Florida Suncoast Dome in St. Petersburg in 1990 and was renamed the ThunderDome in 1993 while serving as home ice for the NHL's Tampa Bay Lightning. The name was changed to Tropicana Field with a sponsorship in 1996. But even before the Tampa Bay Devil Rays threw out the first pitch on April 1, 1998, in their new home stadium, the Dome had established some attendance records.

When the Tampa Bay Lightning played there between 1993 and 1996, they drew the 20 largest NHL crowds of all time. The Tampa Bay Storm of arena football fame also attracted the biggest turnouts in that league's history while calling the Dome home. The arena additionally played host to nearly 26-thousand fans for an NBA exhibition game between the Chicago Bulls and the Seattle Supersonics in 1990, then brought us worldwide attention during the NCAA Men's College Basketball Final Four championships between UConn and Duke in March 1999 as 40-million television viewers looked on.

Tropicana Field is a 45,360-seat, climate-controlled domed ballpark with all-dirt base paths and artificial turf. It was the first tension ring cable-supported domed stadium built in the United States and it is one of the largest in the world. While designed primarily for baseball, Tropicana Field has the flexibility to accommodate arena events from 10,000 to 50,000 people, depending on the event and configuration requirements.

Across the Bay, the 65-thousand seat Raymond James Stadium opened in Tampa, with a win for the NFL Tampa Bay Buccaneers against the Chicago Bears on September 20, 1998, after 22 years of Bucs play in the old Houlihan Stadium, affectionately referred to as "the big sombrero." Raymond James Stadium has comfortable seating for over 65,000 fans, 52,000 of those are in general seating with 12,000 club seats, two air-conditioned club lounges, 71 suites and 100 luxury suites.

A 103-foot long pirate ship is the centerpiece of Buccaneer Cove in the north end zone. It is a replica of an

Preceding pages: St. Petersburg's Tropicana Field is home to the Tampa Bay Devil Rays and holds attendance records for NHL hockey and NCAA men's basketball.
Right: Florida Power Park, home of Al Lang Field and the Spring Training facility of the Tampa Bay Devil Rays.

HERB SNITZER

122

TY HESTON

Sports, Leisure & Recreation

early 1800's pirate ship and has a 9'x7' skull and crossed swords facing the playing field. Buccaneer touchdowns are celebrated by the firing of eight cannons that send mini-footballs and confetti into the stands.

Owned by the Tampa Sports Authority the stadium is also home for the Tampa Bay Mutiny, which features some of major league soccer's most exciting International stars and American superstar players. It is home to Tampa Bay's own Division I college football team, the University of South Florida Bulls who took the field for the first time in 1997. And on New Year's Day the Outback Bowl is played at Raymond James Stadium, the site of Super Bowl XXXV.

In the Garrison waterfront district of downtown Tampa, the Ice Palace was completed in the fall of 1996 as the new home of the NHL Tampa Bay Lightning. Here spectators can get close to the action in the seven-level structure which seats 19,500 for hockey, 20,500 for basketball and 21,500 for concerts. The Tampa Bay Storm also play their home games at the Ice Palace and have won four league championships in Arena Football.

While the Tampa Bay Devil Rays are the first Major League Baseball team to host regular season games in the area, St. Petersburg has a fascinating baseball history. In 1914 Al Lang, a former Pittsburgh laundry owner who had moved to St. Petersburg for his health, lured the St. Louis Browns to come to St. Petersburg. A baseball committee raised $20,000 to buy a large tract of land for a ballpark. The site chosen for the field was Coffee Pot Bayou in St. Petersburg, where a 2,000-seat grandstand was built for the team's spring training.

According to the history books, after a first win in Tampa, the Chicago Cubs played the Browns in St. Petersburg before an estimated crowd of 4,000 including many sitting in their automobiles, parked beyond right field. Schools and most offices shut down at mid-day. It later became custom for merchants to close their doors on Monday and Wednesday afternoons to allow employees and customers to attend games.

Al Lang was elected mayor of St. Petersburg in 1916 and again in 1918. And since that first season, seven other major league franchises have called St. Petersburg their springtime home. In fact more major league spring training games have been played here than in any other city. Here is a brief timeline:

1914 the Grapefruit League is established, in which teams played a five-week schedule of exhibition games. Branch Rickey's St. Louis Browns train in St. Petersburg and stay one year.

1915-1918 Pat Moran's Philadelphia Phillies train in St. Petersburg. After their departure, Lang convinced 20 local residents to each contribute $1,000 to build a new ballpark, Waterfront Park, now the Bayfront Center near today's Florida Power Park.

1919-1920 Florida Spring Training is canceled due to World War I travel restrictions.

1921-1937 Boston Braves arrive and remain through the 1937 season.

1925-1961 New York Yankees (the Bronx Bombers) arrive, except for the 1951 season. The Yankees' dynasty teams of the 1930's, '40's and '50's get their start in St. Petersburg, fueling tourism and making St. Petersburg Florida's hub for baseball in the Spring. The team was headquartered at the now historic Princess Martha Hotel.

1938-1997 St. Louis Cardinals arrive and remain in St. Petersburg until 1998 when they move their spring training camp to Jupiter, Florida.

1943-1945 Again, spring training is canceled due to travel restrictions, this time during World War II.

1947 Al Lang Field was opened on St. Petersburg's downtown waterfront and named in honor of St. Petersburg's fist mayor, "Mr. Baseball," or "Uncle Al" Lang.

1951 New York Yankees and Bronx Bombers swap training locations with the New York Giants, who normally trained in Phoenix, Arizona. That season the Bronx Bombers defeated the Giants in the World Series.

1952-1987 New York Mets train in St. Petersburg.

1977 Al Lang Stadium, an 8,000-seat spring training facility opens, replacing nostalgic Al Lang Field that served as St. Petersburg's spring training headquarters since 1947.

1993-1995 The Baltimore Orioles join the St. Louis Cardinals as St. Petersburg's second franchise holding spring training here.

1995 The Tampa Bay Baseball Partnership is awarded an expansion franchise. The newest major league team of the American League East is named the Tampa Bay Devil Rays and will play in St. Petersburg.

1998 The first regular season gets underway and the Tampa Bay Devil Rays bring professional baseball home to St. Petersburg. The Rays hold spring training at renamed Florida Power Park, home of Al Lang Field, adding to a glorious tradition of baseball in St. Petersburg.

Spring training is still good for tourism as baseball fans follow the Grapefruit League around Florida.

*Above: Albert Whitted Airport, Bayfront Center and Florida Power Park viewed from Tampa Bay.
Below: Namesake plaques at Huggins-Stengel Field.*

Other teams here are the Philadelphia Phillies in Clearwater, the Toronto Blue Jays in Dunedin and the New York Yankees in Tampa. Within an easy drive are the Cincinnati Reds in Sarasota and the Pittsburgh Pirates in Bradenton.

In addition, the Florida State League has two baseball teams in Pinellas County, and the New York Yankees minor-league headquarters are in Tampa. And once a year, the Major League Baseball Players Alumni Association hosts the biggest stand-alone old-timers game in the country, the Legends of Baseball, at Florida Power Park home of Al Lang Field in St. Petersburg.

The City of St. Petersburg runs a competitive slow pitch softball program year round for adult teams in men's, women's and coed divisions. The program is run under the Amateur Softball Association rules with a ten game league season. Across the Bay, the Tampa Bay Firestix play in Women's Professional Fastpitch, a softball league whose season runs from May to August.

And speaking of legends, St. Petersburg is home to the world-famous Three Quarter Century Softball Club, Inc.

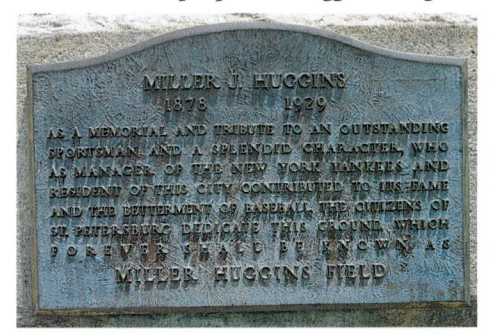

"Kids & Kubs" and the slightly younger half-century men's softball league. Each continues to attract national attention and local crowds for their entertaining brand of softball.

Even baseball, football and hockey fans like a change of pace in the off seasons. Powerboat racing is one of the most popular to watch. Two major happenings are the Gold Cup Challenge Offshore Power Boat Races at St. Pete Beach and the Hurricane Offshore Classic in the waters of Tampa Bay, off The Pier in downtown St. Petersburg. The biggest, fastest and finest offshore racing machines in the world compete for top prizes in this American Powerboat Association two-day event, sanctioned by the Pinellas County based Offshore Powerboat Association.

St. Petersburg's downtown waterfront is also the site for the Olympic Regatta Training programs where competitors from all over the world practice their skills for Olympic sailing events in Tampa Bay waters. In addition, mid-winter regattas for several sailing classes are conducted from the St. Petersburg Yacht Club including the Lightning, Thistle, Sonar, International 14, and Flying Dutchman.

continued on page 131

TAMPA BAY DEVIL RAYS

Field of Dreams

Few cities in America labored longer or harder to attract baseball than St. Petersburg. This 20-year dream was fulfilled in 1998 when major league baseball launched its first season in the Tampa Bay market with the Devil Rays playing in St. Petersburg's Tropicana Field, Florida's only domed stadium, seating 43,800 in comfort and convenience.

Countless comparisons have been made over the years between the game of baseball and the realities of life, emphasizing the teamwork required to succeed, the tremendous rewards and recognition that often follow, and the realization that doing the best and developing talents, whatever they may be, are what truly matter.

Cheering for a Major League Baseball team has been a new activity in the Tampa Bay area, but the spirit needed to work together to attain worthy goals has a long history here. The Devil Rays are pleased to share this spirit by facilitating contact among diverse groups, not just through baseball but through a unifying purpose: making the community a better place to live and work. Sponsors and benefactors who under-

Wade Boggs join the elite 3,000 career hits club with this dramatic home run in his final season of an illustrious 18-year career.

126

write the programs presented by the Tampa Bay Devil Rays deserve a great deal of credit for the assistance in developing, organizing, promoting and presenting them.

For example, in 1999 the Devil Rays provided in-kind donations to more than 400 Tampa Bay area charities and were responsible for raising $1,057,723 for Tampa Bay area charities. Rays corporate partner Volume Services America, in its first three years as the concessionaire at Tropicana Field, donated $1.8 million to local non-profit organizations manning the concession stand at Devil Rays home games.

Few things bring a smile to a child quicker than a personal visit from a favorite sports figure. With a year-round schedule of appearances that includes scores of visits to hospitals and children's clinics, Devil Rays players, coaches, announcers and, of course, Raymond, the Devil Rays' mascot, know that the smiles of those who welcome them reflect inspired hope and happiness. On the average, the Rays provide free guest speakers for more than 300 community events every year.

While baseball is king at Tropicana Field, the Rays have opened the doors for charity events benefiting Abilities, Hillsborough County's TIVY Math competition, Pediatric Cancer Foundation, St. Vincent DePaul Charities, the Pinellas County Education Foundation, the American Heart Association, Suncoast Children's Dream Fund, Big Brothers and Big Sisters of Tampa Bay and Academy Prep in St. Petersburg.

While the team's commitment off the field is manifested by the aforementioned activities, the drive to make the Rays a championship team is most obvious in a minor league system that already ranks as one of major league baseball's best.

www.devilrays.com

TAMPA BAY BUCCANEERS

The Tampa Bay Buccaneers play in state-of-the-art Raymond James Stadium, considered by many to be the "Crown Jewel" of the National Football League. Super Bowl XXXV was played in Raymond James Stadium in January 2001.

A new era in Tampa Bay sports began in 1995 when Malcolm Glazer purchased the Tampa Bay Buccaneers. One of Glazer's first initiatives was to unveil the team's eagerly anticipated new color scheme and logo during a ceremony in downtown Tampa. The new logo, consisting of a red pirate flag with a skull and crossed swords, and colors, Buccaneer red and pewter, drew instant rave reviews from Buccaneer fans around the country. Buccaneer Fever continued to spread throughout the Bay area in 1998 as the Buccaneers kicked off the season in the new state-of-the-art Raymond James Stadium, considered by many to be the "Crown Jewel" of the NFL.

Since the opening day in 1998, every Buccaneers home game has been sold out.

The first professional sports franchise to incorporate in the Tampa Bay area, the Buccaneers organization has been through many changes over the years. Under the leadership of the Glazer family, the Buccaneers have become winners on and off the field.

Tony Dungy joined the Buccaneers in 1996 as the team's sixth head coach, and under his guidance, the Buccaneers have blossomed into one of the best teams in the NFL.

Along with solidifying the team's reputation on the field, Dungy and the Buccaneers are dedicated to improving the quality of life for members of the Tampa Bay area and Central Florida communities. The Buccaneers support a variety of community agencies and are actively involved with a host of charitable organizations, schools and hospitals.

The Buccaneers boast one of the strongest player/coach game-day ticket programs in the NFL. At every home game, the Buccaneers host approximately 20 different groups from local schools and charitable organizations as part of the game-day ticket program. The Buccaneers treat those groups as honored guests during each game, giving them Buccaneers T-shirts, featuring their pictures on BucVision and seating them in specially marked areas of the end zones.

The Buccaneers also have the NFL's only Student Advisory Board. The council is comprised of high school sophomores, juniors and seniors who perform community service projects, create Buccaneer spirit in their schools and develop their leadership skills in preparation for continuing their education.

Community involvement is important to the Glazer family as well, as evidenced by the creation of the Glazer Family Foundation in 1999. The Glazer Family Foundation is dedicated to developing ways to assist charitable and educational causes - focusing primarily on youth - in the Greater Tampa Bay and Central Florida regions. Programs include "Cheering You On," an initiative that gives every child admitted to a Bay area hospital a Buccaneers teddy bear and activity book.

The Buccaneers understand that, to maintain a loyal fan base, the team must excel on and off the field. The organization is committed to remaining a leader within the community for years to come.

Malcolm Glazer, represents the Glazer Family Foundation that works with established not-for-profit organizations to help identify and create programs that advocate positive social development in the Bay area and Central Florida communities.

www.buccaneers.com

TY HESTON

HERB SNITZER

Sports, Leisure & Recreation

Considered one of the most prestigious events in the United States, St. Anthony's Triathlon weekend attracts a competitive field of the top amateur athletes from around the world to St. Petersburg. Over the years St. Anthony's Triathlon has served as a qualifier for the Ironman Triathlon World Championship and is known as the season opener to the 1,800 participants because of its stature as the first major race of the year.

St. Petersburg's Olympic-size North Shore Pool, one of eight public swimming pools, operates two nationally recognized programs, including swim team training and one of the largest masters swim clubs in the nation. Members, ranging in age from 22 to 91, hold national records for the most wins. The club hosts many competitive events and an average of nine northern college swim teams arrive at the pool each winter for "training in the tropics."

Tennis is a year-round favorite sport in St. Petersburg, with numerous public and private courts available and a choice of playing surfaces. Pinellas teams have won national titles and our courts have been graced with many professional players and tournaments including the Davis Cup Finals.

Upper left: St. Petersburg waterfront serves as a site for the Olympic regatta training programs.
Remaining photos: Action shots of St. Anthony's Triathlon including the Meek and Mighty competition shown opposite page.

Sports, Leisure & Recreation

The Women's Tennis Association (WTA) Tour is the premier women's sporting circuit in the world and hosts 59 tournaments around the globe during an 11 month schedule each year. The WTA's Sports Sciences and Medical Division, designed to provide optimal health care to all athletes on the women's professional tennis circuit, is located in downtown St. Petersburg. The Renaissance Vinoy Resort tennis complex serves as a site for tournament play.

Even if you're not a pro, but want to play tennis, there is a St. Petersburg court ready for you, year round. The St. Petersburg Tennis Center is located south of the downtown business district with easy access to Interstate I-275. Opened in 1928, the center features 15 clay courts and four lighted courts. It has also hosted some of the world's best professional players including Martina Navratilova, Bill Tilden and Chris Evert. In addition, the city has 14 more community center locations that have a total of 64 courts available to the public.

With our ideal weather, another favorite activity enjoyed throughout Pinellas County is golf. There are over 40 golf courses both public and private that offer year-round play from sun up to sun down. The city of St. Petersburg maintains and operates three of these courses.

Mangrove Bay Golf Course is an award winning regulation 18-hole championship golf facility that has proven to be a favorite for golfers of all skill levels. The lighted practice range is one of the finest in the area, complete with practice putting and chipping greens. The golf pro shop is fully stocked with the latest golf equipment and apparel and PGA professionals on staff are available for group or individual golf instruction.

The new Cypress Links at Mangrove Bay is a challenging 9-hole, par-3 course designed for golfers of all ages, playing levels and abilities. Players there will find large greens, generous tee boxes, numerous lakes and bunkers, and holes of varying lengths requiring a variety of clubs.

And Twin Brooks Golf Course is a well-maintained par-3 course that is particularly popular with golfing enthusiasts who prefer to walk the golf course. The tees, greens and driving range were completely renovated in 1992 and 1993.

Besides tennis and golf, St. Petersburg has more than 50 athletic fields at 19 locations that are used by recreational adult leagues and youth sports organizations. Like the rest of the cities in Pinellas, St. Petersburg encourages youth sports

St. Petersburg's Olympic-size North Shore Pool and training site of one of the largest masters swim clubs in the nation.

Sports, Leisure & Recreation

Top: With over 40 public and private golf courses, Pinellas County is a golfer's paradise. Below: The Treasure Island Tennis and Yacht Club is one of many excellent facilities serving both recreational and competitive tennis players.

Sports, Leisure & Recreation

participation and there are literally hundreds of teams offering development in soccer, baseball, football, swimming, volleyball, hockey, basketball, tennis, golf, martial arts, sailing, gymnastics and more. Many high school and area college teams, as well as individual athletes, have claimed state and national championships while several local standouts have gone on to professional sports careers, even winning Olympic gold medals!

BMX racing is popular with young riders of various ages and skill levels who compete at St. Petersburg's Walter Fuller Park, while youthful skateboard acrobats make good use of the ramps, half pipes and quarter pipes at two skate park locations. There's an arena at Coquina Key Park in St. Petersburg and one at Central Skate Park nearby on Ulmerton Road mid county.

In sunlight and twilight, Pinellas parks and sidewalks are populated with serious and not-so-serious runners, joggers and walkers of all ages. The Suncoast Runners Club, among others, sponsors weekly events for the novice to the professional. Add bicycle riding and inline skating and the options are even greater.

For pure enjoyment it's hard to beat a ride on the Fred E. Marquis Pinellas Trail, a Rails-to-Trails bicycle-pedestrian path maintained by the Pinellas County Parks Department. This 15-foot wide, paved linear park was built along an abandoned railroad right-of-way and runs for approximately 45 miles – from Tarpon Springs, near the Anclote River in the northern part of Pinellas, to U.S. 19 near 8th Avenue South in St. Petersburg.

Part of the beauty of the trail is that it offers a unique view of the area. You can be near the bustling Tyrone Mall in St. Petersburg, or in Dunedin's downtown Plaza, or in the middle of the city of Clearwater. On the same trail you can also enjoy deep glades of ancient live oaks with trailing Spanish moss, tidal streams with all varieties of land and water birds, even quiet waterways to wet a fishing line.

While the trail is used year round, Florida's cycling season runs from September through April or May, because of cooler temperatures. During those months there is some sort of event nearly every weekend for recreational cyclists. The Tour of Pinellas is an example, sponsored by the Suncoast Cycling Club each April. The St. Petersburg Bike Club also has regular organized rides.

Our city and county parks are a convenient way to enjoy the outdoors. In St. Petersburg, Boyd Hill is an award winning 245-acre preserve with nature trails, environmental studies area and a nature conference center on Lake

continued on page 138

Whether it is sky diving, jet skiing or wind-driven skate boarding, the area is a Mecca for countless forms of good-weather sports activities.

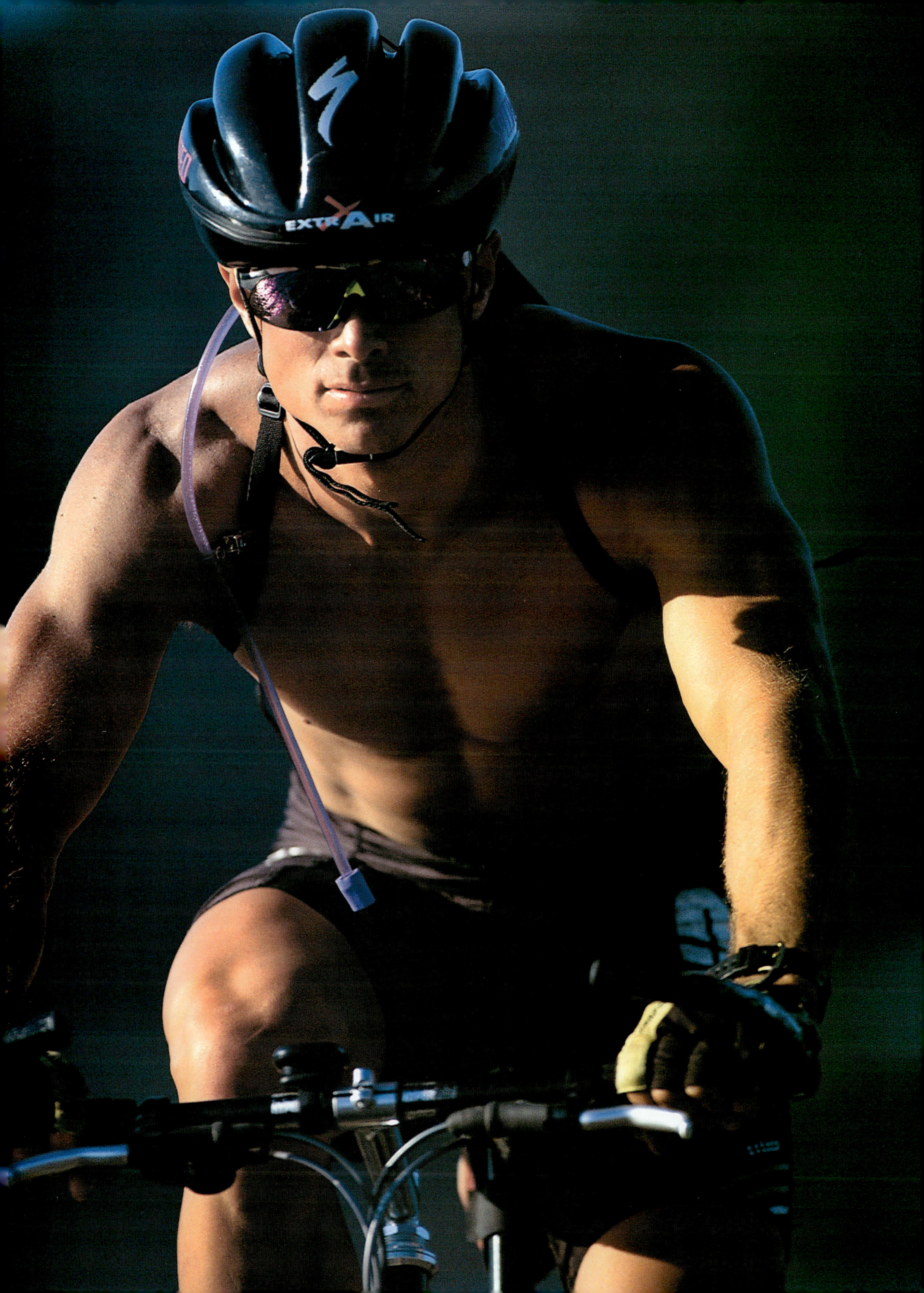
EXTRA AIR

NEW YORK YANKEES LEGENDS FIELD

For as long as there has been baseball, residents of the Tampa Bay area have been avid supporters. America's game has sent teams to Florida for decades during the spring training season, and one of the local favorites has always been the New York Yankees.

The legends of the game – Babe Ruth, Joe DiMaggio, Mickey Mantle and Whitey Ford – made the trek to St. Petersburg from 1925 to 1961 before moving spring training to Ft. Lauderdale. But in 1988 the New York Yankees minor league and Player development complex returned to Tampa. Since George Steinbrenner, the team's principal owner, has been a long time resident of Tampa, the logic of moving the team back to Tampa full time became an obvious choice.

An effort involving individuals from Hillsborough County, the Tampa Sports Authority and the Yankees eventually brought major league spring training back to Tampa in 1996. One of the primary reasons was the newly built training facility, which catered to spring training baseball. Appropriately named Legends Field, this state-of-the-art facility was constructed to incorporate parts of the Bronx's Yankee Stadium with a Florida flavor. The playing dimensions of the field are an exact duplicate of "The House That Ruth Built".

The success of both the Yankees and Legends Field has been nothing short of phenomenal. During spring training, crowds attending the 15 home games are often double that of other area teams. More than 150,000 fans packed the stadium during the 2000 spring training season. But Legends Field has become more than just a showcase for baseball.

Partnering with the Nederlander Organization, which is one of the most successful operators of entertainment facilities in the world, Legends Field has welcomed some of the biggest names in music, including Rod Stewart, Sting, the Moody Blues and Crosby, Sills & Nash. Having a 10,000-seat stadium "without a bad seat in the house" has been one reason for the success.

When the New York Yankees aren't in town, Legends Field is home to the future stars of the team, the Florida State League Class "A" Tampa Yankees. In addition, the Florida High School State Baseball Championships has called Legends Field home for the past 4 years and will continue through 2004. Not including the concert season, more than 300,000 fans visit the complex annually.

The 31-acre complex includes 12 luxury suites packed with all the amenities of a major league park and two practice fields. Legends Field is ideally situated within the Tampa Metro area, located near the intersection of Tampa's Dale Mabry Highway and Dr. Martin Luther King, Jr. Drive.

With Legends Field and the New York Yankees Baseball Complex, America's national pastime and Tampa Bay's long-standing love affair with baseball has created a presence in Central Florida like never before. Baseball fans of all ages agree – the Babe would be proud of Legends Field.

www.legendsfieldtampa.com www.yankees.com

Longitude, latitude and the Gulf Stream

St. Petersburg has a year-round climate that ranks higher than Honolulu's in the number of clear, sunny days, while we share the same average temperature (in the mid-70s). This sunny, tropical weather is moderated by land and sea breezes.

Winters are short and mild. There is usually one day in December and two in January when the temperature drops below 32 degrees. The same occurs once every other February, according to weather forecasters. Summers are warm, and humid. July and August have the most days of 90-degree temperatures with an average of 21 and 22 days respectively.

Fall and spring are usually dry seasons. April and May are sunny 75 percent of the time and the cloudiest months are August and September, with sunny skies only 61 percent of the time. One of the predictable weather factors of summer in Pinellas County is the afternoon thunderstorm, a usual occurrence from June through September that brings soaring temperatures down from mid-day peaks.

Hurricane season coincides with the summer months between June 1 and November 30 officially. Florida is also the lightning capital of the nation and the Tampa Bay area averages 90 days of lightning a year.

Sports, Leisure & Recreation

Top left: Award winning Boyd Hill Nature Park. Top right: Sawgrass Lake Park
Bottom left: Northeast St. Petersburg's 1,500-acre Weedon Island Preserve and resident American bald eagle.
Bottom right: The beauty and serenity of the War Veterans' Memorial Park.

Maggiore. The park has five different ecosystems and conducts monthly nature walks, bird strolls, night hikes, and wildflower walks.

Sunken Gardens, once a privately run tourist attraction that began in 1935, is now owned and operated as a botanical garden by the City of St. Petersburg Leisure Services Parks Department. The landscaped grounds and butterfly aviary have a colorful array of the many plants and flowers that thrive here and can be viewed from the garden's pleasant walkways.

Ft. DeSoto Park is the largest park in the Pinellas County park system and listed in the National Register of Historic Places. It has 900 acres consisting of five interconnected islands with over seven miles of waterfront including three miles of beach. A 235-site family camping area is one of the park's most popular amenities. Its other features include: an 800-foot-long boat launching facility with five floating docks; two fishing piers – one on Tampa Bay and the other on the Gulf; large group picnic shelters; and a four-mile paved loop recreation trail, a favorite with cyclists. Rich in history, a battery of 12-inch mortars and two British cannons of 1890 vintage are located at the fort for which the park was named.

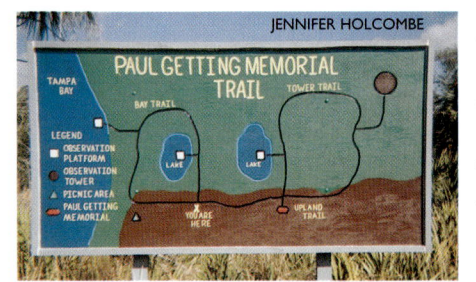

Lake Seminole Park is another Pinellas County park located on the eastern shore of Lake Seminole, near St. Petersburg. In addition to picnic facilities, the park, approximately 255 acres in size, has two ponds that are favorites of model sailboat enthusiasts. There is a large play area and a two-mile recre-

Sports, Leisure & Recreation

ation trail. The park also has a boat ramp accessing the freshwater lake, popular for boating, fishing and water skiing.

Sawgrass Lake Park, just north of St. Petersburg, has been called one of Pinellas County's best-kept secrets. More than a mile of boardwalk meanders through portions of the 360 acres of ecologically sensitive wetlands. Here you can expect to see native flora and fauna in their natural state, including water birds, alligators, turtles and fish. The Pinellas County School Board and the Park Department work together to provide school groups with a unique learning experience by maintaining the park as an on-site classroom.

Another favorite and convenient park for south county residents is the War Veterans' Memorial Park. This 122-acre park is adjacent to the Veterans Administration hospital complex and faces Boca Ciega Bay with access to the Gulf of Mexico. While the park itself closes at sundown, a lighted, public boat ramp is open 24-hours. There are several picnic pavilions, a playground area and an authentic Army tank, plus wide, paved winding roads ideal for bicycling. A 3.5-ton granite sundial was built especially for the park's Memorial Center and is surrounded by five plaques that commemorate the military branches of the U.S.

On the eastern shores of Tampa Bay in northeast St. Petersburg is a group of islands called the Weedon Island Preserve. Boardwalks and trails lead through a mangrove forest to a three-platform 45-foot observation tower with sweeping views of the 1,500 acres. The state of Florida bought Weedon Island in 1974 and opened it as a preserve in 1980. Management was transferred to the county in 1993 and Pinellas forged a financial alliance with the city of St. Petersburg and the Southwest Florida Water Management District for improvements.

The island, once inhabited by the Tocobago Indians, has a history that includes use as a 1930's movie studio, an airport, and a speakeasy. Today a four-mile canoe trail winds among the secluded bayous of the preserve to the open waters of the bay. The trail is excellent for bird watching and there is plenty of shallow water for wade fishing.

continued on page 142

Ft. DeSoto Park is Pinellas County's largest park and is listed in the national register of historic places.

TAMPA BAY LIGHTNING

One of the most exciting young teams in the National Hockey League, the Tampa Bay Lightning provide hard-hitting, high-energy action at the Ice Palace in downtown Tampa. Featuring one of the budding young superstars in the NHL in center Vincent Lecavalier, the Lightning draw fans to Tampa's revitalized Channel District throughout the fall, winter and spring months.

Molded by Senior Vice President & General Manager Rick Dudley, the Lightning are a team with a focus on speed and aggressiveness. Size, skill and character have topped the wish list as Dudley and the Lightning scouting department have scanned the world to find the players that currently fill out the team's roster.

The stability starts at the top with any successful franchise, and much-needed stability is exactly what the Lightning got when the team and the Ice Palace were purchased by William Davidson's Palace Sports & Entertainment prior to the 1999-2000 season. Based in Auburn Hills, Mich., PS&E also controls the Detroit Pistons of the National Basketball Association, the Detroit Shock of the Women's National Basketball Association, the Detroit Vipers of the International Hockey League, the Palace of Auburn Hills and several other sports and entertainment interests.

Starting with the 1992-93 season, the Lightning quickly forged a strong bond with sports fans throughout the Tampa Bay area. NHL hockey came to The Sunshine State for the first time when the Lightning enjoyed one of the most successful expansion seasons ever, playing at Expo Hall at the Florida State Fairgrounds.

The team moved to a new home the following year, routinely drawing record crowds while playing at the ThunderDome (now known as Tropicana Field) in St. Petersburg from 1993 to 1996. Tampa Bay still owns the top nine all-time NHL single-game attendance marks, including an all-time regular-season best of 27,227 for a 1993 match-up with the Florida

140 www.tampabaylightning.com

Panthers. The Lightning provided some of the most exciting moments in Tampa Bay sports history during the 1996 Stanley Cup Playoffs.

While the ThunderDome provided exciting memories, it was only a temporary home while the Ice Palace – built through a unique public/private partnership – was constructed in downtown Tampa. The Ice Palace opened in 1996, and the building's short history has been highlighted by the NHL's choice of the Ice Palace and the Tampa Bay area as host for the 1999 NHL All-Star Weekend. The festivities attracted tens of thousands of visitors and worldwide recognition for the area.

Giving back to the Tampa Bay community has always been a top priority for the Lightning organization. Since the start of The Lightning Foundation, Inc. in 1998, the Lightning have provided support for local youth programs, disabled and disadvantaged children's organizations, cancer research and organizations that provide emotional, financial, and educational assistance for patients with cancer.

THE ICE PALACE

The Ice Palace also features a newly reconstructed sports and entertainment themed eatery, two restaurants on the building's club level and the Nextlink Channelside Club, a private, all-inclusive seating area, whose 550 members are all Tampa Bay Lightning season ticket holders. Decorated in a manner which recognizes all of the performers to play the Ice Palace, the eatery serves as the focal point of activity each and every day at the Ice Palace. Located off of the Chrysler/Jeep Plaza and open for lunch and dinner on a regular basis, the building's new eatery serves as home to television and radios shows before and after many of the building's events.

Medallions, located on the club level, is the Ice Palace's most upscale restaurant, offering the very best in fine dining. Open prior to every event in the building, Medallions features an ever-changing, eclectic menu designed to please Tampa Bay's most discriminating palates. The building's more casual buffet-style restaurant, Icons, has received menu enhancements only overshadowed by new levels of service. The faster paced buffet has extended offerings, a pastry and desert island and rotating live production stations.

The Nextlink Channelside Club offers a beautiful, panoramic view of Tampa's ever-expanding Channel District on one side and private seating over the ice on the other for the Club's members. Offering all-inclusive food and beverage at Tampa Bay Lightning home games for members, the Club is lavishly decorated and designed in hockey's "Original Six" motif. The Club offers members three separate bars and a cigar bar, which overlooks the action on the ice below. Members of the Nextlink Channelside Club are also able to use the 15,000 square foot room for meeting, banquets, presentations and private parties.

www.icepalace.com

Sports, Leisure & Recreation

As a peninsula city surrounded by water and an Intracoastal Waterway, fishing, boating and sailing are almost a way of life in St. Petersburg. Numerous boat ramps give access to the Gulf and inland waters and if you don't have your own boat, private charters and party boats are available. The waters of the Gulf of Mexico hold a treasure of cobia, flounder, redfish, sheepshead, snook, tarpon, grouper, king mackerel, Spanish mackerel and spotted sea trout. Tarpon season runs from mid May through July with tournaments for serious anglers. Bass and other fresh-water fish are found in Pinellas County's two major lakes – Lake Tarpon and Lake Seminole.

If the big ones always seem to get away, check conditions at the track. Pari-mutuel wagering has a long history in the Bay area with the St. Petersburg Kennel Club – Derby Lane which has been in operation since 1925. Races are run live from January through June, with simulcast races the rest of the year. Across the Bay, Tampa Greyhound continues the season with dog races scheduled from July through December. For horse racing, Tampa Bay Downs near the city of Oldsmar offers thoroughbred racing from December to March.

Some days you will never want to be indoors and hopefully you will be able to find a good excuse. The weather here is pretty much ideal year round and for those moments when you simply want the sun on your face, the sand at your feet and the clean air putting fresh wind in your sails, there's always the beach.

The saltwaters of the Gulf of Mexico and Tampa Bay, plus two large fresh water lakes, offer an abundance of fishing choices in Pinellas.

THE TAMPA BAY MUTINY

Carlos Valderrama, the man synonymous with the Tampa Bay Mutiny.

The Tampa Bay Mutiny started a trek to professional sports success

on November 16, 1994, when Major League Soccer (MLS) officially awarded the Bay area one of 10 original franchises. Nearly a year later, on October 17, 1995, the team was given the name "Mutiny," and a logo described as a "cyber-mutant" by the shoe company, Nike.

The Mutiny's first season in 1996 was one of storybook proportions. Tampa Bay compiled a 20-12 record, advanced to the Eastern Conference finals and had three players earn major awards: Carlos Valderrama, one of the most popular players in the world, was the MLS Most Valuable Player. Roy Lassiter, who scored an incredible 27 goals, was the MLS scoring leader and Steve Ralston, who played college soccer at Florida International University, was the Rookie of the Year.

The Mutiny returned to the playoffs in 1997 and again in 1999, after moving into beautiful Raymond James Stadium. Heading into the year 2000, the Mutiny, one of two league-owned franchises, was on the verge of ownership that will ultimately result in a soccer-specific stadium for the team.

Soccer's worldwide popularity carries over into the Bay area with the Mutiny. Nearly 40,000 youth ranging in age from six to under 19 play the game locally and are the current and future fans of the Mutiny and MLS. As active members of the community, the Mutiny originated the popular "Kicks for Kids" program, where local or national corporations purchase season tickets that are in turn donated to charities and schools for use by underprivileged children. The majority of MLS teams have also created similar programs in their cities.

In the first three seasons, the Mutiny's "Kicks for Kids" program helped nearly 100,000 Bay area underprivileged youngsters attend a professional soccer game, many for the first time. Another key component of the Mutiny's community involvement is "Heroes of Tomorrow," where the ticket purchases by corporations leads to monies for charities or aiding youth soccer clubs.

The Mutiny is also actively involved in the growth of TOPSoccer (The Outreach Program of Soccer), that enables disabled youth to participate in the "beautiful game," as well as donating needed items (balls, t-shirts, etc.) so that the children of migrant farm workers in the Bay area may be able to play soccer. Tampa Bay Mutiny players are also individually involved with many charities, camps, clinics, reading and fitness programs, among other activities.

www.tampabaymutiny.com

SUN TIME ENTERPRISES, INC.

It's the seventh inning stretch at a Devil Ray's home game.

Tradition time. A volunteer from the stands takes the public address mike and belts out every baseball fan's favorite song, "Take Me Out To The Ball Game." As a reward, the volunteer is presented with a Devil Ray's wristwatch that plays the same tune (in key). In the background, the Devil Ray's Diamond Vision scoreboard boldly displays this unique watch and its manufacturer – Sun Time Enterprises, Inc.

Sun Time has become the nation's recognized leader in licensed sports timepieces and, through its Linkswalker division, a variety of golf accessories. The company currently holds over 1,000 licenses with Major League Baseball, the National Football League, NASCAR, the National Hockey League, top college programs, and many of the biggest names in sports.

Famous for its unique designs, Sun Time's repertoire of timepieces include musical watches, sound wall clocks, and a "Gripper" alarm clock. Linkswalker, their licensed golf division, produces the latest in golf products and accessories. Recognizing that sports fans come in all ages and genders, Sun Time has something for everyone (including players and coaches).

Sun Time's explosive growth has continued to capture local, statewide and national attention. In 1998 the company was awarded the St. Petersburg Small Business of the Year Award. Inc. Magazine, in its 16th annual ranking, placed Sun Time in the Inc. 500, as one of America's fastest growing private companies. In 1999, the company was the Ernst and Young Entrepreneur of the Year in Florida.

With headquarters in Clearwater, Sun Time maintains a 70,000 square foot warehouse facility and two distribution centers. A team of more than 60 professionals develop, design and ship the company's diverse product line to more than 8,000 customers around the country.

Sun Time and Linkswalker products can be found in small sporting goods retailers, jewelers, gift shops, large national retailers, and many web sites. Not a bad track record for a company that sold its first watch at Super Bowl XXV in January 1991.

Driving this entrepreneurial engine is an ambitious premium and incentive business, meaningful cross promotions, and a goal to continue to strengthen the Sun Time brand nationally. In pursuit of this, Sun Time has also taken the time to remember its roots with a strong commitment to the community and its many sports fans.

That sometimes includes brave Devil Ray fans whose 7th inning song says it all.

Glenn Colangelo, Vice President of Logistics, and David Colangelo, President, discuss the production of the Super Bowl XXXV watch.

www.suntime.com

Chapter 6
Manufacturing & Technology

TY HESTON

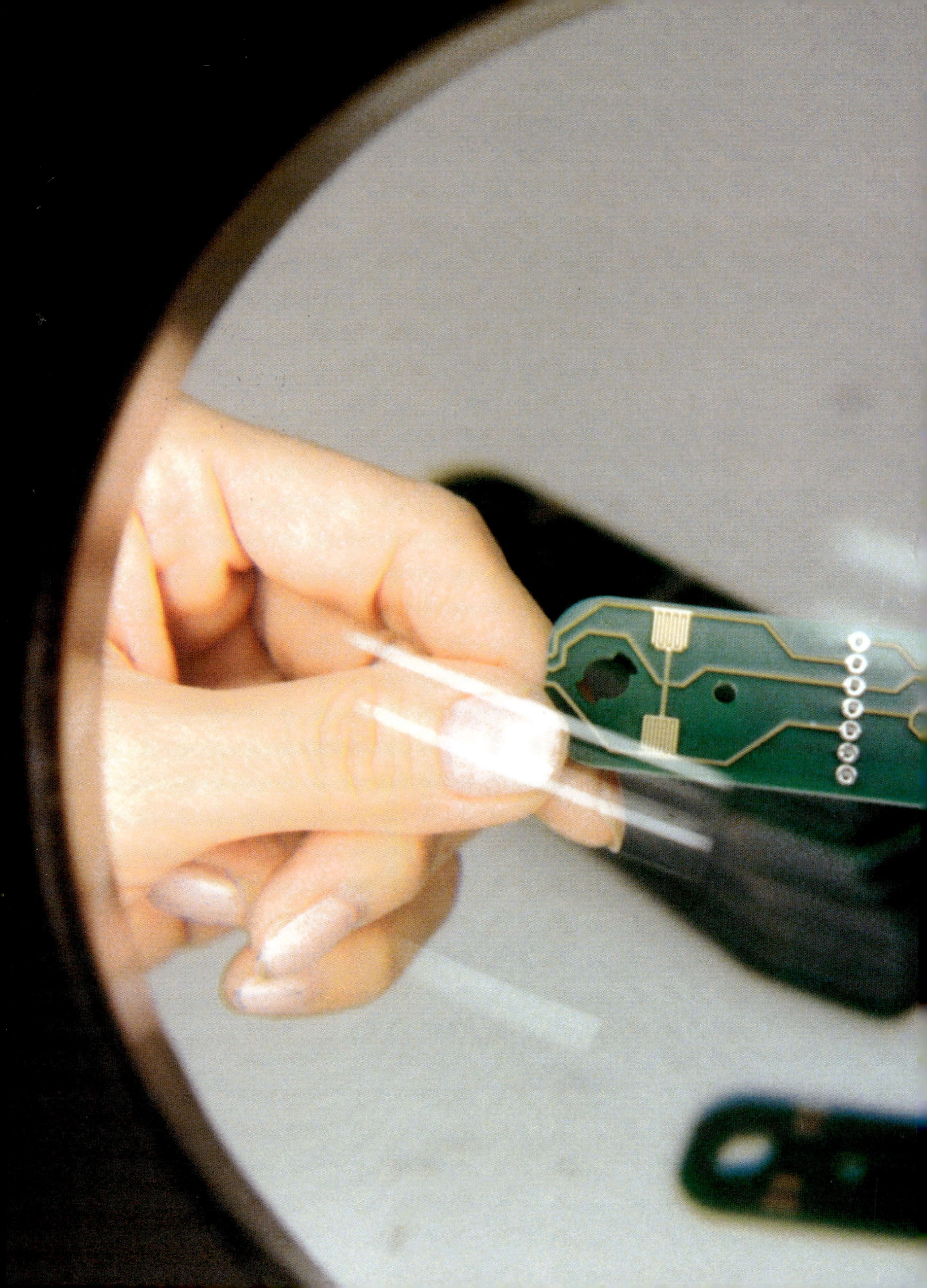

High tech manufacturing dominates the top-50 list of major industries that can be found in St. Petersburg & Pinellas county…

Manufacturing & Technology

To better understand what is happening in the related fields of manufacturing, research and technology, first take a look at the entire state. Florida ranks sixth in the nation in the number of high-tech jobs and is the nation's fifth largest exporter of high-tech goods. It has one of the largest industry clusters of optics manufacturers in the country with 166-plus companies.

Look closer. Companies from microelectronics to optics to medical devices have blazed a new research and manufacturing technology trail across central Florida that stretches from the Gulf of Mexico to the Atlantic Ocean. It has been dubbed the "Florida High-Tech Corridor," and it has the fifth largest high-tech labor force in the United States with 120,000 workers. Two of its key partners are the University of South Florida at the Tampa Bay portal and the University of Central Florida in Orange County.

Studies by the University of South Florida show that the number of information technology companies operating along Florida's High-Tech Corridor grew 60 percent in one year, from 1,033 companies in 1997 to 1,651 in 1998. Pinellas is home to 24 percent of these companies. In fact, there was a 53 percent increase in newly established information technology companies in the Tampa Bay area alone.

A third of Florida's manufacturing companies and 60 percent of the state's high tech companies are in the Tampa Bay area, and Pinellas County ranks number two in all of Florida for manufacturing and number one in the state for manufacturers of computer and office equipment, electronic components, and industrial and commercial machinery.

Along the Florida High-Tech Corridor, St. Petersburg dominates in the medical manufacturing, instrumentation manufacturing, electronics manufacturing, and software development fields. More than half of the medical and biomedical firms, 24 percent of microelectronics companies, 22 percent of laser and optics companies and 18 percent of the information technology firms are in Pinellas County.

While medical device companies, many of which are focused on electronics, became a part of our makeup in the late 60's, downsizing of the military had a major effect on manufacturing in this area, as it did across the country. Pinellas made the most of it.

Sitting on 96 acres in the technology core of Pinellas County is the STAR Center (an acronym for Science Technology And Research), a primary example of a former Department of Energy plant that was saved from oblivion when the Cold War ended. This 730,000-square-foot facility is managed by the Pinellas County Department of Economic Development and has changed with the times from military use to commercial use. It now has 24 tenants including Raytheon's Cable Centers of Excellence, which occupies 352,000 square feet as the anchor tenant.

Research and development firm Concurrent Technologies Inc. moved into an 80,000-square-foot facility at the STAR Center. Part of their work is to reduce pollution in the metal finishing industry. Constellation Technology Corp. occupies another 65,000 square feet and makes a device to detect nuclear weapons. The center continues to accommodate research firms such as these to expand their operations.

Pinellas County enables local businesses to grow with their global markets and stay here. For example, in 1979, Environmental Technologies, Inc. began manufacturing HVAC equipment with 15 employees in a 15,000-square-foot facility near the STAR Center. The firm grew to 1,200 employees and expanded to 600,000 square feet as third world countries began relying on such companies for air conditioning technology.

A line of electro-surgical devices made by Bovie Medical Corp. is now in popular demand in surgery rooms across the nation. The St. Petersburg medical manufacturer has added a newly patented plasma technology to its product line and is planning to ship in larger volumes to the European market.

Circuit board assembly company, Jabil Circuit Inc., established in Detroit in 1966, opened its St. Petersburg headquarters in 1983 and has continued to expand internationally with three facilities on the China mainland, one in Hong Kong, and the opening in 2000 of a facility in Hungary.

Part of the circuit board assembly at Jabil Circuit, Inc.

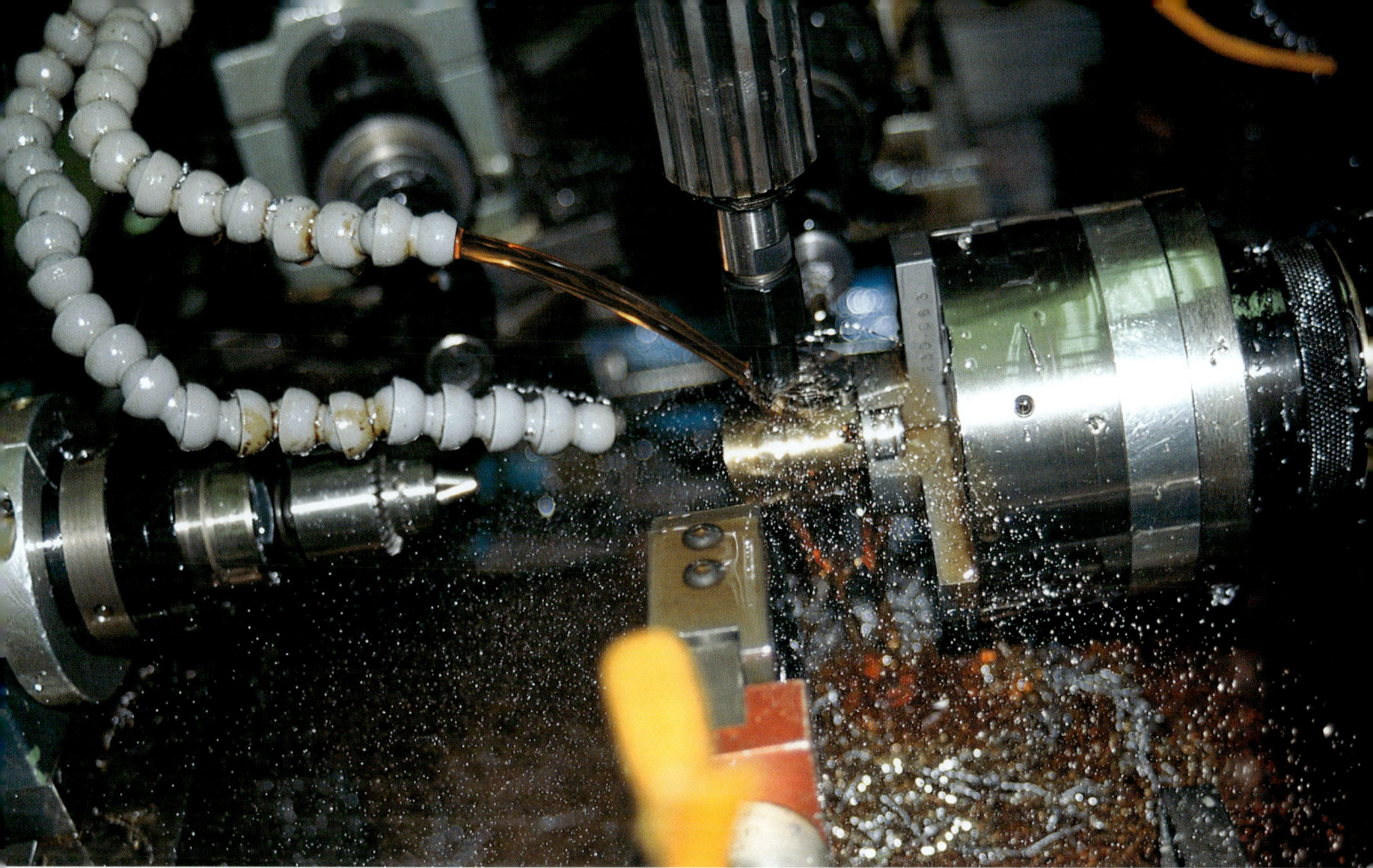

Pinellas County ranks second in the number of manufacturing jobs in Florida.

HERB SNITZER

Jabil is one of several major manufacturing companies, including R.P. Scherer, Compulink Cable Assemblies, Maxxim Medical, Smith Industries, and Eva-Tone, that are located in the mid-Pinellas County area of Gateway. Complementing this manufacturing base are technology firms engaged in research and engineering activities, such as the Tampa Bay Research Institute and the Center for Applied Engineering.

Gateway has been developed over the past three decades and is regarded by most as the leading center of business and industry here. It is sometimes called "St. Petersburg's other downtown." Starting with I-275 as the main artery access, Gateway expansion has been closely related to its interchanges: 4th Street (exit 19), Ulmerton Road (exit 18), 9th Street (exit 17), Roosevelt Blvd. (exit 16), and Gandy Blvd. (exit 15). The area falls within a triangle bordered by 49th Street from the Bayside Bridge to 118th Avenue on the west and Gandy Boulevard and 94th Avenue on the south and includes parts of St. Petersburg, Pinellas Park and unincorporated Pinellas County.

Small and medium-size firms have discovered that they can find development sites and space for expansion in the Gateway environment where existing clusters of manufacturing already exists and rental space is available. Future development is also in place for additional office, industrial and retail space.

Any region for growth needs the infrastructure to produce specialized labor and research, plus access to sources of knowledge. Pinellas has that. The University of South Florida (USF), a key partner in the high tech profile for joint research projects, is the 13th largest university in the U.S. and has more MBA graduates than any Florida school.

In addition, the largest marine science community in the Southeastern United States is located on or near the USF St. Petersburg campus. It includes the USF College of Marine Science; P.O.R.T.S. - Physical Oceanographic Realtime Systems; the Florida Institute of Oceanography; the U.S. Geological Survey Center for Coastal Geology and Regional Marine Studies; Florida Fish and Wildlife Conservation Commission – Florida Marine Research Institute; USF College of Marine Science Center for Ocean Technology; Tampa Bay Estuary Program; Florida Sea Grant; Center for Marine Conservation; and the Marine Science Program at Eckerd College.

Research studies indicate that manufacturing areas designated for the fastest growth all are involved in international trade. These same studies show that overseas companies will license more U.S. manufacturers to build and distribute their products. To benefit, even small manufacturers are joining the global market by partnering with larger firms in Pinellas County who have the means to invest in the technology that enables them to do so, quickly.

Ours is a corporate address of growing world importance, and we're not the only ones who share that opinion. *Employment Review* ranked Pinellas County sixth in the nation; the annual Florida Statistical Abstract places the St. Petersburg/Clearwater area second in the state for manufacturing employment and third for number of manufacturing firms; and *Money* magazine has ranked the St. Petersburg and Clearwater areas fourth out of 300 "best places to live."

JABIL CIRCUIT, INC.

Move over Silicon Valley, Tampa Bay is hot

with high-tech, and when it comes to electronics manufacturing, St. Petersburg's Jabil Circuit, Inc., is a multi-billion dollar powerhouse setting the standard. As one of the world's leading providers of electronic manufacturing services for electronic product companies, Jabil Circuit has proven to be a magnet for talented young executives ready for a different beach.

With its corporate headquarters located in St. Petersburg, Jabil's multi-building campus epitomizes Florida's laid-back lifestyle. Located on a private lake, the company's facilities – including an over-the-lake cabana – are home to more than 3,000 employees. The abundance of sun and fun however, is a fitting balance for a company whose growth has been, and continues to be phenomenal.

Jabil was founded in 1966 by James Golden and William E. Morean, in Morean's Detroit, Michigan garage. The company's name was derived from the founders' first names – James and Bill. Jabil's initial contract was for the manual assembly of replacement circuit boards for Control Data, a computer manufacturer.

Within a year the company had moved into a small facility, incorporated in 1969, moved to yet larger facilities in 1978 and then began to rewrite the growth charts. Currently Jabil Circuit maintains a growing number of highly automated manufacturing facilities in the U.S. and around the globe. International facilities are currently located in Brazil, China, Mexico, Italy, Malaysia, Hungary, and Scotland. Over the past five years Jabil's compound annual growth has grown 40 percent. Prior to the year 2000, Jabil's revenues rose 258 percent while profits soared 1,156 percent between 1995 and 1999.

Success has obviously not been accidental. In 1977 William D. Morean joined the company as Vice President and assumed management of day-to-day operations, implementing the use of automated equipment in order to attract larger high-volume customers. Morean also expanded the company's range of services and formed an aggressive sales effort.

As a result, Jabil began electronics manufacturing for machine controls, voice synthesizers and control automation. Within two years Jabil inked a high-volume turnkey manufacturing relationship with General Motors requiring a strategic commitment to advanced assembly technology and highly automated manufacturing.

Today, companies involved in the communications, personal computer, computer peripherals, automotive and consumer industries utilize a broad range of services from Jabil Circuit. The company offers circuit design, board design from schematic, mechanical and product design, sourcing and procurement, prototype and volume board assembly, complete system assembly services, design and implementation of product testing, end-user distribution and extended repair and warranty services.

The true secret to Jabil Circuit's success has to do with a corporate culture that challenges its employees. As a natural manufacturing extension for customer companies, Jabil's organizational structure gives business unit managers the authority to make on-the-spot decisions in the best interest of the customers and their products. In addition, Jabil dedicates a permanent "workcell" of test, manufacturing and quality engineers, along with purchasing agents, production control analysts and staff to each customer. This workcell team stays in place during the entire product life cycle, essentially forming a "company within a company."

At Jabil, manufacturing and design work hand in hand. The team that designs a product also manufactures it. In doing so, workcell teams blend with customer teams to take on the customer's concerns and goals. The results have led to innovation, zero-defect standards, continuous improvement, technological breakthroughs and unparalleled responsiveness.

After 20 years of refining the workcell team concept, the benefits have paid off in both the company's growth methodology and to its dedicated employees. Jabil has focused on robust internal growth with the emphasis on building facilities from the ground up.

As a result, Jabil's workforce is highly motivated. Many who started on the production floor have worked their way into management positions. Considering that the smallest of the company's 30 teams does about $20 million annually, the impetus for dedication to the team concept is obvious.

For St. Petersburg and Pinellas County, Jabil Circuit continues to set the benchmark for high-tech success. The company is consistently a top performing, local, public company in the Tampa Bay area. From the employees standpoint, an attractive stock purchase plan, full benefit package, tuition reimbursement and an opportunity to receive additional training are what make Jabil one of Tampa Bay's top employment prospects.

Jabil Circuit is one of the premier engines driving Pinellas County's metamorphosis from a tourist-based beach environment into a serious climate for business. ✻

www.jabil.com

DIGITAL LIGHTWAVE, INC.

Reaching Inside the Light

Digital Lightwave, Inc., is a leading provider of fiber-optic monitoring and analysis equipment for the fast growing optical networking industry. Located in a new state-of-the-art corporate headquarters near the St. Petersburg / Clearwater airport, the company is strongly positioned for continued growth in Pinellas County's high-tech corridor.

The company was founded in 1991 on the premise that high-speed optics would play an increasingly important role in global communications network development due to light's superior capacity and speed as a communication transport medium. Indeed it has. The demand for additional bandwidth and higher speeds in recent years, driven by the explosive growth of the Internet, has fueled the growth of optical networks.

As a result of this escalating growth, the company has evolved from a single product company to one that provides a complete suite of products and technology that monitor, maintain and facilitate the management of these high-speed fiber-optic networks. Digital Lightwave's industry-leading products are used to cost-effectively verify and qualify service during network installation and to proactively monitor deployed networks to ensure optimal performance.

The company's products are sold to end users through a direct sales force. Customers include leading telecommunications service providers and equipment manufacturers, such as AT&T, Cisco, MCI WorldCom, Nortel, Qwest Communications, Sprint and Tellabs.

Expanding from a core group of engineers focused on research and development in the first few years of the company's history, Digital Lightwave now has nearly 200 employees with some of the world's premier technical talent in fiber optics. Digital Lightwave's Clearwater corporate facilities maintain sales, marketing, treasury, development, quality and production. Being located in sunny Clearwater, the company easily attracts new recruits from around the world.

Digital Lightwave has consistently ranked among the top performing public companies in the Tampa Bay area. Digital Lightwave's growth is a trend in the fiber optics industry worldwide, and has provided the company with a unique market position and continued opportunities for growth in the near future. Things couldn't brighter for Digital Lightwave, the company that provides technology "to reach inside the light."

www.lightwave.com

ELREHA PRINTED CIRCUITS CORPORATION

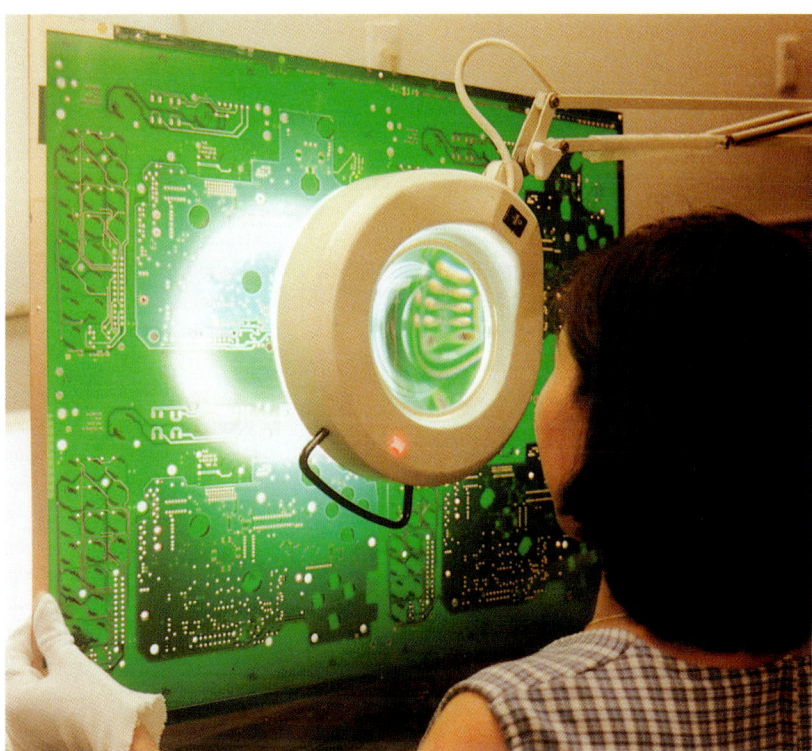

During the mid-1970s, Abdul Hamadeh, a German-based electrical engineer, took notice of the rapidly expanding technological universe and the extreme promise it exhibited. Hamadeh decided to open a small manufacturing plant in the German city of Hockenheim, geared toward creating electronic control systems.

In 1990, to support rapidly expanding business, a decision was made to open a U.S. facility. Pinellas County and St. Petersburg were desirable for several reasons: the close proximity to Tampa International Airport, the strong labor force and the positive family atmosphere. The rapid growth of the technology industry in the Tampa Bay area was the final element confirming that Elreha Printed Circuits Corporation had found a home.

Today manufacturing takes place at Elreha's 65,000 square foot facility located near downtown St. Petersburg. This facility has evolved into a dedicated, in-line manufacturing operation geared specifically to the technical and environmental needs of printed circuit board fabrication.

Elreha is committed to being the premier circuit board manufacturer in North America. The company's dedication to quality and service is a major component in efforts to make Elreha something special in the circuit board industry. Elreha takes the customers product challenges as it's own and continually seeks ways to assist them in producing their products in a quicker, more efficient manner.

The applications for Elreha's products are endless. Elreha's boards are used in the most sophisticated, state-of-the-art automotive applications, including turbo-boost controllers, travel computers, verbal warning systems and anti-skid devices. Additional uses include computers, electronic toys, telecommunications equipment and scanning devices. The merchandise manufactured by Elreha Printed Circuits can be used in almost every piece of electronic equipment.

Elreha now represents a firmly established fixture in the circuit board manufacturing community. Elreha maintains QS-9000 and ISO 9002 certification, ensuring that the company adheres to the highest standards of quality. The company is also a member of the Institute for Interconnecting and Packaging Electronic Circuits (IPC). IPC is an organization dedicated to furthering excellence in the circuit board industry.

For four years running, the Tampa Bay Partnership selected Elreha Printed Circuits as one of the "Tampa Bay Technology Fast 50", representing the largest growing technology firms in the region.

In an increasingly shrinking world, Elreha strives to create a network throughout the global community. Offices currently exist in England, Austria, Italy, Germany, France and the Netherlands.

www.elreha.com

AMERICAN TOOL & MOLD

Whether the average consumer drives a car on the German autobahn, listens to music from a compact stereo system in Tokyo or clicks open a disposable ink pen in Clearwater, chances are parts of these products have come from American Tool & Mold. Literally millions of parts have been produced by the Clearwater-based company specializing in the design and production of custom injection molds and molding.

American Tool & Mold's 135,000 square foot facility might well be likened to a very large space-age clean room equipped with the latest tool-building technology, including the extensive use of robotics. But what separates the company from its competitors is an overriding and all pervasive belief in quality and customer satisfaction. In a business where tolerances are measured in microns, it pays to be perfect.

Maintaining such high standards starts at the top with President Demetre Loulourgas, whose hands-on approach and dedication to excellence is directly passed to the company's 200 employees. Adopting a unique method of project management, Loulourgas directly involves employees in the company's decision-making processes. The results have ensured steady growth for the company.

While the business of injection molding requires the delicate machining of an actual mold into which a plastic is injected, the first critical step in the process is the engineering and design of the mold itself. American Tool & Mold's skilled in-house Engineering and Design team translates customer's products by using three-dimensional and solid CAD/CAM computer programs.

These programs create a "virtual" mold - complex engineering drawings – from which the actual mold is then machined. These molds can include multi-cavity (for producing up to 128 parts in one mold), or two-color and unscrewing molds - an ATM specialty. In an age of e-commerce, it is interesting to note that American Tool & Mold also has the ability to provide complete in-house design services, or transfer customer's existing design data via modem, disc or e-mail through IGES and DXF translators.

To maintain its competitive edge, ATM's quest for perfection begins with its design team and ends with a Quality Control Department unparalleled in the industry. Utilizing the latest in quality systems, philosophies and equipment available, American Tool & Mold ensures that each part meets or exceeds customer expectations.

Fine American craftsmanship is, after all, defined by the satisfied customer. That's the only way American Tool & Mold does business.

www.a-t-m.com

AMERICAN TECHNICAL MOLDING

The difference between American Tool & Mold and its sister company, American Technical Molding, is the difference between finesse and force. The fine line between concept and creation can sometime require the application of 500 tons of pressure. A high-stress job, indeed.

Once a mold has been machined, it must go to work, and American Technical Molding has a vast array of 22 presses that pump out a dizzying array of products. These include pens and markers, caps and closures, power tools, computer, photographic, electronics and automotive parts, as well as packaging, medical devices, disposables and office products.

On the low end, custom injection molding presses owned by American Technical Molding can run in the tens of thousands of dollars. On the high end, for precision plastic parts, the computer-controlled molding machines can run in the hundreds of thousands. What it takes to get a job done – and done correctly – is the philosophy that continues to make American Technical Molding an industry leader.

While there are numerous interfaces between the two companies, including engineering/design and quality control, American Technical Molding is the robotic muscle whose language includes multiple core pulls, melt temperature and pressure monitoring, and ejection on the fly. The translation simply means one quality part produced to customer specifications multiplied by a million.

There are, of course, people behind the presses (even robots need a human touch now and then). President Demetre Loulourgas is one of those people who understand the working relationship between man and machine. "It's our policy," Loulourgas explains, "to promote continuous education and quality improvement programs for all employees. Education and knowledge is key to both personal and company growth."

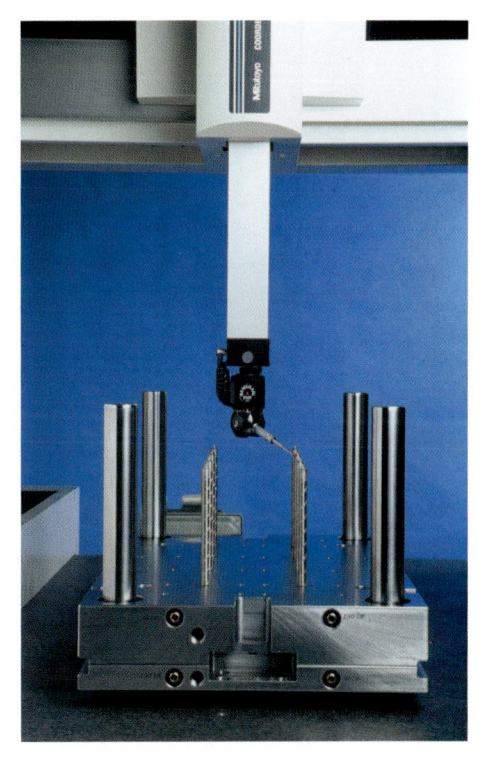

As in any competitive business, finding the edge – whether through mechanical superiority, computer prowess or human innovation – is the keystone of success. American Technical Molding has found that edge, making it one of Pinellas County's, if not America's most progressive manufacturers.

www.a-t-m.com

HONEYWELL

Smarter. Faster. Stronger.

If the Space Shuttle were to pass directly over Clearwater and the Kennedy Space Center during a routine orbit, the 130-mile trip would last a bit less than one-half second. Hardly enough time to cast a downward glance at Honeywell, manufacturing home of the shuttles' main engine controllers.

Large enough to be seen from space, Honeywell's multi-acre Clearwater campus houses more than a million square feet of facilities and is headquarters to Space Systems, a leader in the design, development, and production of control subsystems and equipment for manned and unmanned space applications. The campus is also home to the company's Guidance and Navigation Operation (GNO), which supplies guidance and navigation systems for military aircraft, missile and surface applications, as well as an emerging commercial market for surface products.

The company's Clearwater facility was established in 1956 to take advantage of Pinellas County's available labor pool. Today, Honeywell in Clearwater is more than 2,000 employees strong.

The Space Systems division contributed to the success of such historic programs as the X-15 Rocket Plane, Project Gemini, the Apollo Missions, the Viking Mars Lander, Atlas Centaur and, most recently, Space Shuttle, International Space Station, and Titan IVB. GNO's products were effectively deployed during the Persian Gulf War's Operation Desert Storm, guiding troops, machines and munitions to their desired destinations.

Honeywell products manufactured at other locations around the world range from high-tech components for computers and cell phones, state-of-the-art industrial plant controls to home carpeting fibers, aircraft avionics and engines to automotive products. Honeywell and AlliedSignal's 1999 merger resulted in the blending together of two companies, further expanding the list of innovative products and trusted brands. Today's Honeywell provides such well-known brand names as Fram®, Prestone® and Bendix® in its diverse product line.

As one of the 100 largest companies in the United States, Honeywell is a $24 billion diversified technology and manufacturing leader with over 120,000 people in 100 countries. Although the company can trace its roots back to 1885, the modern Honeywell has continued to grow by providing solutions and products to industry, including aerospace, transportation, as well as homes and buildings.

A major part of Pinellas County's growing high-tech corridor, Honeywell continues to capture awards for its quality work, including the Governor's Sterling Award - Florida's highest quality award - and the George M. Low, NASA Quality and Excellence Award.

www.honeywell.com

MELITTA USA, INC.

The quest for the perfect cup of coffee has perhaps been around for as long as coffee has been recognized as a beverage. But it wasn't until 1908 that history was made when a German housewife punctured the bottom of a tin cup and lined it with her son's blotting paper. Filter drip coffee making was born. Her name was Melitta Bentz, and the company that she founded continues to improve the world's most-loved beverage.

A subsidiary of the privately-held Melitta Group of Minden, Germany, Melitta USA, Inc., maintains its executive offices in Clearwater, Florida, and is responsible for the sale of branded coffee, filter paper and coffeemaking systems, as well as private label paper, to all retail channels in the U.S. and Canada.

Clearwater is also home to the Melitta's filter paper and non-electric coffeemaking systems. The company maintains a 72,000 square foot manufacturing facility with 78 employees. All coffee roasting and packaging operations are located in Cherry Hill, New Jersey.

Recognizing that the ultimate evaluation of a great cup of coffee often rests with the coffee itself, Melitta entered the coffee business after WW II, acquiring one of the pioneering coffee businesses founded in Bremen, Germany. Bremen is recognized throughout the world as one of the seats of coffee culture.

This purchase provided Melitta the opportunity to finally control all the elements of the coffee making process - the filter holder, the filter paper and the coffee - and truly deliver on the quest for a better cup of coffee. Melitta USA continues to search for "coffee perfection": a strategy that continues to win converts in not only America, but also 100 countries worldwide.

The Melitta Group manufactures and markets a wide variety of consumer products including foils and wraps, air cleaners and humidifiers, vacuum bags and cleaning products, and, of course, under the Melitta brand name, the full range of coffee preparation products for which the company is best known.

Constantly mindful of the legacy of Melitta Bentz, the company continues to set its standards high as Melitta USA delivers on the quest for coffee excellence.

Melitta Bentz, inventor in 1908 of the filter drip coffeemaking system.

www.melitta-usa.com

AVAYA COMMUNICATION
(FORMERLY LUCENT TECHNOLOGIES)

Tampa Bay Avaya Communication Knowledge Center

Pinellas County and St. Petersburg have earned the reputation as the main portal to the growing high-tech corridor stretching from Florida's Gulf Coast to the Space Coast. One of the major anchors to this dynamic portal is Avaya Communication's state-of-the-art Knowledge Center in St. Petersburg.

Avaya Communication is the market leader with enviable customer relationships and manages some of the largest enterprise voice networks in the world. It remains the worldwide leader in call centers and enterprise voice messaging as well as the U.S. leader in voice systems. Avaya continues to take share in these core markets as it introduces leading-edge, next-generation networking platforms in areas such as e-business applications and Internet Protocol (IP) networks.

Avaya offers businesses complete end-to-end networking services, including design, installation, integration, maintenance and management. The 100,000 square-foot service center in St. Petersburg houses 550 employees who assist customers globally with the management of complex data networks. Remote monitoring of customers' networks is achieved through advanced "intelligent" technologies. Avaya's philosophy is to enable customers to concentrate on running their core business rather than running their networks.

Avaya products, as well as products from many other vendors, such as Bay Networks, Cisco, and Cabletron are supported from the Center. Skilled technical teams offer remote around-the-clock network diagnosis, troubleshooting and management to any business location. These services virtually eliminate the need for a business to have their own network expertise on site.

Investment in advanced service technologies is a key differentiator of Avaya Communication. This is one of the few companies in the data networking industry that has a research and development budget devoted to developing new services technologies.

Industry experts project that the worldwide market for network-oriented professional and support services will continue to grow about 18 percent annually. Investments of $15 to $20 billion in 1997 will rise to more than $40 billion in 2000. Avaya's Professional Services already ranks among the top four providers of this type of sophisticated communications services.

There are many reasons why Avaya chose the St. Petersburg area. First, the presence of numerous other technology companies in the vicinity facilitates collaboration and partnerships. Within this high-tech community, companies readily interact, purchase equipment, license technology, share resources, and partner in a variety of ways for mutual benefit and accelerated response to market demands.

Excellent educational institutions located throughout the Tampa Bay area work cooperatively to meet the need for specialized personnel. With affordable housing, outstanding schools, and optimal weather conditions for year-round outdoor activities, Pinellas County represents an ideal location for maintaining a world class corporate facility.

Avaya Communication recently established two other data facilities in Florida: in 1999 the company opened its Advanced Data Networking Training and Support facility in Pompano Beach, on Florida's East Coast; and in 2000 Avaya opened a facility in Altamonte Springs designed to provide training in the latest network management techniques.

The establishment of three Avaya sites in the past three years St. Petersburg, Pompano Beach, and Altamonte Springs reaffirms the continuing expansion of the high-tech, sophisticated corporate environment in central and southern Florida.

www.avaya.com

PRIMEX TECHNOLOGIES, INC.

Primex Technologies, Inc. is an ordnance and aerospace contractor that has chosen Florida as home to four of its operational centers. The St. Petersburg facility houses both the Corporate and Ordnance and Tactical Systems (OTS) Division Headquarters. Primex's business operations are organized into two divisions that correspond to its primary products and services. The OTS Division designs and manufactures tank and other large caliber ammunition and medium caliber ammunition for U.S. and friendly foreign government customers. These products are used in ships, aircraft, tanks, and fighting vehicle based weapons. This ammunition contributed to the success of U.S. Forces in Operation Desert Storm and subsequent deployments of U.S. troops around the world.

Additionally, the OTS Division designs and produces shaped charged warheads that are used in various weapons, manufactures precision metal components and provides explosive load, assemble, and pack services for a variety of tactical missile and rocket programs. BALL POWDER® propellant, which is sold to U.S. and friendly foreign militaries, commercial ammunition manufacturers, and sporting and recreational customers, is also manufactured by the OTS Division, with more than 95% of all U.S. military small caliber ammunition loaded with propellants from Primex.

The Aerospace & Electronics (A&E) Division, which designs and manufactures rocket engines and electronic products used in space applications, has delivered approximately 10,000 rocket engines for spacecraft applications, including orbit insertion, maneuvering, and attitude control, as well as launch vehicle and upper-stage attitude and velocity control. This Division, with headquarters in Redmond, WA, also produces solid propellant products used in munitions dispensing and inflation devices.

As government and commercial needs evolve, so will the capabilities of Primex Technologies. Current trends in defense and commercial procurement are focusing on products delivering increased value and effectiveness through advanced technological sophistication. U.S. and Allied armed forces are increasingly called upon to conduct new, more varied missions with highly specialized needs. In support of these trends, Primex is applying its extensive R&D, testing and manufacturing base toward meeting future customer needs – and delivering proven, superior products and systems. By integrating and sharply focusing its diverse technical and personnel resources, Primex is strategically positioned to take a leading role in developing the products and services critical to solving the challenges of the future and meeting the needs of both government and commercial customers worldwide.

www.primextech.com

RAYTHEON COMPANY

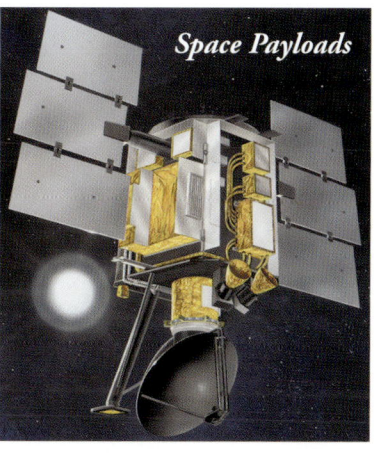

Located in the heart of Pinellas County, Raytheon's St. Petersburg and Largo operations employs more than 2,300 technical and support professionals in world-class manufacturing, engineering, design and development of high-technology command, control and communication systems. The company's 600,000 square foot facility situated on some 30 acres in St. Petersburg, houses sophisticated capabilities that include advanced laboratories for microelectronics design, computer-aided design and development, software development and computer modeling and simulation.

Raytheon's products include secure networking systems, state-of-the-art radios and terminals, satellite communication systems and battle management systems. The manufacturing facility in Largo occupies almost 400,000 square feet of the Pinellas Science, Technology and Research (STAR) Center, providing world class production operations for Raytheon's engineering facilities throughout the U.S.

For more than four decades, Raytheon's primary mission has been to provide the U.S. Government and allies with key command, control and communications systems that support the national defense. The company expects to continue expanding this leadership role in defense electronics while leveraging expertise into commercial markets.

Space Payloads

Secure Networks

Communications

Switching Systems

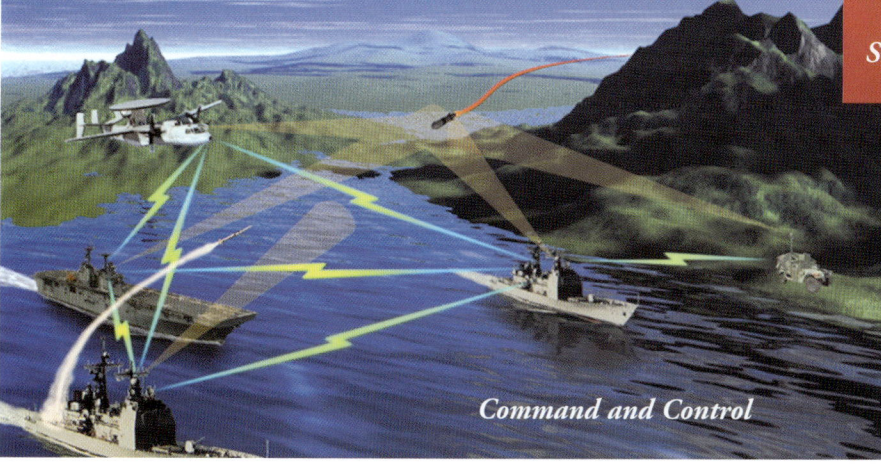

Command and Control

Raytheon Company is a global technology leader that provides products and services in the areas of commercial and defense electronics and business and special mission aircraft. Headquartered in Lexington, Massachusetts, the company employs a diverse, multidisciplined work force of more than 100,000 employees at operations throughout the U.S. It serves customers in more than 70 countries and has annual sales in excess of $20 billion.

Raytheon is committed to demonstrating the highest levels of integrity in partnerships with employees, customers and local site communities.

The company promotes a sense of citizenship that challenges employees to help those in need, support educational activities and organizations, and serve as conscientious environmental stewards.

Employees fill a variety of elective and appointive roles in both governmental and educational venues, participate at the front line in large and small charitable events, and contribute financial resources through the United Way and other fund-raising activities. Raytheon is proud to support and acknowledge the generosity of employees in contributing talents for the good of local, state and national communities.

Raytheon considers human resources to be the company's greatest asset and continuously strives for recognition as an employer of choice. By attracting and retaining only the most qualified and dedicated employees in a highly trained diverse work force, Raytheon continues to exceed industry standards, product quality goals and customer service objectives.

www.raytheon.com

R.P. SCHERER

Partnering for Success

You may not know it, but chances are there's a product manufactured by R.P. Scherer in your medicine chest.

Since Robert Pauli Scherer pioneered softgel technology more than 65 years ago, the company that bears his name, R.P. Scherer, has manufactured capsules in virtually every size, shape and color. As the world's leading supplier of soft gelatin (softgel) capsules, R.P. Scherer's innovative technology and drug delivery expertise has resulted in some of the most popular products in the pharmaceutical and nutritional industry. Scherer now produces nearly every major over-the-counter softgel in the cough and cold sector; and the list of products R.P. Scherer produces in St. Petersburg includes Advil® Liqui-Gels®, Alka Seltzer® Cold Medicine and Robitussin® Nighttime to name just a few.

A recent completion of a 205,000 square foot expansion to the existing pharmaceutical plant incorporates state-of-the-art oral dosage manufacturing technologies to create a world class facility just over 400,000 square feet in size. And, in combination with the company's two other manufacturing facilities in St. Petersburg, R.P. Scherer employs more than 950 people.

In addition to the company's three facilities in St. Petersburg, Scherer also has 12 other manufacturing sites in ten countries serving five continents. And, while to many people the name Scherer is synonymous with softgel, Scherer also is the name behind technologies like Zydis®, the instant-dissolving wafer technology used in Schering-Plough's best-selling allergy medication Claritin® RediTabs®.

The purchase of the company by healthcare giant Cardinal Health Company in 1998 further enhanced Scherer's ability to partner with its customers, helping to give Scherer the stability, capacity and flexibility needed to meet the growing demands of the dynamic pharmaceutical market.

www.rpscherer.com

TECH DATA CORPORATION

Local Origin, Global Vision

Tech Data Corporation, the world's second-largest wholesale supplier and shipper of information technology products, is located in Pinellas County, right in the heart of Florida's Suncoast. In fact, it has always been a Pinellas County business. Founded in 1974 by Edward C. Raymund, father of current Chairman and Chief Executive Officer Steven A. Raymund, the company considers its Florida location to be a tremendous incentive when recruiting sales, marketing, technical and other business talent.

In its formative years, Tech Data employed about a dozen people and handled all customer orders from a small office/warehouse building in Clearwater, not far from the company's current headquarters campus. From ten associates in 1983 to more than 3,000 associates today (10,000 worldwide), Tech Data has emerged as one of the area's largest employers.

During this period, the company's business has evolved from a "pick, pack and ship" operation into an Internet-centric, integrated supply-chain organization relied upon as a true outsource partner by technology makers and sellers. While continually expanding its offering of vital industry services such as technical support, education and custom configuration, Tech Data has also become a highly successful international entity.

In 1989, the growing Pinellas company expanded into Canada through an acquisition, and in 1993 launched a Miami-based export division to serve the Latin American market. Tech Data entered the European market in 1994 through the acquisition of Paris-based Softmart International, S.A, France's largest distributor of personal computer products. In 1997, the company opened its first Latin American office. Located in São Paulo, TD Brasil's distribution facility provides select products to all of Brazil - the region's largest market for PC technology.

One of the most significant developments in Tech Data's history occurred in July 1998 when it acquired a majority interest in Munich-based Computer 2000, Europe's leading provider of IT products to resellers. Computer 2000 also afforded the Pinellas company a market position in the Middle East through a United Arab Emirates location and broader coverage of Latin America with its operations in Argentina, Chile, Peru and Uruguay.

In May 1999, the company doubled its size in the Canadian market by acquiring Globelle Canada. In addition to positioning Tech Data for even greater success in this key market, the acquisition included a subsidiary in Israel that further bolsters the company's growing business in the Middle East.

For the fiscal year ended January 31, 2000, the Clearwater-based company achieved sales of $17 billion. In all measures, Tech Data maintains a market position that has never been stronger. And its ranking of 102 on the FORTUNE 500 listing for 2000 presents a future that looks as sunny as a typical Florida day.

www.techdata.com

WEST PHARMACEUTICAL SERVICES

A World of Healthy People

West Pharmaceutical Services of St. Petersburg has been an integral part of Pinellas County's growing medical manufacturing industry since 1970. As part of a global company with 18 manufacturing facilities spanning Europe, Asia and both North and South America, West Pharmaceutical's St. Petersburg facility produces rubber closures for pharmaceutical products.

Specializing in the precision molding of elastomers, West Pharmaceuticals manufacture plungers, dropper bulbs, sleeve stoppers and other custom designed components able to withstand prolonged contact without compromising drug integrity. With a list of customers including Pfizer, SmithKline Beecham and Merck & Co., Inc., the company maintains ISO 9002 certification. In compliance with this certification, West utilizes the standards of Good Manufacturing Practices and Statistical Process Controls for quality assurance.

Like many other companies in Pinellas County, the concept of locating a manufacturing facility in Florida originated in the late 60s when West Pharmaceutical was having labor shortages in the northern states. As a result, the company purchased seven acres of property on St. Petersburg's western city limits and constructed a 150,000 square foot facility. Today the company operates three shifts with 260 employees.

As a dedicated Total Quality Management plant, West Pharmaceutical stresses the team concept for the development, manufacturing and regulatory aspects of its business. Similarly, part of the company's mission is to be environmentally responsible and a good corporate citizen to the community.

West's employees provide support to the United Way, and also hold a blood drive every six weeks for Florida Blood Services. The company sponsors youth soccer teams and annually holds an aluminum can drive with all proceeds used to buy bicycles for Toys for Tots at Christmas. West Pharmaceutical's recycling program is one of the best in Pinellas County and has won numerous awards for their efforts.

With its corporate headquarters located in Lionville, Pennsylvania, West Pharmaceutical continues to generate significant growth in its global markets. As an example of its continuing spectrum of product development, the company recently introduced the Weststar Product, a fully validated, ready to sterilize elastomer pharmaceutical closure to the industry.

The company's vision for the future is best encompassed by its mission statement promising to provide customers with products and services that continuously improve safety, comfort and convenience of pharmaceutical, healthcare and consumer products.

In short, West Pharmaceutical Services is striving for A World of Healthy People. As an integral part of the St. Petersburg medical manufacturing community, their vision and hope for the future is one shared by all.

www.westpharma.com

SMITH & NEPHEW, INC.

Wound Management Division

Smith & Nephew's dedication to healthcare is far-reaching, striving to make a difference for patients as well as the caregivers and institutions that serve them. The simple beginnings of Smith & Nephew lie with British pharmacist T. J. Smith who dispensed cod liver oil, and, later, wound dressings and bandages along with his nephew, H. N. Smith, more than 140 years ago.

Now a global company with business concentration in the areas of orthopaedics, endoscopy and wound management, Smith & Nephew employs over 12,000 people with operations in 36 countries. The company's Largo facility has approximately 350 employees.

The Wound Management Division in Largo has some of the brightest people in the industry in all disciplines – from Manufacturing to Quality Assurance and Regulatory Affairs, New Product Development, Sales, Marketing, Medical Education, Finance, Information Services, and Human Resources. This talent pool is made up of a global workforce from local USF graduates to the top universities in Europe.

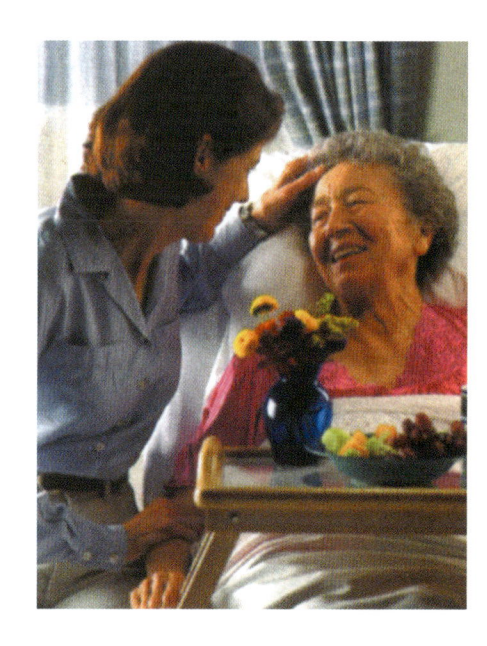

As a worldwide leader in wound care, Smith & Nephew's technological strengths are in the management of both acute and chronic wounds. The company focuses on advanced products and the ability to accelerate healing rates, reduce hospital stay times and reduce the cost of nursing time and aftercare.

Throughout the years, Smith & Nephew has increased investment in research with a current focus in biotechnology and tissue repair. Partnering with Advanced Tissue Sciences, Smith & Nephew has introduced TransCyte™, Human Fibroblast-Derived Temporary Skin Substitute for the treatment of burn wounds. The company's newest and most exciting biotech product, Dermagraft®, is in the final stages of FDA approval and will provide a solution for the 50,000 – 75,000 diabetic foot amputations that occur each year in the U.S.

Smith & Nephew also has a history of making exceptional and innovative contributions to the community through its products, employment opportunities, and by its support for healthcare, education and charitable organizations. The company's partnership with the surrounding communities is a long-cherished tradition.

Smith & Nephew's challenge is to stay at the forefront of innovation and market leadership. Focusing on customer driven technology and innovation, the company's goal is to anticipate the future direction of wound care and create innovative products to provide creative solutions for patients and improve their quality of life.

www.snwmd.com

PINELLAS SCIENCE TECHNOLOGY AND RESEARCH CENTER

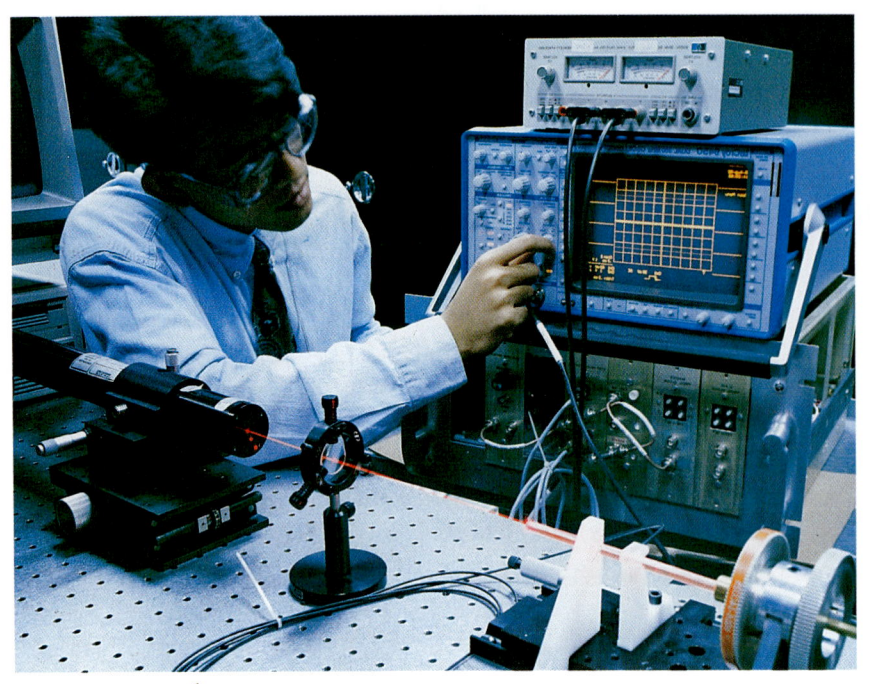

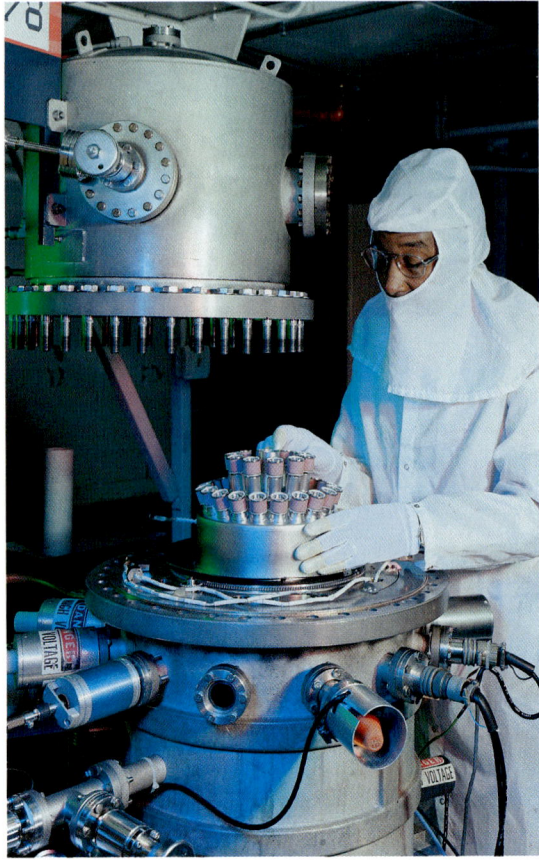

A World Class Facility for High Technology

From its inception, the Pinellas Science Technology and Research (STAR) Center has been a unique undertaking for Pinellas County. Formerly a Department of Energy nuclear weapons manufacturing plant, the STAR Center represents the first and only conversion of such a facility, resulting in the centerpiece of Florida's West Coast high-tech portal.

Owned by Pinellas County, the STAR Center showcases the synergy of government and industry cooperating to create a dynamic atmosphere where leadership companies push advancements in technology. The 96-acre site is located in an unincorporated area of Pinellas County near the City of Largo. The campus houses over 20 technology firms including Raytheon, Constellation Technology, Concurrent Technologies, Pace Technologies and National Technical Systems, to name a few.

But the STAR Center's uniqueness does not end here. Not only is the Center a designated Foreign Trade Zone, the facility has an on-site director committed to facilitating business resources between the Center's tenants and area businesses. The STAR Center has evolved into a true "technology resource" for all West and Central Florida.

Individual companies within the STAR Center have highly specialized equipment that may be underutilized. By promoting and matching these resources to area businesses, a win-win situation has developed. Consider, for example, the types of services that are available: real-time x-ray, ultrasound and environmental testing, ASTM certified testing and Florida's only ISO-9000 Standards laboratory. Many companies formerly shipping products out of state for testing or problem solving now find the necessary resources close at hand. For STAR Center tenants, capacity problems are eased, and for businesses, tough answers come quickly and often at a saving.

The results have been startling growth. Within the STAR Center itself, 17 separate buildings house approximately 730,000 square feet, with more than 80 percent housing laboratories, production space and offices. Three of the Center's former tenants experienced such growth that relocation to larger facilities nearby was necessary.

With a combined workforce of over 1000 people, the Center continues to provide not only high-tech solutions to businesses, but educational opportunities to area students as well. Both St. Petersburg Junior College and the University of South Florida utilize STAR Center facilities for computer, laboratory, graduate level studies and other educational training programs. Information technology is also alive and well at the STAR Center. A number of firms are on site providing Internet services, e-commerce training and technical support. ✤

www.siliconbay.org

JENNIFER HOLCOMBE

Chapter 7
Business & Service Industries

From the bleachers to the boardrooms

throughout St. Petersburg and Pinellas County, there's a spirit that can't be fully depicted in pictures or words or measured in a multitude of demographic charts…

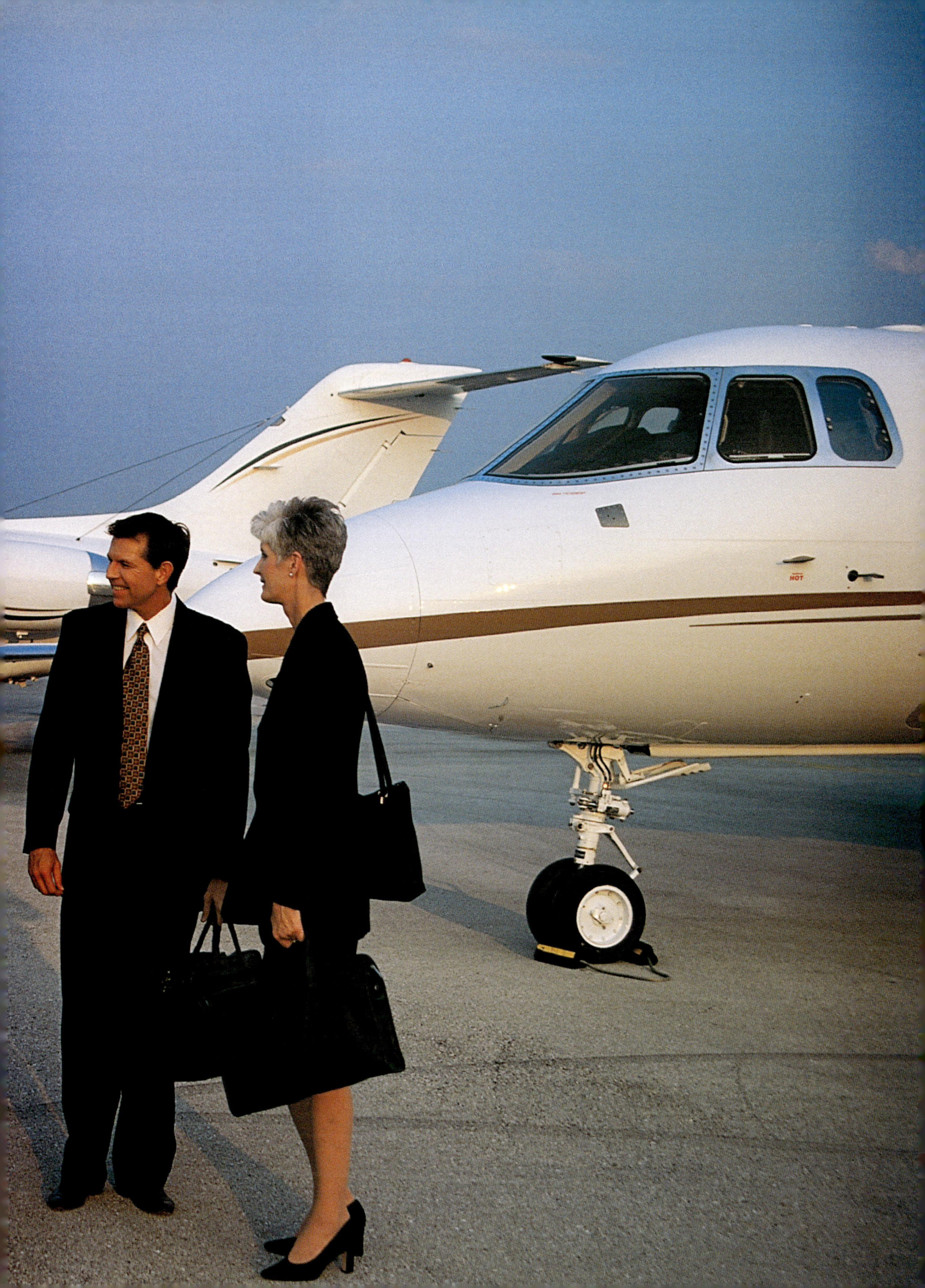
HOT

Business & Service Industries

It is the spirit of entrepreneurship that got us to where we are today and will keep us going well into the future.

The next time you grab something to eat at a Checkers Drive-In, a Crabby Bill's or Hooters, think of us. These national restaurant concepts began right here in Pinellas.

Fortune 500 company Tech Data Corp., one of the world's largest distributors of computer systems, is also a Pinellas County success story. Founded here in 1974, by Edward C. Raymund, with about 12 employees, Tech Data's distribution now includes shipments of its products to 70 countries in Latin America, Europe and the Middle East.

There's more. *Entrepreneur* magazine consistently ranks Val-Pak the number one direct mail franchise system. The company, now a subsidiary of Atlanta based Cox Enterprises, Inc., pioneered local cooperative direct mail in Pinellas in 1968 and today has a network of over 250 field offices in the US, Canada, Puerto Rico and Buenos Aires, Argentina.

Bay area entrepreneurs have something in common – fortitude – which apparently thrives in our business-friendly environment. They may begin from different starting places, but once they are off and running, stay focused and remain willing to work hard for their goals, success seems to follow.

Peter Demens had it when he brought the Orange Belt railroad to the eastern shores of the Pinellas peninsula in 1888. Gus Stravos had it when he started Better Business Forms in 1959 with three employees and developed it to an $80-million business when he retired as CEO in 1989.

In 1898, the first Eckerd Drug Store, begun by J. Milton Eckerd in Erie, Pennsylvania, sold prescription drugs at a discount. In the early 1950s, J. Milton's son, Jack Eckerd chose St. Petersburg to open more drugstores under the family name, and added self service shopping. Eckerd's is now ranked number four in sales in the nation with 2,900 stores in 20 states.

Catalina Marketing Corp. is the brainchild of five friends who went sailing and came back with an idea and a name for the company they launched in 1985. Combining their strengths in marketing, retailing and scanner-based technology, they created the supermarket check out equivalent of the better mouse trap – register tape coupons related to shopping habits. Yet they brought their know how (and 40 percent of their employees) from California to Pinellas County and have expanded the concept to the Internet.

In 1987, James MacDougald and his wife, Suzanne, moved to Florida with the beginnings of a benefits management company launched five years earlier from their New Jersey garage. Applied Benefits Research became ABR Information Services and quickly outgrew its north Pinellas home. Meanwhile, Florida Power Corporation moved its corporate offices from one part of St. Petersburg to another in downtown, and ABR found the vacated facility an ideal headquarters.

Today the company is a unit of the nation's leading benefits administrator – Ceridian – which has turned their new 383,000 square foot campus, in south St. Petersburg, into a state-of-the-art facility with the potential for 2,000 employees.

The face and voice of most large companies in the Tampa Bay area is the receptionist at the front desk.

Business & Service Industries

The U.S. Bureau of Labor Statistics shows the Tampa Bay area had the largest percentage increase in employment of the nation's large labor markets in 1999, adding 56,800 jobs. Employment in St. Petersburg's Gateway area alone, in the year 2000, totals more than 33,000 jobs with manufacturing, marketing and financial service companies especially prominent. In fact, once the final frontier of available land, Gateway has become our high-growth area for companies that want to expand operations to the land of sunshine and opportunity.

In the service category, which includes financial services, insurance, communications, research and professions, Gateway employment figures total about 14,000 in such companies as Equifax, MCI, and Raymond James. The largest of those employers is Raymond James and Associates, with approximately 1,600 employees.

Another 10,000 jobs make up commercial employment for Gateway, including retail sales, restaurants and wholesale trade. The largest employer in the commercial sector is Home Shopping Network, which broadcasts 24 hours a day from studios in the Gateway area. The subsidiary of USA Networks has 5,000 employees.

So what has made Tampa Bay and Pinellas County in particular so attractive? Where other states have higher taxes and higher costs, Florida has no personal state income tax, no state ad valorem or property tax, inventory or goods-in-transit tax, no sales tax on boiler fuels used for industrial processes and no corporate income tax on estates, partnerships, individuals or private trusts.

New and expanding companies find that real estate is not only available, but also very affordable in St. Petersburg and Pinellas. In 1997 and 1998, the city of St. Petersburg recorded two of its best construction years in history with $600-million in new projects. More than three million square feet of new industrial and office space came online.

The new growth, including strong employment, has in turn attracted major national and regional builders to the Tampa Bay area who are filling in the blanks with both single-family homes and rental apartment construction for our new workers. One example is downtown where luxury waterfront condominiums are changing the look of the waterfront in St. Petersburg. Corporate relocations have also created a demand for hotels, especially extended-stay lodging which is predominant in the Gateway area.

Yet, just as the City of St. Petersburg preserved its downtown waterfront in the early 1900s, several large parcels of land in northeast Pinellas were purchased for preservation in the late 1980s and early 90s for the assurance that they can be enjoyed for generations to come. We are aware and protective of the natural beauty that surrounds us in our Florida Paradise. It is important to us and apparently to our potential newcomers.

Visit the web sites of some of the major corporations located here and you will find some unique Florida features among the incentives to join their ranks – our climate, our attractions, our lifestyle, and our natural amenities. Business and beauty, from beaches to bay.

Pinellas and Tampa Bay are home to more than 50 call centers represented here by Time Warner.

CERIDIAN

A Landmark for the New Millennium

Ceridian is proud to be a major partner in the St. Petersburg business community. With the company's completion of extensive renovations to a longtime landmark - the Florida Power building – Ceridian has been welcomed as a new Pinellas County landmark.

Ceridian's St. Petersburg facility acts as the national Benefits Administration Service Center for Minneapolis-based Ceridian Corporation, a $1 billion company with more than 12,000 employees. Ceridian ranks as one of the Tampa Bay area's largest employers and is the nation's leading provider of employee benefits administration services - serving more than 40,000 clients of all sizes, including nearly one quarter of the Fortune 500.

Ceridian helps employers regain core business focus by outsourcing various benefits administration tasks. The firm's service bureau approach provides a cost-effective, efficient, and secure method of administering employee benefits programs. Ceridian is a leader in the field, entrusted to perform complex and time-consuming administrative duties in a consistent and responsive manner. The company is by far the largest COBRA and HIPAA administrator in the United States and is recognized as the nation's largest independent Flexible Spending Account administrator as well. Ceridian ranks among the nation's top Retirement Plan Administrators (including 401K services), and the company's HRIS/Payroll Systems rank among the most sought-after in the services industry.

Over the last 13 years, Ceridian's Benefits Administration operation has created millions of personalized communications, processed millions of life event transactions and answered millions of benefits questions. The company has created hundreds of electronic interfaces to make data sharing with clients straightforward and trouble-free. Ceridian offers economies of scale, location and technology that result in lower cost and higher quality services. A large customer base enables Ceridian to invest in cutting-edge technology, allowing the constant improvement of services.

Large-scale automation of administrative functions is key to quality services. State-of-the-art technology allows Ceridian to offer a single source of integrateable benefits solutions. At the heart of Ceridian's system is a real-time database accommodating the nation's most extensive repository of rates, benefits and eligibility criteria. The system is event-based and reacts automatically to changes sent via electronic feeds, interactive voice response, or the Internet. Ceridian's procedures and materials are time-tested and have been developed with the help of leading ERISA attorneys and an on-staff government affairs expert. A fully staffed compliance department monitors transactions and processes.

Ceridian's ability to deliver "Best in Class" customer service is also enhanced by advanced technology. Automated access is available 24 hours a day via the Internet or Interactive Voice Response systems. Personal assistance is provided through dedicated toll-free telephone numbers, and TDD terminals are maintained for the hearing-impaired. Backed by this technology, Ceridian's experienced customer service representatives are empowered to resolve problems with excellent analytical and service skills. Ceridian's training program is extensive and involves familiarization with each client company's distinct culture, history, and benefit plans. Customer service representatives are adept at servicing participants and are dedicated to providing accurate information in a timely manner. Effective communication is a skill, and Ceridian's customer service team is truly "Best in Class."

Named by Fortune Magazine as one of America's fastest-growing companies, and by Forbes Magazine as among the "100 Best Small Companies in America," Ceridian's Benefits Administration organization (under its previous name, ABR) has enjoyed considerable recognition. The firm relocated to St. Petersburg in 2000, and is poised for continued strong performance into the new millennium.

Seeking out an environment conducive to efficient business activities, Ceridian chose a 51-acre campus located in St. Petersburg. The facility provides a home to the most advanced benefits administration operation in the country and was redesigned to support and enhance Ceridian's central business purpose. Critical systems are housed in areas designed to withstand virtually any natural disaster. Surrounded by hardened concrete and supported by redundant power supplies and backup systems, the continuity of critical operations is assured under nearly any circumstances.

Ceridian thoroughly realizes that the contribution of employees drives economic success, and providing a safe and beautiful working environment is just one of the ways Ceridian endeavors to provide exceptional compensation for associates' efforts. In an inviting atmosphere, employees can enjoy the shady jogging trail or dine in the company's two-story cafeteria. Open-air pergolas offer a breezy place to take a break, and the availability of on-site daycare allows associates with children to work with peace of mind. To further ensure that associates' careers work in harmony with personal needs, Ceridian has made a commitment to flexible working hours, compressed workweeks, and solid health-care benefits.

Prominent in the city's skyline, Ceridian makes a contribution to the community that goes far beyond a physical presence. The company feels that a high level of involvement is the best way to help the community grow and prosper. Ceridian takes on a role not only as a new St. Petersburg landmark, but also as a champion of the community's best interests.

www.ceridian.com

THE HOME SHOPPING NETWORK

Lights... camera... action!

The Home Shopping Network is an exciting, 24-hour live television studio, generating more than $1 billion in sales every year. Located in St. Petersburg, HSN reaches over 70-million households, offering innovative products, qualified demonstrations and entertaining celebrity guests.

As the company that first pioneered the electronic retailing industry from a small radio station in Clearwater, HSN is constantly expanding its horizons - most recently launching HSN.com. HSN has also gone global with successful shopping channels in Germany, Japan and the wildly popular Home Shopping en Español. In order to bring viewers exclusive and often limited-edition products, HSN has partnered with many exciting organizations, including the NFL, NASCAR, Christie's, Tupperware, Marie Claire and many more.

All this creative energy means an exciting workplace for the company's family of nearly 3,000 local employees. Imagine working in newly renovated call center filled with cutting-edge technology, and a "backstage" packed with guests like Diane von Furstenberg, Suzanne Somers, Joe Montana and Jennifer Flavin-Stallone. Many employees have called HSN home for 10 to 15 years. With perks like great on-air discounts, an employee store chock-full of the latest merchandise, professional development programs, flexible scheduling, wellness events, interactive town meetings and sponsorship in many local events and charities, HSN offers employees many reasons to love coming to work each day.

Whether your in front of the camera or behind it, everyone's a star at HSN.

HSN is one of the area's major employers of seniors and the disabled in both full- and part-time positions. Nearly 30 percent of new job openings are filled internally, making HSN an incredible company in which to grow. Centrally located between St. Petersburg, Tampa and Clearwater, Home Shopping's 53 acres include executive offices, a sales and service center with live broadcasting facilities, a Quality Assurance division, commissary and HSN.com. There is also an off-site telemation department in Clearwater, as well as several fulfillment centers throughout the country.

The Home Shopping Network is a division of USA Networks, Inc., a newly-designated, growing Fortune 500 company which also includes film studios, manufacturing facilities, USA Network, the SciFi Channel, Ticketmaster and CitySearch.com.

Tune in soon. That's a wrap!

ECHELON

Echelon is a privately owned real estate company which develops, owns and manages multi-family residential and commercial real estate through Echelon Development LLC, Echelon Residential LLC, and Echelon Real Estate Services, LLC. Echelon has a highly experienced management team and strives to set the standards for excellence in residential and commercial development.

Echelon has a distinguished track record in commercial development with many nationally recognized clients including Franklin Templeton, Raymond James Financial, Aegon/Western Reserve, Xerox, Allstate and Catalina Marketing. The development team can provide custom solutions to client needs and manage the entire development process from land acquisition through property management.

Commercial assets include Class A office space such as the Bank of America Tower, a 26-floor luxury high-rise located in the heart of downtown St. Petersburg's business and retail district and the office park development Carillon. Carillon, strategically located at the very center of the Tampa Bay business market is within 15 minutes of both the Tampa International Airport and the St. Petersburg/ Clearwater Airport. Carillon offers an existing infrastructure with highly improved areas including lighted and landscaped boulevards, underground utility systems, fiber optics telecommunications capability, and master stormwater retention system.

Echelon has a number of multi-family residential properties located throughout the southeast and southwest United States. Each multi-family community is uniquely designed for the particular market, providing a full range of amenities which include clubhouses with office/business centers, pre-wired "smart" apartments for home offices, gated access, fitness facilities, concierge services and garages.

Echelon at The Reserve, Echelon's flagship multi-family development in Carillon was recently awarded the Pillars of the Industry Award for Best Luxury Multi-Family Project by the National Association of Home Builders. In addition, *Echelon at Bay Isle Key*, also located in the Gateway area of St. Petersburg, was named the 1999 Apartment Community of the Year by the Bay Area Apartment Association, and was recognized in 2000 with the "Gold Award" for the second year in a row and was just awarded an Aurora award by the Southeast Home Builder's Association.

Through a wholly owned subsidiary, Echelon Real Estate Services, LLC, Echelon provides a full range of brokerage services and one-stop property, asset and facilities management. Brokerage services include leasing and sale of Echelon owned and third party assets. Property asset and facilities management encompasses financial analysis and all aspects of operations.

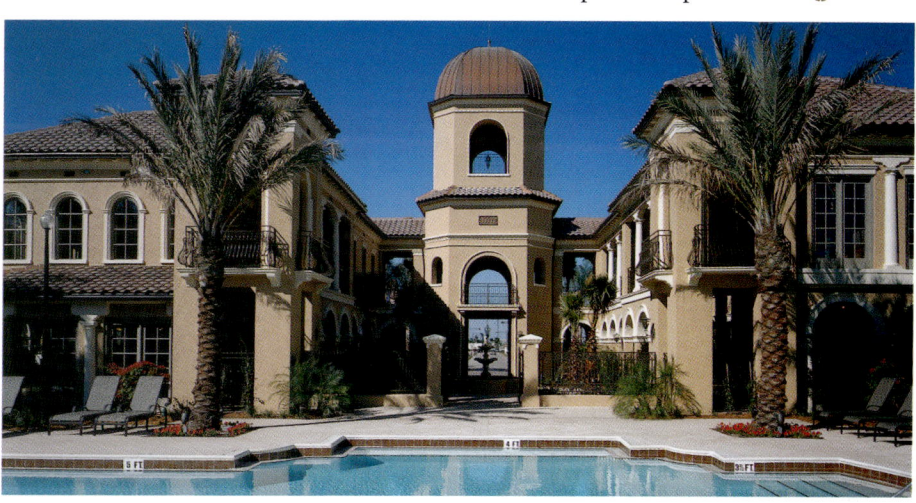

Above, Echelon at Bay Isle Key; Center, Echelon at The Reserve; Top, Castille at Carillon

www.echelonre.com

CATALINA MARKETING CORPORATION

St. Petersburg's Catalina Marketing Corporation, the leader in in-store electronic marketing, is proof that not all innovative business ideas are spawned in the corporate boardroom.

This company was the brainchild of five friends in the related fields of marketing, retailing and scanner-based technology who made the decision to start the company during a boating trip to Catalina Island off the California coast.

The group – which included Mike O'Brien, Brian Yeatman, Tom Mindrum, Mike Scroggie, and current chairman George Off – agreed that mass couponing methods were no longer sufficient in what had become a fragmented, retailer-oriented market, and that customer behavior could be changed in the store at checkout. What began as a discussion about supermarkets and the clutter, misredemption and waste of traditional coupon delivery systems developed into an idea that led to the creation of the company's core program, Checkout Coupon®.

The founders used their combined market research, packaged goods and scanner technology experience to lay down the framework of the system that would enable manufacturers and retailers to identify customers based on actual purchase behavior and distribute incentives at the point of scan. Today that system is called the Catalina Marketing Network's.

In 1984, the Checkout Coupon program went from the drawing board to the marketplace in a highly successful pilot test – the actual sales of couponed products increased up to 60 percent for a 16-week period, and the average redemption rate was eight to 14 percent, more than four times higher than traditional couponing methods. As a result, the system began a national rollout in 1986.

In the 17 years since that fortuitous sailing trip, Catalina Marketing has grown at a fantastic rate. The company has expanded its range of marketing services with new applications of Checkout Coupon and completely new programs. One of the company's most successful product introductions has been Checkout Direct®, the company's database marketing program, capable of increasing both the volume of purchases and brand loyalty of consumers over time. The program now boasts the world's largest electronic real-time database, tracking more than 50 million households for more than 8,000 retail stores.

Catalina Marketing has also diversified its ventures, forming four operating business units. Catalina Marketing

Services delivers the company's core base business on which it was founded. Health Resource Publishing Company reaches pharmacy customers with targeted laser-printed publications offering condition-specific health information and direct-to-consumer advertising. SuperMarkets Online, Inc., partners major retailers and manufacturers to deliver secure promotional services to shoppers via the Internet through its ValuPage® service (www.valupage.com). Catalina Marketing International entered the European marketing arena in 1992, and today is installed in more than 2,500 supermarkets in Europe and Japan.

Catalina Marketing also acquired several companies to expand its expertise and portfolio of services it provides for manufacturers and retailers. The company acquired Market Logic, a targeted direct marketing agency, in July 1998, DCI Cardmarketing, a card production company, in January 1999, and Alliance Research, which conducts research surveys on consumer attitudes, in August 1999.

The results of this strategic growth are phenomenal. To date, billions of Checkout Coupon certificates have been dispensed in nearly 13,500 supermarkets, representing more than 176 grocery divisions nationwide. The Catalina Marketing Network now reaches more than 165 million shoppers every week in the U.S. In the all-important bottom line, revenues have grown steadily each year, rising from $6.5 million in 1988 to $350.9 million in 2000.

Catalina Marketing operates more than 22 offices worldwide, with its headquarters located in St. Petersburg, Fla. Catalina moved its headquarters office from Anaheim, Calif., to St. Petersburg in 1993 in order to develop better relationships with its clients. Employee count has grown to more than 1,400 worldwide, with more than 300 working out of the St. Petersburg office. In addition to providing employment for the Tampa Bay area, Catalina is committed to improving the community through various projects such as blood drives road clean-up, fund-raisers and other services.

Catalina Marketing has been named to the Honor Roll of Forbes' Top 200 Small Business and has earned a place in the permanent collection of the Smithsonian Institution's National Museum of American History, as well as a permanent place in the food industry. In simply "building a better mousetrap," the company has changed the way packaged goods are marketed forever, and literally touched millions of people's lives. ❋

Dan Granger
President, CEO and Chairman

David Diamond
President of Emerging Business and Chief Vision Officer

Sue Klug
President Catalina Marketing Solutions and Chief Marketing Officer

www.catmktg.com

177

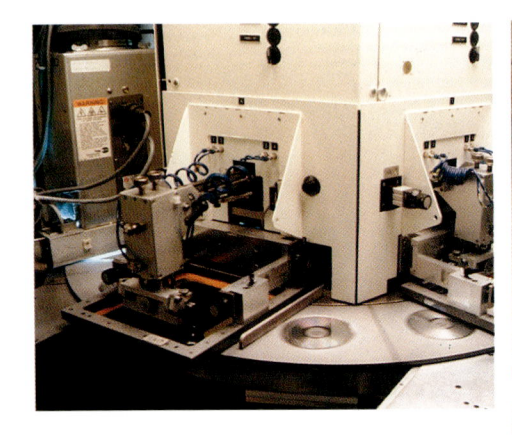

EVA-TONE

We Make It Right

The evolution of Clearwater-based Eva-Tone is a fascinating case study of a family-owned business that began in 1925 making rubber stamps and printing plates by molding rubber into sunken metal type. Later, the company adapted as offset printing replaced letterpress. It also branched into audio products, using its molding techniques to produce plastic phonograph records called soundsheets.

But this was just the beginning. Maintaining a firm grasp on the technology curve of the 1980s and 90s, Eva-Tone's natural progression of innovation has moved the company into the digital millennium as one of the premier manufacturers of print, audio, data and multimedia products.

Capable of taking a client's idea through initial development to fulfillment, Eva-Tone's array of services and products include printing (both conventional and digital), CD and cassette manufacturing, multimedia presentations, CD-ROM development, website design and complete packaging/mailing options. The company's impressive list of clientele includes Readers Digest and Walt Disney Records.

The fact that Eva-Tone has remained a family business - now transitioning into the third generation - speaks volumes about the company's ability to focus on positive growth. Capable of maintaining internal harmony by involving family members in the strategic planning process has translated into a unique decision-making process that benefits the company and its clients.

Eva-Tone's growth (the company is consistently listed in Tampa Bay's Top 100 list) continues to ride on its ability to provide each customer with a customized project solution. The company's suite of services makes it a single source for media production and marketing needs, including companies venturing into e-commerce via the Internet. The company is uniquely positioned to offer a single service, such as cassette or CD-ROM production, or a virtual package ranging from creation to packaging to distribution. Originally located in Illinois, Eva-Tone made the move to Florida in 1979 because of the promise of a better quality of life for its employees, a lower cost of living and lack of a state income tax. The move was propitious for both the company and Pinellas County. Today Eva-Tone has grown to 450 employees and serves customers not only the Tampa Bay area, but in national markets as well.

From art to music to the printed word and the digital revolution, Eva-Tone's motto of "We Make It Right" make the company one of Pinellas County's premier communicators.

PAYMENT SYSTEMS FOR CREDIT UNIONS, INC.

Partnering for Success

Payment Systems for Credit Unions, Inc. (PSCU), is a member-owned cooperative providing financial services to more than 500 credit unions. Established in 1977, PSCU is the largest credit union service organization in the nation.

PSCU maintains both headquarters and an Operations Center in St. Petersburg's Carillon Center. Through a wholly owned subsidiary, PSCU Service Centers, Inc., the association facilitates credit and debit card processing services for more than 5.5 million cardholders across the United States.

More than just a connection to popular credit cards, PSCU is also a strategic planner, business consultant and marketing advisor. To achieve this, PSCU stays close to member-owner credit unions through five regional service centers. Each service center has an experienced full-time member relations, member services and training staff who understand credit unions as well as credit and debit cards.

From cardholder services to technical support, to account settlement processing and marketing advice, PSCU helps credit unions improve the economic lives of members through cooperative thrift and the wise use of financial resources. These resources can include share savings and personal loans, or state-of-the-art financial services.

The association's strategic partnerships have been instrumental in the development of those services. First Data, for example, is one such partner and also the world's largest transaction processor for debit and credit cards. First Data offers over 3,000 card processing options and system variables to PSCU members, as well as bi-monthly enhancements to continually update the processing system.

Another strategic partnership has resulted in ePSCU, the associations' Internet initiative. In conjunction with U.S. Central Credit Union, Cisco Systems and CheckFree, members can conduct Internet banking and bill payment transactions over the Internet. In addition, PSCU provides the EasyToCU suite of Internet-based products, allowing members to receive account information and service online.

As a result, PSCU has created tremendous value for credit unions by leveraging existing member service core competencies in defining, developing, marketing and servicing a set of credit union solutions that address the pressing needs for complete, integrated web-based financial services and member offerings.

PSCU's quality of service, flexibility and state-of-the-art technology represents a powerful tool for America's credit unions. Making members successful is, after all, just another way of making the nation successful. PSCU represents the service foundation and technology path that empowers credit unions to compete successfully now, and in the future.

www.pscusci.com

COX TARGET MEDIA

In 1968, a St. Petersburg area entrepreneur conceived the idea of distributing discount coupons for goods and services to consumers in neighborhoods surrounding those businesses. Clearly, it was an idea whose time had come. Val-Pak - now a familiar blue envelope of discount offers mailed up to 12 times yearly across North America - was born.

Today Val-Pak is the largest local cooperative program in the country with projected malings to consumers of a half-billion envelopes in 2000. It is sold to advertising clients through a franchise network of 250 dealerships in the continental U.S., Canada, Puerto Rico and Argentina. Val-Pak is the flagship product of privately held Cox Target Media, the Largo-based subsidiary of Cox Enterprises Inc. of Atlanta.

Cox purchased Val-Pak in 1991 and added Carol Wright, a highly targeted cooperative envelope for packaged goods, manufacturers and retailers, in 1996, moving operations to Pinellas County where the company was on a growth curve.

Product sampling and Internet promotions divisions were launched in 1999. Sampling, in solo and cooperative mailing format, was a staple of the company prior to its divisional status.

Cox Target Media has a growing presence on the Internet. Through its newly formed Interactive Promotions Group, it re-sells cutting-edge technology which permits retail and manufacturing clients to launch promotional offers from their own Web sites.

ValPak.com, the Internet's largest coupon site, is an extension of the Val-Pak envelope, enabling computer users to access and print local discount coupons whether at home, at work or in travel destinations (www.valpak.com). In addition, Val-Pak coupons for local neighborhoods throughout the U.S. can be accessed and printed via www.Coupons.com.

In 1998 the Val-Pak product was launched in Argentina through an equity stake in a Buenos Aires company that now mails 'Cupones Val-Pak.

Cox Target Media's corporate offices, design center and state-of-the-art printing plant occupy 330,000 square feet in mid-Pinellas County and provide more than 1200 jobs for the local economy. The USPS maintains an employee on-site to provide assistance for the huge bulk mailing programs. Company-owned distribution centers, employing 800, are located in Elm City and Washington, NC, and Las Vegas, NV.

Cox Target Media has a history of involvement with civic and charitable projects – United Way, the Muscular Dystrophy Association, the Pinellas County Education Foundation and All-Children's Hospital - providing avenues for corporate contributions to the area that has nurtured its growth.

www.valpak.com

EQUIFAX PAYMENT SERVICES

Changing the Shape of Global Commerce

Many people are familiar with Equifax as the provider of financial information for their loan application or mortgage approval. Yet one of Equifax's fastest-growing divisions doesn't simply track credit information, it actually processes credit and debit transactions for financial institutions, and gives merchants the ability to approve checks at the point of purchase. Equifax Payment Services, based in St. Petersburg, makes it easier for consumers to make purchases with their checks, credit or debit cards, and even online via the Internet.

Equifax's mission is Changing the Shape of Global Commerce, and Equifax Payment Services plays a vital role in the process. To do so, its strategy revolves around Equifax's four cornerstones of Growth, Innovation, Technology and People.

In 1999, Equifax Payment Services had an exceptional year, marked by continual growth not only in the United States but also in Brazil and the United Kingdom. All of this contributed to a more than 20 percent increase in revenue, making it one of Equifax's strongest divisions.

In today's electronic environment, innovation increasingly means delivering products and services via the Internet. In addition to providing the means for more than 1,800 financial institutions to offer complete Internet account access to their customers, Equifax Payment Services introduced a new product that enables e-commerce companies such as Ameritrade to accept checks online.

With its emphasis on innovation and Internet applications, Equifax Payment Services is dedicated to using the most advanced technology available to serve its customers. Over the past year, Equifax used the most state-of-the-art mainframe system incorporating the latest technologies, to process more than 850 million payment transactions.

As one of the Tampa Bay area's largest employers, Equifax Payment Services employs 2,000 professionals in a variety of specialties. Positions range from customer service associates, who answer cardholder, merchant and financial institution calls, to information technology experts, who program the complex software that runs the processing systems. Not only does Equifax strive to be the area's employer of choice, but it also makes it a priority to give back to the community. For the last three years, Equifax was a title sponsor of Bowl for Kids' Sake, benefiting Big Brothers Big Sisters of Tampa Bay.

Equifax Inc., a world leader in shaping global commerce, brings buyers and sellers together through its information, transaction processing, and customer relationship management businesses. Equifax operates in 16 countries with sales in nearly 50 countries. Founded in 1899 in Atlanta, Equifax today has more than 15,000 employees around the world.

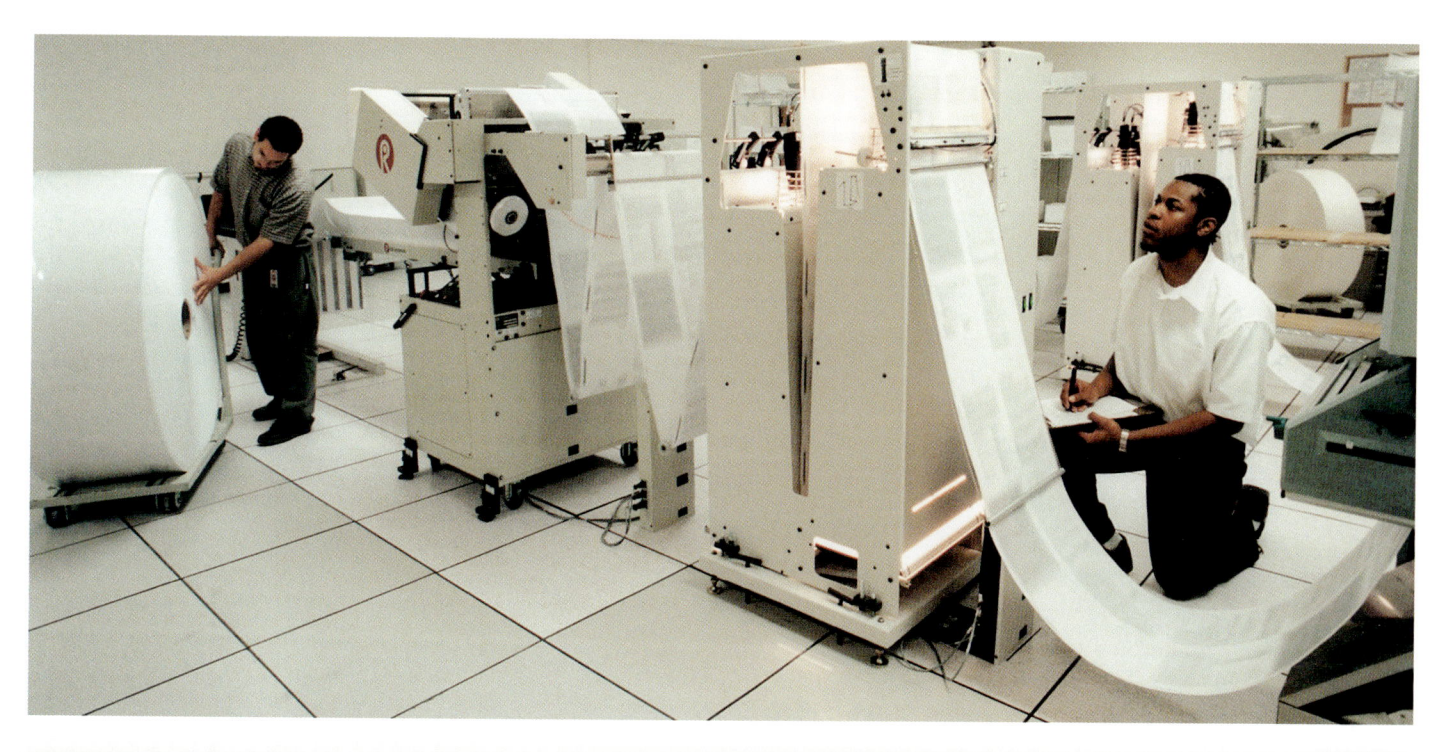

www.equifax.com

CAPITOL MARKETING CONCEPTS

Capitol Marketing Concepts is an incentive marketing company skilled in designing deluxe travel promotions clients use to increase sales, motivate employees and gain competitive advantages in the marketplace. The company began with ten employees in January 1995, with only 1,000 square feet of office space at Bayfront Towers. In 1996 Capitol purchased Bill Brown's Plaza Travel, and in 1997, opened Capitol Cruises. By the summer of 2000, the company had grown to 130 employees occupying 13,000 square feet of space.

In September 2000 the company continued to expand, purchasing a building in downtown St. Petersburg, locating all divisions at One Capitol Center, 696 1st Avenue. The Capitol Group now owns one half of a city block in downtown St. Petersburg. Future plans include construction of another building within the next five years.

Capitol has fulfilled vacation awards for over 75,000 families. When asked what Capitol Marketing Concepts is all about, CEO Brian Bell stated, " We sell pieces of paper that result in a sales promotion or employee incentive programs to improve the income and profitability of clients. This, in turn, creates a lot of happiness for thousands of people and helps fill empty rooms in resort hotels, generating revenue for them."

Capitol's mission is to provide customers with creative, results-oriented, reliable and cost-effective travel promotion solutions while simultaneously becoming the industry leader in product innovation, promotion design and execution, customer service and profitability.

Capitol Marketing Concepts' employees participate in and contribute time and money to a wide variety of civic and church organizations. Last year, Capitol employees contributed 2,688 hours of time as volunteers, members and even officers of many different causes and organizations: an average of 24 hours for each of the St. Petersburg employees. This does not include community service by an additional 47 outside Sales Representatives working in communities throughout the United States.

Capitol Marketing Concepts has experienced tremendous growth in five years because of the products created, the company's dedication to providing excellence in service to customers and because of a strong sense of purpose among the company's employees.

Left to right, Brian Bell, Nicholas Del Corso, Thomas Coffeen and H. John Mejia.

www.capitolmarketing.com

NIELSEN MEDIA RESEARCH

Early every morning, starting at about 3 A.M., the telephone lines to Dunedin are very busy. The reason – more than 25,000 metered households across America are automatically transmitting data to Nielsen Media Research's Operational Center in north Pinellas County. Within a matter of hours, approximately 10 million viewing minutes have been processed for delivery to hundreds of customers.

While the name Nielsen Media Research is synonymous with television ratings and media research, the fact that Dunedin is the central focus for generating those ratings may be a surprise. Since 1972, the Dunedin facility has been providing an objective estimate of television audience size and composition, acting as a barometer of viewing habits.

Originally headquartered in Chicago, the move to Pinellas County gave Nielsen Media Research access to the areas large retiree community – a workforce suited to the company's often hectic needs during "sweeps" weeks in November, February, May and July. Although the population base has become somewhat younger since the 1970s, Nielsen Media Research continues to provide part-time employment to over 2,000 area teachers, students and retirees during sweeps week.

With more than 3,000 full time employees nationwide, the company's local operations, which include five separate facilities in Dunedin, Clearwater and Palm Harbor, are staffed with almost 1,500 full time employees. Many of those are involved in maintaining, upgrading and operating Nielsen Media Research's high-tech information gathering and processing equipment.

Besides generating television ratings, Nielsen Media Research provides a variety of competitive advertising intelligence based on television, radio and print research, as well as information on interactive television and Internet usage. As new technologies evolve – digital television, interactive television, personal video recording, high definition TV, and expanded cable and satellite programming, to mention a few – Nielsen Media Research continues to find relevant methodologies to measure and report each individual use.

In addition to the company's television ratings for 48 major markets (the 13th largest being the Tampa Bay area), including 210 designated market areas, Nielsen Media Research has created a new service – Nielsen/NetRatings – to provide an extensive measure of Internet usage in the U.S. as well as in other countries.

Considering that commercial expenditures for the U.S. television industry amount to more than $46 billion a year, Nielsen Media Research's independent, third-party measurement system is an integral part of American media. Which shows are watched, which web sites are accessed, which advertisements are most effective – are all questions answered daily by Nielsen Media Research.

www.tvratings.com

DURANGO OAK FIRE STEAKHOUSE

Durango Steakhouse's claim to fame isn't based solely on the restaurant's distinctive oak-fired grilling of choice aged steaks, chicken, ribs and seafood. The sizzle is rather a combination of elements that has resulted in a steady growth, with more than 25 Durango Steak Houses now scattered throughout Florida and Georgia.

Operated by St. Petersburg-based Durango, U.S.A., success has come because of a set of comprehensive strategic initiatives that have positioned each of the company's restaurants in a distinctive market situation. While Durango appeals to a wide variety of customers by offering a combination of both traditional Steakhouse and Mexican menu items, a philosophy of offering customers the highest level of quality food and service at a truly exceptional price has been the key.

Durango's innovative approach to supply contract negotiation has allowed the company to maintain as high a quality standard in the selection of main entrees as some of the finest – and most expensive – restaurants. The result has been a stable and economical menu price for the restaurant's wide variety of cuisine.

Sometimes the smaller touches are also what make a difference in this competitive business. Durango's choice of oak-fire grilling, for example, sears meat to seal in the natural juices and flavor. In addition to the unique flavor, fresh baked bread, a freshly made crisp salad, and a choice of a loaded baked potato, Southwestern rice, BBQ Baked Beans, French fries or garden-fresh vegetable accompany each dinner entrée.

Great food and great prices, however, aren't Durango's only claim to fame. Firmly believing that location is truly everything, the company has adopted an equally unique strategy to new restaurant siting. By carefully identifying high traffic areas not already saturated with competition, each Durango Steakhouse not only experience high traffic from opening day on, but also allows the company to develop new sites at a cost significantly less than that of industry competitors.

The final entrée in Durango's menu of success is management philosophy. Above average compensation, bonuses tied to performance, a full benefits package and the availability of equity positions have allowed the company to hire the best managerial talent in the industry. No member of Durango's executive management has less than 20 years industry experience and all are recognized as leaders in the industry.

As a result, Durango OakFire Steakhouse's casual atmosphere and family-oriented fare is a delectable feast that is keeping the company firmly on a steady growth track.

www.durangosteakhouse.com

CROWN AUTO DEALERSHIP GROUP

Dwayne Hawkins, President of Crown Auto Dealerships, Inc., represents one of St. Petersburg's greater private business success stories.

When Hawkins came to St. Petersburg from Birmingham, Alabama, in April 1969 and purchased Waldron Pontiac on 9th Street downtown, he was an ambitious young man moving up from years as an automobile salesperson into his first dealership. Few would have predicted within three decades he would be representing more than a dozen manufacturers from eight countries with annual sales of $300 million. He is now among the largest multi-franchise automobile dealers in the state of Florida.

"When I was looking for an auto dealership, I was thinking – like a lot of people – I'd like to go to Florida," Hawkins says. "I had an opportunity and took advantage of it."

Certainly Hawkins' tremendous growth and success mirrors the rapid development of St. Petersburg and Pinellas County during the 1970s and 1980s. It also reflects his savvy in acquiring land and anticipating future expansion and shifts in consumer buying habits. And the name he gave his company, "Crown", has played a large factor in lending an air of class and distinction to the product line.

The first indication of Hawkins' plans to expand his company came in 1970, when he relocated the original Pontiac franchise to new and larger quarters on 34th Street. Things mushroomed from there. In 1972 he was among the earliest American car dealers to foresee the country's growing interest in small cars, and Crown acquired a Honda franchise. Two years later came Datsun (now Nissan), followed in rapid succession by Jaguar (1975), GMC Trucks (1983), Mitsubishi (1983), Mercedes-Benz and Suzuki (1985), Acura (1989), Audi (1993) Hyundai (1997), and Kia (1998). Car buyers can now see vehicles from the U.S., Japan, Germany, Korea and England, all within a five-minute drive.

Dwayne Hawkins and the Crown Automotive Group have a long history of community involvement and concern. Mr. Hawkins is on the Board of Directors of the Pinellas County Education Foundation and through this organization, was one of the charter sponsors of Enterprise Village, where elementary students get a first hand taste of American business practices. "It shows them how the free enterprise system works and how business is conducted on a daily basis," says Hawkins.

Crown also participates in the automobile mechanics program at Dixie Hollins High School and St. Petersburg Vo-Tech. "St. Petersburg has been very good to myself, my family, and my employees," Hawkins says. "We work hard to earn the right to do business with the people of St. Petersburg. We have tried to be good to the community, and the community certainly has been good to us."

www.crownautonet.com

R.R. DONNELLEY & SONS COMPANY

Telecommunications Division

R.R. Donnelley & Sons Company is a leading printer, communications services, and logistics company. The company offers a full range of integrated service solutions to help publishers, merchandisers, financial, and health-care companies deliver communications to their customers. R.R. Donnelley's end-to-end solutions include premedia, content management, printing, Internet, and logistics services.

R.R. Donnelley serves a broad range of customers who use words and images to inform, educate, entertain and sell. The company's St. Petersburg facility is one of six divisions that serve the global directory needs of telecommunications providers. The division is geographically positioned to better serve the southeastern United States, the Caribbean and Central American markets. Within a full year of production, the St. Petersburg Division produces in excess of 19 billion printed and bound pages - a lot of telephone books by anyone's measure.

The continuing success of R.R. Donnelley's worldwide ventures begin at home with a dedication to customer satisfaction equaled only by a corporate culture that prides itself in both environmental awareness and community service. Locally, Donnelley's 130 employees are active in a variety of causes benefiting children focusing on literacy and diversity education. Each year the division donates multi-cultural books to local schools.

The company is a sponsor of the Junior League's "Back to School Care Fair", held annually at Tropicana Field. The Fair provides school supplies and an immunization program free of charge to Pinellas County students.

Also, since the company's 230,000 square foot printing facility is located near Tropicana Field and on a railroad siding, R.R. Donnelley made its siding available to the "Art Train" – a traveling exhibit encouraging young artists.

With its corporate headquarters located in Chicago, Ill, R.R. Donnelley is one of Pinellas County's many Fortune 500 companies. Nationwide, Donnelley has contracts to print eight of the top ten U.S. consumer magazines, based on total revenue, and produces an average of approximately half of *The New York Times* Best Seller list annually.

www.RRDonnelley.com

IRWIN CONTRACTING, INC.

In 1981, two innovative young men by the names of Innes and Ian Irwin decided it was time to make a mark on the world of contracting and construction – thus came Irwin Contracting, Inc. Behind the walls of Irwin Contracting is the vision of an uncommon team – Ian and Innes, twin brothers at the forefront of building and developing throughout the Tampa Bay area.

The twins have a history of working well together. Innes is the president of Irwin Contracting, Inc., known for building hundreds of commercial and residential projects in St. Petersburg and throughout Florida. Ian is the CEO of the Southeast Companies, a real estate development and property management company.

The brothers have teamed up to construct hundreds of millions of dollars worth of commercial and residential developments, including more than 400 condominium residences in Pinellas County alone. Together, this dynamic duo has been the backbone

Top: The Columbia Plaza in Daytona Beach was completed by Irwin Contracting in 1995. Above: Sunrise Condominium is located on the beach in St. Petersburg.

of many distinctive area landmarks, such as the historic renovation of The Concord Hotel, the expansion of the Salvador Dali Museum, the build-out of the famous St. Pete Pier, the preservation and restoration of the Studebaker Building and the complete development of the premier residential site in the Tampa Bay area, Vinoy Place.

When asked about the key to Irwin Contracting's success, Innes Irwin says, "hands-on management, experience and integrity. Developing lasting relationships and being able to consistently understand and interpret the client's needs is a must in this business."

From multi-story office towers to highly technical special-use buildings to luxury residences, Irwin Contracting has interpreted the most creative and complex design requirements to perfectly meet the individual needs of the owners or occupants. "I have rarely had the opportunity to work with such a dedicated group of people," said Kathryn King of The Pier Aquarium, "whatever it takes to get the job done seems to be a part of Irwin Contracting."

The reputation for meeting all design criteria, keeping the job on schedule and on budget is the company's hallmark. It is with this innovative and determined mindset that catapulted Irwin Contracting to the forefront of this industry and assures continued success for many years to come.

THE SEMBLER COMPANY

The evolution of America's love affair with shopping and shopping centers has been due, in a large part, to visionary developers. Perhaps one of the most visionary is St. Petersburg's Sembler Company, which, since 1962, has been transforming neighborhoods throughout Florida and the southeastern U.S. Now the company is literally transforming two metropolitan areas.

These landmark projects are BayWalk in downtown St. Petersburg and Centro Ybor in the Ybor City section of Tampa. Both are a departure from Sembler's other projects, which include more than 65 major shopping centers and over 96 free-standing stores in Tennessee, Florida, Georgia, South Carolina and Puerto Rico.

Both BayWalk and Centro Ybor differ from traditional shopping centers in that neither have department store or grocery store anchors. Instead, both feature 20-screen movie theaters, restaurants, retail stores, and entertainment venues. The impact of BayWalk in downtown St. Petersburg has been a dynamic cornerstone to the city's continuing revitalization.

Centro Ybor, the new retail and entertainment center in Tampa's Ybor City.

Guided by the Sembler Company's Chairman, Mel Sembler, and CEO Craig Sher, the BayWalk project represents a combination of canny business sense and civic duty. Sembler and his two sons, Brent and Greg, both of whom are vice-chairmen of the board, have proven over and over the company is not afraid to lead the way with new ideas in retailing.

The Sembler Company began its pioneering efforts by building strip centers on the outskirts of towns across the southeast at a time when the concept of side-by-side retailing was unproven. Some 40 years later, the privately held company has over 4.33 million square feet of retail property under management.

The majority of these projects came into being with typical Sembler finesse – most of the tenants were in place before construction began, lowering the risk factors. Not so with BayWalk or Centro Ybor. Because both projects are based on entertainment as well as retail, Sembler's CEO, Craig Sher, admits the two projects are riskier than the company's usual developments.

Balancing that risk, however, is a creative team that applies ingenuity, energy and experience to each project. Innovative design, quality and attention to detail are an edge that Sembler has relied on to set new standards of excellence. Tailor-made to fit particular communities needs, Sembler Company projects, like BayWalk, while flying in the face of convention, continue to succeed. Quite often the difference is a company that prefers to lead rather than following the crowd.

The Sembler Company Board Members from left to right: Craig Sher, Brent Sembler, Mel Sembler, Greg Sembler, and Jeff Fugua.

TY HESTON

Chapter 8
Finance & Professions

TY HESTON

The financial structure of St. Petersburg and Pinellas County is one of new growth and old stability...

Finance & Professions

Pinellas County has extensive individual financial resources — $13.4-billion deposited in banks and thrifts at the first quarter of this new century, according to the Florida Bankers Association. The area is home to some of the largest banks in the nation — Bank of America, Northern Trust, AmSouth, SunTrust, First Union, SouthTrust and Republic Bank — with Bank of America holding the greatest single market share in Pinellas County.

At the start of 2000, the seven-county Tampa Bay MSA had 976 bank offices with more than $38.7 billion in deposits, including dozens of small banks with one to five offices. The chartering of new banks accelerated in the 1990s, and there are now over 50 locally based financial institutions in the Tampa Bay region. These banks are among the financial sources available not only for well-established firms with large growth, but new businesses that are building their financial foundations.

In addition, those newer, smaller companies have access to other funding resources in the state. Florida legislation provides $150-million over a five-year period as seed money distributed through certified capital development corporations. The good news for new business is that half of the money allocated must be invested in emerging companies that have been in existence less than two years with annual revenues below $3-million.

The University of South Florida's office of corporate development is also involved with fostering venture capital relationships among local businesses. Through venture forums the school provides small business owners the opportunity to present themselves as investment worthy. It helps them develop business plans, executive summaries and multimedia presentations for securing investments, then provides the opportunity to network with investors.

Tampa Bay's banking industry, like that of other areas throughout the country, was affected by the enactment of the Financial Service Modernization Act in 1999. Perhaps the most significant effect this had was to allow banks to get into other lines of business such as insurance and brokerage — generating fee income. Banks, mortgage companies, investment firms and brokerage firms, once completely separate from banks, now compete to sell each other's products with a one stop shopping approach for financial services. The bank on the corner is not just on the corner anymore. You will find them on the Internet, and next to the stack of shopping carts at your favorite grocery store.

When the mega mergers took place in the banking industry across Florida, it gave the Bay area fewer big banks, and as we approached the new century, several new community banks opened. They were started by experienced professionals, many from the larger banking institutions, and all well connected to the community.

In 1999, Pinellas County alone saw the start up of First Home Bank in Seminole, Cornerstone Community Bank in St. Petersburg and Signature Bank in St. Petersburg — new community banks promoting convenience, service and personal atten-

Pinellas County has over $13-billion in bank deposits.

tion as they compete with non-banks for their customers.

Raymond James Bank, started in St. Petersburg in 1992, carried the role of a community bank to the next level by adding the capabilities and services associated with its national brokerage company affiliation. Together, the two entities became the first financial services company with broker/dealer subsidiaries to have received FDIC insurance powers through the full application process; the first and only to have purchased from the Resolution Trust Corporation; and the only one to have received approval to enter all 50 states electronically and telephonically.

Financial services continue to move into the St. Petersburg Gateway area, bringing thousands of jobs and increasing the location's importance as a regional center of business and industry. Raymond James Financial was among the first.

The Franklin Templeton Group is another. The mutual fund company maintains one of its three national data centers in nearly 600,000 square feet of corporate office space in Carillon Park at Gateway. Franklin Templeton employs close to 1,400 at that address, placing it among St. Petersburg's top 20 largest employers. What's more, construction of an eight-story high rise now augments the company's four-building St. Petersburg campus.

Across the Bay, PricewaterhouseCoopers LLP built a $52-million Learning and Professional Development Center near the Tampa International Airport. The training center is a first stop for its new employees from around the world.

Several more of the nation's most recognized financial service firms have added their presence to the area, and their signs to our cityscapes. Names like Capital One, MetLife, Allstate, Citigroup, Wachovia Bank, Chase Manhattan, and

Finance & Professions

Huntington Bank are now part of the financial picture here.

In a related industry, Payment Systems for Credit Unions, Inc. (PSCU), one of the largest credit and debit card service providers for credit unions in the U.S., has a regional service center in the Gateway area. Tampa Bay also houses many of Florida's largest law firms and serves as an important business and legal center for the state. According to the Florida Bar in Tallahassee, there are over 2,580 lawyers in Pinellas County alone who are members in good standing.

How does all this fit into our overall profile? Since population growth affects all industries, it is interesting to note that the highest population group in the St. Petersburg, Clearwater and Tampa MSA ranges in age from 35 to 44. As professionals, building a strong economy and economic base for the Tampa Bay area's future growth has been and is their concern.

Making their way into that future is the second largest category of individuals, the five to 14 year olds. Group efforts spawned from corporate, federal and state funding and Florida's education advancements over the past ten years, have provided new opportunities for this important group to become tomorrow's corporate stars.

Third in the lineup are the 45 to 54 year olds, destined to make their mark for the others to follow. Typically, they were educated outside the Tampa Bay area and relocated to the region based on their own mix of ideas, personal and professional reasoning. Ultimately, the opportunities for employment and quality of life became determining factors.

Next, in a very close fourth ranking, are the 25 to 34 year olds. They include a large percentage of our university and college graduates choosing to stay in the Tampa Bay area where ongoing education opportunities can further develop their potential in the work force arena. Pinellas County is just now realizing the results of many research and development programs implemented over the past decade – group efforts, spawned from corporate, federal and state funding, that will provide us with the talent crop for shaping the local economy.

TY HESTON

Few devices have become more essential to today's professional than the cell phone, used here in the midst of downtown St. Petersburg construction.

TY HESTON

RAYMOND JAMES FINANCIAL

Committed to Your Financial Future

Raymond James Financial, a diversified financial services firm, has been headquartered in St. Petersburg since the company was founded in 1962. From one small office on Central Avenue, the firm has grown to an international corporation with more than 1,800 locations.

Over the past 38 years, Raymond James has added an insurance company, federal savings bank, trust companies and asset management subsidiaries to support the clients of the firms' broker/dealer subsidiaries, Raymond James & Associates and Raymond James Financial Services.

Today, The Raymond James Financial Center is located in the heart of the Carillon office park in the Feather Sound area of St. Petersburg, near the intersection of Roosevelt and Ulmerton Roads. The buildings and 45-acre campus are filled with beautiful paintings and sculptures from the private collection of Tom and Mary

Tom James, Chairman

James. James is chairman of the firm.

Raymond James was founded by Tom's father, Bob James, who believed the number one job was to help people articulate financial objectives and develop investment strategies to achieve personal goals. Although this concept didn't receive an official name until years later, the primary objective gradually became known as financial planning.

Over the years, Raymond James has built an international reputation as a leader in financial and investment planning for individuals, corporations and municipalities. Through Raymond James & Associates and Raymond James Financial Services, the firm has more than 4,400 Financial Advisors throughout the United States and in 11 countries, including Argentina, Belgium, Canada, England, France, Germany, India, Italy, Luxembourg, Switzerland and Turkey.

In 1998, when Raymond James decided to buy the naming rights to Tampa's new community stadium, the company became the first investment firm in the United States to make such a bold move. As the finest sports facility in the NFL and site of the 2001 Super Bowl, Raymond James Stadium is one of the crown jewels of Tampa Bay (see photo, page 128).

But naming the stadium was only

Raymond James Financial Center Campus

one of many firsts for the firm. Raymond James became one of the first to offer clients the alternative of wrap-fee accounts and the first to provide investors with a "Client Bill of Rights," a detailed explanation of an investor's rights and responsibilities.

In 1998, Raymond James achieved another first by becoming the only firm to offer investors exclusive mutual fund research with specific recommendations (highly recommended, hold-under review or not recommended). The firm has top-rated equity, mutual fund and international research teams. An Investment Banking Department assists growth companies with raising capital and completing corporate transactions.

Raymond James was also among the first financial services firms to venture onto the Web. Today, the firm remains a front runner in financial services technology, offering clients an array of capabilities and services in alliance with the individual's personal Financial Advisor.

The firm's Equity Capital Markets Group includes active investment banking, equity research, institutional sales and merchant banking efforts. Raymond James' Equity Research Department, in fact, is one of only 15 in the Zachs Investment Research quarterly survey, as reported in the Wall Street Journal.

Rounding out its services is the Asset Management Group, anchored by Eagle Asset Management and the Heritage Family of Funds.

A key factor in the firm's success is Raymond James' unswerving commitment to client service, embodied in a philosophy called "Service 1st." More than just a slogan, Service 1st is a corporate culture in which the firm's clients and their financial well being always comes first.

Raymond James is also distinguished for civic and charitable support of the Tampa Bay community and other communities in which the company's Associates live and work. In Tampa Bay alone, Raymond James is perennially one of the largest contributors to the United Way. In addition, the firm contributes generously to education by sponsoring a statewide Stock Market Game, contributing to St. Petersburg's Academy Prep and Pinellas County's Enterprise Village, and encouraging Associates to mentor students and volunteer in the schools.

The firm also supports the performing and visual arts in Tampa Bay by sponsoring major art shows, such as the Raymond James Gasparilla Festival of the Arts, and contributing to theaters and museums. Raymond James encourages the firm's Associates around the world to participate enthusiastically in worthwhile volunteer activities that enrich communities.

Raymond James Financial, a public company since 1983, is listed on the New York Stock Exchange under the symbol RJF. The company's shares are currently owned by more than 11,000 individual and institutional investors.

www.raymondjames.com.

AEGON EQUITY GROUP

Respect People, Make Money, Have Fun

The AEGON Equity Group is focused on providing customers with a wide range of investment-oriented products, including variable universal life insurance, variable annuities, and mutual funds. AEGON Equity Group is a trade name representing the Florida operations of AEGON USA, Inc., a subsidiary of AEGON NV, one of the ten largest life insurance, pension, and related financial services organizations in the world. AEGON Equity Group currently employs over 1,500 people in the St. Petersburg office.

Capitalizing on the strengths of proven marketing and operating strategies the companies of AEGON Equity Group can be distinguished from the competition because of high quality, service-oriented customer assistance, along with a product portfolio that is unique for several reasons. AEGON Equity Group companies give many investors a real opportunity to invest with some of the best independent investment managers, many recognized both nationally and internationally, who typically manage investments only on behalf of large institutions. In addition, a strategic focus on distribution systems has enabled AEGON Equity Group to form long term relationships with many top-producing groups as well as attracting new strategic partners.

AEGON Equity Group's member companies include Western Reserve Life Assurance Co. of Ohio (WRL) and its affiliated broker-dealer, InterSecurities, Inc. Other companies serve as the manager, investment advisor, principal underwriter and transfer agent to the IDEX group of Mutual Funds and the WRL Series Fund. Together these mutual funds have more than $18 billion in assets under management. The IDEX Mutual Funds are nationally recognized for their record performance and growth.

The mission for the companies in AEGON Equity Group is to strive to bring superior life insurance, mutual funds, and asset accumulation products and services to customers; provide a reasonable return to shareholders; furnish opportunities for personal and professional growth to employees; and to be a good corporate citizen.

AEGON Equity Group's mission combined with AEGON NV's core philosophy of Respect People, Make Money, Have Fun provide a winning strategy for the employees and the community. AEGON Equity Group is well positioned to continue to expand the company's position in today's extremely dynamic and competitive financial services market.

www.aegonequitygroup.com

BANK OF AMERICA

The new Bank of America is a company rich in history and possibilities. Formed in 1998 through a merger between California-based Bank of America and NationsBank of North Carolina, the union created the first truly nationwide bank with offices coast-to-coast and in 37 countries. One in every three U.S. households banks with Bank of America. The bank is also the nation's top provider of Small Business Administration loans and has corporate relationships with more than 80 percent of the companies in the Global Fortune 500.

The foundation of the new Bank of America began at the turn of the century when waves of immigrants were moving to the new American West with hopes of making a better life for themselves. Most banks in the area weren't interested in immigrant business, so A.P. Giannini, himself the son of Italian immigrants, opened the Bank of Italy in San Francisco in 1904 by knocking on doors to explain to working people what a bank could do. Often he made loans based on nothing more than the calluses on a borrower's hands. Giannini pioneered the concept of statewide branch banking in America, gathering small deposits from working people and moving that capital around California where it was needed most. In 1930, Giannini changed the bank's name to Bank of America. In later years, the bank created Bank Americard, now known as VISA and pioneered the world's first successful use of computers in business operations, an achievement that today is honored in the Smithsonian.

While Bank of America was writing the book on innovation in financial service, in 1960 a North Carolina bank began writing another book on growing a small community bank into a global powerhouse. That year, the American Commercial Bank and the Security National Bank merged to create North Carolina National Bank (NCNB).

Throughout the 1970s and 80s, NCNB expanded its size and geographic scope. In 1992, NCNB changed its name to NationsBank. In the late 1990s, NationsBank merged with other banks, Boatmen's Bancshares and Barnett Bank – making it the dominant force in banking in the South, Southeast and mid-Atlantic.

Today, the new Bank of America is striving to blend the best of its predecessor organizations into a company that will make banking work for clients in ways no bank has ever done before. And, Bank of America has set an unprecedented goal of $350 billion for community investment over the next ten years.

www.bankofamerica.com

CARLTON FIELDS

Civic leadership emanates from the firms ranks as exemplified by Joel Giles, Past Chairman of the St. Petersburg Area Chamber of Commerce, 1999-2000.

Carlton Fields was established in 1901 and is one of Florida's oldest and largest law firms.

Today, with more than 175 lawyers located in St. Petersburg, Tampa, Miami, Orlando, Tallahassee and West Palm Beach offices, the firm is in the unique position of having attorneys statewide to handle the diverse needs of clients in the most efficient and effective manner possible.

Carlton Fields has a proud tradition and history in the State of Florida, with members continuing to serve in numerous public and community positions. Former Governor Bob Martinez heads up the Firm's Government Consulting Group. Edith Osman, in the Miami office, is the Past President of The Florida Bar – only the second woman to be elected to this position in its 50-year history.

For the past century, companies and individuals with business interests or disputes in Florida and across the country have relied on Carlton Fields' dedication to excellence. The firm serves a distinguished mix of national and local corporations (61 of the Fortune 100 companies), state and local public entities, and individuals. 94 law firms on the AmLaw 100 list have referred matters to Carlton Fields.

The breadth of practice areas and client base provides excellent opportunities for lawyers to develop professionally and to grow personally. Carlton Fields is proud of the long-standing relationships with clients - relationships that have been built and have endured as a result of mutual trust and a sincere understanding of clients' needs and goals.

Professionalism and ethics, service to clients, communities and the profession, appreciation of diversity, enjoyment of work, a strong work ethic, teamwork and cooperation, loyalty to clients, firm and each other, and competent effective management are the firm's core values. The production of first-rate legal work is the hallmark of the firm's practice. Carlton Fields seeks lawyers who demonstrate these qualities and values.

Carlton Fields is committed to serving clients effectively, efficiently, and ethically, to developing new business for the firm, and to participating in community activities, pro bono representation, and professional organizations. In addition, attorneys spend time engaged in continuing legal education, firm committees, recruiting, and other events that enhance the individual's legal experience.

Carlton Fields was recently highlighted in the book, America's Greatest Places to Work with a Law Degree. In addition, the Firm received the 1998 Gender Friendly Recognition Award from The Florida Bar. More recently, the Firm was awarded the Business Family Friendly Award by the Greater Tampa Chamber of Commerce.

www.carltonfields.com

AMSOUTH BANK

Meeting customers' needs is not just a marketing slogan. At AmSouth Bank it's the foundation for the way the company does business. "Understanding needs, meeting needs, building relationships" is a corporate philosophy that also perfectly describes how the bank has become one of Pinellas County's most trusted and respected financial institutions.

After arriving in the Tampa Bay area in 1993, AmSouth has grown to more than 40 branches, and the residents of the area have entrusted the bank with more than $2 billion in deposits. All of that growth is grounded on the simple principle of building relationships. But AmSouth's relationships in Pinellas County extend beyond individual customers. The City of St. Petersburg has honored the bank with a "Key to the City" award and the Pinellas Arts Council has given the bank a "Friends of the Arts" award.

All of these relationships are very important to AmSouth's future. Although based in Birmingham, Ala., the bank has more branches in the Tampa Bay area than in its own home town. AmSouth recognizes that Florida is a key to the bank's future, just as the bank is a key to Pinellas County's future.

AmSouth's service capability extends worldwide. The company plays an instrumental role in helping Florida businesses establish and conduct business internationally, especially in developing and promoting exports. AmSouth maintains relationships with financial institutions in more than 100 countries on six continents. For international banking expertise, AmSouth holds the President of the United States', E-Star Award for excellence in export service.

The benefits of a good relationship flow both ways, and AmSouth will continue to help the people of Pinellas County meet financial goals and build the businesses of the booming bay area. Successful relationships will benefit everyone by helping Pinellas County thrive.

To a significant extent, AmSouth's success reflects the economic vitality of the towns, cities and states where the company does business. As a result, AmSouth has a vested interest in the markets served and considers the bank a partner with all who seek the best interests of St. Petersburg's businesses and residents. In addition to contributing to the city's financial well being as productive citizens and taxpayers, AmSouth employees also take leadership roles in a variety of worthwhile civic, charitable and cultural organizations.

St. Petersburg is no ordinary city – nor are the city's needs ordinary. AmSouth is no ordinary bank.

www.amsouth.com

CBB ARCHITECTS

Founded in downtown St. Petersburg in 1992, CBB Architects has grown into one of the largest architectural firms in Florida. Offering a complete spectrum of architecture, interior design, construction management, and facilities management services, CBB's practice is dedicated to commercial projects. The firm has designed attractive and efficient buildings for clients in nearly every industry, including health care, manufacturing, high-tech, broadcasting, financial services, hospitality and government.

CBB has enhanced the ambience of Pinellas County through numerous adaptive reuse projects. The firm converted abandoned "big box" retail buildings in Palm Harbor into headquarters for DOVatron, Inc. (now Flextronics, Inc.) and for Applied Benefits Research Center (now Ceridian, Inc.). CBB also gave the Pinellas Science Technology and Research (STAR) Center a facelift. Recent work includes a major renovation of the International Shrine Headquarters on the Causeway in Tampa. With land prices at a premium, adaptive reuse designs that transform vacant space into viable offices and retail venues make sense in the Tampa Bay area.

In addition, CBB has built and renovated numerous public and private schools. Pinellas projects include the Azalea Middle School and Dixie Hollins High School in St. Petersburg and the Paul B. Stephens Exceptional Center in Clearwater. In fact, CBB's design for the Nina B. Harris School for exceptional children is being used as a national prototype for similar schools.

CBB has a national practice specialty in broadcast design and has designed facilities for FOX, Tribune Broadcasting, Hearst-Argyle and Paxson Communications. Local broadcast facilities include the studios of ABC affiliate WFTS-TV Channel 28 and WUSF-TV Channel 16, the University of South Florida's PBS station.

One of the firm's most unusual projects was "John F. Kennedy: The Exhibition" at the Florida International Museum. CBB recreated portions of the White House as a backdrop for the collection.

The firm's principals William S. Blizzard, AIA; Joseph E. Blouin, Jr., AIA; William N. Criswell, AIA; John R. Cochran, AIA; and Leandro A. Arroyo, AIA, share a deep commitment to the Tampa Bay area and plan to continue building it into a great place to live, work and play.

The International Shrine Headquarters

Applied Benefits Research Center (now Ceridian, Inc.)

ABC Affiliate WFTS-TV Channel 28

www.cbbarchitects.com

MERRILL LYNCH

At Merrill Lynch, financial planning is where everything starts. It isn't necessarily about numbers; it's about the hopes, dreams and needs of people. It's also about families. It's about the future.

Those simple concepts drive the St. Petersburg office of Merrill Lynch. Serving as the headquarters for Florida's West Coast district, extending up the Suncoast to Crystal River, the location also houses the offices of Merrill Lynch Trust Company.

Originally founded in 1885, Merrill Lynch established its goal of "Bringing Wall Street to Main Street." When the St. Petersburg office opened in the 1930's, Charles Merrill, the son of a small town Florida doctor, had already begin to mold the international financial services company into its present form. The goal, however, remained the same and Merrill Lynch's St. Petersburg office quickly became an integral part of the community.

The Company's role in St. Petersburg has continued to evolve as the community has changed. Always involved in assisting retirees, the company has extended its financial planning services to include not only retirees, but also the growing number of high-tech professionals in Pinellas County.

From key-man insurance to 401K's, from financing business expansion to underwriting IPO's, Merrill Lynch continues to be "bullish" about the potential of both St. Petersburg's and Pinellas County's future growth. But the core of the company's business continues to concentrate on the individual and the absolute need for sound financial planning.

As the world becomes ever more complex, a financial road map is absolutely essential. For retirees, this means ensuring the protection of the family from the cost of long-term care, the hopes to bequeath a legacy to family and community, or the desire to help with children and grandchildren's education. On the opposite end of the spectrum, Merrill Lynch provides a wealth of investment strategies and money management techniques for emerging and established professionals.

Merrill Lynch Financial Consultants have both the answers and the alternatives. These can range from explaining a new 401K plan to a company's employees or investigating estate preservation strategies to a retiree; working with a nonprofit to develop an endowment fund or establishing an investment portfolio for a new client. Whatever the need, Merrill Lynch stands ready to provide individual solutions to individual needs.

As part of the process of financial evolution, Charlie Merrill's mission in St. Petersburg might better be stated as "Bringing Wall Street to Central Avenue."

www.merrilllynch.com

MORTGAGE INVESTORS CORPORATION

Mortgage Investors Corporation believes that the strength of the country is dependent on the well being of its communities, that the source of that well-being is the stability of the family, and that the foundation of that stability is home. With that vision in mind, MIC focuses its efforts in the direction which will benefit the homeowners by providing savings in their mortgage and consumer refinancing, hence re-establishing a cornerstone of financial security for the families in the years to come.

The American Dream is alive and well, and Mortgage Investors Corporation is a part of it, especially in St. Petersburg and Pinellas County. As a long established, nationwide company, MIC is one of the largest refinance providers in the USA, offering VA, FHA, and conventional residential mortgages.

In 1995, the company refinanced more that $254 million, and in 1996, $365 million in mortgages. Volume in 1997 was $1.36 billion and in fiscal year 1998, the company exceeded $3.6 billion. MIC achieved 1st position among retail refinancing originators on September 7, 1998, and maintained that ranking as reported by the National Mortgage News on March 22nd, 1999.

Mortgage Investors Corporation has been providing mortgage-banking services since 1938. Such success and extraordinary growth rests on a foundation of outstanding customer service. This service is provided by assessing each client's needs and then offering the best financial alternative available.

Mortgage Investors Corporation's federal endorsements and authorizations rest on the founding of MIC's reputation and good standing within the mortgage industry. The company operates within the strict guidelines set by Federal and State government. Consequently, the company has been authorized by the Federal Housing Administration since 1953 and has been authorized by the Veterans Administration since 1980.

Additionally, the company has been a member in good standing of the Mortgage Bankers Association since 1944 and is a member of the Better Business Bureau at every location it operates.

www.mortgageinvestors.com

NORTHERN TRUST BANK

The Private Bank™

The difference is by design. Downtown St. Petersburg's Northern Trust Bank, while having all the normal trappings of a bank, goes a bit further. There is a quiet elegance, an air of confidence, an assurance of quality that is perceptible. It is implicit that service at this bank is a cut above the norm. Responsive. Innovative. Private.

Northern Trust, founded in Chicago in 1889, has a long tradition of quality and service. One of the country's largest managers of private assets with more than $1.5 trillion in trust assets under administration, Northern Trust entered Florida in 1971 and opened the St. Petersburg office in 1993. Northern Trust offers customized banking, trust and asset management to successful people in 11 counties on both coasts of Florida. As one of the largest managers of private wealth in the state, Northern's growth in Florida did not come about mainly as a result of acquisition and merger but rather from a clearly defined marketing strategy that targets communities where successful people reside. Pinellas County, with more than 7,000 millionaire households, ranks behind only Palm Beach, Broward and Miami-Dade.

Northern stresses personalized, local service provided by career professionals working and living in Pinellas County, not at some remote headquarters. This emphasis on customized money management tailored specifically to the individual caused readers of Worth Magazine to rank Northern Trust the best private bank in the country.

The bank's St. Petersburg customers agree. Not only do the bank's 20+ employees offer financial expertise, but also have social and charitable ties to the community. Since Northern Trust does not have high staff turnover, this continuity of service and community involvement provides a high level of comfort and support to Northern's clients.

Northern Trust is also committed to the financial support of local charitable and cultural organizations. In fact, the bank recently received the Florida Arts Recognition Award from the Secretary of State for its outstanding initiative and leadership to advance culture and the arts in the State of Florida.

The Private Bank has quickly carved out a considerable niche in the St. Petersburg community because of attention to detail, ongoing activities that connect Northern Trust directly to the community, and a belief that superb service is appreciated and rewarded.

www.ntrs.com

FRANKLIN TEMPLETON INVESTMENTS

Many area residents are familiar with the Franklin Templeton Investments offices in the Carillon complex, but may not realize that the investment management company is truly global, with more than 20 offices all over the world.

Franklin Templeton employs close to 1,400 people in St. Petersburg, which makes this one of the largest locations for the nearly 6,500-employee company. This places Franklin Templeton among the top 20 largest employers in St. Petersburg.

A new eight-story building opened in August 2000, completing the Carillon campus that includes four other two-story buildings at the east end of Ulmerton Road. In addition to state of-the-art office space and equipment, the five-building complex includes a high-tech auditorium, fitness centers, cafes, recreational rooms and an outdoor jogging trail.

Franklin Templeton takes pride in offering employees a well-rounded benefits package that includes, but is not limited to, free medical, vision, dental, and life insurance, short and long-term disability, various incentive plans, Profit Sharing, 401K and Employee Stock and Investment Plan. Franklin Templeton also offers an Education Assistance Program, as well as a variety of technical and leadership classes conducted by in-house trainers in the Training and Development Department.

Franklin Resources, Inc., is a global investment organization operating as Franklin Templeton Investments. Through its subsidiaries, Franklin Templeton Investments provides global and domestic investment, shareholder and distribution services to the Franklin Templeton and Mutual Series funds and institutional accounts, as well as separate account management services.

With over 50 years of investing experience, the company has become recognized as a leader for its global stock investments and innovative fixed-income funds. Franklin Templeton is one of the largest mutual fund organizations in the United States, and offers shareholders money management expertise spanning a variety of investment categories.

In 1992, Franklin, recognized as a leader in managing domestic mutual funds, joined forces with Templeton, a pioneer in international investing. Four years later the Mutual Series team, known for a value-driven approach to domestic equity investing, became part of the organization. The addition of these funds further strengthened Franklin's equity fund offerings and created one of the most comprehensive product lines in the mutual fund industry.

Today, Franklin Resources continues to be a major force in the mutual fund industry with over 230 mutual funds worldwide and offices in over 20 countries.

www.franklintempleton.com

KIRKLAND, RUSS, MURPHY & TAPP, PA

Earlier in their careers, while members of the same international accounting firm, Jack Kirkland, Andy Russ, Bruce Murphy and Bill Tapp all had the same goal. Their common objective was to form a professional services firm that was more effective at meeting the needs of a wide range of businesses, both large and small. This was the basis upon which Kirkland, Russ, Murphy and Tapp was formed.

Combining significant international accounting firm experience with technical expertise and a desire to be more actively involved with their clients' business activities has enabled Kirkland, Russ, Murphy and Tapp to attract many clients that were previously served by international firms. Centrally located to effectively serve the entire West Coast of Florida, the firm has a partner-to-staff ratio that makes it more effective at meeting the needs of middle market companies by ensuring a greater degree of client involvement by its partners and managers.

Unlike most local firms, Kirkland, Russ, Murphy and Tapp has not merged their audit and tax functions. By maintaining roles as specialists in these vital areas, and by assigning both an audit and tax partner to each engagement, clients are assured of receiving superior service throughout the year – not merely at year-end or when tax returns are filed. The firm's collective experience and leverage provide for more time and energy to be directed to substantive business issues. This has enabled Kirkland, Russ, Murphy and Tapp to function as valued business advisors to their clients.

Kirkland, Russ, Murphy and Tapp provides a broad range of tax, audit and business advisory services. These services include audit, review, compilation and accounting services for both public and private companies, as well as business and individual tax compliance and planning services.

Understanding the client's business and industry is critical to KRMT's success.

The firm works very closely with clients in the area of estate and succession planning, helping to maximize the value of their businesses, both for themselves and their heirs through effective tax planning, including business valuation services. The firm frequently represents clients before federal and state regulatory agencies, including the Internal Revenue Service and the Florida Department of Revenue. In addition, the firm has extensive experience in the analysis and evaluation of accounting systems and internal controls and in conducting industry-based performance reviews for clients.

Kirkland, Russ, Murphy and Tapp's breadth of experience and depth of involvement has enabled them to develop expertise in a variety of specialized areas, including professional services to the automotive industry, the manufacturing and distribution industries, growth companies and publicly traded entities.

As a local firm with extensive national firm experience, Kirkland, Russ, Murphy and Tapp is uniquely qualified to provide professional accounting services to both large and small businesses that will help them grow and prosper. ✺

KRMT works closely with clients to help them achieve current and long-term goals.

www.KRMTCPA.com

SOUTHTRUST BANK

You're Not Just Another Customer

We're Not Just Another Bank

SouthTrust Bank is banking on excellence in the south, with excellent people, excellent products and excellent results. Strong employment growth as well as expanding per capita income levels have made the south a great place to do business.

SouthTrust's professionals provide the kind of leadership that sets SouthTrust apart form the rest.

SouthTrust Bank is a full service financial institution for consumers, small businesses and corporations. SouthTrust Bank operates over 623 banking offices and several bank related affiliates in Alabama, Florida, Georgia, Mississippi, North Carolina, South Carolina, Tennessee and Texas. Florida's Tampa Bay Market encompasses over 57 offices in 6 counties, with over 500 dedicated employees. Bank related subsidiaries located in the Tampa Bay Market include SouthTrust Securities Inc., SouthTrust Mortgage Corporation, SouthTrust Life Insurance Company and SouthTrust Asset Management.

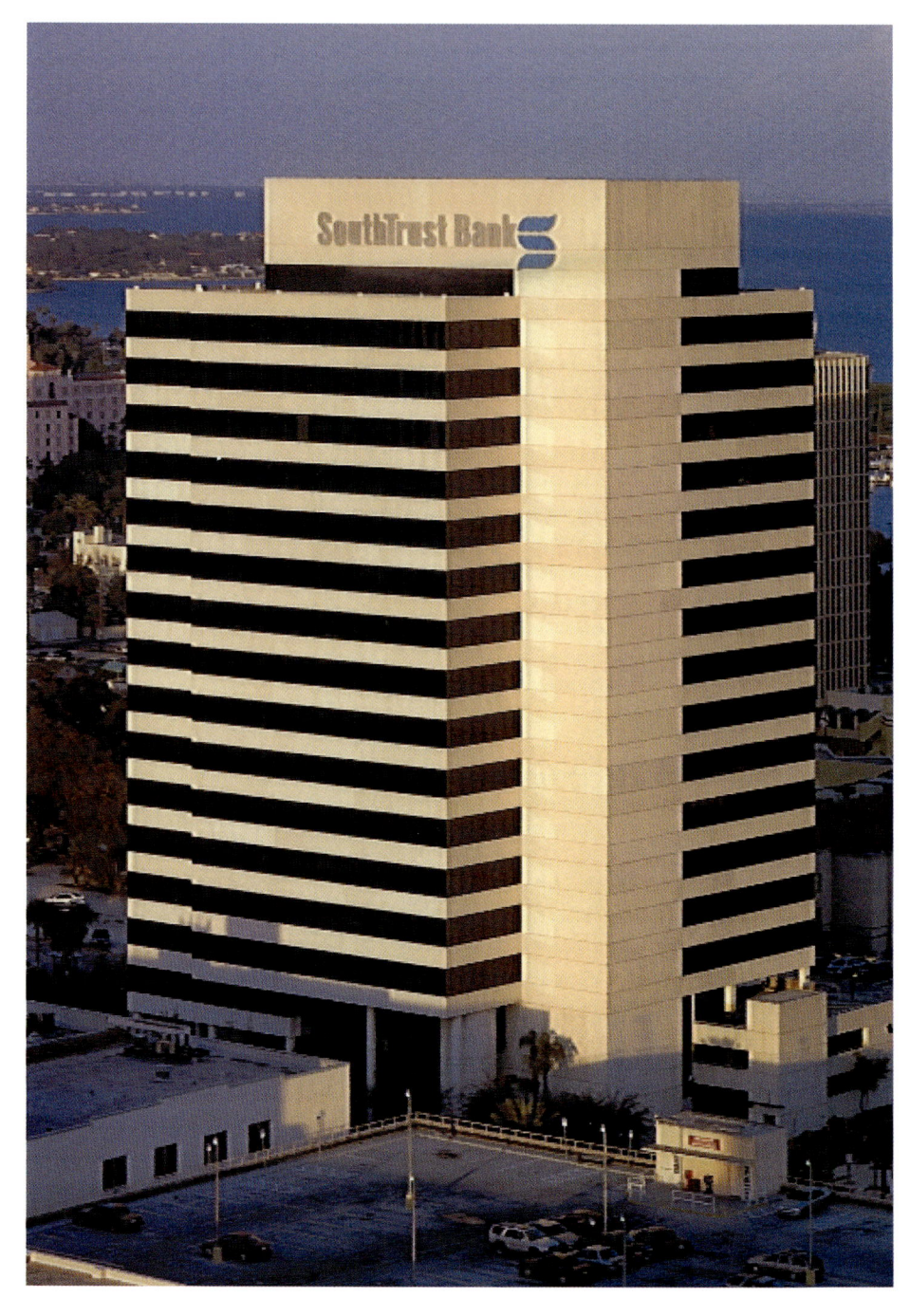

SouthTrust has been serving the South for the past 112 years and has evolved into a leading financial organization by anticipating changes in the marketplace and meeting those changes with innovative products and services. As an example, SouthTrust is keeping in step with changing technology by offering an exciting new distribution channel for the Bank's products and services through the Internet. Future success will continue to be built by excellent people delivering excellent products.

SouthTrust Bank has made a considerable impact in the St. Petersburg community by focusing attention to ongoing activities that connect directly to the community and the belief that You're Not Just Another Customer. We're Not Just Another Bank.

www.southtrust.com

NORTHWESTERN MUTUAL FINANCIAL NETWORK

A relationship built on trust, and strengthened by an individualized planning process, is the objective of every client meeting.

For over forty years Northwestern Mutual Life has provided the Tampa Bay area with the highest quality of insurance-based financial services. As a successful business, Northwestern knows the Tampa Bay environment in which companies operate, and what it takes to succeed. This insight, shared by Northwestern's financial representatives, allows the company to successfully plan the future of clients with a focus on existing needs, and goals and objectives for the future.

Today, the newly named Northwestern Mutual Financial Network provides sound, effective personal and business planning on a broadening basis to clients throughout Tampa Bay. Representatives work closely with the Network's group of trusted financial specialists in areas like retirement planning, estate planning, asset allocation, advanced planning and small business planning to ensure that clients' needs are reviewed from every perspective. This personalized approach leads to customized recommendations, which will help clients make sound decisions that are needs-based for all concerned.

At the heart of Northwestern Mutual Financial Network stands Northwestern Mutual Life, the country's largest provider of individual life insurance. With over $6 billion in life and disability income coverage in force locally, Northwestern represents one of the most significant providers of insurance products and services in the area.

In addition to these primary products and services, the firm utilizes the expertise of affiliated companies, Robert W. Baird & Company, Inc., the Frank Russell Company, and its newest subsidiary, the Northwestern Long Term Care Company. As one of only a handful of insurance companies with the highest possible financial ratings from the four top rating services, the company is an undisputed leader with 140 years of providing strong financial products and unmatched levels of client service and satisfaction.

The company's Representatives have been ranked #1 as the top sales force in the U.S. by Sales and Marketing Management Magazine. Fortune Magazine's annual survey of executives has rated Northwestern Mutual as the "Most Admired" company in the industry for almost two decades.

In St. Petersburg, business and civic leader, David Wilbanks, District Director leads the Network's mission to secure each client's family and/or business' future, to make life better, and to protect what is most important. Each client brings a unique vision, and Northwestern makes it happen. The solid combination of corporate strength and local commitment to serving St. Petersburg and all of Tampa Bay, sets the Northwestern Mutual Financial Network apart in meeting the needs of all the company's clients.

www.northwesternmutual.com

SUNTRUST BANK

Helping You Be Ready For Life

When Linton E. Allen founded SunTrust Bank, his business philosophy was "Build your community and you build your bank." SunTrust has been building its community and growing with St. Petersburg since 1959. On January 22, 1959, SunTrust, then called City Bank and Trust Company, took to the road with unwavering growth and expansion and, in 1973, it was renamed Sun-Banks of Florida, Inc.

SunBank continued to build on a foundation of strong performance and customer satisfaction. In 1985, Sun-Banks of Florida merged with the Trust Company of Georgia and later with Third National Bank Corporation of Tennessee, forming SunTrust Banks, Inc. But it was not until 1995 that all SunTrust subsidiaries, including Florida's SunBank locations adopted the SunTrust name, establishing a connection between local banking institutions and their umbrella organization SunTrust.

With more than $96 billion in assets, today SunTrust Banks, Inc., is the nation's 9th largest commercial banking organization. Operating more than 1,100 banking locations in Alabama, Florida, Georgia, Maryland, Tennessee, Virginia, and the District of Columbia, SunTrust provides a wide range of personal financial services.

SunTrust's role in attracting, keeping and growing businesses in St. Petersburg is legendary. On March 3, 1998, the company presented a check to David Fischer, Mayor of St. Petersburg, in support of the city's cooperative efforts with the Small Business Administration to create the "Community Business Development Center," a resource center that would benefit all of Pinellas County.

SunTrust is also involved with the St. Petersburg Chamber's Small Business of the Year Award, the Chamber's Membership Drive and other Chamber activities. As SunTrust has evolved, its strength has helped St. Petersburg earn its spot as a national and international destination for businesses and visitors alike. Other civic endeavors in which SunTrust and its leaders have assisted include the United Way of Pinellas County, the St. Petersburg Family YMCA, Eckerd College, All Children's Hospital, the American Cancer Walkathon and Suncoasters, along with many others.

SunTrust's commitment to service extends beyond daily business calls. By working with leaders in government, health and human services, business, industry, education, and the arts, SunTrust actively searches for creative solutions to economic and social challenges. Philanthropy, through financial and in-kind donations, volunteering time and talent, and board involvement, is a significant part of SunTrust's past, present and future contributions to Pinellas County.

WILLIAM R. HOUGH & COMPANY

William R. Hough entered the securities industry in 1948 after receiving a master's in business administration from the University of Florida. His dedication to the industry and his general enthusiasm for developing an aggressive securities firm led to the establishment of William R. Hough & Co., specialists in state, county and municipal bonds in 1962. The firm's principal objective was to provide complete underwriting and financial advisory services to governmental issuers in the state of Florida.

Under the leadership of William R. Hough and W. Robb Hough, Jr., named president of the firm in 1994, William R. Hough & Co. developed into a leading underwriter of municipal bonds. During the 1990s, the company expanded the scope of its business beyond municipal finance, offering a wide range of services to customers. In 1992, Hough started WRH Mortgage Inc., an affiliated company designed to trade in the commercial mortgage secondary market. The Hough Group of Funds was launched in November 1993, in an effort to diversify the company whose focus had been on underwriting municipal securities.

William R. Hough & Co. is also deeply committed to the arts as pictured below and above featuring the beautiful Palladium Theater.

Today, with headquarters in St. Petersburg, William R. Hough & Co. has been a part of the Tampa Bay community for nearly four decades. The company's growth and expansion into various client-oriented services has called for locations throughout Florida and the United States. While maintaining its status as a leading investment banking firm and developing as a full service investment firm, William R. Hough & Co. has continued its involvement in the St. Petersburg community. Since the firm's founding, the range and depth of the company's commitment to the community has expanded immensely. As the years progress, the firm continues to recognize the importance of contributing to arts and culture organizations in the bay area as well as other not-for-profit charities and education foundations. Advertising, marketing and public relations dollars are invested in such community organizations in lieu of general corporate commercial awareness. Through this public support, William R. Hough & Co. has incorporated the community into virtually every aspect of its corporate culture.

As William R. Hough & Co. continues its expansion into the new millennium, the firm will continue to build on client relationships as well as uphold its commitment to community service. William R. Hough & Co. prides itself on its commitment to its customers. The firm's dedication to knowledge and development will continue to strengthen the services provided. As technological advances continue, William R. Hough & Co. will further develop cutting edge services – services ready to meet the needs of a demanding financial market place.

William R. Hough & Co. will continue to strive to maintain the sound business and investment philosophies and strategies that have established the company as a leading full-service investment firm.

209

JMC COMMUNITIES

Waterfront Living at its Finest

Throughout the width and breadth of Pinellas County the vistas of open water, whether Tampa Bay or the Gulf of Mexico, are a commodity in high demand by residents who wish to take advantage of this natural beauty. JMC Communities helps connect individuals to these natural amenities with more than a home, but a sense of community as well.

Since the company's inception in 1978, the mission of JMC Communities has been to give each homeowner both an exceptional community and a superior home that will provide a lifetime of security, comfort, beauty and friendships. Nothing in JMC's success story is more compelling or gratifying than listening to how homeowners appreciate the quality of life at a JMC community.

According to St. Petersburg native, builder and JMC owner J. Michael Cheezem, "Homeowner's satisfaction tells us we've built more than just a good home. We've shaped a better way to live." Over all the years of sending out customer satisfaction surveys, 99 percent of the homeowners would recommend JMC to their friends.

Top: Dolphin Cay's Casino Clubhouse looks out over Spoonbill Lake. Above: Florencia, on St. Petersburg's beautiful downtown waterfront.

This kind of satisfaction isn't an isolated occurrence because JMC is a builder of numerous high quality condominiums – over 3,500 homes, including downtown St. Petersburg's new luxury high-rise, Florencia. Other JMC properties include The Grande on Sand Key and Meridian in Clearwater, Dolphin Cay, Bacopa Bay, HarbourSide, Pasadena Cove and Winston Park NE, all in the St. Pete area; Pinebrook and Wood Park in Bradenton. The company is currently developing Villaggio at Tierra Verde, Mandalay Beach Club on Clearwater Beach and Minorca in New Smyrna Beach.

Consistently on the forefront of design, features and amenities for homeowners, JMC Communities was named 1998 Builder of the Year by the Contractors and Builders Association of Pinellas County, and the Grand Overall Winner of Suncoast Parade of Homes five of the past six years. The company is also the winner of numerous Aurora Awards from the Southeast Building Conference.

www.jmccommunities.com

GEORGE F. YOUNG, INC.

Turning Vision into Reality

Martin T. Lott, R.A., Sr. V.P. and Lewis H. Kent, President (right), discuss on site, the plans of one of their many projects.

Pinellas County's peninsular geography – actually a microcosm of the majority of Florida – creates a multitude of challenges for any builder or developer to overcome. Understanding the myriad of design and permitting problems that can stymie the efforts of even the experienced local developer, and providing innovative solutions to those problems, is what sets George F. Young, Inc. apart.

Founded in 1919 in St. Petersburg by pioneer engineer and surveyor George Fleming Young, the company has grown steadily to become a full service consulting firm offering architecture, engineering, subsurface utility engineering, landscape architecture, planning, and surveying services to clients in both the private and public sector. In addition, George F. Young, Inc. provides its clients environmental and real estate services through its subsidiaries, Commercial Partners Realty, and Environmental Analysis & Permitting. With offices located in St. Petersburg, Bradenton, Gainesville, North Palm Beach, Sarasota, and Tampa, Florida, George F. Young, Inc. is now a statewide consulting company.

George F. Young, Inc.'s full service capabilities minimize the hassles associated with today's complex projects. The in-house team of architects, engineers, planners, landscape architects, ecologists, surveyors, and real estate professionals work together to provide clients with a seamless project from concept to completion.

Anyone needing professional consulting services from a small residential, office, commercial, or industrial development to a large master planned project or a municipal, regional, or state project, can be confident that George F. Young, Inc. will perform. The company's value oriented approach has resulted in a long history of satisfied clients. Over 80 percent of the company's business comes from repeat clients.

If you are new to the area and need advice or assistance in site selection, land acquisition, land development, permitting, environmental analysis, or building design, do not hesitate to contact the George F. Young, Inc. team of professionals who will help turn your vision into reality.

www.georgefyoung.com

COLLIERS ARNOLD COMMERCIAL REAL ESTATE SERVICES

The mission of Colliers Arnold is to be a superior supplier of real estate services and solutions with an absolute commitment to ethics and integrity... where the client's interest is best served. Founded in 1974, the firm's focus on commercial real estate with a commitment to clients through education and process management, quickly distinguished the company from its competitors.

CEO, Lee E. Arnold, Jr., was one of the youngest commercial real estate professionals to receive the CCIM (Certified Commercial Investment Member) designation and to become a CCIM instructor. He published two books, "Commercial Real Estate Marketing and Management – Book I and Book II," which became best sellers and the core text material for CCIM marketing classes and many national companies internal training programs. In 1983, the firm developed and launched REALBase (the first PC based commercial real estate database system.) The system was implemented by over 800 commercial real estate firms.

In 1990, the firm expanded its service lines to include valuation, consulting, asset management and related value-added services. In 1991, the firm acquired an interest in Real Estate Research Consultants in Orlando, the largest independent real estate consulting firm in the state.

In 1996, the firm joined Colliers International, which offered the ability to leverage the firm's internal capabilities with one of the finest commercial real estate services firms in the world. Concurrent with joining Colliers, new offices were opened in Orlando and Fort Myers, recruiting some of the most experienced professionals in each of those markets. This expansion completed the plan to allow the firm to service the I-4/I-75 corridor.

Today, with over 100 employees, including 60 real estate professionals with an average of 16 years of experience in commercial real estate, the Colliers Arnold offices in Clearwater, Tampa, Orlando and Fort Myers offer first-class commercial real estate services to virtually every market in Florida. Colliers International provides clients with instant access to local market experts throughout the world. The focus on process, technology, best practices and an uncompromising commitment to ethics and the client's best interest, continue to serve as the basis for the growth and success of Colliers Arnold.

The company has established itself as a regional force and a national leader in the industry. Colliers Arnold is committed to continuing their 25-year history of superior results through superior service. Their clients have been loyal and well served. The future should bring continued success.

www.colliersarnold.com

HERB SNITZER

Chapter 9
Networks & Shopping

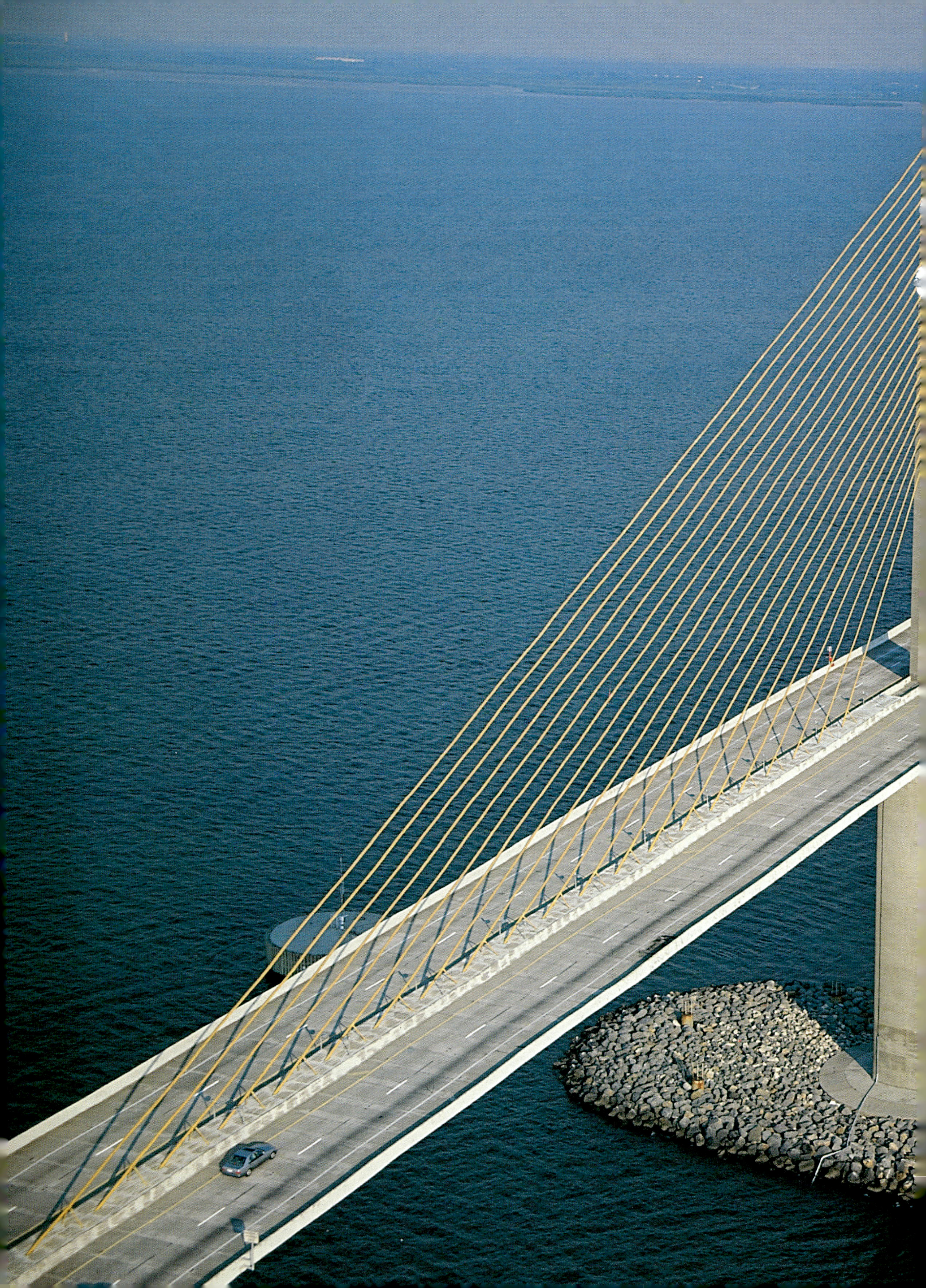

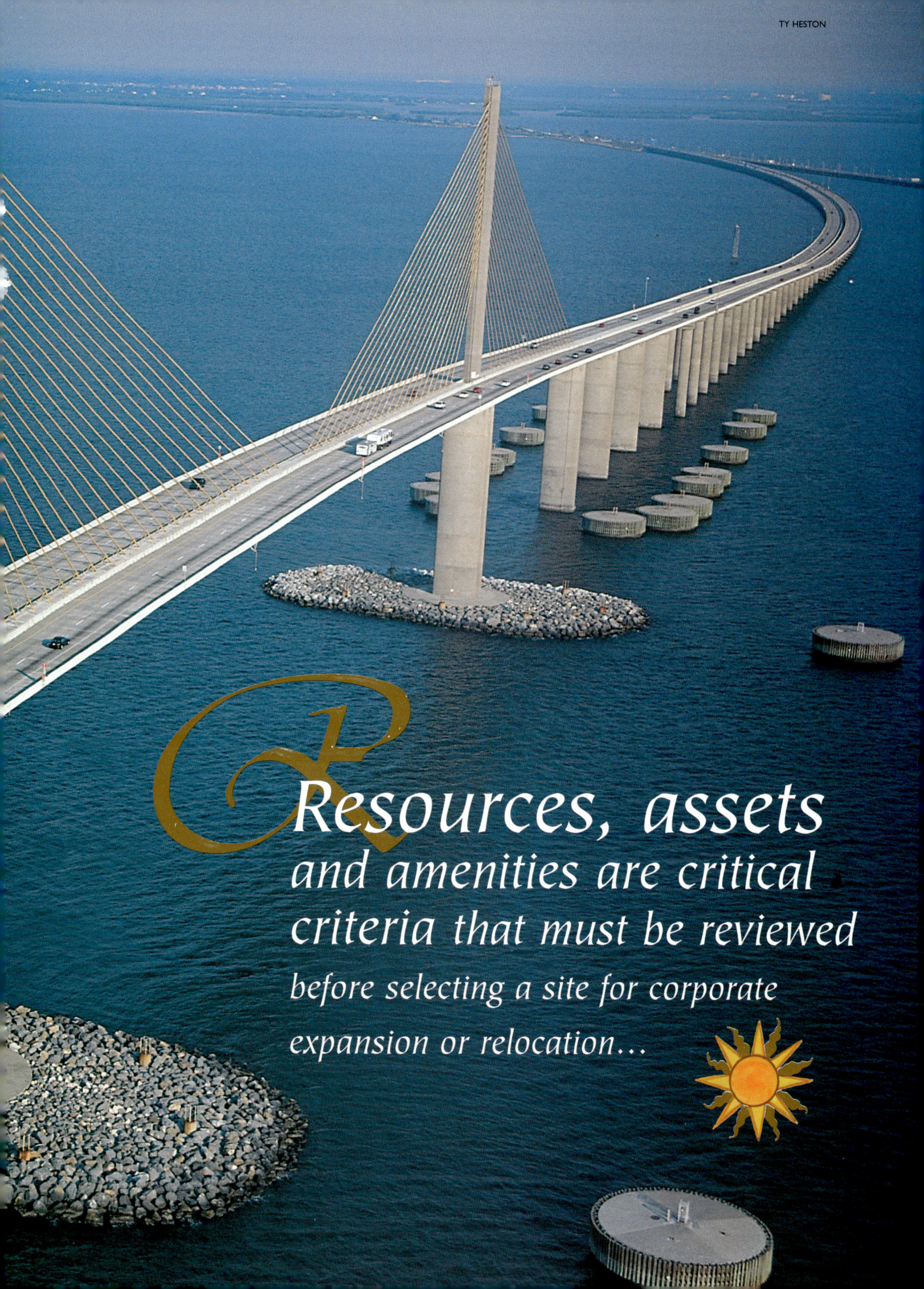

TY HESTON

Resources, assets and amenities are critical criteria that must be reviewed before selecting a site for corporate expansion or relocation…

Networks & Shopping

Pinellas County Court House built in 1960 contains the county administrator's office, commissioners' offices and commission meeting room.

Meeting that criteria and coming out on top is Pinellas County – in one of the nations premier markets, well positioned for a global economy and, equally important, one in which employees like to live.

Get out your check list. The Tampa Bay region has an efficient Interstate system, the largest bulk port in the southeast and one of the finest international airports with an adjacent Free Trade Zone.

Half of all U.S. freight destinations are within a day's drive. The World Trade Center, Tampa Port Authority headquarters, and the University of South Florida's Center for International Business are all located in one new facility.

More reasons to locate here – technology, research and development companies like the way we do business; Florida offers support programs and tax incentives; our workforce is skilled and diverse; and, not to be overlooked, our weather is mild, our beaches are beautiful and our cost of living low.

Pinellas County is a community of 24 incorporated cities and towns sharing all of these attributes in the region known as Tampa Bay. Of its approximately 439 square miles, 280 square miles of Pinellas are land and the balance water.

With a population of approximately 900,000 Pinellas County is one of the most densely populated in Florida, ranking fifth in the state, with the second smallest total land area. St. Petersburg is its largest city and Clearwater, the County seat, is the second largest. Of the county's total population, approximately 280,000 reside in unincorporated areas. Together we enjoy many resources, assets and amenities in an unequaled environment for work and play.

Pinellas County has a charter government with a seven-member commission that sets policies, passes laws, enacts ordinances and establishes countywide property tax rates. The Commission is also charged with approving the annual billion-dollar county budget. County districts elect commissioners to four-year terms. An appointed county administrator handles day-to-day operations and implements policy.

The Board of County Commissioners also serves as the Emergency Medical Services Authority, Fire Protection Authority, Mosquito Control Board, and the Water and Navigation Authority. While each municipality in Pinellas has its own government structure, all local government entities in Florida operate "in the sunshine" whereby council meetings and workshops are open to the public.

Residents of Pinellas County towns and cities are privileged to have a countywide library system. The exceptions, those living in Kenneth City and South Pasadena, choose to remain independent, but can pay a fee to use the system. Use of the Internet is available on the Suncoast Free-net, accessed from every public library in Pinellas and Hillsborough counties along with an available personal e-mail address.

Local phone service is provided to residents by Verizon Communications (a merger of Bell Atlantic and GTE in 2000), while several start-up telecom and smaller phone companies are also available to business customers. NewSouth, Adelphia and Florida Digital Network, for example, have built competitive local networks here that market everything from wireless to high speed Internet. KMC Telecom launched

continued on page 220

Networks & Shopping

Above: The "Old" Courthouse has civil courtrooms, offices and Pinellas County's law library. It has been restored in detail to its original 1917 splendor. Below: The Criminal Justice Center, located in mid Pinellas County, houses criminal and juvenile courtrooms in a modern, nearly half-million square foot facility completed in 1996.

ST. PETERSBURG TIMES

Local news. National standards.

On a muggy Florida morning more than a century ago, three Pinellas pioneers turned on a switch of enlightenment for the Tampa Bay area. In the back room of a Dunedin pharmacy, J.M. "Doc" Baggett, M. Joel McMullen and Dr. J.L. Edgar began publishing the *West Hillsborough Times,* a four page country weekly designed to help settlers keep up with area developments.

One hundred sixteen years later, the *St. Petersburg Times,* now Florida's largest daily newspaper, continues to shape its efforts around in-depth local reporting held to the nation's highest standards. Deeply rooted in the principles of integrity, opportunity and independence, the *Times* remains one of the last and largest independently owned newspapers in the country.

That independence allows the *Times* the freedom to serve readers and support the community based on beliefs instead of budgets. Different from newspapers that are one of many in a conglomerate of media organizations with decision-making headquarters located thousands of miles away, the *Times* is owned by the Poynter Institute for Media Studies, a school for journalists that sits blocks away from its downtown St. Petersburg building. That means decisions about coverage, community efforts, and business are made by people who live and work in the communities affected by those decisions.

Nelson Poynter, the last man to own the *Times,* recognized the importance of a newspaper preserving an independent voice decades before the industry began to feel the effects of corporate ownership. In a visionary act that remains unmatched anywhere in the world, Poynter left the newspaper to a school that works to elevate and uphold the standards of journalism. Professional journalists from around the globe travel to the Institute to learn from the nation's leading experts. The *Times* is unique in many other ways. Serving readers in more than five counties, the *Times* produces 16 regional editions that provide readers in all 24 Pinellas communities and beyond with in-depth information about their neighborhoods.

The *Times* is ranked among the nation's top 10 newspapers, and its journalists have won the Pulitzer Prize six times, each for local stories that worked to shed light on events happening in and around Tampa Bay. *Times* coverage saturates the state's most populous metro area and, the fourteenth largest media market in the country, making it the first choice for advertisers trying to reach the largest number of consumers.

These uncompromising standards of excellence work to serve the com-

Shadowing the growth of the community, the newspaper reaches more than 718,000 readers every day and almost 900,000 on Sunday. Thousands more access the paper online.

Sometimes community support merges with the newspaper. An award-winning Newspaper In Education program brings the world to hundreds of Bay area classrooms every week. Newspapers donated by readers and many businesses add real-life to learning, filling in the gaps between textbooks and experience. And every November the *Times* champions literacy with the *St. Petersburg Times* Festival of Reading. Critically acclaimed authors and journalists come together on St. Petersburg's Eckerd College campus to celebrate the world of books and reading.

Other community support includes the S*t. Petersburg* Times Turkey Trot, an annual race that raises money for charity, and the *St. Petersburg Times* Scholarship program. This Scholarship program is one of the *Times'* newest and most promising endeavors. In 2000, college scholarships were awarded to four high school students from cities throughout the newspaper's coverage area. These students, recognized for a commitment to excellence, even in the face of challenges, will each receive up to $15,000 a year for four years. Such scholarships will be awarded to deserving students annually.

This most recent investment in the future illustrates the *Times'* innovative history of encouraging excellence from within, and throughout the community. From the three original employees to today's more than 3,000, the *Times'* uncompromising standards and commitment to community have and will continue to provide readers with all of the news, information and analysis they have come to expect from Florida's finest newspaper.

munity in other ways as well. The *Times* partners with many of Tampa Bay's corporate entities to sponsor more than 200 entertainment, sports and other events for area residents. These partnerships include sponsorship of the Tampa Bay Devil Rays, shows and concerts at the Ice Palace, and much more.

The company's philanthropic support includes more than 100 organizations each year. These gifts add up to more than $1 million annually, extending from performing arts organizations to hospitals, to universities and the United Way.

"Sometimes the support is money. Sometimes it is advertising. Sometimes it is manpower. The specifics change, but the underlying belief is constant: we believe in our communities and we will do everything possible to help them grow and prosper," says Andy Barnes, Chairman.

www.tampabay.com

219

Florida Power Corporation has provided electric service for over 100 years. Opposite page: The I-375 interchange to downtown St. Petersburg. Note the prominent domed Tropicana Field, home of the Tampa Bay Devil Rays.

its fiber optic network in Pinellas County in 2000, becoming the first competitive, facilities-based, local telecommunications company. In addition, several nationally recognized names offer long distance service.

Florida Power Corporation provides electricity for all of Pinellas County, except in Oldsmar, which is served by Tampa Electric Co. (TECO). Both utilities are investor-owned and provide several programs and rate schedules to suit business and industry needs, as well as free counseling for companies in need of reliable, uninterrupted power sources and energy efficiencies. Local provider Florida Power has comparably lower rates than many other areas of the country, and generally the lowest rates in all of Florida. Electric rates fall under the jurisdiction of the Florida Public Service Commission, which approves all rate adjustments.

Natural gas is available to most industrial and commercial areas of Pinellas County and to many private homes in residential areas. TECO/Peoples Gas System provides Service to the area south of Ulmerton Road (SR 688), which includes St. Petersburg and St. Pete Beach. They offer propane gas service to areas not served by natural gas. The city of Clearwater Utilities Department provides natural gas service to Clearwater, Dunedin and Largo through the Clearwater Gas System. Communities north of Clearwater and Dunedin do not have natural gas available.

Water systems are operated by Pinellas County, St. Petersburg, Clearwater and Belleair. Pinellas pipes the majority of its water supply from wells it owns and operates in Pasco and Hillsborough counties and St. Petersburg boasts award-winning, high quality tap water for its residents, which is from the Cosme Water Treatment Plant, where it receives a five-step treatment including aeration, lime softening and filtration.

Pinellas County operates a resource recovery plant that, when opened in 1983, revolutionized our waste disposal process by turning garbage into electricity. The facility can burn up to 3,000 tons of garbage daily to produce enough electricity to service 45,000 homes. The plant also recovers 55 tons of metal each day, which is sold for recycling. In addition, a variety of sanitation services can be found throughout Pinellas, controlled by each of the municipalities and the unincorporated areas. Some cities, such as St. Petersburg, provide garbage pickup, while others contract with private companies.

Incorporated cities in Pinellas County have their own police departments with some exceptions. The cities of Belleair Bluffs, Belleair Shore, South Pasadena, Seminole, Safety Harbor and Oldsmar rely on the Pinellas County Sheriff's Department as does the unincorporated areas of the county. Pinellas contracts with 17 fire departments to provide fire and rescue service in those same unincorporated areas and cities without their own fire and rescue service share with those that do. A 911 emergency telephone number reaches a central dispatcher for police, fire and rescue.

The county also contracts with one private company to operate 50 paramedic ambulances countywide. 911 calls are transferred electronically from the 911 center to the ambulance dispatch facility.

Florida has one of the lowest tax rates in the nation, and is the only state in the southeast with no personal income tax. In Pinellas there is a seven percent sales tax on non-food items – one percent more that the state's six percent. That's because Pinellas County had the vision and commitment to help itself with "Penny for Pinellas" – a one-cent sales tax to be used for capital expenditures in our own backyard.

Pinellas County residents voted overwhelmingly, in 1997, to extend the "Penny for Pinellas" 10 more years. The county's first alternative high school is planned for the 2002-03 school year using a portion of these funds. Road projects,

HERB SNITZER

Networks & Shopping

endangered land purchases and park expenditures are all on the list of improvements planned for the years 2000 to 2002, utilizing the "Penny for Pinellas."

Pinellas County property owners pay a mileage rate of roughly $22.15 per thousand dollars of taxable property value. This amount funds city, county and school budgets. Those living outside city limits, in unincorporated areas of the county, pay no city taxes but are assessed a special tax for services payable to the county tax collector.

The Florida State Constitution requires all property to be appraised at fair market value. A $25-thousand homestead exemption is available to homeowners. If a homeowner has title or record to their property as of January first, and resides permanently on the property, the first $25-thousand of value is deducted from the total appraised value for figuring taxes.

An extensive network of roads and highways traverse Pinellas County, joining one community with another. The Pinellas County Metropolitan Planning Organization (MPO) is a countywide transportation planning organization, created by law to provide a forum for cooperative decision-making concerning countywide transportation issues.

Interstate-275 connects Pinellas with Manatee County to the south via the Sunshine Skyway Bridge, and with Hillsborough County to the northeast via the Howard Frankland Bridge. I-275 also links with I-4 east to Orlando from Tampa and I-75 going north or south. U.S. 19 runs the entire length of Pinellas and serves as one of its major roads, while the Bayside Bridge, designed to ease congestion off of U.S. 19, is a three-mile north-south link between St. Petersburg's Gateway area, the St. Petersburg/Clearwater Airport, and Clearwater.

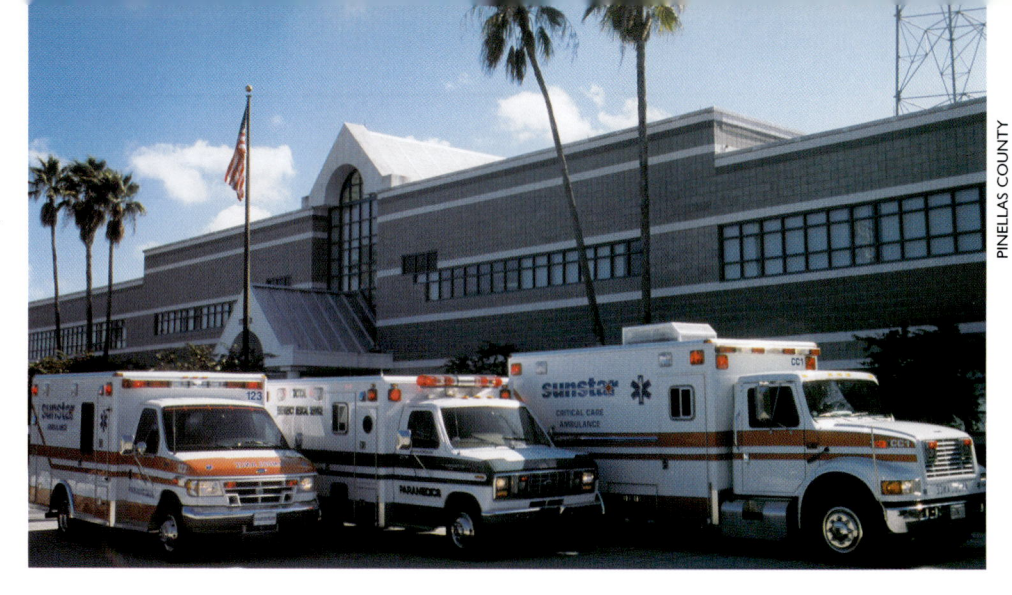

In addition to the state's Department of Transportation (DOT) Howard Frankland Bridge, two other routes make Pinellas County an easy commute from Hillsborough and Tampa – the Courtney Campbell Causeway runs east-west to Clearwater (SR 60) and the Gandy Bridge connects St. Petersburg to Tampa and the Crosstown Expressway.

In north county, near Oldsmar, the East-West Parkway also connects Pinellas and Hillsborough entirely over a land route. Running cross-county, from the Howard Frankland Bridge west to the Gulf beaches, is Ulmerton Road (SR 688) and crossing Ulmerton are numerous roads to virtually all other areas.

Buses provide local mass transit by way of the Pinellas Suncoast Transit Authority (PSTA), which has a fleet of 147 buses on more than 40 strategic routes throughout the county. With the popularity of the Pinellas Trail recreational bike path, and the area's ongoing invitation to enjoy the scenery, all busses are equipped with bicycle racks so passengers can continue their journey off the road and at their leisure.

For longer distances, Pinellas County and the entire Bay Area are served by Greyhound-Trailways Bus Lines as well as several charter bus companies. A strategic infrastructure of world-class airports, deep-water ports, rail and highway systems enables rapid inter-county transit or world wide shipping.

continued on page 224

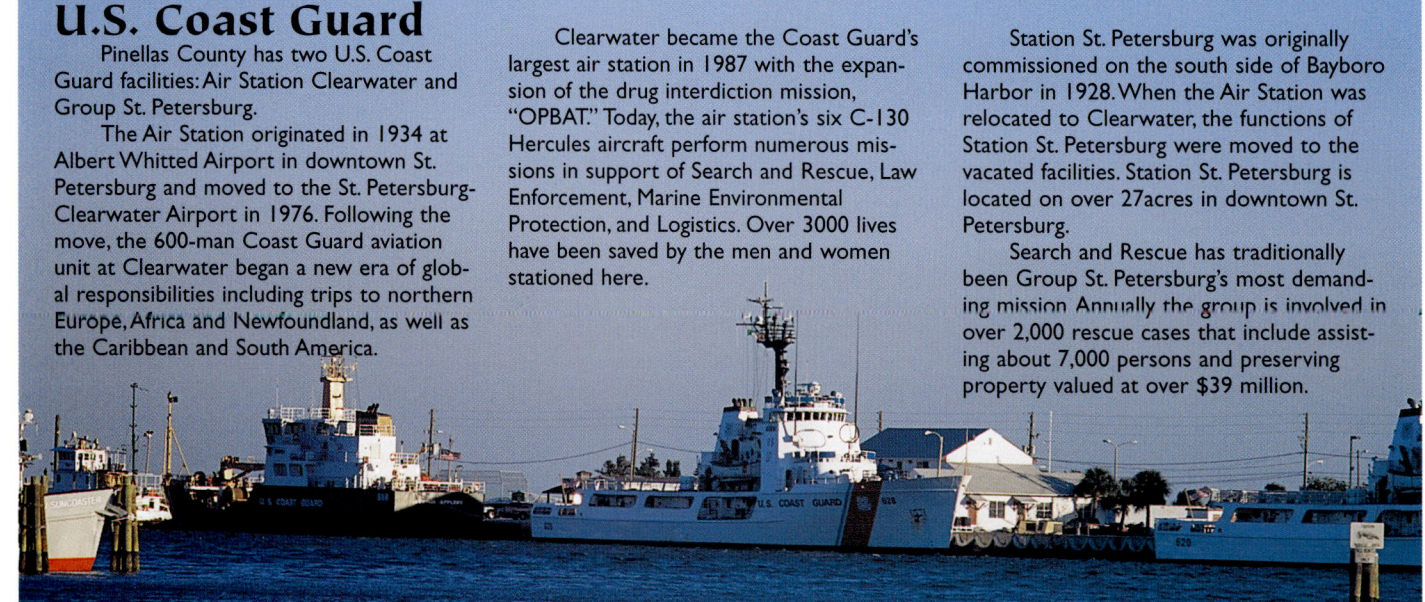

U.S. Coast Guard

Pinellas County has two U.S. Coast Guard facilities: Air Station Clearwater and Group St. Petersburg.

The Air Station originated in 1934 at Albert Whitted Airport in downtown St. Petersburg and moved to the St. Petersburg-Clearwater Airport in 1976. Following the move, the 600-man Coast Guard aviation unit at Clearwater began a new era of global responsibilities including trips to northern Europe, Africa and Newfoundland, as well as the Caribbean and South America.

Clearwater became the Coast Guard's largest air station in 1987 with the expansion of the drug interdiction mission, "OPBAT." Today, the air station's six C-130 Hercules aircraft perform numerous missions in support of Search and Rescue, Law Enforcement, Marine Environmental Protection, and Logistics. Over 3000 lives have been saved by the men and women stationed here.

Station St. Petersburg was originally commissioned on the south side of Bayboro Harbor in 1928. When the Air Station was relocated to Clearwater, the functions of Station St. Petersburg were moved to the vacated facilities. Station St. Petersburg is located on over 27 acres in downtown St. Petersburg.

Search and Rescue has traditionally been Group St. Petersburg's most demanding mission. Annually the group is involved in over 2,000 rescue cases that include assisting about 7,000 persons and preserving property valued at over $39 million.

PEOPLES GAS

When TECO Energy acquired Peoples Gas in 1997, the acquisition gave the company an immediate presence throughout Florida. Striving to give the lifestyle, comfort and value homeowners deserve with natural gas technologies, the company's presence in the state has not only strengthened, but grown as well.

To capitalize on Florida's underserved market, Peoples Gas completed expansion into southwest Florida in 1999. Experts predict that more than 100,000 new homes and businesses will be built in this area over the next decade. As a result of the Peoples Gas expansion, consumers and businesses in key cities like Fort Myers, Naples and Cape Coral have natural gas as an energy option for the first time.

Peoples Gas also completed an expansion to serve the U.S. Naval Station at Mayport near Jacksonville. Natural gas service "went live" at Mayport in October 1999: 14 buildings at the navy base are now using natural gas. When fully operational, the Mayport station is expected to use more than 2.6 million therms of natural gas annually.

Peoples Gas expanded to St. Johns County with the planned community of The Neighborhoods at World Golf Village. Construction began in April 2000, on the first two miles of pipeline.

In Martin County, variety and the opportunity to provide natural gas to a thriving area led to a Peoples Gas pipeline expansion project there. Existing contracts include several restaurants, two residential developments with a total of 184 homes, a high school, manufacturing plants and several research and development facilities. A new Peoples Gas office is also under construction.

A southwest Broward pipeline expansion has progressed along with the county's commercial and residential growth. Adding more than one million therms annually since it began in 1998, the area is expected to generate customers representing another 750,000 therms a year. Peoples Gas also secured a franchise agreement and began serving gas customers in the city of Brooksville north of Tampa.

Along with expansion efforts, Peoples Gas has undertaken a number of branding efforts throughout the state. To increase TECO Energy's statewide presence, Peoples Gas secured the naming rights to the home of the Florida Everblades hockey team. TECO Arena is located near Fort Myers in Estero, Florida. This sponsorship has meant increased brand recognition for Peoples Gas and for TECO Energy.

It is no surprise that as businesses and homeowners look at remodeling or building, natural gas remains the energy preference. As long as Floridians demand the energy source that delivers lifestyle, comfort and value, Peoples Gas will continue to deliver natural gas service statewide.

www.peoplesgas.com

Networks & Shopping

Two commercial airports – Tampa International (TIA) and St. Petersburg/Clearwater International – carry more than 14 million passengers annually with non-stop service to over 105 cities in the U.S., Canada, the Caribbean, South American and overseas. Access to either airport from any point in Pinellas County is often less than 20 minutes.

The St. Petersburg-Clearwater International Airport serves over one million passengers a year with commercial airline service to U.S. and international destinations. Over 23-million pounds of cargo are shipped annually through the airport, which is owned and operated by Pinellas County. This 2,000-acre complex is a fully certified facility with an ILS-equipped 8,500-foot runway and two 5,500-foot runways. A series of improvement projects begun in 2000, will lengthen the main runway and construct a new one, expand the cargo ramp, and build six jet bridges while keeping five ground-level gates.

The airport provides U.S. Customs and FAA-operated control tower facilities, private/corporate aviation hangars, airplane rental, and flight instruction and is home of the busiest U.S. Coast Guard Air Station in the world. United Parcel Service, Air Cargo and General/Corporate Aviation are also major activities, while the airport's industrial park is a Foreign Trade Zone for international commerce.

By sea, the Port of Tampa and Port of Manatee (Florida's fourth largest deep-water port) offer warehouse and stevedore facilities. Both are served by excellent rail connections. The Port of St. Petersburg, equipped with a 1,500-foot wharf, a 1,000 foot turning basin, 40,000 square feet of warehouse space and full dockside services, is actively being studied for redevelopment as a port for small cruise ships.

Amtrak provides intercity rail passenger service to Tampa, with a bus shuttle from the Tampa station to mid Pinellas County. Commercial rail service between Pinellas and points north and south along the Atlantic coast is provided by CSX.

The Sunshine Skyway

The famous bridge that connects St. Petersburg and Manatee County over Tampa Bay is part of the Interstate 275 system. It is a cable-stayed bridge, rising more than 180 feet above the water, crossing the shipping channel with a 1,200-foot span.

For 30 years travelers crossed these waters via The Bee Line Ferry, which operated from 1924 until 1954 when the first span, a steel girder bridge was completed. Seventeen years later a sister span, similar in design, opened adjacent to the original bridge in 1971.

Early on the morning of May 9, 1980, in a downpour of rain, the phosphate freighter, Summit Venture collided with the northbound bridge in a tragic accident that claimed 35 lives. The old Skyway spans were torn down in 1991 and their causeway approaches were preserved and converted to fishing piers. At over four miles in distance, these are the longest fishing piers in the world.

Construction of the new Sunshine Skyway began in June 1982 and the bridge was opened to traffic on April 30, 1987.

When it comes to being well informed, Pinellas County and the rest of Tampa Bay residents are well served by a variety of quality media, including 15 television stations, cable networks and local access channels, dozens of radio stations, two daily newspapers, numerous weekly and monthly newspapers, magazines and special interest publications.

The St. Petersburg Times is owned by the Poynter Institute for Media Studies, itself a world-renowned journalism center located in downtown St. Petersburg. The four-time Pulitzer Prize winning paper is Florida's largest and boasts a daily circulation of nearly 400,000 with an additional 100-thousand readers on Sundays.

The Tribune is owned by Media General and is also a Pulitzer Prize winner. The Trib publishes 13 daily sections and a local edition for Pinellas County. Media General also owns WFLA-TV, Channel 8, manages its coordinated website Tampa Bay Online, and in 2000, after a move to spacious

The renown Poynter Institute nonprofit teaching and research institution for journalists.

continued on page 226

THE ST. PETERSBURG-CLEARWATER INTERNATIONAL AIRPORT

Tampa Bay's Other Great Airport

The St. Petersburg-Clearwater International Airport is the closest international airport to the area's award-winning beaches and St. Petersburg's downtown. An average of 1.1 million people a year choose it over any other airport for convenient, hassle-free flying.

Passengers arriving and departing receive free parking, a single baggage pickup for international flights and hassle-free, quick access to ticketing and the boarding gates.

The airport offers low fares and over 30 daily non-stop flights to Chicago, Toronto, Milwaukee, Minneapolis and Indianapolis aboard ATA/American Trans Air, Sun Country, Canada 3000, Air Transat, Royal Airlines and Casino Airlink.

With around-the-clock security, FAA weather monitoring systems and a multimillion-dollar U.S. Customs facility, the airport has been rated one of the best airports in the country in handling charter and scheduled flights, as well as corporate and private aircraft.

The airport's runway complex provides access for virtually any size aircraft from jumbo jets to charter planes to private aircraft. The airport features a fully stocked gift shop, a duty-free shop, comfortable cocktail lounges, and newly restyled restaurants. And there is a broad selection of hotels and meeting facilities within minutes of the facility.

And when it comes to business needs, it's fair to say the sky's the limit.

The airport's 2,000-acre complex provides office space, show rooms, research/development facilities, light manufacturing, and distribution centers for large and small businesses who want to take advantage of the airport's full-service hub.

Ample warehouse space and sophisticated loading operations enable St. Petersburg-Clearwater International to handle several national and international shippers with ease. In fact, one of the largest UPS hubs in the Southeast is located at the airport.

Complete facilities include a FAA-operated tower, an around-the-clock flight service station, and a flight standards district office located adjacent to the main terminal. Pilots will find two full-service, fixed-based operators, a paint and refinishing shop, tie down and hangar spaces, charter flights, a flight instruction school, aircraft sales and services, aviation fuels 110-115 and Jet A, and FAA-approved repair shops.

For convenience and efficiency, the Airport Industrial Park is centrally located between the area's three bay cities and convenient to major transportation networks and seaways.

www.stpete-clwairport.com

Networks & Area Shopping

new headquarters overlooking the Hillsborough River in downtown Tampa, added simulcast newscasts on AM radio station WTM 570, combining newspaper, television, radio, and online news.

Another force in the bay area media market is Clear Channel Communications Inc., which in 1999 added to their existing bay area stations in a merger with Jacor Communication already on radio airwaves here. By FCC standards, Tampa Bay is in the second 10 market and listeners enjoy the results of competitive formatting by having so many choices. There are 52 radio stations (28 AM and 24 FM) available to 1.5 million potential listeners, earning the Bay Area a reputation as one of the more competitive radio markets.

Television broadcasters have gone from analog to digital signals in Tampa Bay, which has seven broadcast network affiliates, two Hispanic outlets, two public television stations, a Christian broadcast station and an independent. We are the 15th largest television market in the nation. In addition to regularly-scheduled newscast, anchored by favorite local personalities on our NBC, CBS, ABC and Fox affiliates, Time Warner Communications, now owned by AOL, has a 24-hour, all-news channel "Bay News 9."

The ability to have content and to go across the Internet with video modes has opened up a whole new world in communications now enjoyed in the Tampa Bay area.

Tourism continues to fuel our economy. The county's St. Petersburg/Clearwater Area Convention and Visitors Bureau is the county's tourism management and marketing organization responsible for developing and promoting the area as the leisure, business, convention, conference, sports and film production destination that it is.

In its brief ten-year history that bureau's film commission also assisted moviemakers with such productions as Health, Cocoon, and Summer Rental all filmed on location here. And if you stayed until the very end of Lethal Weapon III, you saw one of St. Petersburg's former landmark hotels, The Soreno, adding its visual impact behind the credits as it was imploded into history.

Restaurants and Retail are alive & well in Pinellas County where the names of nationally-recognized stores anchor our malls and new combination entertainment/ shopping districts revitalize our downtowns. In fact, the Tampa Bay area is the tenth largest retail market in the nation, the largest and richest consumer market in Florida and number two in the Southeast. Its 56 million square foot retail market has continued strong leasing activity throughout 1999.

Regional malls, a product of the 1950's, are strategically located to serve the greatest number of shoppers and ours have been modernized with the times. In Pinellas County, the largest enclosed mall is Simon's Tyrone Square Mall at 22nd Avenue North and the intersection from which it gets its name – Tyrone Boulevard – in St. Petersburg. With 1.2 million square feet of retail space, it is a major retail destination.

In north Pinellas, Countryside Mall, on U.S. Highway 19 North at State Road 580, features 166 stores and an ice

continued on page 230

From power lunches and corporate gatherings to impromptu dinners out with the family, the wonderful variety found in St. Petersburg and Pinellas County restaurants is an added plus to living in a resort location that caters to visitors. There are casual eating spots to be found along the beaches, in the malls, and throughout the Tampa Bay region. There is international cuisine prepared by some of the finest chefs in the world and served in the elegant surroundings of our hotels and resorts. And, especially for boaters, waterside dining includes many local favorites and the only McDonald's in the United States with a dock!

WTSP-TV

There are four television stations covering local news in the Tampa Bay region, but WTSP-TV, Channel 10, is the only one licensed to St. Petersburg and headquartered in Pinellas County. WTSP-TV is owned and operated by Gannett Television, a broadcast company known nation-wide for commitment to the communities served. The station is the CBS affiliate designated for the ten-county Tampa Bay area, but WTSP-TV's ties to Pinellas County are strong.

The 10 News team of news anchors Reginald Roundtree and Sue Zelenko, and Chief Meteorologist Dick Fletcher is very active in the Pinellas County community. Frequent participation in such fields as local education, the environment and social and family services keep the team in contact and informed with the important issues facing all of Tampa Bay. This serves each of the broadcasters well in reporting on news and developments pertaining to the area.

Pinellas County's vulnerability to hurricanes and severe tropical weather is exceptionally important to all residents, which is why the station maintains an unmatched commitment to weather coverage and forecasting. WTSP is the only station with 10 Double Doppler radar, a powerful weather-monitoring tool that gives WTSP a significant edge in warning viewers as potentially dangerous weather moves across the area.

10 Double Doppler isn't the only technological advantage that WTSP can claim over the competition. The station is committed to continual and substantial investment in the very latest forecasting technology. Far too much rides on dependable and accurate weather forecasting, and WTSP is determined to be the best source of weather information for all of west central Florida.

WTSP-TV's ties and commitment to Pinellas County are all evident, but the ability to cover the big news stories anywhere in the Southeast United States also benefits local viewers. The station's large, experienced news team is also affiliated with the Florida News Network for fast and in-depth coverage of breaking news across the state.

Additionally, ties to Gannett's USA TODAY gives the station unique and fascinating insight to national and international stories that have impact on the Tampa Bay region.

WTSP-TV's pride, commitment and unique abilities to reach out of the area to cover news that is important to all Florida residents make the station an invaluable resource for all residents of Pinellas County and Tampa Bay.

Evening News Anchors, Reginald Roundtree (above) and Sue Zelenko (below) discuss the next broadcast with members of the production team.

www.wtsp.com

TIME WARNER COMMUNICATIONS

Recognized as a technological leader in providing information and entertainment services, Time Warner Communications provides cable television, high-speed Internet access and 24-hour local news and weather to a growing area of West Central Florida.

In Pinellas County, the company provides state-of-the-art digital multimedia service to over 300,000 homes and it employs over 800 highly skilled customer service specialists, technicians and engineers. Time Warner's sophisticated fiber optic network is one of the most complex in the country – delivering over 200 channels of video programming and lightning-fast Internet access via Road Runner Online Service. In addition to Road Runner service deployment in 1997, Time Warner introduced their exclusive, local 24-hour, 7-day/week news channel – Bay New 9. Local residents can tune to Bay News 9 anytime day or night for the latest local news and weather. For total weather information, Channel 109 (Bay News 9 Weather NOW), provides continuous, 24-hour reports.

Committed to providing quality service is only the beginning. The company is committed to the communities it serves in Pinellas County and is actively involved in partnerships, projects and special event sponsorships that are meaningful to the residents of the County. The company's number one priority is Education. Time Warner has taken a leadership role in providing resources for Enterprise Village and the Pinellas County Education Foundation, along with providing complimentary cable service and Cable in the Classroom programming. Students in Pinellas County also stay connected to the world through Road Runner's high-speed Internet access.

Time Warner's Employee Volunteer Program provides thousands of volunteer hours to various projects throughout the County. In addition, The United Way of Pinellas County is beneficiary to strong employee, corporate and leadership giving campaigns and serves as the cornerstone of the company's philanthropic support.

Time Warner community partners also include Ruth Eckerd Hall, the Bayfront Center, Mahaffey Theater Foundation and the Largo Cultural Center. The organizations supported by the company are broad-based and reflect the diverse nature of the communities in Pinellas County.

Time Warner Communications is committed to the growth of Pinellas County and is ready to expand and fulfill the growing needs of its consumers.

THE BUSINESS JOURNAL SERVING GREATER TAMPA BAY

The width and breadth of business booming in the Tampa Bay area is indicative of an economy that encompasses a diverse range of commercial interests - everything from high tech to service sector to international trade. Keeping up with the ebb and flow of this rapidly changing information is the domain of The Business Journal Serving Greater Tampa Bay.

As Tampa Bay's only weekly newspaper devoted exclusively to business, the Journal has become a vital tool for small and medium-sized business owners and executives interested in health care, manufacturing, technology, real estate, medical and other news pertinent to the economy. More than 213,000 adult readers utilize the Journal each month to track events, trends and breaking news.

Each week the Business Journal spotlights top stories affecting Bay area businesses, along with such popular features as Bridging the Bay; Strategies, regular reporter columns, and a front section packed with breaking business news. The Business Journal also publishes specific business listings that rank local companies by a number of economic factors. These lists are then complied into a comprehensive Book of Lists that is released once each year.

As one of 41 local business newspapers owned by American City Business Journals, The Business Journal Serving Greater Tampa Bay has an editorial staff of more than 14 professional journalists. With national resources to draw upon, The Business Journal provides succinct reporting of outside influences effecting Tampa Bay businesses. For local input, the newspaper also maintains bureaus in both Pinellas and Hillsborough counties.

As an active member of the community, The Business Journal sponsors a variety of special events throughout the year

www.bizjournals.com/tampabay

Networks & Area Shopping

skating rink. Anchor stores at both Countryside and at Tyrone include Burdines, Dillard's, JCPenney and Sears. The next largest mall is Clearwater Mall at U.S. Highway 19 North and Gulf-to-Bay Boulevard (SR 60). Further south on U.S. 19 at Park Boulevard in Pinellas Park, ParkSide Mall counts about 46 stores with room for more surrounding its 60 by 120-foot ice skating rink.

A revitalized Gateway Mall on Dr. MLKing (Ninth) Street North in St. Petersburg features Target, Eckerds, TJ Maxx, and Office Depot. And Central Avenue, the pedestri-

continued on page 234

Convenient shopping can be enjoyed in stores such as these at Coconut Grove (Above) near downtown and Tyrone Square Mall (Below) in St. Petersburg.

TYRONE SQUARE MALL

Simply the Best Shopping There Is

For over 28 years, Tyrone Square has been the most powerful shopper magnet for the majority of Pinellas County. The super-regional shopping center, anchored by Borders Books and Music, Burdines, Dillard's, JCPenney, Sears and AMC Theatres is the home to more than 170 of the country's finest specialty stores and restaurants including Ann Taylor Loft, Gap, Gap Kids, Victoria's Secret and Tia's Tex Mex. The exceptional variety of merchandise and entertainment allows shoppers to find just what they are looking for.

As one of over 220 properties across the United States managed by Simon Property Group, Tyrone Square's exceptional amenities reflect the advantages of a premier shopping destination. The Simon Marketplace (information center) provides shoppers with helpful assistance including Simon gift certificates which are accepted at more than 220 shopping centers nationwide, *S* magazine — a free exclusive Simon Magazine filled with shopping, fashion and time saving tips, tourist information — including a store directory and special mall discounts as well as money-saving offers through MALLPeRKS, Simon's exclusive members only reward program. MALLPeRKS allows shoppers to earn points toward discounts on mall merchandise, special offers, even travel.

Additionally, as an added convenience, Tyrone Square offers access to mall information from anywhere through the use of its Direct Connect Shopping Line and web site. Both contain information on mall events, hours, stores, job openings and directions. The web site, shopsimon.com, also provides shoppers with store leasing information, MALLPeRKS members account information including rewards offered by the mall, Simon Gift Certificates and *S* magazine home delivery.

Tyrone Square is close to the beach and easy to reach, located at the intersections of Tyrone Boulevard and 66th Street, the mall's strategic location serves as a popular shopping destination for both locals and tourists alike.

Simon, Simply the Best Shopping There Is!

www.shopsimon.com

VINTAGE ANTIQUES & EMPORIUM ANTIQUE MALL

A trip through Vintage Antiques & Emporium Antique Mall is a bit like a day at one of Florida's many theme parks – so much to see, so many discoveries to make. This is no ordinary antique shop. Vintage Antiques offers an eclectic selection of objects d'art that range from the sublimely elegant to the ridiculously simple.

The 15,000 square foot "Multi-Dealer Mall" is the showcase for Kathie and Peter Schuckert's endless travels around the globe searching for the unusual. The results are a improbable aggregation of decorative items, European and reproduction furniture, architectural artifacts, and assorted items that include oriental, nautical, kitchenware, glassware, deco, a fantastic selection of Hummels from Germany and an amazing collection of Coca-Cola paraphernalia.

The labyrinth of individual rooms and grottoes, each filled with a particular genre of collectible, inexorably leads to Vintage Antiques newest addition, a back room filled with "Big Toys for Little Boys", although one immediately suspects the boys interested in these artifacts may not be so little. A magnificent bar of immense proportions is the centerpiece for a wildly accentuated wonderland of statues and shtick, definitely toys for boys – and girls – of all ages.

The concept for Vintage Antiques has come about as an evolution of the Schuckert's own personal collecting skills and a home which eventually ran out of room. Deciding to turn the art of collecting into a business led the Schuckert's to Vintage Antiques current incarnation in St. Petersburg.

Customers come from all over the world in search of collectibles for their homes, offices or friends who appreciate something more. It will take the better part of a day to fully grasp just how extraordinary Vintage Antiques & Emporium Antique Mall truly is. And better yet, it's free, open seven days a weeks with no long lines waiting to get in, so there's no excuse not to stop by and see "The Best of Tampa Bay."

PARKSIDE

The City of Pinellas Park is located in the heart of Pinellas County, and ParkSide is surely the heart of Pinellas Park. In 1997, John Hancock Life Insurance Company initiated multi-million dollar renovations at ParkSide, which have transformed the two-level mall into one of Florida's most exciting new shopping and entertainment experiences. There is something for everyone, including a spectacular ice skating rink.

ParkSide is located on the corner of U.S. Highway 19 North and Park Boulevard. This busy intersection offers a combined annual average of 110,000 cars per day, with easy access from I-275. There are over 43,000 households with an annual income in excess of $50,000 residing within a 7-mile radius of ParkSide. Over 1,000 new apartments are being constructed within 3 miles of the mall.

The ice skating rink, located in the center of the mall on the lower level, offers skating classes through the Tampa Bay Skating Academy. ParkSide boasts its own precision ice-skating team as well as a "Learn to Skate Hockey class." There are public skating sessions for adults only and children. A party room is available for private birthday parties.

Specially themed courtyards and fun game areas are located in front of the three major department stores - Dillard's, the JCPenney Outlet Store and Wards, where exciting, weekly events are held for the entire family. Exterior renovations to the mall entrances give the mall a bright, inviting look.

A 16-screen megaplex movie theater provides a state-of-the-art movie experience complete with stadium seating, surround sound and the latest in technical advances. Access from within the mall and from the exterior give the ParkSide shopper the convenience of enjoying a movie, shopping, and enjoying lunch or dinner in the 200-seat Food Court, which over looks the ice rink, while the kids are skating!

ParkSide offers a variety of services at the Customer Service center, which include a facsimile machine, copy machine, rental of "Frog Strollers" and wheelchairs, and the sale of mall gift certificates. Gift Certificates are sold in denominations of $10, $25 and $50 and are good for any purchase made at any store at ParkSide. Information on special events and job opportunities is also available at the Customer Service Center.

Weekly special events include beauty pageants, entertainment for children, auto shows, sports card and memorabilia shows, school exhibits, blood drives, and a variety of exhibitions and community events. Divaris Property Management Corporation manages ParkSide. Divaris Real Estate maintains an office on-site at ParkSide.

www.parksidemall.com

Above: A favorite with visitors are the shops at John's Pass Village, Madeira Beach. Left: Dessa's is one of many antique shops found on 4th St., 9th St. and Central Ave. in St Petersburg.

an-friendly street that connects Tropicana Field to the downtown St. Petersburg waterfront, has been rejuvenated with an eclectic mix of shopping, dining and after-hours favorite places, while BayWalk, our brand new 150,000-square-foot entertainment destination has added still another shopping and dining choice to St. Petersburg's downtown.

Clusters of antique shops can be found throughout Pinellas County, from Tarpon Avenue in picturesque Tarpon Springs to Central Avenue in St. Petersburg. Antiques abound in shops along Main Street in downtown Dunedin, on the Ninth Street and Fourth Street corridors north of downtown St. Petersburg, even in Belleair Bluffs just off Indian Rocks Road, and at frequent stops in Safety Harbor.

John's Pass Village at Madeira Beach is popular with visitors and residents alike for its variety of shops and restaurants along a boardwalk and waterfront setting. And for true bargain hunters, weekends at the Wagon Wheel Flea Market, billed as the "world's largest" flea market, can be not only entertaining, but also rewarding.

Our food markets include such grocery giants as Albertsons, Publix, Winn Dixie, Kash 'n' Karry and Food Lion. For home improvement supplies Home Depot and Lowe's compete for customers. Completing the picture of familiar names in new places are the discount chains of Big K-Mart, Wal-Mart and Target.

Bottom: Indoor ice skating is a cool amenity found at ParkSide Mall in Pinellas Park.

COUNTRYSIDE MALL

This is true shopping

The Countryside area of central Pinellas County and Clearwater was once the pastoral site of grazing cattle and orange groves. Dynamic growth, however, has replaced such sights with the signs of progress, and none is more progressive than Countryside Mall, the super-regional center for smart shopping in Clearwater and the surrounding Tampa Bay area.

Anchored by Burdines, Dillard's, JCPenney and Sears, this two-level shopping center has over 170 specialty stores, a 15-unit food court, and a multi-screen movie theater. Countryside Mall also features a center court indoor ice skating rink that has become a popular attraction to both permanent residents and visitors alike.

With an ambitious expansion program begun in 2000, Countryside Mall will ultimately boast more than one and one-quarter million square feet of shopping paradise for mall visitors. Strategically located on U.S. 19 between State Road 580 and Countryside Boulevard in Clearwater, the Mall sits almost in the center of one of the fastest growing metro areas in the U.S.

Considering the thousands of tourists visiting from both nearby beach and bay resorts, the average Countryside customer has a household income well above the metro average. From Tarpon Springs to the north, to Bellair, Indian Rocks and north St. Petersburg to the west and south, Countryside Mall is in the heart of Pinellas County's shopping action.

While the unique mix of retail, leisure and entertainment facilities have combined to make Countryside Mall an outstanding destination, continuing improvements and expansion represent the leadership position the Mall enjoys in the community. Extensive renovations to the indoor ice skating rink, for example, further upgrades its appeal to the many residents and visitors who, while enjoying a tropical lifestyle, prefer sports and leisure activities more suited to colder climates.

In addition to its physical facilities, Countryside Mall is also a center for the nearby communities because of a wealth of ongoing activities that support many of the area's social and charitable organizations. Whether as a place to shop or a fun place to gather, Countryside Mall has proven itself to be a place for all ages and all seasons.

Although the grazing cattle and orange groves are gone, Countryside Mall has replaced them with a pastime more in keeping with modern America – shopping. And at Countryside Mall, this is *true* shopping.

ST. PETERSBURG/CLEARWATER AREA CONVENTION & VISITORS BUREAU

Florida's Beach

Business suits or swim suits. Ties or tie-dye. Gourmet dinners by candlelight, or a hot dog and soda at the ballpark. The alternatives never seem to end for visitors to Florida's Beach. Perhaps that's what makes Pinellas County so special.

The area's superb year-round weather, sparkling blue waters, and pristine white-sand beaches have long attracted those wishing to escape cold-weather climates and the hectic pace of less relaxing areas. Tourism is the driving force of the area's economy, drawing more than 4.54 million overnight visitors each year, directly responsible for over $2.3 billion in expenditures annually and accounting for more than 66,000 jobs.

The area organization responsible for maintaining this vital economic engine is the St. Petersburg/Clearwater Area Convention & Visitors Bureau. The CVB is the countywide tourism management and marketing organization responsible for developing and promoting Pinellas County as a leisure, business, convention, conference, sports and film production destination.

Through a broad, innovative, and industry-leading variety of efforts, the CVB has helped provide the area with its ninth straight year of record visitation.

One such example is the Bureau's innovative website. The CVB was the first Visitors Bureau in the nation to offer not only destination information to potential visitors on the Web, but to provide a means of booking accommodations online.

With nearly 25 percent of all visitation to the area related to business meetings or conferences, the CVB has increased its marketing focus to this growing sector, expanding its services to aid the businesses and organizations considering meeting in or holding an event in the area. Through the CVB's efforts, the number of meetings in the area has increased more than 300 percent.

The bureau's over $9.5 million marketing budget, including a $5 million advertising budget, is among the highest in Florida and the country. In fact, it is larger than many state tourism promotion budgets. This budget is funded by a Tourist Development Tax levied on visitor accommodations (hotels, motels, condominiums, campgrounds, etc.) that are rented for a period of six months or less. These tax revenues are used exclusively for marketing to prospective tourists and promotion of Pinellas County and its communities.

With the area enjoying an ever-growing international reputation, the CVB maintains international offices in the U.K., Germany, and Canada; and directs its efforts in Latin America through an office in Miami.

www.floridasbeach.com

Chapter 10
Beaches & Resorts

HERB SNITZER

The Beaches

of Pinellas County,
give new meaning
to the phrase
"unwind and relax"...

TY HESTON

They are something you can count on when the world gets tough and you want to feel the sand under your feet, see tall patches of protective sea oats sway in the breeze, hear the sound of a gentle surf punctuated by a seagull's call, or be amazed at the sandpipers who scurry away from your path as you reach for yet another shell that has washed ashore.

The beaches are postcards brought to life with people jogging, walking, or stretched out on beach towels, their backs to the sun, and children creating fortresses of sand turned out of paper-cup molds, and couples exchanging marriage vows at sunset.

Sunsets at the beach are truly awesome sights that accompany so many perfect days. In a final show of color they render a blue sky gold and amber, topaz and pink, lavender and, when atmospheric conditions are just right, an emerald green. This "flash of green" is an elusive mirage that appears very briefly, though brilliantly, the moment the sun goes below the horizon. There are scientific explanations for the phenomenon that is even more pronounced here at sea level, but few have actually witnessed it.

Spectators often applaud a sunset, especially if they are in a casual restaurant, bar or lounge with at least a glimpse of the western horizon. It is quite a show and it signals the beginning of nightlife on the beaches. Beach bars with thatched roofs are the gathering places for visitors and locals alike. And you don't have to wait long before you'll hear someone with a guitar and wearing a Hawaiian shirt do the vocal of a Jimmy Buffett song. Buffet is not a native of Tampa Bay, but his music is as much a part of being at the beach as a SPF 15 sunscreen.

Several public access points are located along the beaches with metered parking spaces close by. Guests who choose one of the many resorts, condos, motels and hotels on the west side of Gulf Boulevard have beach access directly at their doorstep, while those staying on the east side need only to cross the street to reach the beach. By Florida law, the entire coastline is open to the public; therefore long walks are not only possible but also popular.

As a vacationland, St. Petersburg and the beaches are truly enhanced by water and the incredible variety of things there are to do. There are dolphin-watch cruises and sailboat trips, leisurely lunch and dinner cruises, scuba diving adventures, and not to be missed, the excitement of casino gambling aboard one of the pleasure boats that venture into international waters of the Gulf. Deep sea fishing party boats and private charters go out daily and each May marks the beginning of the Suncoast Tarpon Roundup, a 70-day annual tournament along 70-miles of coastline from Anclote Key to New Pass on Florida's west coast.

Pinellas County has 400 miles of shoreline, including 35 miles of beach. The Gulf is generally calm, making it ideal for swimming, yet there are enough breezes for windsurfing and parasailing. Boat rentals are readily available as well as jet skis and wave runners.

We have nearly year-round sunshine, ideal temperatures and attract 4.5 million tourists and visitors each year making tourism the largest and most important industry in Pinellas County. According to the St. Petersburg-Clearwater Convention and Visitors Bureau there are 25,131 accommodation units in all of Pinellas. This includes rooms in 73 hotels, 235 motels, and 79 rental condominiums. In addition there are approximately 1,800 restaurants here.

Winter is still the primary time of year for most visitors to come to Florida, but a summer season exists as well. Each May a huge, outdoor beach festival weekend begins the summer season with a line up of food, entertainment and sports events such as The Taste of the Beaches, the Madeira Gulf Beach Triathlon, and the Bud Light Pro-Am Beach Volleyball Series.

Of course, you can live at the beach and thousands do. The nine cities and towns that form the beach communities of Pinellas County are connected by one major road, Gulf Boulevard, which extends from Pass-A-Grille to Sand Key. Clearwater Beach is part of the city of Clearwater and is included in another section of this book.

ST. PETERSBURG / CLEARWATER CVB

TY HESTON

Beaches & Resorts

St. Pete Beach

The seven-mile beachfront that is one of the most popular vacation destinations in the world is also the front yard of St. Pete Beach, a city of approximately 10,000 permanent residents. It is connected to St. Petersburg by the St. Petersburg Beach Causeway at the north and the Pinellas Bayway to the south where there is direct access to I-275.

As far back as the 1830's Cuban fishermen camped on the beaches of Long Key. In fact Pass-A-Grille, the historic district that encompasses the southern end of the island, probably got its name from those fisherman who smoked and salted their catches on the beach before returning to Cuba. Pass-a-Grille was the first established town on Florida's West coast barrier islands and is a registered National Historic District.

St. Pete Beach is composed of three islands, the largest being Long Key, surrounded by the Gulf of Mexico, Tampa Bay and the Intracoastal Waterway. In 1957 it became St. Petersburg Beach through consolidation of four independent communities and in 1994 shortened its name to the more popular St. Pete Beach.

The picturesque community of Pass-A-Grille is at the southern tip of St. Pete Beach. Mapmakers recorded the pass as Pass-aux-Grillard as early as 1841, and the island was first settled in 1884. In 1905 the St. Petersburg trolley service extended its tracks to nearby Gulfport and ran a ferry service to the beach. By 1919 the first bridge to connect the mainland with any barrier island opened, which enabled the people of St. Petersburg to live on the island and commute to the city.

Pass-A-Grille has no condominiums or high-rise buildings keeping it a unique slice of old Florida. The peninsula is only two blocks wide and features a historical museum and 22 historic structures including the first homestead dating back to 1886.

The Don CeSar Resort & Spa is the beginning of several blocks of some of the finest accommodations to be found anywhere. When built in 1927, the resort positioned the island of St. Pete Beach as one of the leading tourist areas in the Gulf Coast a distinction that remains today.

continued on page 248

243

THE DON CESAR BEACH RESORT & SPA

The Pink Lady of St. Pete Beach sounds like the title of an aria for good reason. The Moorish-Mediterranean castle bears the name of the hero in the 17th century opera La Maritana – Don CeSar. It's therefore no surprise that the lyrics inspired by the Don CeSar Beach Resort & Spa have been captured by travel writers since it opened in 1928, but the melody, like the structure, is unique.

This is a song sung different on purpose. It revels in chords unusual, both tropical and yet old-world European. The Don, as it is affectionately known, sings its way into the hearts of travelers by building on its elegance, offering the unexpected and proving that a renaissance-laden past can totally accept a high-tech future. The Don is a blending of these things and much more.

Remaining aloof from the standardization of modern hotel chains, the Don CeSar Beach Resort & Spa is free to be what it needs to be: an intricate boutique of rooms and suites, boardwalk shops and world-class restaurants. The service, much like the setting, is a masterpiece. Expect the unexpected.

Consider, for example, a call to confirm reservations and inquire about what other needs might be fulfilled – a car reservation, tee time, tickets to upcoming events. Consider the Chef's Table in the Four Diamond rated Maritana Grille, an intimate, private dining area located in the main kitchen where the chef and culinary team provide a potpourri of specially selected and prepared food and wine. And this is but the opening stanza. The Don CeSar's international spa pampers in European methodologies that invigorate and innovate.

Accommodations are equally unusual. For those seeking a beach home away from home, the 70-suite Beach House offers one bedroom suites complete with full kitchen, living room and balcony overlooking the Gulf. The Don CeSar itself holds 275 guest rooms, including 43 spacious suites and two luxury penthouses.

When work needs to be mingled with pleasure, the Don offers 39,000 square feet of function space for groups as large as 750 or as intimate as 10. Two ballrooms and seven executive boardrooms are available, plus a Conventions Services Department attuned to orchestrating the most creative meeting needs.

But creativity is what the Don CeSar is all about. First run movies at the pool with underwater speakers. Kids, Ltd. provides ages 5 to 12 with supervised games and activities. And miles of white sand beaches awaiting a footprint.

There are memories here waiting to be made, indelibly different, deliciously unique. The Don CeSar is simply a song that, once sung, will pleasantly haunt the mind forever.

www.doncesar.com

TY HESTON

TRADEWINDS ISLAND RESORTS

An island nestled within an island. Paradise redefined within paradise.

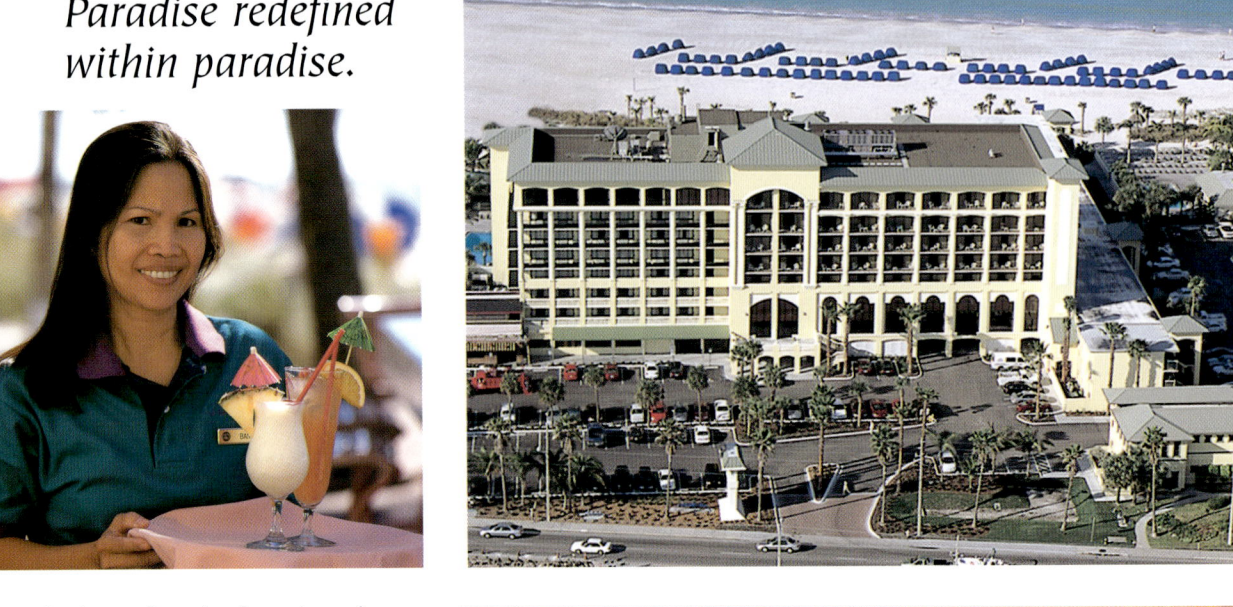

A place where business is a pleasure and pleasure is always at hand. What sounds too good to be true is, in reality, the trilogy of the TradeWinds Island Resorts, St. Pete Beach's ultimate getaway.

The TradeWinds are a larger than life canvas upon which the masterpiece is presented. They are a painting encompassing both tropical imagination and practical necessities. Businessmen come to do business. Families come for fun. They all find that the TradeWinds are art for the soul.

The Island Grand. The Sandpiper. The Sirata Beach. The trio representing the TradeWinds Island Resorts provides 35 acres of beachfront beauty, each inhabiting their own stylistic realm, yet a part of the whole. They are as divergent as the needs of those they serve, whether groups conventioning or newlyweds hiding away.

The TradeWinds have an array of contemporary facilities ranging from intimate tropical chic to ballroom masterpieces - a total of 61,500 square feet of meeting space for as few as 50 or as many as 1,000. Accommodations are equally special, with 630 rooms and 480 full suites, each with its own brand of TradeWinds uniqueness.

That uniqueness is called service, and the TradeWinds service is legendary. From people to amenities, there is a culture of hospitality that is measurable. The TradeWinds are not just hotels, they are homes. The staff is family. Employees will literally smile their way into the heart of the most seasoned and travel-weary guest. The smile says welcome and the proof just keeps coming.

Each room, for example, has its own refrigerator, coffee maker, and desk. Each meeting and conference has seasoned professionals who are dedicated to doing nothing more than making the business experience a complete and total success. Call it pampering. Call it comfort. By any other name, it's business as usual.

The reason is simple. Prior to 1999, the TradeWinds Resort was the largest employee owned resort in the world, and although now under new

TRADEWINDS ISLAND GRAND • SANDPIPER BEACH RESORT
SIRATA BEACH RESORT & CONFERENCE CENTER

ownership, the lessons learned are still applied liberally. Success breeds success, and the TradeWinds maintains an attitude of absolute can-do that does… and does.

What more can a guest ask? Silly question. Breezy gazebos, a waterway that meanders throughout the resort, four heated swimming pools, beachfront cabanas and hammocks, whirlpools and saunas, are all there for the enjoying. Not including, of course, miles of pristine white sand beaches and a Florida sun never accused of being shy.

For the sports inclined, year round leisure opportunities include preferential tee times at nearby golf clubs, tennis at the resort's four har-tru courts, or volleyball on the beach. A staff of more than a dozen professional recreational counselors can introduce guests to sailing, windsurfing, parasailing or fishing excursions. For groups, team-building activities and icebreakers are the counselor's specialty. Afterwards, the fitness center is staffed with personal trainers, while Body Works, the resort's on-site salon, pampers with aroma-therapy and massage.

And then there's the fun stuff. For kids, there's the KONK Club (Kids Only, No Kidding!), complete with Beaker, the TradeWinds' own mascot. For families, a fun shuttle connects all three of the TradeWinds resorts, and for a nominal fee, the Explorer Value Pass opens the doors to every recreational facility available, including use of the business center for fax, computer or Internet services.

Fuel for this fun is also abundant. Ten restaurants are sprinkled liberally throughout the resort with venues that range from absolute elegance to Key West casual. After fresh seafood and decadent desserts, relaxation runs the gamut from live entertainment, dancing or simply sampling a tropical drink at the piano bar.

At the end of the day, the TradeWinds Island Resorts certainly reflect the Island Grand's four-diamond reputation. Sometimes it's hard to believe the Island Grand, Sandpiper and Sirata Beach are only 25 interstate miles from Tampa International Airport. Paradise may be elusive, but this world-class resort threesome goes a long way to making it very, very accessible. ❋

www.tradewindsresort.com

247

Beaches & Resorts

Treasure Island

Treasure Island incorporates five separate islands into one city 1.3 square miles in size. It is both residential and touristy and has grown from a community of 320 in 1940 to a mature beach city of nearly 7,500. Treasure Island is immediately west of St. Petersburg, connected by a causeway from Central Avenue, and is home to four miles of wide, flat Gulf of Mexico beach that in part is owned by the city of St. Petersburg.

In the 1950's, a plan was formulated to consolidate many of the small towns established in the area into one large community. And like St. Pete Beach, this eventually led to the incorporation of Treasure Island in 1955.

Developers visualized the creation of man-made land masses with luxury homes on them, then realized those dreams when major landfill efforts created the Isle of Capri, Isle of Palms and Paradise Island, all part of the Treasure Island of today. The finger landfills became a building technique applied to most of the shoreline communities in Pinellas County, enabling homebuyers more waterfront choices than ever before.

John's Pass on the north end of Treasure Island and Blind Pass on the south provide boaters with fast and easy access to the Gulf of Mexico from Boca Ciega Bay. Along the main Gulf Boulevard, Treasure Island's many hotels and restaurants provide a Florida vacation atmosphere year round along with events such as the Taste of the Beaches food festival in April, and a weeklong Pirate Days extravaganza during the July 4th weekend.

The Treasure Island Tennis and Yacht Club organizes the Budweiser Cup, one of the largest sailing events in Florida, each year. And each February the St. Petersburg Shell Club sponsors a shell exhibit at Treasure Island, presented by private collectors. It is recognized by the national organization Conchologists of America as well as by the Smithsonian Museum.

There is over a mile-long sidewalk on the beach and a public boardwalk along Sunset Beach located on the south end of Treasure Island and the city has a complete range of public services including a parks and recreation department, a community center and a city transit system.

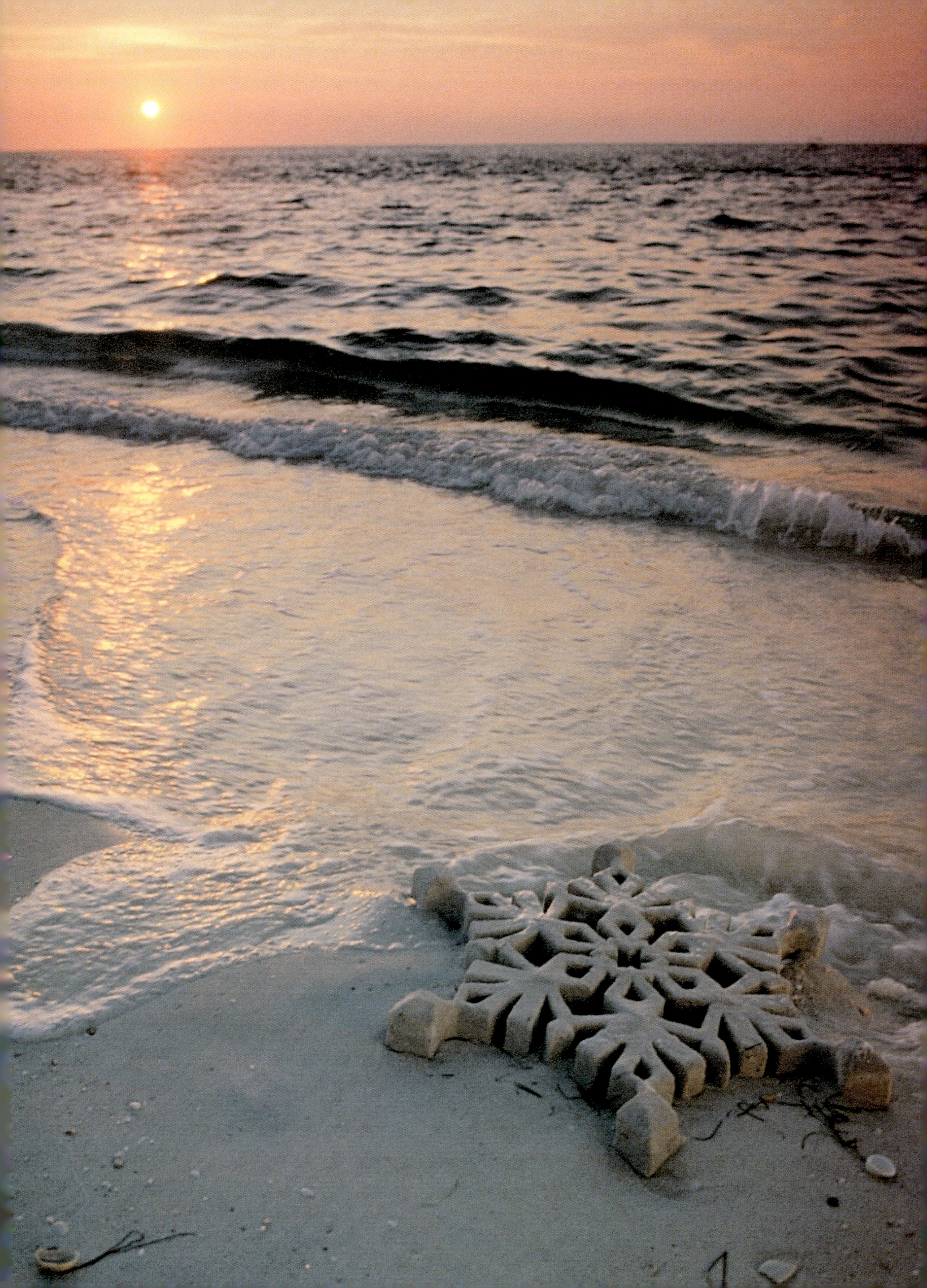

Beaches & Resorts

Madeira Beach

Madeira Beach began as a fishing village, and because of its location at John's Pass with direct access to the Gulf of Mexico, there is a large commercial and charter fishing fleet as well as casino cruises.

The city of just over 4,000 occupies a 1.5-mile stretch along the Gulf of Mexico and, like the other beach communities, the population more than doubles during the winter months as seasonal residents return to Florida. It connects to the mainland near St. Petersburg by a free causeway and to the other barrier islands by bridges.

Madeira Beach is widely known for the famous John's Pass Boardwalk Village, a quaint shopping district that overlooks John's Pass. Art galleries, restaurants, boutiques are located in the area and the boardwalk provides a scenic view of the waterfront. It is the site of several festivals and special events, including the John's Pass Seafood Festival in October, which draws more than 100,000 people each year.

John's Pass was created by the gale winds and tidal surge of a major hurricane that altered the entire area in September 1848. As for the seafood, more grouper is brought into John's Pass than any other place in the state of Florida.

Indian Rocks Beach

Indian Rocks Beach is less than three miles along the Gulf of Mexico and, like its neighboring barrier islands, waterfront property faces either the Gulf or the Intracoastal Waterway. At some points along this narrow piece of land you can view both bodies of water.

A quiet town of approximately 4,000, Indian Rocks Beach was initially developed in the 1920s as a weekend getaway destination for wealthy inland residents. Its 2.7 miles of beachfront are popular with all ages and between its array of motels and condominiums there are more than 20 beach accesses.

Despite its sleepy appearance, Indian Rocks Beach is home to some of the best-known restaurants along the Gulf Coast, and holds an Arts and Crafts Festival every November and April. The city's tourist population, especially in the winter months, is one of its greatest assets.

Left: The bridge connecting Treasure Island with Madeira Beach. Above: Shops at John's Pass Boardwalk Village.

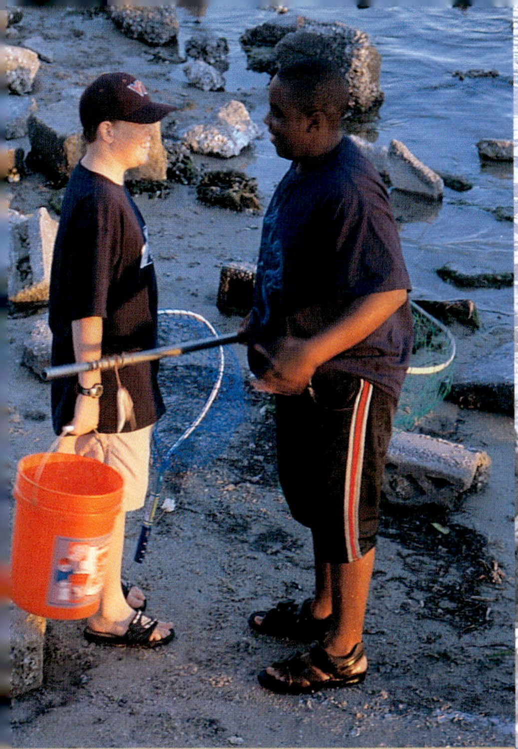
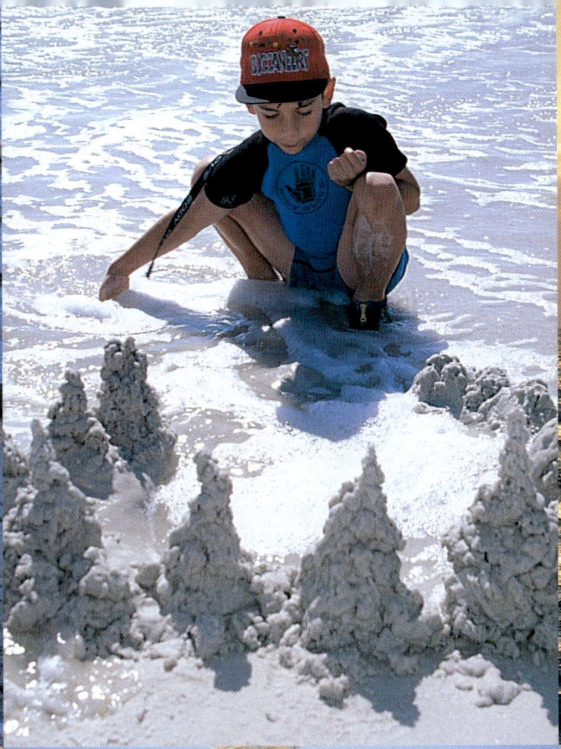
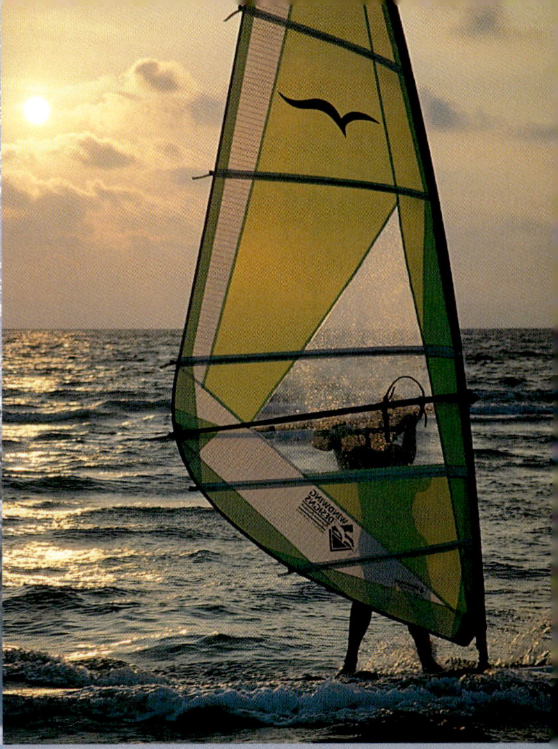
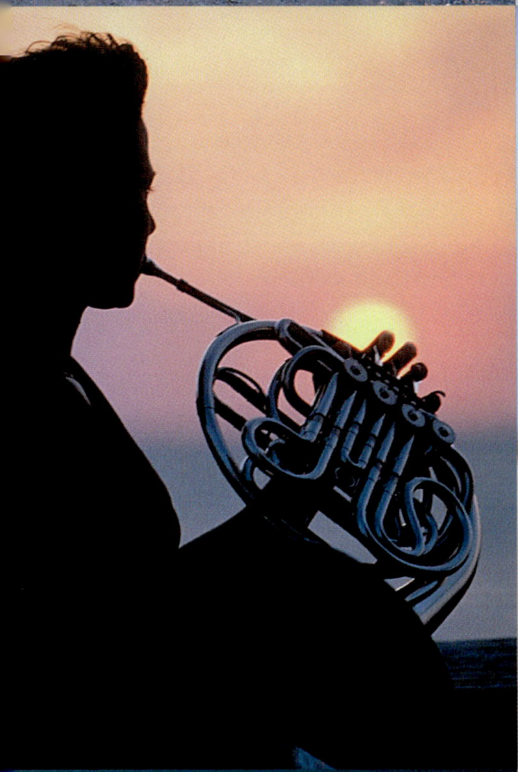
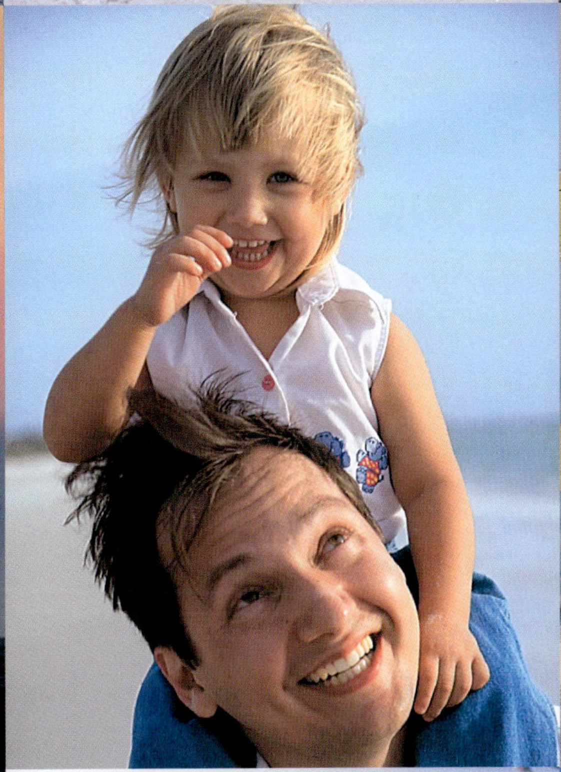
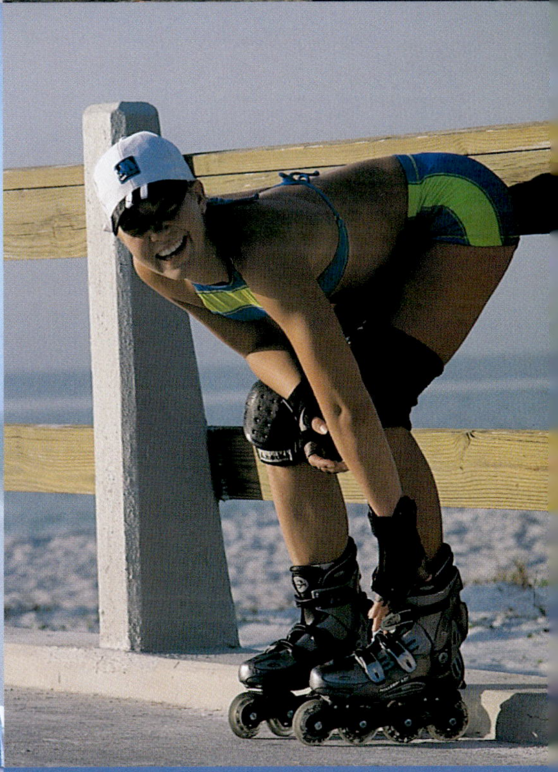
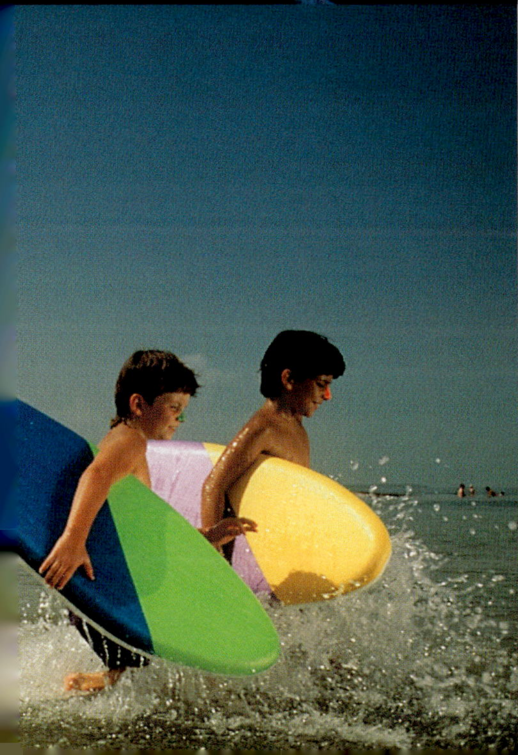
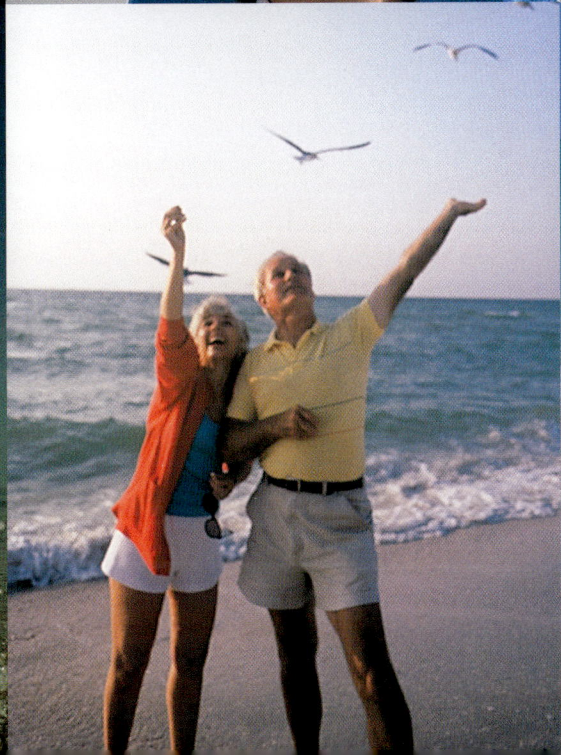
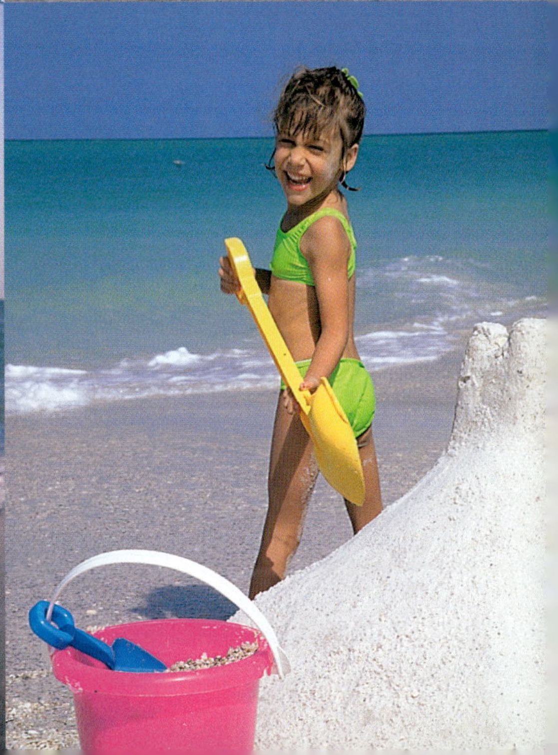

Beaches & Resorts

Redington Shores

This one-mile long community has a census population of 2,700 that also doubles during the winter season. It provides accommodations for tourists in the form of condominiums, hotels, motels and apartments.

Single-family homes have long been established in the quiet community that welcomes the winter influx of return visitors from England, Canada, France, Germany, Italy and Denmark. The community has some of the area's best restaurants with casual dining within walking distance to many area properties.

Several recreational and nature parks offer areas for cookouts, picnics, fishing, tennis and playgrounds for children, while avid fisherman seek out the Redington Long Pier which extends 1,021 feet into the gulf and is open 24 hours a day.

Belleair Beach

Belleair Beach is one of the northernmost communities on Sand Key. Chartered in 1950, it is two miles long and has a population of a little over 2,000. It borders Clearwater and Sand Key Park on the north side and Belleair Beach on the south.

Originally a "second home" location, Belleair Beach could be considered a bedroom community. Housing is primarily single-family homes with some condominiums and a couple of motels. Many of the condos are rented on a seasonal basis. There is no commercial property at all. Beaches are public, but access is private.

Redington Beach

This residential beachfront town of less than two square miles has a brand new skyline with the construction of a six-story, 214-unit condominium complex. The new Tides Beach Club fronts a quarter-mile of Gulf of Mexico beach in a town of approximately 1,700.

Yet the residential character of Redington Beach remains. Beaches are private with no public parking and the town has only three motels on its main road.

The popular pier at Redington Shores.

HERB SNITZER

Indian Shores

Indian Shores is a town of less than 1,500 with 2.65 miles of newly renourished sandy beach on the Gulf of Mexico. A number of public beach access parking areas are available and a public fishing area and playground are located on the Town Hall property.

Residential is primarily low to medium-rise condominiums and town houses with a sprinkling of single-family homes on the beach. Nothing may be constructed in Indian Shores that is more than five stories.

As a result of a winter population, which reaches 5,000, the town has a variety of shops and restaurants including Chinese, Spanish, Scandinavian and Italian, along with upscale to budget-priced seafood, steak and other menu items. Accommodations range from low-priced motels to high-end condos, offering short-term, long-term rentals and time-shares.

North Redington Beach

With nearly one mile of frontage on the Gulf of Mexico and a population of over 1,100, North Redington Beach offers a blend of single family homes, mid-rise condominiums, resort hotels, motels, restaurants and retail shops. There are several public accesses to the beach with curbside parking and no meters.

Many homes are owned by people from other countries and used for vacations. These are mostly on the inner bay waters with ready access to the Intracoastal Waterway where boating and fishing are popular pastimes.

continued on page 258

SUNCOAST SEABIRD SANCTUARY

The Gulf coast of Pinellas is abundant with birds not found in other climates, such as the white egret, brown pelican and cormorant. One place to not only see these species up close, but to contribute to their future, is at the Seabird Sanctuary.

This non-profit organization is dedicated to the "rescue, repair, recuperation and potential release" of rehabilitated, sick and injured wild birds and operates solely through public contributions. It is located directly on the beach at Indian Shores.

SHERATON SAND KEY RESORT

The poetry of Sand Key is written on endless white powder sand beaches with footprints as stanzas, rearranged endlessly by the rhythmic wash of blue-green waters, accentuated by a warm, tropical sun. Idyllic, this barrier island, this expression of paradise found. Such is the page upon which the Sheraton Sand Key Resort sits.

The panorama of beach and sky encompassing the Sheraton Sand Key Resort belies its proximity to the hustle and bustle of nearby Clearwater Beach, just across the channel. Adjacent to the Sand Key Park and Preserve, the 390-room resort is immersed in its own solitude, an ideal stress-free haven for work or play.

Like a verse rewritten and improved, the Sheraton Sand Key Resort's $7.5 million renovation had added amenities upon amenities for guests, conferences and meeting environments. As one of west central Florida's top meeting hotels, the resort now offers more than 24,000 square feet of conference space, including 14 meeting rooms and a 8,500 square foot ballroom.

Equally exceptional is the Sheraton Sand Key's staff, from chef to director of convention services, all adept at satisfying the most particular taste or need. Nationally recognized service is commonplace, from formal dining to high-tech meeting facilities. Consider, for example, the Sand Key Beach Club, an exclusive environment for senior executives offering private conference space, a full range of business services, membership to the Resort's state-of-the-art fitness facility, and access to a private rooftop hospitality suite overlooking the Gulf of Mexico.

Of course, families and fun have not been forgotten. When the beach does not beckon, there's the pool, whirlpool and children's pool, with a playground for organized children's activities. Lighted tennis courts, sailing, wind surfing and bicycle rentals are at hand. Over 30 shops are just steps away. Golf, fishing and boat rentals are within easy reach.

At day's end, guests unwind at the Suncoast Fitness Center for a sauna or massage. Then there's fine dining at award winning Rusty's. Try the Island Grille for casual cuisine or watch one of Florida's famous sunsets from the comfort of the Poolside Café and Turtle Bar. For just plain fun, there's the Mainstay Tavern. Excellent room service is also available, or snacks 24-hours a day from Bluewater Provisions

The cadence of life experienced at the Sheraton Sand Key Resort is made for memories. The sights, sounds and experiences of the key remain like prose for the soul, and whether visitors come for work or play, return is inevitable.

www.beachsand.com

TY HESTON

TY HESTON

TY HESTON

HERB SNITZER

Besides the well-populated islands that form our many beach communities, there are still more barrier islands. Three miles west and offshore of Tarpon Springs is Anclote Key State Preserve. It is the northernmost island off the Pinellas peninsula and you need a boat to get there. It offers beach lovers the beauty of an undeveloped, less-traveled shoreline though there are a few tables and barbecue grills, but no running water or other amenities.

Another northern barrier island state park, accessible by car, is Honeymoon Island. It is connected to the mainland by the Dunedin Causeway and features a popular beach and nature trail, plus facilities for fishing and picnicking.

West of Dunedin is 650-acre Caladesi Island State Park with a largely undisturbed beach on the Gulf of Mexico side and a dense mangrove shallow on the Bay side. The island is alternately covered with windswept dunes topped with sea grasses and pine, scrub palmetto and large, moss-draped oak trees. A concession store offers some snacks and supplies, while a ferry service from either Honeymoon Island from the north or the Clearwater docks from the south provides access for those without a boat.

Egmont Key is a three-mile island located halfway between

Above: Fort Dade at Egmont Key. Opposite top: The 650 acre Caladesi Island State Park west of Dunedin. Opposite bottom: Egmont Key, an island paradise south of St. Pete Beach.

Anna Maria Island in Manatee County and St. Pete Beach and is accessible only by boat. Egmont Key offers some of Florida's best beaches and also claims a 136-year-old working lighthouse and the ruins of Fort Dade. The ferry to this spot can be caught from John's Pass Village in Madeira Beach.

These unspoiled refuges are ideal for swimming, shelling, fishing, picnics and nature study. Caladesi Island is one of the last remaining undisturbed barrier islands on the Gulf Coast and was named the sixth best beach in the United States in a 1999 national study. The islands are also refuges to several rare and endangered birds.

ST. PETERSBURG / CLEARWATER CVB

TY HESTON

WESTIN INNISBROOK RESORT

No, it's not Scotland, but the rolling hills, lakes and woodlands certainly give the feel of the Highlands. So do the golf courses – one of the Westin Innisbrook Resort's signature attractions. Internationally known as a golf and conference destination, Innisbrook's four championship courses are laid out over 1,000 acres of terrain unusual for Florida.

The warm, hospitable style of the Innisbrook experience is apparent in its 689 suites, each featuring a fully equipped kitchen and private patio or balcony. The suites are linked to dining and conference facilities by climate controlled shuttles, and, of course, to Innisbrook's legendary links.

The Island course has tight fairways, abundant bunkers and intimidating water hazards. Highlands South features well-bunkered greens reminiscent of Pinehurst. Highlands North course promises tight fairways, placing a premium on accuracy. The par-71, Lawrence Packard-designed Copperhead course stretches 7,230 yards for tournament play. The Copperhead course hosts the PGA Tour's Tampa Bay Classic in 2000.

The Innisbrook Troon Golf Institute offers a year-round series of comprehensive instructional programs for all levels of play and features a variety of daily clinics, private instruction and three practice facilities. Innisbrook's Tennis and Racquet Center provides 11 HarTu tennis courts and three racquetball courts, locker rooms, exercise and fitness equipment and supervised fitness programs. The Recreation Center is designed with both parents and children in mind and includes a children's play area, miniature golf, video games, basketball and volleyball equipment and fishing rod and bicycle rentals.

For a little fun and relaxation, visit the Loch Ness pool and spa. Designed with a natural feel, the pool is located in the center of the resort in the midst of a three-acre fun park complete with water slides. The adult spa seats up to 36 people. Dining and entertainment take place at the resort's clubhouses and pool. Savor culinary delights in casual and formal settings and experience a level of service that is distinctly Innisbrook's.

Meetings and conferences from around the globe convene at the Westin Innisbrook Resort. With 36 conference rooms totaling over 85,000 square feet, these expansive facilities offer a professionally unique experience.

Westin Innisbrook Resort is located near Tarpon Springs, a charming Greek fishing and sponging community where sponge docks are loaded with shops and restaurants. Several beaches are only minutes away via the resort's complimentary shuttle service.

www.westin-innisbrook.com

Chapter 11
Around Pinellas County

Pinellas
County is one of the most desirable places to live in the nation says popular opinion, from market studies to the most casual observer…

CITY OF ST. PETERSBURG

Preceding pages: Photo taken from space shows Pinellas County and the barrier islands of the Gulf of Mexico, with Tampa Bay and Hillsborough County to the right. Above: An overpass on The Fred E. Marquis Pinellas Trail.

The Pinellas peninsula covers a land area of approximately 280 square miles, the second smallest county int the state of Florida. A population of approximately 900,000, makes it the most densely populated county in Florida. Ulmerton Road (SR 688) is often referred to as the dividing line between north and south Pinellas County. Not that we differ so much from place to place – we share the same county government services, public school system, county park facilities, and transportation networks. And we all enjoy the natural amenities that go along with living in a tropical paradise.

Like any other region that has experienced the tremendous growth that Pinellas County has, our cities and towns, because of their history, the people, and the various industries they attract, have characteristics that distinguish and separate them.

There are 24 incorporated cities and towns in Pinellas County. Nine of them make up most of the barrier islands and the beaches along the Gulf of Mexico that are so familiar to sun worshippers. The largest city in Pinellas, of course, is St. Petersburg and even we have a municipal beach on Treasure Island. Clearwater is the next largest city and the county seat. It also has a beach of its own.

There are fourteen more cities and towns, including Clearwater, plus a large area of unincorporated Pinellas, that are neighbors to St. Petersburg and the beaches. All are important to Pinellas County. Let us show you around.

Clearwater

Clearwater, the county seat of Pinellas County, was incorporated as Clearwater Harbor in 1891. Twenty-four years later it was chartered as a municipality and now, with a population of approximately 105,000 it is the second largest city in Pinellas County, occupying 26.4 square miles on the highest bluffs along Florida's west coast, standing 30 to 75 feet above sea level.

The city was originally the site of Fort Harrison where wounded soldiers recuperated after fighting Indians on the Florida frontier. The U.S. Army opened the fort in 1841 during the Second Seminole War. It closed in less than six

The award-winning Pinellas Trail is a gleaming example of the Rails-To-Trails program. The popular trail winds for nearly 50 miles through scenic Pinellas County, from St. Petersburg to Tarpon Springs.

months and the area was opened to settlers. It's namesake, the Fort Harrison Hotel is home to the Church of Scientology which has recently added another component to its expanding headquarters in downtown Clearwater.

From downtown, the city stretches north to the large planned community of Countryside and its surrounding environs that offer residents a country club, golf course, tennis courts, swimming pool, a community park, churches, schools and a two-story shopping mall. To the east are the waters of Old Tampa Bay and the Courtney Campbell Causeway leading directly to Tampa International Airport.

Also on the east, just north of St. Petersburg by way of the Bayside Bridge, is Ruth Eckerd Hall, one of the area's finest venues for the performing arts. The hall is part of the Richard B. Baumgardner Center for Performing Arts and is noted for its excellent sightlines and the quality of its acoustics for audiences of up to 2,173 in a continental seating arrangement. The PACT Institute for the Performing Arts at Ruth Eckerd provides a varied year-round educational program in theater, music and dance.

Clearwater's endorsement of the arts is evident during its annual four-day Clearwater Jazz Holiday, which draws thousands of visitors and residents alike to hear the best of jazz in the outdoor, waterfront setting of Coachman Park downtown. And the Octagon Arts Center, actually a church sanctuary, serves as an outreach to the community for the visual and performing arts while its mezzanine functions as an art gallery.

Many know the area because Clearwater's Jack Russell Stadium is the spring training home of the Philadelphia Phillies. For community recreation and amateur sports competition, the Long Center in Clearwater, has the only indoor Olympic-size pool on the west coast of Florida. The multi-use center is world renowned for hosting a variety of athletic trainings and competitions and included in the 150-thousand square foot facility is a 25-yard instructional pool that is handicapped accessible.

On the west, Clearwater connects to its own beach and the rest of the Gulf of Mexico beaches via the scenic Memorial Causeway. Along the way is the Clearwater Marine Aquarium where visitors can observe the rehabilitation and care of rescued dolphins, otters and sea turtles. The aquarium also offers Marine Life Adventures, an interactive marine experience in Clearwater Bay.

Opposite: The City of Clearwater is proud of its new Roundabout, dramatic Beach Entryway and Pier 60 Park.
Above and below: Open year round, beachfront settings like these at Clearwater Beach offer nonstop fun along the water's edge.

Always a popular vacation destination, Clearwater has more than 250 hotels and motels. The Harborview Center opened in 1996 in the heart of downtown and supports this thriving business of tourism with convention and meeting facilities. Clearwater's Fun 'n Sun Festival is the city's annual salute to Spring, and an invitation to browse through art shows, attend auctions, concerts, parades and sporting events.

More than 100 boats set sail from the Clearwater Yacht Club to Key West for the annual Conch Quest Regatta, one of Florida's longest, best attended point-to-point distance sailboat races. The Kahlua Cup International Yacht Races also sail from the yacht club, an annual event that draws racing yachts in four classes from around the world. While the Clearwater Municipal Marina has the largest fishing fleet on the west coast of Florida.

Clearwater's Beach was ranked "best city beach" by Conde Nast Traveler and consistently ranks among the best American beaches. This wide, sun-drenched, inviting stretch of sand and water is popular during Spring break and is the sandy court for the annual Miller Lite AVP Beach Volleyball Tournament. Nearby is Pier 60 Park, a popular gathering spot that features nightly musical entertainment.

While tourism is an important element in the economy of the area, Clearwater welcomes new industry and is the address for several high-tech businesses, including the corporate headquarters of Information Management Resources, a computer technology company, located on a 14-acre complex on the eastern part of downtown.

continued on page 273

HERB SNITZER

IMRGLOBAL CORP.

Corporations today are faced with a multiplicity of new challenges – challenges like finding the best ways to leverage emerging technologies, addressing the threats posed by new competitors and becoming flexible enough to deal with the certainty of change. These are the challenges that have driven IMRglobal Corp. (IMRglobal) to become a business solutions provider in an IT-dependent world and to amass a suite of solutions designed to meet customers' complete business and technology needs.

IMRglobal helps customers around the world realize competitive business advantages by adding value through innovative, cost-effective IT solutions. Founded in 1988, IMRglobal has grown through the successful delivery of solutions for Fortune 500 and Global 2000 companies – solutions developed in IMRglobal's network of offices and state-of-the-art, ISO 9001-certified software delivery centers. The company combines strategic and tactical approaches to provide end-to-end business and technology solutions.

IMRglobal has the vision to identify, develop and implement the next wave of IT solutions that will help advance customers' businesses, while at the same time optimize the return on existing technology investments. The company's expertise is integrating new systems with old systems, Web-enabling legacy systems, and designing and implementing front ends that seamlessly interact with back ends.

In just over a decade, IMRglobal has grown to more than 3,000 employees with global operations on 4 continents and in 7 countries. The Clearwater, Florida-based company's success is based on a clear vision of the business and technology solutions customers need as well as on the ability to deliver results that help customers establish and maintain a competitive edge.

With business expertise in key industries, including financial services, healthcare, government, utilities, retail and manufacturing/distribution, IMRglobal provides a wide variety of technology solutions.

Business Technology Consulting, for example, aligns the customer's business and IT systems strategies to identify the technology choices that will best support objectives and goals. E-business Services include planning, designing, developing and implementing e-business initiatives.

In the Application Management suite of solutions, Application Development provides customized applications to automate business processes using rapid application development (RAD) and component-based development (CBD) methods. Application Modernization often involves performing conversions, migrations and updates

268

for legacy systems, including mining existing systems for viable components to be used in updated systems. Application Maintenance provides maintenance and support for enterprise information systems, thus freeing the company's IT staff to focus on mission-critical projects.

Depending on the client's specific needs, any or all of these services can be a part of the overall solution.

These end-to-end services are supplemented by traditional IT-related professional services, which are offered to help address customers' short-term IT resourcing needs. These services, which include readiness assessments, requirements analyses and staff augmentation, enable IMRglobal to accomplish two very important goals – optimizing the productivity of IMRglobal's billable resources and, at the same time, establishing credibility with new clients.

IMRglobal's suite of products and end-to-end services have been carefully assembled to help customers throughout the world successfully untangle interwoven business and information processing challenges. And, based on IMRglobal's years of IT experience, the company can provide these solutions cost effectively – delivering real value for each IT dollar invested.

IMRglobal accommodates fixed-price/fixed-time contracts as well as time and materials contracts, giving customer's a choice of billing options. Another flexible option the company offers is a network of global delivery centers located in different time zones to accelerate the delivery of customer solutions. Using this network to supplement onsite resources, IMRglobal has created a "24x7 virtual workday," literally working around the clock to deliver high-quality solutions and support when and where they are needed.

This global delivery model is ideal for establishing the close relationship management IMRglobal customers have come to expect from the company.

To ensure the quality of the company's solutions, IMRglobal's development facilities in India and the UK are ISO 9001 certified. In addition, the company's development facilities in India were recently appraised at Level 4 of the Software Engineering Institute's Capability Maturity Model. Highlighting the significance of this certification is the fact that, of the 734 organizations that underwent this rigorous assessment from 1995 to mid-1999, only 4 percent received this distinction.

From planning and design, to development and integration, to training and support, IMRglobal delivers the business and technology solutions customers need to be competitive.

www.imrglobal.com

CLEARWATER MUNICIPAL MARINA

Like No Place Else in the World

From whichever direction, by whatever means of transportation, the Clearwater Municipal Marina is a destination in the absolute heart of fun, sun and sand. By land, air, or particularly by sea, visitors will quickly discover the award-winning Clearwater Marina is part of an oasis like no place else in the world.

Located on Clearwater Harbor, the Marina is one of the best-equipped and most attractive marinas in Florida, capable of accommodating vessels up to 125 feet. With no drawbridges to the Gulf of Mexico, it's a natural for boaters headed to or from other Gulf Coast locations. Gasoline and diesel fuel, free pump outs, showers, 24 hour security, free cable TV for visiting boaters, weather monitor, free fishing pier and waste oil disposal are all available.

For landlubbers and water enthusiasts alike, the Clearwater Marina houses the largest and finest fishing fleet on the west coast of Florida, offering sailing charters, sight-seeing boats, dinner cruise boats, parasail boats, dive boats and boat rentals. The marina is also home to restaurants, a gift shop, barber shop, nautical shop, collectible shop, post office, newspaper, bait house, and a dental clinic.

If location is truly everything, the Clearwater Marina's location is a dream come true. Situated on Causeway Boulevard, visitors are just steps away from miles of white sand on Clearwater's famous beaches. After a walk or a day in the sun, gourmet restaurants, a 1000-foot long fishing pier and the City of Clearwater Community Sailing Center are close at hand. The Sailing Center provides a variety of classes for all ages, ranging from basic to intermediate. The Center is also home to the Annual JY 15 Mid Winters and Clark Mills "Optimist" Regatta.

Renowned for dazzling sunsets, nearby Clearwater Beach is famous for its Sunsets at Pier 60 festival held two hours before and after sunset year round. The festival features local artists, crafters and performers to help end yet another perfect day.

Clearwater Municipal Marina is the place where the visitor can do it all, or do nothing at all. Whichever, the heart of fun, sun and sand is right here.

www.clearwater-fl.com/marine

CLEARWATER MARINE AQUARIUM

Forget the normal concept of aquariums

While the Clearwater Marine Aquarium provides an opportunity to view aquatic life, it does so with a unique twist. The aquarium's displays are filled with water from Clearwater Bay, sustaining sea life indigenous to the bay. But the majority of the facility is dedicated to education, one facet of which is the rescue, rehabilitation and release of sea creatures.

On any given day, the Clearwater Marine Aquarium is a haven for injured or sick whales, dolphins, otters and sea turtles. It is also a haven for people who want an opportunity for a hands-on approach to marine and environmental education. Put succinctly, the show is not necessarily inside, but outside, in the environment of the Gulf of Mexico and Clearwater Bay.

For the visiting tourist, the not-for-profit marine facility offers a compelling glimpse into Florida's marine eco-system and its inhabitants. But residents of Pinellas County (or tourists who plan ahead) can take advantage of a wide variety of educational programs not normally associated with an aquarium.

The Clearwater Marine Aquarium offers on-water excursions - Marine Life Adventures - for individuals, groups and families. The internationally recognized "Full Circle" program provides animal-assisted therapy for children with physical and emotional difficulties. Off-site educational presentations are often made with a mobile touch tank, allowing a close up view of many animals seen within local waters.

The aquarium also fulfills a research role and is deeply involved in studies of dolphin populations, sea turtle nesting research and projects with North American river otters.

www.CMAquarium.org

RUTH ECKERD HALL
AT THE RICHARD B. BAUMGARDNER CENTER FOR THE PERFORMING ARTS

Since opening in 1983, Ruth Eckerd Hall has set the standard for excellence among presenters and performing arts centers. It was the first performing arts center in Florida to be designated a Major Cultural Institution by the State of Florida, in 1992, and recently was ranked #1 in the same program. The Hall provides a variety of spaces to serve the public on its 4-acre campus. The Frank Lloyd Wright Foundation designed its 2,173-seat auditorium with superb acoustics.

Now celebrating its 17th season, Ruth Eckerd Hall has become one of the Southeast's most honored and emulated arts institutions. From commissioning a modern dance piece celebrated around the world to serving over 130,000 children and adults each year through its unique and comprehensive arts education program, Ruth Eckerd Hall is creating a legacy of quality performing arts and a new generation of arts patrons for the future.

Many of the finest in nationally and internationally renowned artists and companies held their premiere performances in the State of Florida at Ruth Eckerd Hall, including Jessye Norman, Yehudi Menuhin and Andres Segovia. More than 5.5 million people have experienced over 4,000 performances since the Hall first opened.

Ruth Eckerd Hall also commissions new works such as "Bachiana," a modern dance work by choreographer David Parsons, and the musical number "I Have a Little Shadow" by Dave Brubeck. In addition, more than 20 original scripts have been created, produced and performed by Eckerd Theater Company. The Florida Playwrights' Process also develops new scripts: a 1997 winner, Dunedin student Monica Wrobel, went on to win the national Discovery Program's Young Playwrights competition and, as a result, had her script produced at the Kennedy Center, Washington D.C.

From the beginning, Ruth Eckerd Hall has been committed not only to bringing the finest performances to the area but to educating all segments of the community in the performing arts. Its extensive arts education program, honored in 1990 with the first Kennedy Center Arts Partnership Consortium established in the State of Florida, extends well beyond the walls of Ruth Eckerd Hall via outreach classes and its own professional children's theater troupe. With the creation of Eckerd Theater Company (ETC) in 1988, PACT became a theater producer with significant impact around the state (Florida touring began in 1991-92) and nationally (national tours began in 1993-94).

As it enters its 17th season, Ruth Eckerd Hall will continue to create successful new programming mixes, including the very finest of the classical arts; to pursue innovative partnerships with other organizations to provide expanded programming off-campus; and to reach across cultural barriers through arts education programs to unite communities. Ruth Eckerd Hall remains central to the quality of life in southwest Florida – and a leader in the nation's arts industry.

www.rutheckerdhall.com

Jack Russell Memorial Stadium is the spring training home of the Philadelphia Phillies.

Largo

Much of the history of Largo dates back to seven McMullen Brothers from Georgia who settled in the Largo area between 1848 and 1871. The family had cattle ranches and many citrus groves. Referred to as "Citrus City" in its early years, Largo's extensive orange groves provided the livelihood for several of its pioneer families.

In 1888 it was established as the railroad's halfway point between Clearwater and St. Petersburg. Today, Largo covers about 14.1 square miles and has enjoyed rapid growth, extending west to the bay waterfront, and east to Highway 19 in the heart of Pinellas County and near the outer island beach communities of Belleair Shore and Belleair Beach.

Largo was officially given its status as a city in 1974 and currently has a population of approximately 69,000. Promoting commerce is an important part of recent efforts of its City Commission. Among projects has been the redevelopment of old downtown Largo, along West Bay drive between Seminole Boulevard and Clearwater-Largo Road. Voluntary annexation is a crucial part of the city's recent growth, bringing in hundreds of acres of commercial land, and new residents.

A variety of year-round recreation and athletic programs are available at eight public facilities, eight parks and four sports complexes. The award-winning Largo Central Park and Largo Cultural Center has become a mid-Pinellas landmark for special events and entertainment; the Bay Area

continued on page 276

The Long Center in Clearwater has a 50 meter indoor Olympic sized heated pool and a 25 yard instructional pool.

PINEWOOD CULTURAL PARK

Like any great work of art,

Pinewood Cultural Park is a masterpiece in progress. Located in the heart of Pinellas County at the intersection of Ulmerton and Walsingham Road, the 200-acre development represents an interdisciplinary project that is the only one of its kind in the country. The Pinewood Cultural Park partnership involves the Florida Botanical Gardens, the Gulf Coast Museum of Art and Heritage Village.

The Florida Botanical Gardens, a total campus environment of over 180 acres, features native and non-native Florida plants, plus non-invasive ornaments well adapted to the local climate. Moreover, an essential part of the Garden's educational objective is keeping the Gardens as natural as possible, preserving what isn't already disturbed and restoring what has been altered.

Recent accomplishments include re-meandering a natural creek that passes through the Gardens, introducing islands for wildlife nesting habitats, and the restoration of wetlands. Other priorities include creating habitats for wildlife in transition zones between the more formal gardens and natural areas and preserving the native canopy.

In 2000, the first formal gardens opened to the public. The Tropical Garden features a Tropical Courtyard and Tropical Walk while the Wedding Garden includes a Cottage Garden, Rose Garden, Topiary Garden and Jazz Garden. A Shade Garden and Palms Garden incorporate the formal Palm Walk and Informal Beach Gardens that have become living displays for the public's enjoyment.

Located adjacent to the Florida Botanical Gardens is the Gulf Coast Museum of Art (GCMA). Accredited by the American Association of Museums, the GCMA's new 45,000 square foot campus is designed to accommodate the Museum's mission

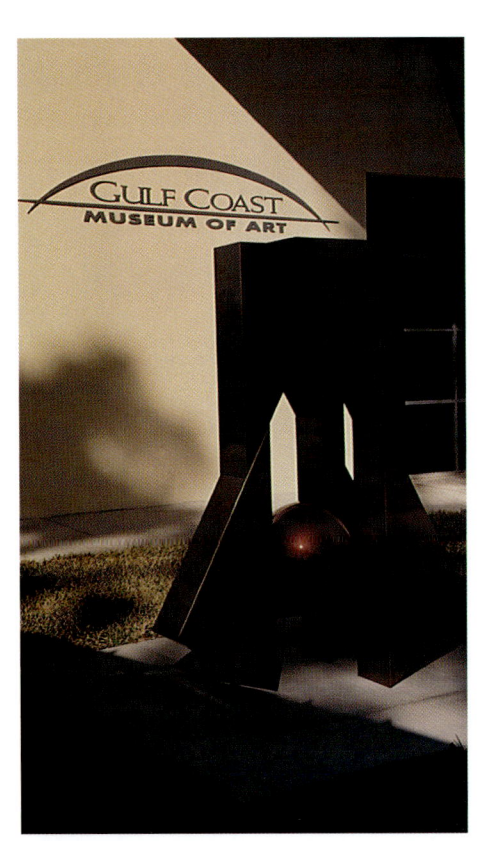

www.gulfcoastmuseum.org   www.fbotanical.e-builder.net

of collecting, exhibiting and teaching in the visual arts. The facility includes galleries for permanent and changing exhibitions; two major sculpture gardens; a 100-seat teaching auditorium; studio buildings for painting, photography, ceramics and metalsmithing; a kiln house with a foundry; a studio manageris office; a materials' supply room; a Museum Store; an administrative wing; library; collections management; and security office. In addition, future phases of the campus will include a classroom building for sculpture, woodworking and glassblowing as well as studios for fiber arts and printmaking; a four-bedroom, four-bath artist-in-residence house and a 75-seat restaurant/café.

Each year, the Museum presents a significant and diverse schedule of exhibitions including traveling/temporary exhibitions organized by the GCMA and exhibitions from national museums and private collections. In addition, The Museum's permanent collection is often on view and consists of contemporary art created by Florida artists from 1960 forward, and a special focus on fine contemporary craft media objects from the Southeastern United States.

With a strong commitment to Education, the GCMA offers year round programs, classes and workshops for students of all ages, including a summer art camp. Also, the Museum has developed a prestigious Master Artist Workshop series, which brings artists of national and international significance to the Bay area for three to five day workshops in their area of expertise.

Neighboring the GCMA is Heritage Village, a 21-acre, open-air historical village and museum. The natural pine and palmetto landscape is home to some of Pinellas County's most historic buildings. First opened to the public in 1976, Heritage Village features 23 structures, some dating back to the mid-19th century. The village includes a school, church, railroad depot, and store, as well as a variety of historic homes. The homes range from the McMullen Log Cabin, the oldest existing structure in the county, to the magnificent Victorian-era Seven Gables House.

While each element of Pinewood Cultural Park is, in itself, a valuable asset to the citizens of Pinellas County and the Tampa Bay area as a whole, the interdisciplinary melding of art, gardens and history is totally unique.

www.coop.co.pinellas.fl.us/bcc/heritag.htm

Renaissance Festival is one. For six consecutive weekends, this springtime event depicts life in a 16th-century village during a country fair with entertainment by more than 350 costumed artisans, musicians, street characters and royalty.

The Gulf Coast Museum of Art, accredited by the American Association of Museums, has a 45-thousand square foot campus facility in Largo at Pinellas County's new Pinewood Cultural Park, which also features Heritage Village, a historical complex, and the Florida Botanical Gardens.

Pinellas Park

Pinellas Park was founded in 1913 as an agricultural community and is now home to nearly 45,000 residents. Voluntary annexation has brought Pinellas Park to a size of 14 square miles and over 70-percent of the city's tax base is provided by businesses, including a considerable portion of industry not visible to people driving through the city. Portions of Gateway Centre, a 600-acre office and industrial park are located in Pinellas Park.

More obvious are the businesses along its major artery, Park Boulevard that runs east and west through the heart of the city. On the far east is one of Pinellas County's larger malls, ParkSide, which has several department stores and an indoor ice-skating rink. To the far west is the Wagon Wheel Flea Market, which attracts thousands of shoppers to its weekend bargains. The annual Pinellas County Fair is held on grounds adjacent to the flea market.

A progressive attitude toward business has not dampened a strong community spirit evident throughout the city. Each

Photos this page: Brown pelican and friend at the Suncoast Seabird Sanctuary; Quiet and informative intersection along the Pinellas Trail at Dunedin's old train station.; Happiness is finding a bargain at the Wagon Wheel Flea Market in Pinellas Park.

spring the City of Pinellas Park, along with the Mid-County Pinellas Park Chamber of Commerce, sponsors a festival to showcase that spirit called Pride in The Park. In addition the community still holds to its agricultural roots with Country in the Park and International Harvest Festival celebrations each year.

For stock car fans, there is racing every Saturday night at the Sunshine Speedway, just south of the St. Petersburg/Clearwater Airport, and drag racing on week nights at the Tampa Bay Dragway, at the same location.

Like the rest of the mid-county area, Pinellas Park offers a wide range of housing, from modest starter homes to luxurious executive residences. A sizable number of the residential areas allow owners to keep riding horses. In addition, several adult retirement communities, including the golf course condominium homes in Mainlands, can be found in Pinellas Park.

Around Pinellas County

Dunedin

The city of Dunedin rests along the shores of St. Joseph Sound and the Gulf of Mexico. Richard L. Garrison recorded the first land deed in 1852; only seven years after Florida became a state. A petition in 1882 by two Scottish merchants, J.O. Douglas and James Somerville, officially named the Post Office, then the town itself. Dunedin meaning "castle on the rock" became incorporated in 1899, and a city in 1925.

Dunedin reflects the rich American and Scottish heritage of its founding fathers. This charming village-like town of approximately 38,000, features natural wooded and subtropical settings, three miles of picturesque waterfront and a relaxed lifestyle. It was recently named one of the five most walkable downtowns in America by *Walking Magazine,* and 4.2 miles of the Pinellas Trail wind through the heart of downtown.

The city is quick to give credit to special efforts by developers, contractors, architects, planners and individual property owners to enhance the aesthetic value of their property. Almost 50-percent of land use is single-family residential. Multi-family units and mobile homes comprise the rest of the area, which is fast becoming an antique center.

Dunedin is a city so proud of its Scottish heritage that the City Pipe Band holds regular concerts at Highlander Park and a weeklong springtime celebration and Scottish Festival culminates with the piping, dancing and drumming contests of the Highland Games. The city has a Bluegrass Festival each Labor Day weekend, a First Night celebration on New Year's Eve, and in November, The Dunedin Art Harvest is one of the largest juried fine arts shows on the West Coast of Florida.

The Toronto Blue Jays hold Spring Training at Dunedin's Grant Field.

More art can be found at the Dunedin Fine Art Center – 18-thousand square feet of exhibition space, studios, three galleries, the Gladys Douglas School for the Arts and the only children's art museum in Pinellas, the David L. Mason Children's Art Museum.

Once Dunedin was a major citrus producing area and the birthplace of the citrus concentrate industry. The Minute Maid Company still has a large citrus packaging facility there. Dunedin was the first home of the prestigious Professional Golfers Association (PGA). Now it is home to the master computer system of the A.C. Nielsen Company, responsible for the Nielsen television ratings. Baseball fans know Clearwater's Jack Russell Stadium as the spring training home for the Toronto Blue Jays.

Tarpon Springs:

With the arrival of the Orange Belt Railway, Tarpon Springs enjoyed great success as a winter destination for wealthy northern tourists. Hamilton Disston had developed the area around Spring Bayou into a thriving winter resort and health center.

Incorporated in 1887, Tarpon Springs is the oldest and northern most city in Pinellas County. It is located 30 miles west of Tampa and 30 miles north of St. Petersburg with a population of nearly 20,000.

The special atmosphere of Tarpon Springs is an outgrowth of one of the state's most fascinating, one-of-a-kind industries –

Below: The Sponge Docks in Tarpon Springs. Right: Greek Orthodox Archbishop blesses cross retriever during the annual Epiphany celebration.

Around Pinellas County

Historic Indian mounds can still be found in the 122 acres of Philippe Park in Safety Harbor.

sponge fishing. The Greek population of Tarpon Springs grew rapidly after 1905 as the sponge industry grew. Today the city is enriched by the Mediterranean heritage brought here by Greek sponge divers and their families whose customs, religious practices, and language their ancestors have maintained.

The Sponge Docks are listed as a National Historic District and visitors to the area will find authentic Greek food in many of the more than 20 restaurants, as well as shops, cruise boats for day-trips or fishing trips, and authentic Greek clubs.

On the edge of the historic business district, with its antique shops, art gallery-studios, boutiques and restaurants, are the beautifully restored Victorian homes built by the founders of Tarpon Springs. Other delightful residences are on the city's bayous and waterways, plus there is a charming mix of new subdivisions in Tarpon Springs and new development along the Anclote River.

The leading industry is tourism – Tarpon Springs hosts some one million visitors a year. There is also a 350-seat Performing Arts Center and a Cultural Center that houses two galleries for exhibits and an 84-seat theater for concerts and viewing of films. Several annual events and festivals are held in Tarpon Springs, including the Arts and Crafts Festival, an all-media juried show featuring the works of artists and craftsmen from all across the United States.

The Greek Orthodox Epiphany Celebration, always on January 6th, is the largest Epiphany celebration in the United States. Following religious services at the St. Nicholas Greek Orthodox Church, a procession through the streets of Tarpon springs leads to Spring Bayou where young men of the community dive to retrieve a gold cross. According to tradition, the diver who finds the cross is blessed with a year of good luck.

Safety Harbor

Safety Harbor's written history dates to the 1539 when Hernando de Soto, in his search for the legendary Fountain of Youth, discovered five mineral springs near a large Tocobaga Indian village in the area. The Indians believed the springs had healing qualities, and the legend persisted into the early 1900's drawing tourists to the area.

The Safety Harbor Resort & Spa, with its pampering accommodations, is built over the springs and continues to use the legendary therapeutic waters as a marketing tool. It is the city's most famous landmark. Located just over a footbridge from the spa is Philippe Park, a tree-lined 122-acre setting on Old Tampa Bay.

Safety Harbor was first homesteaded by Count Odet Philippe, a French surgeon in Napoleon's navy, who introduced citrus growing to Florida. Established in 1823 the Count's homestead is now the site of the park and a protected ceremonial mound from the ancient Indian settlement exists there today. The city also has a small Historical Museum on the site of several remaining Native American shell mounds and features artifacts from the area dating back some 10,000 years.

Primarily a residential community of about 15,000, the population of Safety Harbor's incorporated 4.46 square miles has nearly peaked. Where grapefruit once grew, many housing developments now attract a young, affluent commuter populace who want the quaintness and small-town charm of this historic area to remain intact, while having access to nearby larger cities.

Incorporated as a city in 1917, Safety Harbor has maintained its family oriented community while preserving its environmentally sensitive lands and revitalizing its historic Main Street and downtown business district.

Gulfport

In 1884 Hamilton Disston came to the area with plans to develop a city on thousands of acres of land he owned on the lower Pinellas peninsula. For a few years Disston City was a reality, until the railroad went into St. Petersburg instead.

Renamed Veteran's City, a later promotion encouraged Civil War veterans to retire there. Gulfport was officially incorporated on October 12, 1910; five years after the trolley from St. Petersburg reached the town and helped it survive.

Gulfport Casino, built in 1905, is a community favorite for ballroom, line and swing dances.

Around Pinellas County

Primarily residential, Gulfport occupies a compact 2.8 square miles adjacent to St. Petersburg and has a long shoreline along Boca Ciega Bay. It is the oldest settlement in the southern part of Pinellas County and has an approximate population of 12,000. For a small town there is an impressive support of the historical and art communities in Gulfport.

The Gulfport Arts Village is the largest organized art community in the Tampa Bay area. It is comprised of shops and galleries that represent work in all media and is an indirect result of the many working artists who live in the community. On the first Friday of each month the galleries stay open throughout the evening for an Art Walk as visitors are encouraged to browse and buy.

Along the sandy beach of the waterfront is the Gulfport Casino, a landmark built in 1905. Swing bands, ballroom and country music alternate on stage throughout the week attracting dancing couples of all ages.

In addition, the Southeast Little League Regional Headquarters is in Gulfport and once a year youthful players and supportive parents come from other regions of the country for the final series competition.

Seminole

The City of Seminole, incorporated in 1970, is 12 miles northwest of St. Petersburg and just south of Clearwater. It is characterized by a strong sense of community and is attractively located within the greater metropolitan area.

Occupying 2.2 square miles of Pinellas County, and with a population of around 10,000, Seminole is home to St. Petersburg Junior College's largest and most technologically advanced campus. It also borders the western shores of Lake Seminole, one of only two fresh water lakes in Pinellas.

Seminole Park is a 259-acre county park on the lake with individual and group picnicking facilities, a large play area, and a two-mile recreation trail. The park also has a boat ramp accessing the lake for boating, fishing, and water-skiing.

Each May a Bluegrass and Arts Festival helps raise money for children's charities. Sponsored by the Seminole Junior Women's Club the folk, country and bluegrass music event features top names and local artists.

Lake Seminole covers 684-acres.

Oldsmar

Oldsmar is the only city in Pinellas County that is contiguous with Tampa and Hillsborough County. It was established in 1918 and is named for its founder, Ransom Eli Olds, father of the Oldsmobile.

In 1913, Olds designed and modeled the city after Washington, D.C., with tree-lined boulevards leading from the northern edge of Old Tampa Bay to downtown. He envisioned a city of 100,000, but the population was only about 200 when Mr. Olds left having lost millions of his investments.

Oldsmar today has a population of over 9,000 and its location is near one of the fastest-developing areas of west central Florida. Race Track Road remains a picturesque drive past green pastures and racing stables, but new residential development can be seen all around including nearby East Lake with some of the most luxurious neighborhoods in Tampa Bay.

Surrounding beautiful Lake Tarpon, East Lake has blossomed with new housing, apartments, villas and condominiums. The area is known for its natural beauty and many of these new communities have set aside preservation areas.

There are 34 acres of protected wetlands in the Harbor Palms Nature Park of Oldsmar, which has also set up a distribution system for reclaimed storm water in recognition of the resource conservation needs of the region. The area boasts thoroughbred horse racing at the Tampa Bay Downs, a racetrack just outside the city, in Hillsborough County. In addition, the 30-acre Oldsmar Flea Market draws thousands of shoppers to the area each weekend. Oldsmar is also home to the Tampa Bay Skating Academy, which has an Olympic size ice rink.

South Pasadena

This small community of 6,000 is nestled on Boca Ciega Bay just west of Gulfport and St. Petersburg. The city features several shops and restaurants, one of the largest private hospitals in Pinellas County, and a drawbridge to St. Pete Beach.

The anchor of the residential area of the Pasadena area is the Pasadena Yacht & Country Club. Technically in an unincorporated area of Pinellas, this gated property has a clubhouse, historic links originally designed by PGA tour great Walter Hagen, and a marina providing access to Boca Ciega Bay and the Gulf of Mexico.

Kenneth City

Kenneth City is a land-locked area tucked near the Northwestern corner of St. Petersburg and south of Pinellas Park, with only a few identifying signs to offer clues of its separate and independent status.

Incorporated in 1957, Kenneth City has a population of about 4,500 people who are mostly retirees. It was named Kenneth City after the son of its developer, Sidney Colen and the city's two square miles were formed around a shopping center, park and city hall. Part of the campus of Dixie Hollins High School is in Kenneth City and part in St. Petersburg.

Around Pinellas County

Belleair

Part of Belleair's prestigious personality lies in its brief but colorful history. In the 1890s, railroad magnate Henry B. Plant constructed the Belleview Biltmore Hotel in what is now known as Belleair. The hotel, one of the largest wooden structures in the world, is listed on the National Register of Historic Places and continues to offer guests the finest amenities and golf packages.

Belleair incorporated in 1923 and is one of the smallest cities in Pinellas County. It consists of two square miles between the Intracoastal Waterway, Clearwater and Largo and has just over 4,000 residents. Rows of towering palms and handsome landscaping in front of elegant homes contribute to the lavish look of Belleair

Belleair Bluffs

The second smallest community in Pinellas, Belleair Bluffs is three-quarters of a mile square bordering the Intracoastal Waterway with no frontage on the Gulf. The Belleair Beach Causeway has a free boat launch and pet-friendly beach.

Nestled between Largo and Belleair, the city has a population of around 2,400 and a mix of single-family homes, condominiums and apartments. There are retail stores, small boutiques and a good selection of antiques. It also is home to some of the area's good restaurants.

Belleair Shore

Belleair Shore is a private residential community with no public beach access. It consists solely of several large homes on the west side of Gulf Boulevard. between Indian Rocks Beach and Belleair Beach. The town is .0043 square miles and is dedicated to preserving the quality of a quiet, residential life for its less than 60 residents who participate in and support the commercial activities of neighboring communities.

Palm Harbor

Palm Harbor was supposed to be one of the original towns in Pinellas County, but it is a town in name only. In the 1880s the area was plotted for a city to be named Sutherland. The area changed its name to Palm Harbor in 1925, but the depression kept it from developing into a city and it was never incorporated. However, it is a thriving community with over 65,000 residents and great natural beauty.

The 33 square miles of Palm Harbor stretches from Curlew Road (SR 586) above Clearwater and Dunedin to Klosterman Road, below Tarpon Springs. On its west are the waters of the Gulf of Mexico, St. Joseph Sound, and the residential communities of Crystal Beach and Ozona, known for its Florida Cracker-style houses and restaurants. On its east are Lake Tarpon, the lake's outfall canal, and the sprawling developments along East Lake Road all the way to the Hillsborough county line.

Palm Harbor is governed by the Board of County Commissioners, protected by the Pinellas County Sheriffs Department and has four fire stations in its district. A well-balanced economy has firm roots in retail business, the service industries, financial institutions and the building trades.

Unlike most of coastal Pinellas, the terrain here is not flat. Palm Harbor rises gently from the Gulf to an average elevation of 25 feet, with some land as high as 80 feet above sea level.

A popular area in Palm Harbor is John Chestnut Park on the shores of Lake Tarpon. The park features nature trials, canoe trails and a boat ramp. Ranked as one of the Top 10 bass waters, Lake Tarpon is a popular fishing spot for visitors and residents alike.

Today Palm Harbor thrives on its small-town friendliness. Much of the old downtown has been preserved and many historical items are featured in the historical museum. Palm Harbor hosts three fine arts, crafts and music festivals annually: Palm Harbor Day in May, The Palm Harbor Arts, Crafts & Music Festival held in early December and the Downtown Merchants Arts, Crafts and Music Festival in February.

Florida's natural beauty can be found in many areas such as Crystal Beach in Palm Harbor.

Brooker Creek Preserve

is over 8,500 acres of wilderness in the East Lake-Palm Harbor northeast corner of Pinellas.

Species of white-tailed deer, wild turkey and bobcat thrive in this natural environ which is managed by Pinellas County's Department of Environmental Management. Since 1972, Pinellas County has set aside 5,000 acres of environmentally sensitive land and plans to acquire 2,500 more acres.

Chapter 12
Tampa Bay Treasures

HERB SNITZER

The Hillsborough River runs for fifty-six miles through Hillsborough County, winding its way through wilderness, parks, residential communities, campuses and the very center of Tampa's downtown…

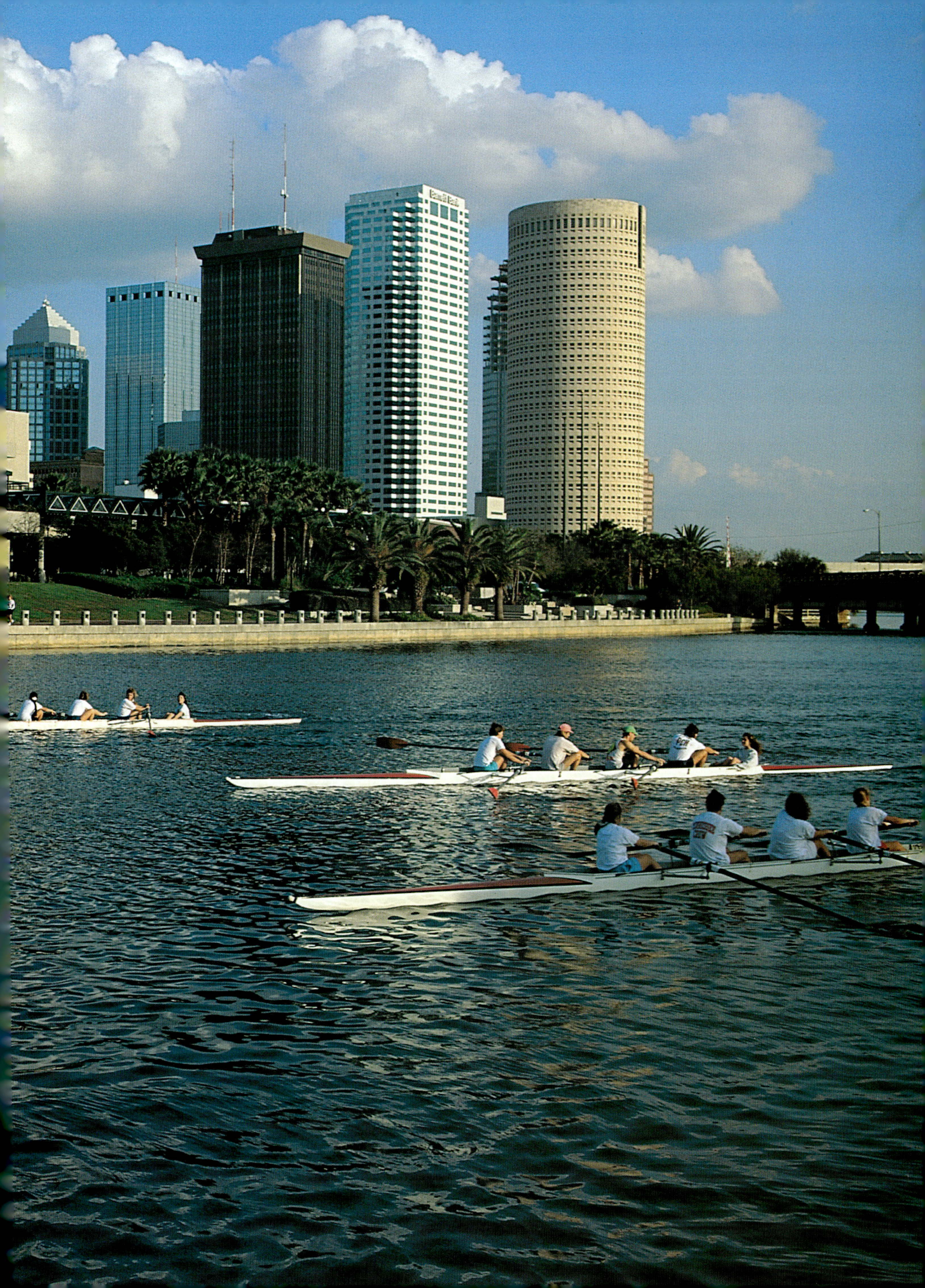

Tampa Bay Treasures

You can camp in the Hillsborough River State Park and take a canoe adventure through a 16,000-acre wilderness, the habitat of white ibis, alligators and turtles. Or you can reach for your tickets to a Sir Andrew Lloyd Webber production at the Tampa Bay Performing Arts Center as you walk near the river's banks and see the reflected city skyline of towering steel, concrete, glass and marble, the habitat of Tampa's business and financial decision makers. You can wonder at the history the river has seen.

Tampa is a cosmopolitan city of approximately 290,000 people in a county of more than 900,000. It is part of Hillsborough County, which was originally formed in 1834 from a massive tract of land that encompassed 8,580 square miles or roughly over five million acres – an area which now is divided into nine separate Florida counties and includes the Tampa Bay region.

St. Petersburg was part of Hillsborough County until 1912, when an independence bill went into effect making the peninsula west of Tampa Bay to the Gulf of Mexico officially Pinellas County. It was a separation initiated entirely by St. Petersburg out of a need for roads, bridges and other improvements it did not get while Tampa controlled the tax dollars.

While schooners ran regular runs between the two cities, and the Benoist Airboat Line was launched in 1914, it wasn't until 1924 that the Gandy Bridge linked the two cities for auto travel across the Bay. A new span opened in the early 1970's, and the original Gandy Bridge is now used as a recreational path, dedicated in 1999 and appropriately renamed The Friendship TrailBridge.

In 1934 the Davis Causeway, now the Courtney Campbell Causeway and Route 60, created a second access to Pinellas from Hillsborough, connecting Tampa to Clearwater, and in 1960 the Howard Frankland Bridge, now part of I-275, provided the most direct route to St. Petersburg and Pinellas.

Tampa's recorded history, like St. Petersburg's, began when

Left: Conductor Michael Stern rehearses with his father Isaac Stern and the Florida Orchestra at the Tampa Bay Performing Arts Center. Opposite: The Gandy Bridge and the pedestrian Friendship TrailBridge join St. Peterburg and Tampa.

284

TY HESTON

Tampa Bay Treasures

Spanish explorers mapped the region in the 1500's and Panfilo de Narvaez named what is now Old Tampa Bay, Espiritu Santo or Bay of the Holy Spirit. According to legend, when Hernando DeSoto arrived in 1539 he signed a peace treaty with Native Americans at the site of what is now the University of Tampa. But DeSoto soon left, and for more than a century, throughout the 1600's and much of the 1700's, Europeans largely ignored Tampa Bay.

A few early settlers farmed the region in the 1700's, when Spanish and Cuban fishermen peacefully coexisted with the Indians. Following England's acquisition of Florida from Spain in 1763, another mapmaker Bernard Romans, penned in the name Hillsborough Bay for Lord Hillsborough, British Secretary of State for the Colonies.

It was a time when pirates sailed along Caribbean waters to the Florida coastline. And pirate legends die hard. One in particular involves Jose Gaspar who is thought by some to be merely the creation of an ambitious promoter of pirate maps for tourists. None the less, he is the pirate behind one of Tampa's most popular annual celebrations when the city's business, social and civic leaders, dressed in full pirate regalia, reenact the conquest of the Cigar City by this rogue of the high seas, with a Gasparilla Pirate Invasion and Parade.

In 1824, two months after the arrival of the first American settler in Tampa, Colonel George Mercer Brooke was sent to establish Fort Brooke on the strategic harbor of Tampa Bay. It was part of the U.S. Army's network of military outposts throughout the state to oppose the Indians. The farming and fishing village that grew just outside the military post was also called Fort Brooke. It eventually was known as Tampa, meaning "sticks of fire," a name that had been given to the area by the Caloosa Indians many years before. The city was incorporated in 1855 with a population of approximately 800.

Unlike St. Petersburg, which had little involvement in the Civil War, Confederate troops occupied Tampa's Fort Brooke in 1861, eventually yielding to federal troops in 1864. The Union forces remained in Tampa until the end of the Civil War in 1865. Both cities however, got their first economic boosts with the arrival of the railroad. For Tampa, it was Henry B. Plant; a northern tycoon turned Florida landowner who, after the Civil War, bought several small bankrupt rail companies serving the South and put them together to form The Plant System of Railways. The Plant System provided service from

Top: University of Tampa and H.B. Plant Museum, as seen from across the Hillsborough River. Bottom: The Victorian style Plant Museum was originally one of Henry B. Plant's railroad destination resorts in 1891. Opposite: The classic minarets of the University of Tampa lend old-world drama to the modern city skyline of Tampa's downtown.

TAMPA / HILLSBOROUGH CONVENTION & VISITORS ASSN.

Tampa Bay Treasures

Charleston, S.C., through Georgia, Florida and Alabama. Connections were also provided to New York and the entire northeast.

Plant recognized that his railroad would be a greater success if combined with steamship and steamboat service. In 1886, the Plant Steamship Line was organized with service to Bermuda, the Bahamas, Cuba, Boston, New Orleans, Jamaica, and Nova Scotia. Plant extended his railroad from Sanford to Tampa in 1884, four years before St. Petersburg became an incorporated city.

He began to build magnificent hotels, eight in all, along his Florida rail lines, including the Belleview Biltmore Hotel in what is now Belleair, across the Bay in Pinellas County and the Tampa Bay Hotel, in Hyde Park on the Hillsborough River in Tampa. The Plant System accommodated winter visitors, and enhanced a valuable new industry for the Tampa Bay area called tourism.

The Tampa Bay Hotel, completed in 1891, is now occupied by the University of Tampa whose crew teams can be seen on the Hillsborough River. The elaborate building is a recognizable Tampa Victorian landmark with Moorish revival

continued on page 290

Top: Hand-rolled cigars are still made in Ybor City, a National Historic Landmark district, once known as the cigar capitol of the world.
Above: Twelve cannons fire smoke and confetti from the 103-foot pirate ship at Raymond James Stadium, home of the Tampa Bay Buccaneers.

HILLSBOROUGH COUNTY AVIATION AUTHORITY

Tampa International Airport

A recent *New York Times* article stated that "as the (Tampa International) Airport is currently undergoing remodernization, it is more convenient in its time of upheaval than most airports at their most settled. Bright, close in, with plenty of elevators and escalators and lots of easily understood signs, Tampa ought to be cloned nationwide."

Long recognized as America's favorite Airport, Tampa International's continuing objective is to provide the Tampa Bay area with "world class" transportation. Both the Airport's mission and vision statements emphasize customer service and Tampa International has provided this community with transportation services and facilities necessary for safe, efficient and dependable air service.

Over the past few years, the Airport's initiatives have resulted in many customer-friendly services, including paramedic emergency medical response services within the terminal complex. Most recently, valet parking became available to improve the level of service and to provide alternative parking to Airport customers.

Similarly, Tampa International strives for a "traveler friendly" atmosphere by offering a variety of perks, such as a "Smarte Carte" program for first-class baggage service, and a flight information system and electronic signage which provide information regarding flights and their respective baggage belt systems.

The uniqueness of the Tampa Bay area is also highly visible, with a renovated Landside Terminal depicting a Florida ambiance providing passengers with maximum comfort and convenience, as well as marine exhibits in the baggage claim area. A Public Art Program allows local artists to exhibit their diverse works on a rotating basis. Also, a non-denominational Airport chapel is available for use by passengers and employees.

Tampa International houses a galleria of 15 shops featuring a wide variety of national brands, creating an Airport shopping experience for over 15 million passengers who travel through the Airport each year. An Airport hotel and six restaurants complement the shopping experience.

The Hillsborough County Aviation Authority has been serving the Tampa Bay area for over 54 years and remains an important catalyst for the community. It is the 5th fastest growing Airport in the U.S. for total passenger traffic and ranked as the 29th busiest out of 149 airports in the nation. Currently, Tampa International Airport offers nearly 300 daily nonstop scheduled departures to 53 domestic destinations and 46 weekly nonstop scheduled departures to eight international markets.

www.tampaairport.com

Half a million passengers a year sail on cruise ships from the newly expanded Terminal 2 at the Port of Tampa.

architecture and ornate silver minarets. The Henry B. Plant Museum is housed in the south wing of the university's Plant Hall, an administration building.

An 1880 census shows that Tampa's population had actually declined during the decade before, with the closing of Fort Brooke. Plant's railroad changed all that, and by 1885 the population had increased to nearly 3,000. On May 7, 1885 Tampa's Board of Trade was organized, determined to transform the community from a tiny fishing village into a productive metropolis. One of its first accomplishments was to underwrite $4,000 needed to finalize the purchase of land bought by V. Martinez Ybor to establish what became Ybor City and a flourishing cigar town.

Spanish, Cuban, and Italian families first settled Ybor to work in its world-famous cigar factories. In the late 1800's, another man, Jose Marti, known as the George Washington of Cuba, would urge cigar factory workers to take up arms against Spain. In 1898 the Spanish-American War was fought and Tampa became a military post where 30,000 troops were staged for debarkation to Cuba. The Tampa Bay Hotel became an officer's headquarters, including that of Col. Theodore Roosevelt who was to gain fame later in Cuba as leader of the Rough Riders.

The Depression and a new smoke of choice, cigarettes, slowed the demand for cigars and by the early 1950's Tampa's cigar factories were mostly empty brick buildings. Today's Ybor City is an area of about two square miles and one of only three National Historic Landmark Districts in Florida. By day it is popular for history and walking tours, and by night is the hot spot for jazz and other live music in its many restaurants, bars and clubs along Seventh Avenue.

In the fall of 2000, an entertainment-retail complex called Centro Ybor opened, featuring a 20-screen movie theater, shops and restaurants. A transportation link, planned by the city to connect Tampa's downtown convention hotels with the refurbished Channelside waterfront area, will have a stop in Ybor's historic district.

Around the same time the cigar industry took hold in Tampa, the discovery of phosphate in the area created new mining and shipping industries that prompted a boom of growth and wealth that lasted through the 1890's. A 20-foot channel was dug from Tampa Bay and Hillsborough's port development began in earnest in the early 1900's. During World War I, Tampa became a shipbuilding center, an activity repeated two decades later in World War II.

Today, the deepwater Port of Tampa is the tenth largest bulk port in the nation handling more than 50 million tons of phosphate, citrus concentrate and scrap metal cargo each year. In return, it receives imports of petroleum, coal, liquid sulfur, and steel.

In addition, approximately 500-thousand cruise passengers dock at Tampa's Garrison Seaport Center's terminals each year, with itineraries to the Caribbean and Latin America. A recent $6.5 million renovation doubled the size of Cruise Terminal 2 and the Tampa Port Authority is very involved in a remaking of the entire Garrison Waterfront District, downtown Tampa's focal point for new development.

Tampa, like St. Petersburg, was attractive to real estate speculators and showed incredible growth during the Florida building boom of the 20's. A man named D. P. Davis dredged Hillsborough Bay, created man-made islands, and sold $1.68-million worth of lots for his Davis Islands development in one

continued on page 292

THE FLORIDA AQUARIUM

A Walk on the Wild Side

Imagine getting so close to a shark, you could actually count all its teeth. Have you ever stood so close to a gator, you could see its eyes blink? Do all this and more – all in air-conditioned comfort – at The Florida Aquarium, downtown Tampa.

The Florida Aquarium opens a window to the side of Florida few ever get to see. Located in the booming waterfront district, the Aquarium offers a dramatic and unique look at all that swims, floats, preys, and crawls in and around Florida waters and beyond. Follow a drop of water from its source in freshwater springs, all the way out to the open ocean, encountering over 10,000 aquatic plants and animals along the way.

The signature 1,100-panel, seven-story high glass dome crowning the 152,000-square-foot facility is where your journey begins. Enter the first of four major presentations, the Wetlands Gallery and come across freshwater fish, free-flying birds, Florida alligators, playful river otters and a host of other inhabitants of Florida's wetlands. Climb a giant staircase up to the 2,500-square-foot mezzanine which houses Frights of the Forest, an exotic exhibit showcasing creepy creatures from wet forest habitats around the world.

Next, the Bays and Beaches Gallery takes you for a walk under a bridge, a stroll by the beach, and encounters with stingrays, bonnethead sharks, a 190 lb. grouper and spiny lobsters – without ever getting wet. On the way to the next gallery, you'll encounter the latest addition located on the second floor lobby: the NoBoneZone, a kid-friendly exhibit exploring the fascinating world of invertebrates. The main feature is the "S.C.U.M" touch tank – a 600-gallon hands-on experience with sea stars, crustaceans, urchins, mollusks and other invertebrates from the world's oceans.

Your next stop is an incredible underwater world simulating a 60-foot dive in the Coral Reefs Gallery. This 500,000-gallon tank offers a one-of-a-kind look at a coral grotto featuring giant green moray eels, rainbow parrotfish, black tip sharks and other colorful reef inhabitants. The spectacular 42-feet wide, 14-feet high Panoramic Window is the stage for three dive shows held daily.

Enter the Aquarium's awesome Aussie exhibit – Dragons Down Under – starring rare, leafy sea dragons from Australia, along with some of their relatives, seahorses, pipefish and trumpetfish. Your journey concludes at the Offshore Gallery for a look at the mysterious world of the open sea. Discover one of the most popular exhibits at the Aquarium, Awes & Jaws, featuring spine-tingling sharks from all over the world, as well as moon jellies, giant isopods, golden crabs, large sea turtles and gliding rays..

www.flaquarium.org

Tampa Bay Treasures

day! The stately homes of this self-contained community, with its own executive airport, are well maintained today and close to downtown.

In the 1930's a WPA project enabled $1-million worth of improvements to Tampa's Bayshore Boulevard, including its famous balustrades along what still is the world's longest continuous sidewalk. Runners today can enjoy the 4.5-mile stretch, that fronts some of the city's most prestigious homes in the Old Hyde Park neighborhood, which includes an upscale shopping area of boutiques, restaurants and bistros.

Another 1930's WPA project allowed work on the airfield now known as MacDill Air Force Base, which officially began operation in 1941. There has always been a military presence in Tampa. Before it was a frontier town it was a military outpost called Fort Brooke. During the Spanish-American War, the city was the primary outfitting port for U.S. troops bound for Cuba. In 1991, during the Persian Gulf War, MacDill Air Force Base was home of U.S. Central Command under General Norman Schwarzkopf.

Today, MacDill is the headquarters of the Defense Department's U.S. Special Operations Command and hosts the supporting 6th Air Base Wing. It is the 6th largest public-sector employer in the Tampa Bay MSA, serving more than 7,000 military and civilian personnel. Each spring the public has an opportunity to visit MacDill during its annual Air Fest, where precision flying demonstrations and a history of military aviation attracts thousands.

Another airfield, Drew Field, was renamed Tampa International Airport (TIA) when Eastern and National airlines moved to the hub in 1945. Twenty-six years later, in 1971, TIA got an $80-million makeover, including a new air terminal, and soared to one of the highest-ranking airports in the nation. TIA routinely earns top ratings by the International Foundation of Airline Passengers Association, and Conde Nast Traveler magazine. It ranks 30th nationally in terms of total passenger traffic, which reached 13.4 million in 1997 – a figure that is expected to reach 40-million annually by the year 2020.

Tampa International is essential to the infrastructure of the entire Tampa Bay area. It handles more than 130 million pounds of cargo a year, and is considered a major shipping point for tropical fish, one of Hillsborough County's established industries. Next to the airport is a 28-thousand square foot U.S. Postal Service Center, open 24 hours a day, which handles 9 million pieces of mail daily.

Passenger figures at TIA peak in the tourism months of March, April and December when Europeans and vacationers from colder, northern U.S. cities head for the warmth of the Florida sun and Tampa Bay's many attractions. And while the City of Tampa does not depend on tourism as its primary industry, it has plenty of first class entertainment and theme parks to offer its visitors. It is also a convention destination served by the Tampa Convention Center, which opened in 1990 with 600,000 square feet of meeting space overlooking the Hillsborough River in downtown, and augmented in recent years by several new convention hotels.

Channelside Drive is a growing down-
continued on page 294

Runners compete in the Gasparilla Distance Classic on Bayshore Blvd., the world's longest continuous sidewalk.

TAMPA CONVENTION CENTER

There's a good reason why the Tampa Convention Center is one of the hottest convention destinations in the country. With major visitor attractions, nearby Gulf beaches and outstanding sports, the Convention Center mirrors the vibrancy of the Tampa Bay area as a whole.

As "TCC" enters its 10th year, conventions and trade shows have had a major impact on the community. An estimated 200,000 out-of-town delegates participated in a convention or trade show during 1999. Partnering with the Tampa/ Hillsborough Convention and Visitors Association (THCVA), Tampa hosted 38 conventions and trade shows, generating an estimated $178 million economic impact to the community.

But the facility is not just for out-of-town business – the 600,000 square foot coral and glass facility accommodates local meetings and public trade shows as well. Well over half a million attendees walk through the doors annually. More than half those are local residents.

Since the waterfront Convention Center opened in 1990, the Florida Aquarium, the Ice Palace, and the Tampa Marriott Waterside – the city's largest meeting hotel – has followed. Located on Florida's beautiful Gulf Coast, just minutes from one of the world's top-rated airports, the Tampa Bay area is a meeting planner's paradise, offering a harvest of amenities.

The 36,000-square foot ballroom provides theater seating for 3,800, banquet seating for 2,400, and can be divided into four smaller rooms.

Eighteen meeting rooms (six are waterfront) total another 63,000-square feet which can accommodate 60-7,500 people simultaneously. The 200,000 square foot exhibit hall (that's four football fields) can accommodate up to 1,015 10'x10' booths, or be divided to a 50/50 or 60/40 split.

Whether it's a trade show, convention, consumer show, large delegation, an intimate, roll-up-your-sleeves roundtable or a waterfront wedding reception, TCC is the perfect spot. As a matter of fact, The Tampa Convention Center was awarded the Planner's Choice Award in the Convention Center category from Meeting News.

Planning is currently underway for a $6 million meeting room expansion, adding 18 more breakout rooms. This will help Tampa attract more high-end national, professional, and trade organizations as well as national corporate business. Together with the community, TCC has created a sound business atmosphere conducive to meetings at the international, national, state and local levels and has become part of the fabric of this dynamic region.

www.ci.tampa.fl.us

Tampa Bay Treasures

The Ice Palace is home to the Tampa Bay Lightning, Tampa Bay Storm and numerous entertainment events and concerts.

town Tampa destination with construction of the new Garrison Seaport Center, a 130,000 square foot urban entertainment complex that includes a movie theater, waterfront restaurants, retail shops and offices. The center is near the convention hotels, the Ice Palace, the Florida Aquarium and the cruise ship terminal, all easily linked by shuttle to the Ybor City entertainment district a few minutes away.

The Ice Palace, built in 1996 for NHL's Tampa Bay Lightning, is a modern hockey arena also used year-round for concerts, basketball games and exhibits. Next door is the 152,000-square-foot Florida Aquarium, which opened in 1995. This enclosed facility is designed as a walk through exhibit that follows a drop of water through Florida's diverse aquatic ecosystems, from its underground source to the open sea, in a series of living galleries including a 43-foot wide panoramic window with over 1,500 coral reef aquatic species. It is marketed as part of the "Tampa Trio," which includes the Florida Aquarium, the Museum of Science and Industry (MOSI), and the Lowry Park Zoo.

MOSI is the largest science center complex of its kind in the southeast. It is located on a 70-acre campus across from the University of South Florida (USF) in north Tampa and evolved from a series of predecessor museums to become a visionary, high-tech facility. Accredited by the American Association of Museums and by the Association of Science-Technology Centers, MOSI features dozens of scientific and interactive exhibits – from a backwoods trail and a three-stories-tall sauropod dinosaur, to a flight simulator and a planetarium. The museum's IMAX Theater was the first to open in the state of Florida.

Tampa's first zoo was established in the late 1930's on the banks of the Hillsborough River with a small collection of animals. The city moved the zoo to Lowry Park in 1957 where it was maintained by the Tampa Parks Department until the 1970's. As the collection of animals continued to grow and include more exotic species, the Lowry Park Zoological Society was formed dedicated to building a first-class zoological garden.

Reopened in 1988 and recognized today as one of the top three mid-sized zoos in the country, the Lowry Park Zoo is accredited by the American Association of Zoological Parks and Aquariums. It has 41 acres of natural habitats in five main exhibit areas: the world-renowned Florida manatee and aquatic center, a native Florida wildlife center, the Asian domain, a primate world, free-flight aviary and children's petting zoo.

One of the most popular destinations for visitors to Tampa is Busch Gardens Tampa Bay. Busch Gardens is a 335-acre family entertainment park that grew from a brewery tour and bird sanctuary in 1959. It is one of the world's premier zoological parks with hundreds of African animals, birds, a nursery and petting zoo and features thrilling rides and live entertainment. It is here that the adventuresome can ride an inverted roller coaster called "Montu," and a new double wooden roller coaster named "Gwazi," billed as the southeast's largest and fastest double wooden roller coaster.

Next door is the 25-acre water park Adventure Island, another of The Anheuser-Busch Adventure Parks, which offers some fun ways to cool off during a hot Florida summer including 500 feet of open flumes and closed tubes called the "Splash Attack."

St. Petersburg goes to Tampa for the fun of the theme parks, for much of the nightlife, and for the outstanding performances booked in the Tampa Bay Performing Arts Center. This dramatic cultural center, on a nine-acre site along the

continued on page 298

University of South Florida Athletics

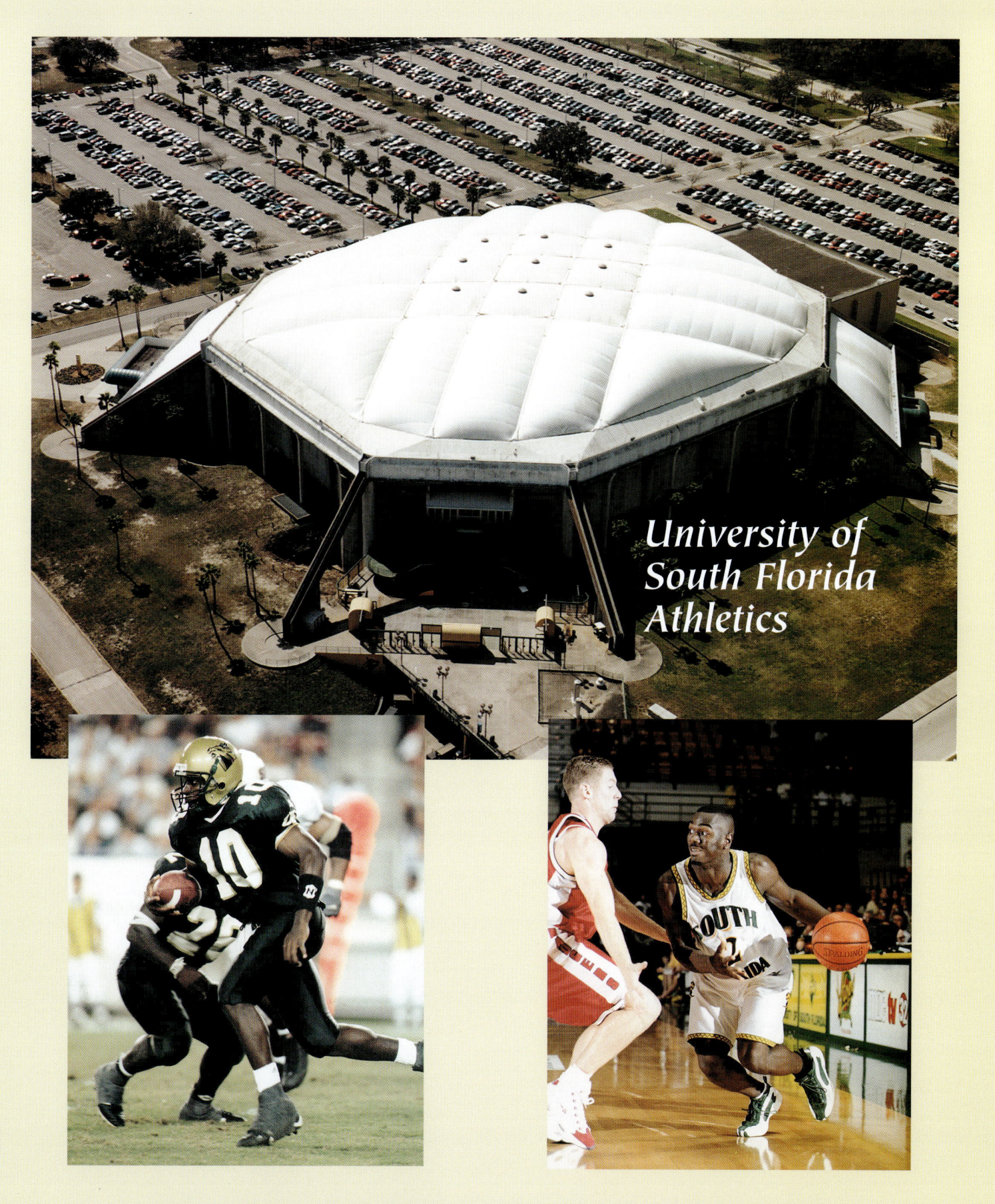

Home to USF Basketball, the Sundome seats 10, 411 and is a great venue for seeing outstanding Division I basketball. A major athletic step was taken by USF as they launched their football program at the Division I level in 1997 and moved rapidly toward full Division I bowl eligibility status in 2001. A member of Conference USA, the green and gold Bulls are fast becoming a major competitor in all of the 8 men's and 8 women's sports.

The football Bulls, from their first full season, have ranked at or near the top in attendance nationally at the IAA level and have positioned themselves to be a very competitive gridiron program in a state known for outstanding pigskin success.

MUSEUM OF SCIENCE & INDUSTRY

In an age of continuing technological wonders, providing a hands-on learning approach to science, as well as industries' use of that science, is a rare opportunity for youngsters and adults alike. The Museum of Science & Industry (MOSI) is Tampa Bay's answer to that opportunity. In a word, MOSI's approach to providing such a unique experience borders on the awesome.

Upon entering MOSI's science center, it is apparent that this is a place from which dreams are generated. Encompassing more than 260,000 square feet on 76 acres, MOSI is a feast of sights and sounds: a springboard for inspiring the imagination of young and old alike. This largest science center in the southeastern United States delivers what it promises - to make a difference in people's lives by making science real. More than 605,000 visitors a year couldn't agree more.

This is innovative learning coming from all directions and all scientific persuasions - from dinosaurs to butterflies, down-to-earth ecology to the wonder of the heavens. There is no limit to the inspiration. Designed programs range from pre-school to the elderly and are too countless to mention here. Needless to say, MOSI has something for everyone.

Consider, for example, that MOSI houses The Saunders Planetarium, Florida's only IMAX® *Dome* Theatre, the Back Woods Nature Center, the Southwest Florida Water Management District/Bank of America BioWorks Butterfly Garden, the GTE Challenger Learning Center and the Coleman Science Works Theater. MOSI also features 60,000 square feet of permanent exhibit space, 5,000 square feet of temporary exhibit space, a 450-seat auditorium, an outdoor amphitheater, a store and a restaurant. Definitely a place to spend an entire day, then return again and again.

Located in Hillsborough County opposite the University of South Florida campus in northern Tampa, MOSI draws visitors from a five county region with a total population of 2.1 million. As a part of its mission, MOSI offers a selection of 15 different interactive learning experiences geared to a variety of audiences. These range from continuing education enrichment, corporate computer learning to programs for disadvantaged, at risk and minority audiences.

But most of all, MOSI has a predilection for making the basic act of discovery - learning - fun, regardless of age or audience. It is Tampa Bay's field of dreams, and people have come to treasure MOSI. One trip will explain it all.

www.mosi.org

LOWRY PARK ZOO OF TAMPA BAY

Tampa Bay's "wild side" has been in residence at the Lowry Park Zoo, since the late 1930's. Recognized as one of the top three mid-sized zoological parks in the country, Lowry Park Zoo features 41 acres of lush, natural habitat comprising five main exhibit areas: the Florida Manatee and Aquatic Center, Native Florida Wildlife Center, Asian Domain, Primate World, Free-Flight Aviary and the Children's Petting Zoo.

Not only a place for wild creatures, the Lowry Park Zoo accommodates Tampa Bay's human population in a variety of exciting venues. The Saunders Pavilion is a 10,000 square foot area for meetings, banquets, educational programs and special exhibitions. The Harrell Discovery Center is an interactive area featuring hands-on displays, exhibits, artifacts, videos and a small insect zoo.

The adjoining Saunders Amphitheater houses the Zoo's "Reptile Encounter" programs, and a Birds of Prey Amphitheater allows visitors to soar with a variety of owls, hawks, eagles and falcons. The new Florida Environmental Education Center will house 11 classrooms, a library, lecture/meeting hall and an outdoor amphitheater. This 21st century facility will be equipped for distance learning on the Internet.

The Lowry Park Zoo also provides a variety of conservation and preservations programs for endangered wildlife. The world-renowned Manatee Aquatic Center and Rehabilitation Hospital cares for Florida's injured West Indian manatees. As the only not-for-profit hospital in the area, the Manatee Center has treated over 70 injured manatees and been the site of the area's first manatee birth in captivity. Lowry, a male manatee, was born in 2000.

Located in North Tampa, the Lowry Park Zoo has added a number of "creature comforts" for Zoo visitors, including a fully air-conditioned Paradise Café featuring an extended Key West Deck with an exciting view of the Manatees. Shade canopies also protect visitors at the Reptile and Birds of Prey amphitheaters.

Named for General Sumter L. Lowry, Jr., who donated an 18 year-old Asian elephant to the zoo in 1960, the Lowry Park Zoo is managed by the Lowry Park Zoological Society. Supported by the city of Tampa and the community, the zoo continues to be a central focus for a variety of imaginative functions, including an annual black tie event.

www.lowryparkzoo.org

Concerts on the Mighty Wurlitzer organ often precede the showing of film classics at the restored 1926 Tampa Theatre.

east bank of the Hillsborough River, is the largest complex of its kind south of the Kennedy Center. Built in 1987, its centerpiece is the 2,557-seat Carol Morsani Hall with enormous onstage and backstage areas that easily accommodate major productions of Broadway musicals, operas, ballets and orchestra concerts.

The Tampa Bay Performing Arts Center also has an elegant 1,034-seat Playhouse, the 300-seat Robert and Lorena Jaeb Theater, and the more intimate 150-seat Off Center Theater. The Center and its programs are sponsored in part by the Department of State, Division of Cultural Affairs and the Florida Arts Council; the Arts Council of Hillsborough County; and the Tourist Development Council/Hillsborough County and the City of Tampa.

The Tampa Theatre is another local landmark and a theater tradition since it opened in 1926. Here moviegoers can expect to find independent and foreign films viewed in one of the most ornate settings of its time and on some days have the added bonus of a pre-movie concert on the theater's Mighty Wurlitzer.

In 1973 its owners donated the Tampa Theatre to the City of Tampa, which continues to restore the building created by noted theatre architect John Eberson. Its design has been described as "Florida Mediterranean," which includes touches of Italian Renaissance, Byzantine, Spanish, Mediterranean, Greek Revival, Baroque, and even English Tudor. It is listed in the National Register of Historic Places.

Art knows no boundaries in the Tampa Bay area. The Tampa Museum of Art, with 7,000 works in its permanent collection, and the University of South Florida Contemporary Art Museum, with changing exhibits of regional, national and international works, are just two more examples.

Tampa is a city with its own government, utilities, transportation system, libraries, public school system, and neighborhoods, yet many of the resources located in Tampa, like those located in St. Petersburg, bridge the bay between us. Higher education, for one, health care for another, and sports. You will see Devil Rays caps on the heads of many Tampans just as you will see the flag of the Buccaneer pirate flying from the aerials of cars bearing Pinellas County plates. Whether it was St. Petersburg hosting the men's NCAA Final Four in 1999 or Raymond James Stadium hosting the 2001 Super Bowl, both sides of the Bay rally together to bring these natiional sports spectaculars to our doorstep.

When companies study our region to consider an expansion or relocation they are given statistics that include Tampa Bay demographics – those of an MSA that encompasses the cities of Tampa in Hillsborough County and St. Petersburg in Pinellas including our strengths and our differences. And when you consider the sum of these parts and factor in the weather, it proves to be an unparalleled environment for work and play – a matter of business and beauty, from beaches to bay.

TAMPA BAY PERFORMING ARTS CENTER

Make it a special night out!

Situated in the heart of Tampa Bay, the Tampa Bay Performing Arts Center is the home of world-class entertainment. As the largest performing arts center in the Southeast, it boasts one of the nation's leading Broadway series and is nationally respected for producing grand opera as well as a wide variety of performance art.

Opened in 1987 and continually renovated, the facility is state of the art. Four venues of various sizes and configuration ensure audiences the best environment for the particular production.

The stage of Carol Morsani Hall (a 2,600-seat auditorium) has launched several of the country's leading Broadway tours. In addition to its Broadway reputation, the Tampa Bay Performing Arts Center's producing arm, Opera Tampa, draws internationally recognized opera stars for principal characters and spotlights local talent in supporting and chorus roles. Audiences in Louise Lykes Ferguson Hall (1,050 seats) see dance, from ballet to daredevil, and concerts from classical ensembles to jazz and rock. The Jaeb Theater (300-seat, cabaret-style) lets the audience sit comfortably at a table with refreshments while they enjoy original cabaret productions by The Center Theater Company of Tampa Bay. And the Off Center Theater (150 seats) has a black box design adaptable for configuration to the performance. In the Off Center, The Center Theater Company produces a play series and a women's works series as well as presents poets, performance artists and comedians.

Located on a picturesque nine-acre site on the east bank of the Hillsborough River in downtown Tampa, the Tampa Bay Performing Arts Center is just off exit #25 on Interstate 275. Valet parking is available on-site and self-parking is available adjacently. Make the night complete with a visit to Maestro's, an onsite fine dining restaurant, and stop by The Center Store to enjoy some favorite theater memorabilia.

www.tbpac.org

BUSCH GARDENS

Busch Gardens Tampa Bay combines unforgettable thrill rides, live entertainment and one of North America's largest zoos within an exotic African adventure. In June 2000, Busch Gardens premiered a 29-acre enhanced portion of its famous Serengeti Plain habitat where giraffes, zebra, bongo, ostriches and other African species can be seen closer than ever before in majestic settings. Up-close animal encounters abound with more than 2,700 animals in naturalistic environments such as Edge of Africa, Myombe Reserve and Lory Landing.

Gwazi, the Southeast's largest and fastest double wooden roller coaster challenges guests through six crossings at combined speeds of 100 mph. Experience World Rhythms On Ice, a whirlwind tour of seven countries including England, Brazil, Germany and the United States. This ice-skating extravaganza features authentic costumes, dazzling special effects and world-class skaters blended into an unforgettable live performance.

www.buschgardens.com

ADVENTURE ISLAND

Adventure Island is Tampa's sizzling, tropical water park featuring 18 drenching water play areas including exciting thrill slides, white sand beaches and championship volleyball courts.

New in 2000 is Wahoo Run, a state of the art tunnel raft ride that sends adventurous riders down six stories and more than 600 feet of unforeseen drenching twists, drops, back-to-back curves and turns. Whether your cruising down Key West Rapids or floating down the Rambling Bayou, Adventure Island is the ultimate water destination for sun-seekers of all ages.

www.adventureisland.com

TAMPA BAY PARTNERSHIP

The Climate Is Right For Business

Like most major metropolitan areas, Tampa Bay comprises more than just one city, or one county. From beaches to orange groves to downtown high-rise office buildings, the Tampa Bay area is a diverse collection of unique cities and business opportunities.

To highlight this diversity, the Tampa Bay Partnership, a regional business-led group for economic development, brings together the counties of Pinellas, Hillsborough, Pasco, Hernando, Polk, Manatee, and Sarasota to collaborate on issues of economic growth for the entire region.

Since 1994 the Partnership has worked closely with economic development groups and chambers to increase "brand" visibility for Tampa Bay while helping facilitate the site selection process for relocating and expanding companies.

The Partnership's major objectives include business image enhancement, including advertising, targeted events and a premium Internet presence, and advocacy for infrastructure to regional solutions in transportation, water supply and education. Another objective, workforce development, helps recruit skilled workers to Florida's High Tech Corridor, stretching from the Gulf Coast to the Space Coast. The fourth objective is business attraction, including trade shows and a highly effective lead generation and referral process.

As one of the hottest economic engines around, Tampa Bay consistently creates one-third of all new jobs in the Sunshine State and is in the top echelon of major metro labor markets in the U.S. The high tech workforce in Tampa Bay helps propel Florida to number six among states in terms of high tech jobs and output.

Talent is found in a wide variety of fields, from manufacturing and materials management, to software design and development, network engineering, information systems management, telecommunications, and biomedical engineering. St. Petersburg and Pinellas County, in particular, have a growing cluster of biomedical companies that make Tampa Bay the state leader in producing and acquiring medical patents.

The University of South Florida is crucial to the region's high tech potential, and research programs have spun off an increasing number of startup companies. The acclaimed marine science program is a major reason the Florida Institute of Oceanography, the U.S. Geological Survey and the Florida Department of Environmental Protection are all located on or near the USF Bayboro campus in St. Petersburg.

"The Climate Is Right For Business" is a promise used globally by the Tampa Bay Partnership to capture the truly diverse advantages offered by St. Petersburg and west central Florida. There's much to be gained by building a strong regional community that will thrive in this digital age.

www.tampabay.org

Chapter 13
Vistas of Tomorrow

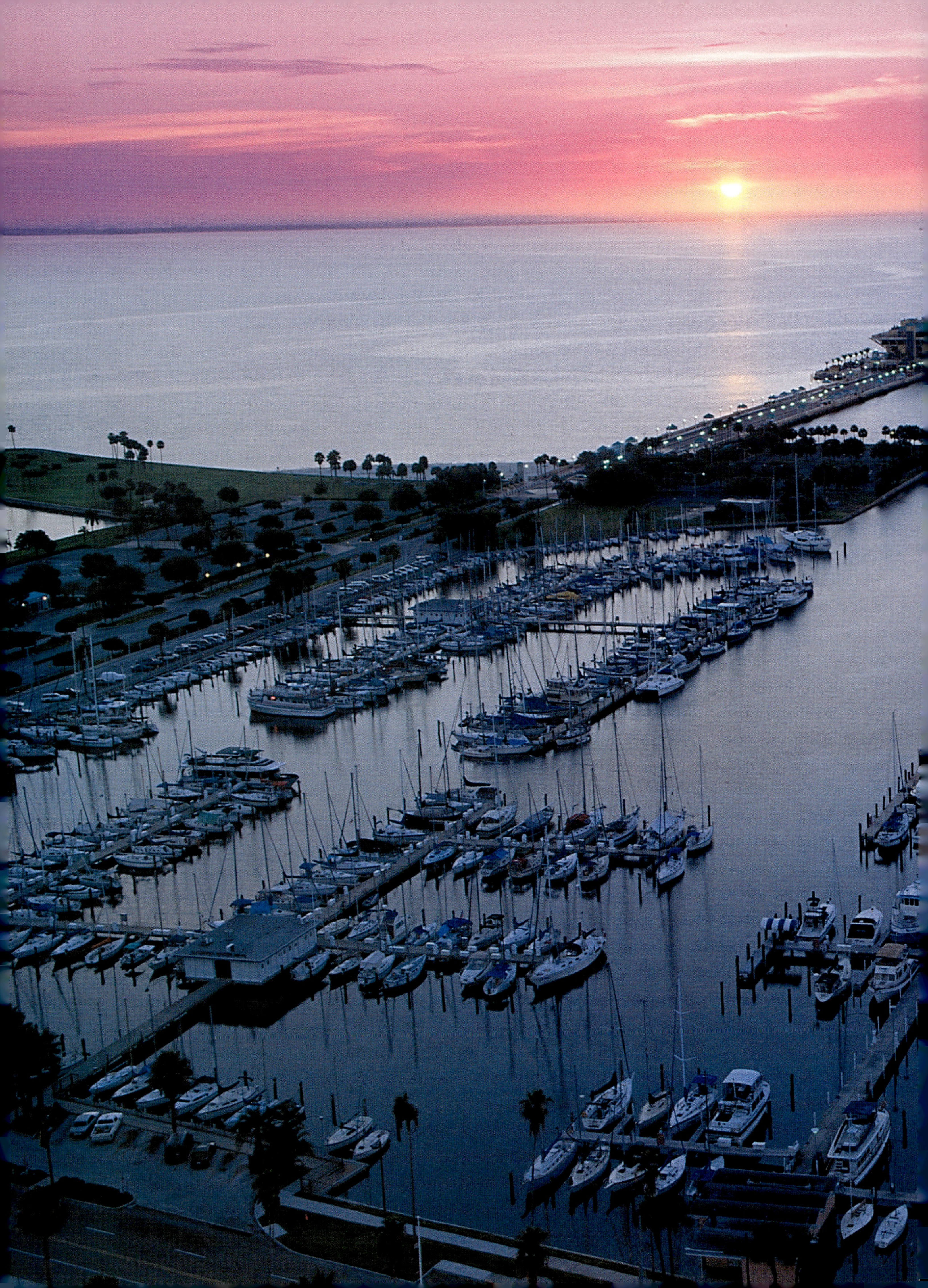

When the curtain rose on the twenty-first century, the overture was in digital sound and the image was in pixels. St. Petersburg took its cue…

Vistas of Tomorrow

Here was a city well prepared, confident, and poised to take the leading role. We had waited quietly in the wings like a hopeful understudy, whose full potential was often underestimated and true talent sometimes obscured by stereotyping.

Now the millennium had arrived and technology was looking for a home. Ultimately the spotlight fell on Tampa Bay, a place more familiar with sunshine than the limelight. Standing center stage was the vibrant, young, innovative St. Petersburg and Pinellas County, a place where corporate dreams could grow.

For more than a century we have nurtured business ideas and welcomed entrepreneurs while remaining true to a sense of community and quality of life. No longer restricted to the limits of geography and communication, today we are connected by efficient transportation systems, and by internet technology and e-commerce. As the world was getting smaller we got better!

Near the close of 1999, the U.S. Bureau of Labor Statistics reported that the Tampa Bay area had the largest percentage increase in employment of all the nation's big labor markets. The next study, released in July of 2000, showed that things hadn't slowed down and that for over two consecutive years our local job growth rate averaged 4.9 percent over each six month period.

At the center, the Tampa-St. Petersburg-Clearwater area topped the bureau's rankings of all 24 U.S. metropolitan areas with employment levels of one million or more. We are now home to the largest civilian work force in the state of Florida and consistently maintain a low unemployment rate. That could change, but experts predict that most likely it will not.

Unlike other heavily industrialized or industry-specific areas in the U.S., Tampa Bay's moderate wage scale reflects the nature of our diverse businesses. From our earliest history, St. Petersburg and the beaches have been known for superlative scenery and abundant sunshine – responsible for our initial growth. The services industry is still the largest employer in Pinellas County, a trend expected to continue as tourism and financial service providers thrive in our healthy business climate. In St. Petersburg, the majority of business growth comes from our own homegrown and small businesses. New economy industries like information technology, high technology and manufacturing, and marine science have further diversified this profile.

As we accommodate new business, corporate relocations and expansions, the commercial real estate market in Pinellas has been positively affected by additional service, retail trade, and construction industries, especially in the last decade, and is expected to continue. Tampa Bay offers low construction costs – and because of climate, year-round construction opportunity – an abundance of existing office and industrial space, and ample available acreage in top quality business parks.

We are in the fourth largest state in the U.S. with over 14 million people. State and local governments see the business community as the main source of prosperity and security, so they work to provide legislation and regulations that encourage economic activity. Florida's tax structure has always been attractive to business and the state offers a substantial package of financial incentives and business assistance programs.

As St. Petersburg expands its economic base, it too has established more resources to assist existing and start-up businesses. The forward thinking city has one of Florida's 30 targeted Enterprise Zones, which covers a 9.4 square mile section of the city including all of downtown. Businesses in the Enterprise Zone receive valuable state tax credits and refunds when they create new jobs, purchase equipment, make building improvements or hire employees who live in the immediate area. They also can receive a 50% credit on Florida corporate income tax or insurance premium tax by donating to community development projects in the Enterprise Zone.

The City of St. Petersburg's median age has dropped ten years over the last two decades, establishing a young and energetic workforce for our growing business community. More than half of those who attend college in the Tampa Bay area continue to live and work in the area after graduation, providing more than 10,000 highly educated workers each year.

Pinellas County's four-year public university, the University of South Florida (USF) – St. Petersburg, now admits freshmen and sophomores on a regular basis and offers full academic programs for undergraduates and graduates at its downtown Bayboro campus, including a doctoral degree in Marine Science – all recent changes.

St. Petersburg Junior College's new University Center is the first of its kind in Florida and one of only a handful nationwide. It offers access to junior and senior level courses for bachelor's and master's degrees through an alliance with the University of South Florida, Florida State University, Florida A&M University, University of Central Florida, Eckerd College, Saint Leo University, Florida Gulf Coast University, and Florida International University. Still more universities are being considered to bring additional degree programs to the school.

The college population also provides a potential pool of over 110,000 skilled part-time workers in a state that has demonstrated their productivity. In fact, studies show that all our workers add an average of $2.54 to the value of manufactured goods for every $1 spent on payroll. Florida is a right-to-work state by constitutional provision, with strong employment at-will legislation. Only 8.2 percent of the Florida's workforce is unionized, compared to 15.5 percent nationally. And while our strong research and high education institutions are growing our high tech base, our mature vocational training programs continue to offer a large and superior labor base.

From our educational research labs to the galleries of our

continued on page 308

ST. PETERSBURG AREA CHAMBER OF COMMERCE

Considering St. Petersburg's accommodating climate, "Chamber of Commerce weather" is a year-round delight. Without the burden of winter woes, the St. Petersburg Area Chamber of Commerce™ has turned its vision to the business climate, an equally invigorating phenomenon, with dynamic and innovative partnerships.

The year 2000 not only welcomed a new millennium but also began the Chamber's second century of service as the vibrant voice of business and the catalyst for community development. For the past 100 years, the Chamber has been a leader in tourism, economic development, transportation and in most major community projects.

Located in the heart of downtown St. Petersburg, the Chamber Building has witnessed an abundance of new construction on all sides. Representing Florida's fourth largest city is both rewarding and challenging. With 80 percent of new jobs emanating from existing businesses, the Chamber's partnership with the City of St. Petersburg has a specific focus in solving problems of current businesses relating to survival, expansion or discontent.

The Chamber's showcases provide the leading network and exposure opportunities for businesses in Pinellas County. Offering some 35 committees and task forces, the Chamber has five geographic councils and addresses major issues in transportation, education, the environment, minority entrepreneurship…to name just a few.

Other major programs of the Chamber include the second oldest chamber leadership program in America, an orientation program for new to the area CEO's, the only Entrepreneurial Academy in Florida and the staffing of three welcome centers at key visitor points in the greater St. Petersburg area.

The Chamber's website receives over four million hits a year and offers a wealth of information ranging from employment opportunities, to where to stay and what to do in sunny St. Petersburg, Pinellas County and the Tampa Bay area. With over 2000 business members, the St. Petersburg Area Chamber of Commerce is an organization governed by a Board of elected directors and staffed with dedicated professionals.

www.stpete.com

Vistas of Tomorrow

museums, generous donations of public and private funds have also, without question, given our community the opportunity to develop. For example, the St. Petersburg Museum of Fine Arts sits on 4.5 acres of downtown waterfront that the city gave to the institution in the early 1960's. A 50,000 square-foot, three-story wing is now planned to be built on the existing parking lot, providing two floors of new galleries and rooms for more educational programs. The expansion, the third since the museum first opened, will more than double the existing space, and will depend on community support.

In addition, the Salvador Dali Museum is proceeding with plans to build an addition onto its waterfront site in the Bayboro District, and Great Explorations, the Hands-On Museum is expected to move from its temporary location at The Pier to a larger space in city-owned Sunken Gardens.

St. Petersburg's Bayboro District has seen many improvements in recent years, made possible, in part, by generous benefactors. A new $12-million Pediatric Research Institute, built on land donated by the city to USF-St. Petersburg, received enough help from private contributions to establish two research chairs and endowments when it opened in 2000. Ultimately as many as 100 scientists will work at the institute.

Water, of course, is an essential resource to Tampa Bay's economy, environment and way of life. We are, after all, a resort area that advertises the pleasures of swimming, boating and fishing. Drinking water is essential to life. For a region of two-million people it is a 247-million gallons-a-day fact of life, from a mostly groundwater supply that could be threatened by population increases.

To address this, a Master Water Plan was approved, in 1995, to produce new or alternative sources of potable water for the region. Tampa Bay Water, a wholesale water supplier, is now executing that plan in a regional partnership with the governments of Hillsborough, Pasco and Pinellas counties and the cities of St. Petersburg, Tampa and New Port Richey. One method included in the plan is "reverse osmosis" at a seawater desalination plant to be built, owned and operated by a private developer.

Though environmental impact studies are still being conducted, the plant site would be at Tampa Electric Company's Big Bend Power Station near Apollo Beach in southern Hillsborough County with a target completion date of December, 2002. When constructed, it would be the largest desalination plant in North America.

Future modes of transportation for a changing Florida are also in the works. A proposed high-speed rail system, the Florida Overland Express, would link the Gulf Coast Tampa Bay area, central Florida's Orlando and south Florida's Miami as never before. Service between Miami and Orlando – an estimated 55-minute trip – is targeted to begin in 2004 and Tampa Bay service – 93 minutes to Miami – would begin in 2006.

The seven county Tampa Bay area has more total households than the twenty-county Atlanta metropolitan area, and is projected to add an average of 50,500 persons per year, reaching nearly 3.7 million people by 2005.

Preparing to manage this rate of growth while maintaining our natural attributes is a challenge set before county and city councils and commissions throughout the region where any change in population and environment affects us all.

To adapt to the changing nature of both population demographics and business diversity we not only share the very things that make all of Tampa Bay so attractive, but rely on the support of our education networks, government tax incentives, and business programs. It is this very partnership, the private sector working with the universities and local governments, that will sustain us through the decades to come.

We invite you to be a part of our future and experience the brilliance that is St. Petersburg and Pinellas County – The Gulf Coast Jewel of Tampa Bay.

TY HESTON

CITY OF ST. PETERSBURG ECONOMIC DEVELOPMENT

A City for the New Millennium

St. Petersburg has enjoyed record levels of growth in recent years; for example, the value of new construction over the last three years prior to 2000 ($885 million) exceeded the total for the prior 6 years ($873 million). Over $1 billion dollars of public and private investment has occurred in the City's downtown area since adopting the Intown Redevelopment Plan in 1982, and that portion of the City's tax base has grown by 29 percent since 1995.

The City's downtown tax base has also seen significant growth, with a 17.5 percent increase in taxable value occurring in three downtown tax increment financing districts in 1999. Over $130 million in new residential construction, representing 475 new dwelling units has been initiated in the downtown area, with more anticipated through 2001.

Downtown St. Petersburg represents the largest concentration of businesses in Pinellas County and third largest in the Tampa Bay region. More than 1,500 businesses employ some 25,000 people in the downtown area. BayWalk, a $40 million new mixed-use urban entertainment center, opened in late 2000. More than 9 million people visit the downtown area each year to attend special events, baseball games and attractions.

The largest oceanographic research center in the Southeast, featuring the University of South Florida's Department of Marine Science and United States Geological Survey, is located in the City's downtown area. More than 10 marine institutes employ nearly 1,000 scientists, engineers and support staff.

Business opportunities throughout the city continue to be extremely positive. Numerous corporate offices, manufacturing facilities and residential development projects have occurred in the City's Gateway area in recent years, including $302 million of private investment to date and $100 million more in progress. The City is enhancing the Dome Industrial Park and developing a $7.5 million 19-acre industrial park pilot project to bring new industries to this area. The Dome Area Businesses, along with many others, lie in the City's Enterprise Zone which have received nearly $2,500,000 in state corporate income tax credits and refunds. In 1999, the City in conjunction with several partners, opened a one-stop Business Development Center to assist existing small businesses and encourage the formation of new businesses

According to Cushman & Wakefield's 1999 year-end reports, St. Petersburg had the lowest vacancy rate of industrial space among Florida's seven largest cities, and the third lowest office space vacancy rate among the same seven cities (Fort Lauderdale, Jacksonville, Miami, Orlando, Palm Beach, St. Petersburg, Tampa).

GULFCOAST CERTIFIED DEVELOPMENT CORPORATION

The Money that Makes Your Business Work

Bessolo Design Group Inc.

Successful small businesses provide more jobs than any other sector of the economy. Considering the majority of Pinellas County's more than 30,000 businesses fall into this category, St. Petersburg's GulfCoast Certified Development Corporation (GCDC) is ready to help guide many of those businesses into a prosperous future. As a partner with the U.S. Small Business Administration (SBA), GCDC provides access to the 504 Loan Program.

Founded in 1982 as the St. Petersburg Certified Development Company, GCDC has since grown to serve a broader area of Florida's Gulf Coast. As a 501c-3 private, non-profit corporation, the company now provides assistance to businesses throughout Pinellas, Manatee and Pasco counties.

GCDC represents a partnership of the public and private sectors with the primary purpose of creating job opportunities and fostering economic development. Governed by a board of directors, the GCDC offers an alternative financing source with low down payment, below market interest and long term fixed rate financing. GCDC utilizes a seven-person loan committee with a volunteer, community-oriented membership composed of 30 small business owners, community leaders, governmental representatives and industry professionals.

While the SBA was created in 1953 under the Eisenhower Administration, the GCDC is quick to point out that "it's not your father's SBA anymore." Now streamlined to function as a grass roots economic development tool, the GCDC, as an Accredited Lender, can provide a three-day turnaround on loan applications. Typically, the 504 loan program is for the purchase and use of long term fixed assets such as land, building, or capital equipment.

Many eligible for the 504 loan program can receive up to 90 percent financing with a long term, fixed interest rate for up to 20 years. Projects are financed through a public-private partnership with financial institutions covering 50 percent of the cost, the GCDC picking up 40 percent of the project through the sale of debentures, and the small business investing at least 10 percent. One new permanent full-time job or part-time equivalents must be created for every $35,000 of debenture funds.

For small businesses in Pinellas, Manatee and Pasco counties, the GCDC is quick to remind prospective borrowers that many small companies have profited greatly from the 504 loan program. Names like Federal Express, Apple Computer and Outback Steak House were all started with SBA loans.

Not bad company by any stretch of the imagination.

Lasting Impressions Interiors

www.gulfcoastcdc.com

PINELLAS COUNTY ECONOMIC DEVELOPMENT

Economic Development in progress at Carillon in St. Petersburg, one of Florida's most attractive and dynamic business parks.

See Business in a Whole New Light

Pinellas County's invitation to see business in a whole new light offers a spectrum of possibilities for those who come for the business climate and stay for the lifestyle. But behind this prism of possibilities lies a dynamic engine of growth powered by the high-octane fuel from a progressive economic development team.

Pinellas County Economic Development represents a unique and synergistic partnership between people and businesses that extends from the mom and pop corner store to corporations involved in multinational operations. In between these entities are needs ranging from simple to complex, and Pinellas County's Economic Development team provides an open conduit for solutions to these needs.

Economic Development addresses a wealth of diverse human needs ranging from welfare-to-work programs, business-driven education and training, and workforce issues, as well as business assistance and expansion activities. Focusing each need is a professional dedicated to understanding the cause and effect relationship between the economy of Pinellas County and the tens of thousands of businesses that call it home.

Business Assistance Specialists pave the way for success. This can be as simple as solving a permitting issue, helping to find financing opportunities or providing a cohesive economic development vision for the County's diverse municipalities.

Pinellas County Economic Development continues to expand international trade, illustrated by the opening of the Pinellas-Mexico Trade Office in Mexico City. Pinellas was the first U.S. county to achieve this.

A premium is placed on active partnerships and a two-way line of communications. In-person business surveys continually gauge the pulse of business. A sophisticated Internet website provides linkage to businesses and critical information databases. The cable television show and AM radio broadcast, *Good Business Pinellas,* produced by Economic Development, are lively mixes of education and entertainment created to make doing good business easier.

Contained within this dynamic environment are individual business initiatives that continue to drive Pinellas County full speed forward. The County leads Central Florida in the number of biomedical firms, in microelectronics concerns, in laser and optics businesses and in information technology companies. This is business at its finest, in a county at its best.

At the heart of Pinellas County Economic Development's efforts are more and better jobs starting at a living wage and low cost, high quality living for the people of Pinellas.

Seeing success in a whole new light is more than just an advertising slogan. For Pinellas County Economic Development, it is a crystal clear vision of the future that is happening now.

www.siliconbay.org

A child of a new century. We can only imagine what wonders she will see and experience as she grows up in this alluring environment. Few cities and counties in America offer a better mix of industry, technology, recreation, culture, attractions and enviable quality of life. St. Petersburg & Pinellas County – Truly The Gulf Coast Jewel on Tampa Bay.

Production Team

Editor-In-Chief
RUSS SLOAN

Russ Sloan has been President/CEO of the St. Petersburg Area Chamber of Commerce™ since 1994. Having led three major chambers, Sloan's career also encompasses three championship years as a collegiate head football coach, four years as Director of Motor Vehicle and Licensing for the State of Missouri, athletic director at S.E. Missouri State and Fresno State, and executive director of the California Bowl.

Russ Sloan assembled the talented team to produce this publication and worked with them on all aspects of the book's production.

Creative Consultant, Illustrator
JUNE ALLARD BERTÉ

June Allard-Berté is an established portraitist and creative designer with a background as a commercial artist. Her visionary design sense and drawing skills are the foundations for her creative projects, ranging from portraits for the Western Massachusetts Judicial Society to serving on event committees and juried art shows. A published artist, Allard-Berté represented the United States in International Artist Magazine, April '99. Her work also appears in Becoming A Successful Artist, Being An Artist and Energizing Your Paintings with Color, published by North Light Books. Allard-Berté teaches classes at the Gulf Coast Museum of Art.

Writer/Editor, Narrative
RUTH BROSS

Ruth M. Bross has researched and written editorial content for the Chamber's publications since 1995. She began her communications career as an advertising copywriter in the Hartford, then Indianapolis markets and, as a St. Petersburg-based freelancer, has written for print, broadcast and electronic media. In the late 1980s her weekly newspaper column, Time Out, received the Florida Press Association's first place award for humor, a style she says evolved from her family's homelife. Today, she is happy to be living in the information age.

Writer/Editor, Business
E.L. HARRIS

E.L."Gene" Harris began his career as senior public relations writer for a multinational corporation traveling the globe. The grail of communicating in written English eventually led him to free-lance where, for nearly a quarter-century, Harris has produced appropriate verbiage for foreign governments, corporations, businesses and individuals. He and his wife, fine artist Cassandra Gordon-Harris, now are proud to call St. Pete home. Harris continues to produce the written word for local and national businesses and web-based e-commerce enterprises.

Photo Editor/Chief Photographer
HERB SNITZER

Herb Snitzer's 45 years of image-making has earned him a reputation as one of America's most respected photojournalists. His work has appeared in the pages of Life, Look, The Saturday Evening Post and other respected national publications. As photographer and later associate editor of Metronome, America's leading jazz magazine, Snitzer met, photographed and became friends with the great jazz musicians of our time. Author of five books, Snitzer's work appears in museums across the country and in many private collections. Snitzer resides in St. Petersburg where he maintains his studio.

Design Director & Production
JUDY FALLON

Judy Fallon designs and produces brochures and collateral materials for many Tampa Bay Businesses under the name, Marketing By Design. She has an extensive background in magazine publishing and provides graphic design and production for several local publications. Fallon has been the winner of over a dozen Addy Awards and has received awards for magazine design excellence from the Florida Magazine Association. She operates her business in Tarpon Springs, where she also has a retail shop, Global Folk Arts, offering crafts, beads and jewelry from third world countries.

Index

A
A.C. Nielsen Company, 277
Admiral Farragut Academy, 33, 108, 312
Adventure Island, 294, 301
AEGON Equity Group, 196
Al Lang Field, *14*, 52, 124, 125
Albert Whitted Airport, 12, 52, *60, 63, 131*, 222
Allendale, *32*
Allendale United Methodist Church, *46*
All Children's Hospital, 72, 76, 93, 94
American Stage, 66
American Tool & Mold, 154
AmSouth Bank, 192, 199
Amtrak, 16, 224
Anclote Key State Preserve, 258
Andersen Consulting Solution Works, 72
Army Air Corps, 13
Arts Center, 64, 86
Artspace, 64
Asian Family and Community Empowerment Center, *46*
Avaya Communications, 158, 159
Azalea, 34

B
Bahama Shores, 34
Baltimore Orioles, 124
Bank of America, 72, 192, 197
Bankers Insurance Group, 69, 72
Barcley Estates, 28, 29
Bay Isle Key, 27
Bay Pines VA Medical Center, 12, 94
Bay Plaza, 18, 68
Bay Point Elementary School, 103
Bay Point Middle School, 103
Bay View Tower, 72
Bay Vista Fundamental School, 106
Bayboro District, 308
Bayboro Harbor, 16, 52
BayCare Health System, *90*, 92, 94
Bayflite, 94
Bayfront Center, 16, 52, *60, 66, 94, 98*, 24
Bayfront-St. Anthony's Health Care, 72, 92, 96
Bayshore Boulevard, *292*
Bayside Bridge, 149, 222, 265
BayWalk, 18, 54, 70, 72, 234
Bayway Isles, 38
BeeLine Ferry, 14
Belleair Beach, 252, 273, 280
Belleair Bluffs, 220, 234, 280
Belleair Shore, 220, 229, 280
Belleair, 13, 220, 280, 288
Belleview Biltmore Resort & Spa, 13, 19, 280, 288
Benoist Airboat Line, 284
Bethel Community Baptist Church, 39
Board of County Commissioners, 216, 280
Board of Trade (St. Petersburg), 50
Board of Trade (Tampa), 290
Boca Ciega Bay, 7, 33, 37, 38, 94, 139, 248, 279
Boca Ciega High School, 103
Booker Creek, 36
Boston Braves, 9, 124
Bovie Medical Corp, 148
Boyd Hill Nature Park, 16, 134, *138*
Brightwaters Boulevard, *29*
Broadwater, 37
Brooke, Colonel George Mercer, 286
Brooker Creek Preserve, *280*
Bruce Watters Jewelry, 15
Bunce, William, 5
Busch Gardens - Tampa Bay, 294, 300
Business Journal Serving Greater Tampa Bay, 229

C
Caladesi Island State Park, *258*
Caloosa Indians, 286
Canterbury School of Florida, 109
Capitol Marketing Concepts, 182
Carillon Park, 192
Carlton Fields, 198
Catalina Marketing Corporation, 170, 176, 177
Cathedral Church of St. Peter, 40, *41*
Cathedral of St. Jude the Apostle, 40

Caya Costa, 28
CBB Architects, 200
Center for Marine Conservation, 149
Central Avenue, *70*
Central Plaza, 32
Central Skate Park, 134
Ceridian, 170, 172, 173
Chenault, General Claire, 33
Chicago Cubs, 124
Christ United Methodist Church, 40
Christian Science Reading Room, 44
Church of Scientology, 265
Church of St. Bartholomew, 40, 43
Church of the Holy Spirit, 43
Cincinnati Reds, 125
Civil War, 40, 286
Clear Channel Communications, 226
Clearwater Beach, 241, *266*
Clearwater Discovery School, 110
Clearwater Gas System, 220
Clearwater High School, 104
Clearwater Mall, 16, 230
Clearwater Marine Aquarium, 271
Clearwater Mission of the Methodist Church, 40
Clearwater Municipal Marina, 266, 270
Clearwater Yacht Club, 266
Clearwater, 6, 8, 11, 13, 16, 106, 110, 125, 134, 193, 216, 220, 222, 230, 241, 252, 258, 264, 265, 266, 273, 277, 279, 280, 284, 306
Cloisters on Beach Drive, 18, 68, 74
Coachman Fundamental School, 106
Coachman Park, 265
Coconut Grove, *230*
Coffee Pot Bayou, 28, 29, 52, 124
Colen, Sidney, 279
Coliseum, 11, *13, 66,* 68
Colliers Arnold, 212
Community Resource Centers, 26
Compulink Cable Assemblies, 149
Concurrent Technologies, Inc., 148
Congregation B'nai Israel, 44
Constellation Technology Corp., 148
Coquina Key Park, 134
Coquina Key, 36, 37, 134
Cornerstone Community Bank, 192
Cosme Water Treatment Plant, 220
Council of Neighborhood Associations (CONA), 27
Countryside Mall, 16, 226, 235
Countryside, 16, 92, 226, 230, 235, 265
Courtney Campbell Causeway, 222, 265, 284
Cox Target Media, 180
Creative Clay Cultural Art Center, 64
Crescent Lake Field, *11*
Criminal Justice Center, *217*
Crossroads, 34
Crosstown Expressway, 222
Crystal Beach, 8, *280*
CSX, 224
Curtis Fundamental School, 106
Cypress Links, 132

D
Davis Cup, 131
Davis, D.P., 290
Davis, Enoch Douglas, 39
Davis, E.A., *4*, 7
Davis, George R., 29
de Narvaez, Panfilo, 4, 286
de Soto, Hernando, 278
Demens Landing Park, 16, *64*
Demens, Peter A., *5*, 6, 170
Dennis Hotel, 10
Derby Lane, 142
DeSoto, Hernando, 4, 286
Dessa Antiques, *234*
Digital LightWave, 152, 216
Diocese of St. Petersburg, 40
Disciples of Christ, 43
Disston City, 278
Disston Ridge, 32
Disston, Hamilton, 5, 277, 278
Dixie Hollins High School, 279
Dolphin Cay, 37

Dome District, 56
Don CeSar Beach Resort & Spa, 10, 13, 43, 243, 244
Donaldson, John, *5*
Douglas, J.O., 277
Downtown Partnership, 72
Driftwood, *33*, 36
Dunedin Fine Art Center, 277
Dunedin High School, 106
Dunedin, 4, 6, 8, 106, 125, 134, 220, 234, 258, 277, 280
Dunedin Train Station, *276*
Durango Oak Fire Steakhouse, 184

E
East Lake, 279, 280
East-West Parkway, 222
Echelon, 72, 175
Eckerd College, 16, 38, 114, 115, 149, 306
Eckerd, Jack, 170
Eden Isle, 29
Edward White Hospital, 94
Egmont Key, 258
Elreha Printed Circuits Corporation, 153
Enterprise Village, *103*
Enterprise Zone, 306
Environmental Technologies, Inc., 148
Epiphany Celebration, *277*
Epiphany of Our Lord Ukranian Catholic Church, *39*
Equifax Payment Services, 171, 181
Eva-Tone, 149, 178
Evert, Chris, 132

F
Feather Sound, 28
Festival of States, 60, *62*
First Avenue Methodist Church, 40
First Church of Christ Scientist, 44
First Congregational United Church of Christ, 43, 102
First Home Bank, 192
First Night, *62*
First Presbyterian Church, 41, 42
First Union Bank, 192
First United Methodist Church, *40, 41*
Florencia, 18, 68, 70, 71
Florida Aquarium, 291, 294
Florida Botanical Gardens, 276
Florida Craftsmen Gallery, 64
Florida Department of Natural Resources, 16
Florida Fish and Wildlife Conservation Commission, 16, 149
Florida high tech corridor, 98, 148
Florida Holocaust Museum, 18, 62, 81
Florida Institute of Oceanography, 72, 149
Florida International Museum, 18, 62, 72, 73
Florida Marine Research Institute, 16, 72, 149
Florida Orchestra, 66, *67, 284*
Florida Overland Express, 308
Florida Power Corporation, 7, 20, 21, 72, 170, *220*
Florida Power Park, 9, 56, *60*, 82, *122-123*, 124, *125*
Florida Presbyterian College, 114
Florida Sea Grant, 149
Florida State League, 125
Florida Theater, 11, 14
Flying Tigers, 33
Fort Brooke, 286, 290, 292
Fort Dade, *258*
Fort DeSoto Park, *38*, 138, *139*
Fort Harrison, 264, 265
Fountain of Youth, 278
Franklin Templeton Investments, 204
Friendship TrailBridge, 18, *284*
Fuller, Walter P., 27, 33, 134

G
Galbraith Marine Science Laboratory, 16
Gallery Walk, 64
Gandy Bridge, 10, 14, 16, 18, 222, 284
Gandy, George S., *9*, 10
Gangplank, 34

Corporate and Institutional Patrons are listed in **bold**. Pictures are indicated in *bold Italic*.

314

Index

Garrison Seaport Center, 290, 294
Gaspar, Jose, 286
Gasparilla, 286
Gasparill Distance Classic, *292*
Gateway Mall, 230
Gateway, 16, 26, 27, 28, 149, 171, 192, 193, 222, 276
George F. Young, Inc., 211
Germain, Anna, 5
Gibbs High School, 104, *106*
Gilchrist, Albert, 8
Gills, Jim and Heather, 32
Gizella Kopsick Palm Arboretum, *27*
Glass Canvas Gallery, 64, 65
Gomez, Captain, 4
Grace Bible Church, *39*
Grant Field, *277*
Grapefruit League, 124
Great Explorations, 52, 308
green benches, *12,* 16
Greyhound-Trailways Bus Lines, 222
Gulf Boulevard, 10, 240, 241, 248, 280
Gulf Coast Museum of Art, 276
GulfCoast Certified Development Corp., 310
Gulfport Arts Village, 279
Gulfport Casino, *278,* 279
Gulfport, 8, 103, 104, 243, 278, 279

H
Hackney, Dr. James, 5
Hall, Charles R., 27, 34
Hamlett, J.C., 28
Harbor Bluffs, 8
Harbor Isle, 28
Harborview Center, 266
H. B. Plant Museum, *286*
HCA, 94
Heritage Village, 276
Hillsborough County Aviation Authority (TIA), 224, 265, 292
Hillsborough River, 226, 282, 284, 288, 294, 298
Hilton St. Petersburg, 77
History of Florida bas relief, *78*
Holiday Inn Heritage, 60
Holiday Park, 34
Home Shopping Network, 171, 174
Honeymoon Island, 258
Honeywell, Inc., 110, 156
Howard Frankland Bridge, 14, 26, 222
Huggins, Miller, 11
Huggins-Stengel Field, *125*
Hurricane Offshore Classic, 125
Hyde Park, 288, 292

I
Ice Palace, 122, 124, 141, 294
IMRglobal Corp., 268, 269
Indian Rocks Beach, 250, 280
Indian Rocks, 8
Indian Shores, 254
Irwin Contracting, Inc., 187

J
Jabil Circuit, 148, 150, 151
Jack Russell Stadium, 265, *273,* 277
Jacor Communication, 226
Jannus, Tony, 8, *10*
Jimenez, Jose, 4
JMC Communities, 210
John Chestnut Park, 280
John Hopkins Middle School, 103, *110*
John's Pass, 250
John's Pass Village, *234*
Jungle Country Club, 10, 33
Jungle Prado, 34
Kenneth City, 216, 279
Kenwood, 32

K
Kennedy, John F., *16*
Keswick Christian School, 111
Kids & Kubs, 125
Kirkland, Russ, Murphy & Tapp, PA, 205
Kopsick, Gizella, 27

L
Lake Maggiore, 138
Lake Seminole Park, 138, *279*
Lake Seminole, 138, 142, 279
Lake Tarpon, 142, 279, 280
Lakeview Fundamental School, 106
Lakeview Presbyterian Church, 46
Lakewood Country Club, 34
Lakewood Estates, 27, 34
Lakewood High School, *102,* 104
Lang, Al, 14, 124, 125
Largo High School, 104
Largo, 6, 8, 103, 104, 220, 273, 276, 280
Lassing Park, 52
Lealman Discovery School, 110
Lighted Boat Parade, *63*
Ling, Jahja, 66
Long Center, 265, *273*
Looper trolley, *52*
Lowry Park Zoo, 294, 297

M
MacDill Air Force Base, 292
Madeira Beach, 11, 234, *250,* 258
Mahaffey Theater for the Performing Arts, 16, 52, 66, 85
Mainsail Art Festival, *63*
Mangrove Bay Golf Course, 132
Mangrove Bay, 28, 132
Mariners Pass, 28
Marti, Jose, 290
Masters Swim Club, *132*
Maximo, Antonio, 5
Maxxim Medical, 149
McAdoo, W.G., 8
MCI, 171
McMullen brothers, 273
Meadowlawn, 28
Mease Health Care, 92, 97, 110
Media General, 224
Mellitta USA, Inc., 157
Melrose Elementary School, 103
Memorial Causeway, 139, 265
Merrill Lynch, 201
Methodist Episcopal Church, 40
Minute Maid, 277
Mirror Lake Christian Church, 43
Mirror Lake, *78*
Mirror Lake Drive, 43
Mirror Lake Lyceum, 44
Mitchell, Noel "The Sandman", *8*
Moffitt Cancer Center, 95, 98
Moffitt, H. Lee, 98
Monte Cristo neighborhood, *39*
Moran, Pat, 124
Morse, Eleanor R. and A. Reynolds, 62, 64
Mortgage Investors Corporation, 202
Morton Plant Hospital, 92, 97
Morton Plant Mease Health Care Systems, 110
Moss, P. Buckley, 64, 75
Mount Zion AME, 39
Municpal Marina, *53*
Museum of Science and Industry (MOSI), 294
Musial, Stan, 52

N
National Airlines, 13
National Association of Professional Baseball Leagues, 76
National Baptist Convention, 39
Navratilova, Martina, 132
NCAA, 122, 298
New York Giants, 124
New York Yankees/Legends Field, 136
Nielsen Media Research, 183
Normile, Martin, "Marty", 72
North Redington Beach, 254
North Shore Park, *27,* 28, 52
North Shore Pool, 131, *132*
North Shore, 27, 28, 52, 131
North Straub Park, *78*
North Yacht Basin, *57*
Northeast High School, 106
Northeast Park Baptist Church, *46*
Northern American Trust, 192
Northern Trust Bank, 203
Northside Baptist Church, *41*
Northside Hospital, 94
Northwestern Mutual Financial Network, 207

O
Oakhurst, 8
O'Keefe, Georgia, painting by, *61*
Olds, Ransom Eli, 279
Oldsmar Flea Market, 279
Oldsmar, 8, 142, 220, 222, 279
Olympic Regatta training, 125
Operation Greenscape, *26*
Operation PAR Inc., 101
Orange Belt Railroad, *5,* 6, 277
Osceola High School, 104
Outback Bowl, 124
Ozona, 6, 8, 280

P
P. Buckley Moss Gallery, 64, 75
P.O.R.T.S., 149
Palladium Theatre, 44
Palm Harbor, 6, 8, 43, 104, 280
Palms of Pasadena Hospital, 91, 94
Park Street, *33*
ParkSide, 16, 230
Pasadena Community Church, 43, 45
Pasadena Fundamental School, 106
Pass-a-Grille, 8, 13, 241, 243
Patrician Point, 28
Paul Getting Memorial Trail, *138*
Payment Systems for Credit Unions, Inc., 179, 193
Pediatric Research Institute, 308
Peoples Gas System, 220, 223
Pennsylvania Hotel, 10, 34, 170
Penny for Pinellas, 220, 222
PGA, 132, 277, 279
Pheil, 10
Philadelphia Phillies, 124, 125, 265
Philippe, Odet, 278
Philippe Park, *278*
Pier 60 Park, *266*
Pinellas Bayway, 38, 114, 243
Pinellas County Aquatic Preserve Act, 38
Pinellas County Court House, *216*
Pinellas County Economic Development, 311
Pinellas County Education Foundation, 105
Pinellas County School Board, 102, 139
Pinellas County Schools, 102, 103, 106, 110
Pinellas County Schools administrative building, *106*
Pinellas County Technical Centers, *106*
Pinellas Declaration of Independence, 7
Pinellas Historical Museum, 278
Pinellas Park High School, 104
Pinellas Park, 8, 110, 149, 230, 276, 279
Pinellas Point, 26, 37
Pinellas Science Technology and Research Center (STAR), 148, 166
Pinellas Suncoast Transit Authority (PSTA), 222
Pinellas Technical Education Centers, 104, 110
Pinellas (Fred E. Marquis) Trail, 18, 134, 222, 277, *264, 265, 276*
Pinewood Cultural Park, 274, 275, 276
pink streets, 26, 37, *30-31*
Piper-Fuller Airport, 33
Placido Bayou, 28
Plant Steamship Line, 288
Plant, Henry B., 280, 286, 290
Plaza Theatre, *9*
Ponce de Leon, Juan, 4
Port of Manatee, 224
Port of St. Petersburg, *63,* 224
Port of Tampa, 224, *290*
Poynter Institute for Media Studies, 76, *224*
PricewaterhouseCoopers LLP, 192
Primex Technologies, 160
Princess Martha Hotel, 124
Punta del Pina, 4

Corporate and Institutional Patrons are listed in **bold**. Pictures are indicated in ***bold Italic***.

Index

R
R. P. Scherer, 149, 162
R.R. Donnelley & Sons Company, 186
Railroad Pier, *7*
Raymond James Bank, 192
Raymond James Financial, 171, 192, 194
Raymond James Stadium, 122, 124, *288,* 298
Raytheon Company, 148, 161
Redington Beach, 252, 254
Redington Long Pier, *252*
Redington Shores, 252
Renaissance Vinoy Resort and Golf Club, 18, 27, 29, 33, 56, 59, 70, 132
Republic Bank, 72, 192
Rickey, Branch, 124
Ridgecrest Elementary School, 103
Riviera Bay, 28
Robinson Challenge School, 106
Roebling, Donald, 13
Rolyat Hotel, 10
Ronald McDonald House, *94*
Roosevelt, Theodore, 290
Roser Park, 36
Roser, Charles, 36
Roundabout, *267*
Rouse, Elva, 27
Ruth Eckerd Hall, 16, 265, 272
Ruth, Babe, *11*

S
Safety Harbor Resort & Spa, 278
Safety Harbor, 3, 5, 8, 220, 234, 278
Saint Bartholomew's, 46
Salt Creek Artworks, 64
Salvador Dali Museum, 16, 62, 64, 79, 308
Sands Point neighborhood, *38*
Sawgrass Lake Park, *138,* 139
Schwarzkopf, General Norman, 292
Science Center of Pinellas County, 34, *114,* 149
SCLC Martin Luther King Jr. Drum Major for Justice Parade, *63*
Second Seminole War, 4, 5
security lizard, 66, *68*
Sembler Company, 70, 188
Seminole, 8, 104, 110, 192, 220, 279
Sheraton Sand Key Resort, 256
Shore Acres, 27, 29
Shorecrest Preparatory School, 107
Signature Bank, 192
SmartCenter, 72
Smith & Nephew, 165
Smith Industries, 149
Snell Isle, 27, 28, 29
Snell, C. Perry, 27, 28
Snell Arcade, *76*
SoHo South Gallery and Custom Framing, 80
Somerville, James, 277
Soreno Hotel, 10, 13, 226
South Pasadena, 94, 216, 220, 279
South Straub Park, *72*
South Yacht Basin, *60*
Southeast Little League Regional Headquarters, 279
Southside Fundamental School, 106
SouthTrust Bank, 192
Spa Beach, *12*
Spanish-American War, 290, 292
Sponge Docks, *277,* 278
St. Andrew Russian Orthodox Church, 43, *46*
St. Anthony's Triathlon, *131*
St. Joseph Sound, 277, 280
St. Joseph's Baptist Health Care, 92
St. Louis Browns, 124
St. Louis Cardinals, 12, 124
St. Mary Our Lady of Grace, 40
St. Mary's Roman Catholic Church, 40
St. Nicholas Greek Orthodox Church, 278
St. Pete Beach, 38, 114, 125, 220, 243, 248, 258, 279
St. Petersburg Area Chamber of Commerce, 50, 307
St. Petersburg Bike Club, 134
St. Petersburg Challenge School, 106
St. Petersburg City Economic Development Dept., 309
St. Petersburg City Hall, *82*
St. Petersburg Fire & Rescue, 27
St. Petersburg General Hospital, 94
St. Petersburg High School, *103,* 104
St. Petersburg Historical Society, 56
St. Petersburg International Folk Fair Society (SPIFFS) *46, 62*
St. Petersburg Junior College (SPJC), 12, 33, 104, 110, 112, 279, 306
St. Petersburg Methodist Episcopal Church South, 40
St. Petersburg Municipal Marina, 52
St. Petersburg Museum of Fine Arts, 16, 61, 62, 308
St. Petersburg Museum of History, 67
St. Petersburg Police Department, 26
St. Petersburg Open Air Post Office, *70*
St. Petersburg Suncoast Association of Realtors, 35
St. Petersburg Times, 7, 50, 218, 219, 224
St. Petersburg Woman's Club, 29
St. Petersburg Yacht Club, *51,* 52, 68
St. Petersburg-Clearwater International Airport, 13, 224
St. Petersburg/Clearwater Area Convention and Visitors Bureau, 226
STAR Center, 148, 166
Stavros, Gus, 170
Sterling Research Group, Inc., 83
Stern, Michael, *284*
Stetson University College of Law, *88-89,* 118
Still, Christopher M., painting by, 82, *fold-out*
Straub Park, 60, 62, 64, 66
Straub, William L., 50
Straub, W.L., painting by, *4*
Stumm, Frank, 34
Summit Venture, 224
Sun Time Enterprises, 144
Suncoast Cycling Club, 134
Suncoast Runners Club, 134
Suncoast Seabird Sanctuary, *255, 276*
Sunken Gardens, 18, *82,* 138, 308
Sunset Beach, 11
Sunshine Skyway Bridge, 14, 16, 37, 222, 224
Sunshine Speedway, 276
SunTrust Bank, 72, 208

T
Tampa Bay Buccaneers, 16, 122, 128, 129
Tampa Bay Devil Rays, 18, 122, 124, 126, 127
Tampa Bay Downs, 142, 279
Tampa Bay Estuary Program, 149
Tampa Bay Firestix, 125
Tampa Bay Lightning, 122, 124, 140, 294
Tampa Bay Mutiny, 124, 143
Tampa Bay Partnership, 302
Tampa Bay Performing Arts Center, *284, 288,* 298, 299
Tampa Bay Skating Academy, 279
Tampa Bay Storm, 122, 124
Tampa Bay Water, 308
Tampa Convention Center, 292, 293
Tampa Electric Company, 308
Tampa International Airport, 265, 292
Tampa Museum of Art, *298*
Tampa Port Authority, 216, 290
Tampa Sports Authority, 124
Tampa Theatre, *298*
Tampa Tribune, 224
Tarpon Springs High School, 106
Tarpon Springs, 4, 6, 8, 18, 106, 110, 134, 234, 258, 277, 278, 280
Taste of Pinellas, *62*
Taylor, Henry, 33, 40
Taylor, Jack, 27
Tech Data Corporation, 163
Temple Beth-El, *44*
Tenet Health System, 94
The Alligator, 13
The Jungle, 27, 33, 34
The Pier Aquarium, 52
The Pier, 9, 11, 16, 40, 52, 82, 308
Thomas Kinkade Signature Gallery, 64
Tierra Verde, 38
Tilden, Bill, 132
Time Warner Communications, 226, 228
Times Bayfront Arena, 16, 52
Times Publishing Company, 72
Tocobago Indians, 3, 37, 139
Tomlinson, E.H., 102
Tomlinson, Peter, 43
Toronto Blue Jays, 125, 277
Tour of Pinellas, 134
Tourtelot Bros. Realty, 22
Tradewinds Island Resorts, 246, 247
Treasure Island Tennis and Yacht Club, 248
Treasure Island, 11, 248, 264
Trinity Lutheran Church, 43
Tropical Shores, 36, 37
Tropicana Field, 18, 56, 122, 234
Twin Brooks Golf Course, 132
Tyrone Square Mall, 16, 33, 226, 231

U
U.S. Coast Guard, 16, 52, 222, 224
U.S. Postal Service Center, 292
University of South Florida (USF), 16, 72, 76, 98, 110, 116, 124, 148, 149, 192, 216, 294, 295, 298, 306
University of Tampa, 286, 288
Updegraff Lasik Vision, 100
Upham, Nathaniel J., 29
USF College of Marine Science, 149
USF College of Medicine, 98
U.S. Geological Survey Center, 72

V
Val-Pak, 170
Van Bibber, Dr. W.C., 7
Vencor Hospital, 99
Venetian Isles, 28, 29
Verizon, 216
Veterans' Administration Center, 12, 72, 139
Vinoy Hotel, 18
Vinoy Park, 10, 13, 33, 60
Vinoy Place, 18, 58, 70
Vinoy Yacht Basin, 52
Vintage Antiques & Emporium Antique Mall, 232

W
Wagon Wheel Flea Market, 234, 276
Walter Fuller Park, 134
War Veterans' Memorial Park, 139
Webb's City, 11
Webb, Doc, 11
Wedding, Stephenson & Ibarguen Architects, Inc., 17
Weedon Island, 3, 139
West Pharmaceutical Company, 164
Westin Innisbrook Resort, 260
WFLA, 11
WFLA-TV, 224
William R. Hough Company, 72
Williams, General John C., 5, 6, 36
Women's Tennis Association, 76, 132
Woodlawn, 32
World Trade Center, 216
World War I, 13, 62, 124, 290
World War II, 13, 62, 124, 290
WPA, 12, 292
WSUN, 14
WTSP-TV, 227

Y
Yacht Club Estates, 38
Ybor City, 290, 294
Ybor, V. Martinez, 290
YMCA, 32

Corporate and Institutional Patrons are listed in **bold**. Pictures are indicated in ***bold Italic.***

Pinellas County Chambers of Commerce

Chambers of Commerce, professionally staffed with memberships of 250 or more, ranked in order by membership size.

St. Petersburg Area Chamber of Commerce
100 Second Avenue N, Suite 150
St. Petersburg, FL 33701
P.O. Box 1371, St. Petersburg, FL 33731
Phone (727) 821-4069, Fax 895-6326
Information line (727) 821-4715
www.stpete.com
email: mcornish@mindspring.com

Clearwater Regional Chamber of Chamber of Commerce
1130 Cleveland Street
P.O. Box 2457, Clearwater, FL 33765
Phone (727) 461-0011, Fax 449-2889
www.clearwaterflorida.org
email: info@clearwaterflorida.org

Gulf Beaches of Tampa Bay Chamber of Commerce
(800) 944-1847
www.gulfbeaches-tampabay.com
email: gulfbchs@gte.net

Indian Rocks Beach Office
105 Fifth Avenue North
Indian Rocks Beach, FL 33708
Phone (727) 595-4575, Fax 595-4575

Madeira Beach Office
501 -150th Avenue, Madeira Beach, FL 33708
Phone (727) 391-7373

St. Pete Beach Office (exec. offices)
6990 Gulf Blvd., St. Pete Beach, FL 33706
Phone (727) 360-6957, Fax 360-2233

Treasure Island Office
152 - 108th Avenue, Treasure Island, FL 33706
Phone (727) 367-4529

Pinellas Park/Mid-County Chamber of Commerce
5851 Park Boulevard, Pinellas Park, FL 33781
Phone (727) 544-4777, Fax 545-1678
www.pinellasparkchamber.com
email: ppmc@ij.net

Greater Dunedin Chamber of Commerce
301 Main Street, Dunedin, FL 34698
Phone (727) 733-3197, Fax 734-8942
www.dunedin-fl.com
email: chamber@dunedin-fl.com

Greater Largo Chamber of Commerce
151 Third Street NW, Largo, FL 33770
Phone (727) 584-2321, Fax 586-3112
www.largococ.com
email: largococ@gte.net

Greater Palm Harbor Area Chamber of Commerce
1151 Nebraska Ave., Palm Harbor, FL 34683
Phone (727) 784-4287, Fax 786-2336
www.palmharborcc.org
email: phchamber@palmharborcc.org

Tarpon Springs Chamber of Commerce
11 East Orange St., Tarpon Springs, FL 34689
Phone (727) 937-6109, Fax 937-2879
www.tarponsprings.com
email: tscc@tbi.net

Greater Seminole Area Chamber of Commerce
8400 113th Street N
P.O. Box 3337, Seminole, FL 33772
Phone (727) 392-3245, Fax 397-7753
www.seminole-chamber.org
email: seminole@seminole-chamber.org

Greater Oldsmar Chamber of Commerce
163 State Road 580 W, Oldsmar, FL 34677
Phone (813) 855-4233, Fx 854-1237
www.oldsmarchamber.org
email: kogartland@juno.com

Safety Harbor Chamber of Commerce
200 Main Street. Safety Harbor, FL 34695
Phone (727) 726-2890, Fax 726-2733
www.safetyharborchamber.com
email: anpiccone@safetyharborchamber.com

Reference Sources

BOOKS AND PUBLICATIONS
Arsenault, Raymond. *St. Petersburg and the Florida Dream 1888-1950.* The Donning Company, Norfolk, VA 1998.
Bothwell, Dick. Sunrise 200, *A Lively Look at St. Petersburg's Past.* Times Publishing Company, St. Petersburg, FL 1975.
Dunn, Hampton. *Yesterday's St. Petersburg.* E.A. Seemann Publishing, Inc., Miami, FL 1973.
Dunn, Hampton. *Yesterday's Tampa.* E.A. Seemann Publishing, Inc., Miami, FL 1972.
Fuller, Walter P. *St. Petersburg and Its People.* Great Outdoors Publishing Co., St. Petersburg, FL 1972.
Grismer, Karl H. *The Story of St. Petersburg.* P.K. Smith & Company, St. Petersburg, FL 1948.
Marth, Del. *St. Petersburg: Once Upon A Time.* The City of St. Petersburg, 1976.
Slaght Gould, Rita. *Pioneer St. Petersburg.* Page Creations, 1987.
Young, June Hurley. *Florida's Pinellas Peninsula.* Southern Heritage Press, Inc., St. Petersburg, FL 1996.
Florida Paradise - Newcomer and Relocation Journal *A St. Petersburg Area Chamber of Commerce publication, 1999.*
1999 Tampa Bay Corporate Guide. *Tampa Bay Partnership publication, 1999.*
2000 Tampa Bay Corporate Guide. *Tampa Bay Partnership publication, 2000.*
2000 Tampa Bay Technology Directory, *Tampa Bay Partnership publication, 2000.*

ARTICLES AND SPECIAL REPORTS
"An Historical Look At A Place In The Sun." Pamphlet sponsored by a grant from the Paradyne Corporation.
"Banking & the Consumer Revolution." *Maddux Report,* April 2000.
City Centennial special edition. *St. Petersburg Times,* June 8, 1988.
"Florida stays on the leading edge." *Business Florida 2000,* published by Enterprise Florida.
"High-rise hopes." *St. Petersburg Times, Neighborhood Times,* August 31-September 2, 1997.
"Hooking Up Business," by Michael Braga. *St. Petersburg Times,* July 31, 2000.
"In the Air and In Your Face." Tampa Bay's *Maddux Report,* December, 1998.
"Lyceum visitors to remember" *Neighborhood Business, Times,* May 7, 2000.
"Market Facts Guide." *The Business Journal,* December 31, 1999.
"Pinellas County Historical Background." Prepared by The Pinellas County Planning Department, April 1995.
"Planning to pack the pews." *Neighborhood Times,* March 16, 2000.
"STAR Bright Land Light." Corporate Report: Pinellas County, *Maddux Report,* December 1999.
"St. Petersburg Sees a New Dawn." *Maddux Report,* September 1999.
"Sunny Skies and Silicon Dreams," Michael Reich, *University of South Florida Magazine,* Winter 1999.
"The Power of Thinking Big." Pamphlet of the University of South Florida.
"The Soul of St. Petersburg," by Jon Wilson. *St. Petersburg Times, Neighborhood Times,* January 2-4, 2000.
"Pinellas County - Preparing for the challenges of the 21st Century." 1999-2000 Calendar: Pinellas County Board of County Commissioners.
Untitled. Archived story on downtown churches by Waveney Ann Moore, *St. Petersburg Times,* April 12, 1998.

WEB SITES
Enterprise Florida, Inc. - http://www.floridabusiness.com (May 2000)
Florida Department of State Division of Historical Resources - http://dhr.dos.state.fl.us (March 2000)
Florida State Archives Photographic Collection - http://www.dos.state.fl.us/fpc (April 2000)
Gateway Chamber of Commerce - http://www.gatewaychamber.org/gccprofiledevelopment.htm (May 2000)
Greater Tampa Chamber of Commerce - http://www.tampachamber.com (April 2000)
Hoover's Inc. - http://www.hovers.com (April 2000)
Pinellas County Economic Development - http://www.siliconbay.org (April 2000)
Pinellas County Government Board of County Commissioners - http://www.co.pinellas.fl.us/bcc (May 2000)
Pinellas County Schools - http://www.pinellas.k12.fl.us (March 2000)
Poynter Institute - http://poynter.org (May 2000)
South Florida Regional Planning Council - http://www.sfrpc.com/websites/menu3.htm (May 2000)
St. Petersburg Area Chamber of Commerce - http://www.stpete.com (March 2000)
St. Petersburg Black History - http://nelson.usf.edu/mclin/about.html (June 2000)
St. Petersburg International Folk Fair Society - http://www.spiffs.org (June 2000)
St. Petersburg-Clearwater Convention and Visitors Bureau - http://www.floridasbeach.com (March 2000)
Suncoast 2000 - http://www.suncoast2000.com/pinellas.htm (March 2000)
Tampa Bay Partnership - http://www.tampabay.org (April 2000)
Tampa Bay Water - http://www.tampabaywater.org (June 2000)
Tampa/Hillsborough Convention and Visitors Association - http://www.thcva.com (April 2000)

Note: This is a partial list. In instances where several pages within a web site were used for reference, only the home page is listed here.

Corporate and Institutional Patrons

Admiral Farragut Academy	108
AEGON Equity Group	196
All Children's Hospital	93
American Technical Molding	155
American Tool & Mold	154
AmSouth Bank	199
Avaya Communications	158-159
Bank of America	197
Bankers Insurance Group	69
Bayfront-St. Anthony's Health Care	96
BayWalk	54-55
Belleview Biltmore Resort & Spa	19
Bruce Watters Jewelry	15
Busch Gardens - Tampa Bay	300-301
Business Journal Serving Greater Tampa Bay	229
Canterbury School of Florida	109
Capitol Marketing Concepts	182
Carlton Fields	198
Catalina Marketing Corporation	176-177
CBB Architects	200
Ceridian	172-173
Clearwater Marine Aquarium	271
Clearwater Municipal Marina	270
Cloisters on Beach Drive	74
Colliers Arnold	212
Countryside Mall	235
Cox Target Media	180
Crown Management Auto Dealership Group	185
Digital LightWave	152
Don CeSar Beach Resort & Spa	244
Durango Oak Fire Steakhouse	184
Echelon	175
Eckerd College	115
Elreha Printed Circuits Corporation	153
Equifax Payment Services	181
Eva-Tone	178
First Presbyterian Church	42-43
Florencia	71
Florida Aquarium	291
Florida Holocaust Museum	81
Florida International Museum	73
Florida Power Corp.	20-21
Franklin Templeton Investments	204
George F. Young, Inc.	211
Glass Canvas Gallery	65
GulfCoast Certified Development Corporation	310
H. Lee Moffitt Cancer Center	95
Hillsborough County Aviation Authority (TIA)	289
Hilton St. Petersburg	77
Home Shopping Network	174
Honeywell, Inc.	156
Ice Palace	141
IMRglobal Corp.	268-269
Irwin Contracting, Inc.	187
Jabil Circuit	150-151
JMC Communities	210
Keswick Christian School	111
Kirkland, Russ, Murphy & Tapp, PA	205
Lowry Park Zoo	297
Mahaffey Theater for the Performing Arts	85
Mease Health Care	97
Mellitta USA, Inc.	157
Merrill Lynch	201
Mortgage Investors Corporation	202
Morton Plant Hospital	97
Museum of Fine Arts	61
Museum of Science & Industry	296
New York Yankees/Legends Field	136
Nielsen Media Research	183
Northern Trust Bank	203
Northwestern Mutual Financial Network	207
Operation PAR Inc.	101
P. Buckley Moss Gallery	75
Palms of Pasadena Hospital	91
ParkSide	233
Pasadena Community Church	45
Payment Systems for Credit Unions, Inc.	179
Peoples Gas System	223
Pinellas County Economic Development	311
Pinellas County Education Foundation	105
Pinellas Science Technology and Research Center (STAR)	166
Pinewood Cultural Park	274-275
Primex Technologies	160
R.R. Donnelley & Sons Company	186
Raymond James Financial	194-195
Raytheon Company	161
Renaissance Vinoy Resort and Golf Club	166
RP Scherer	162
Ruth Eckerd Hall	272
Salvador Dali Museum	79
Sembler Company	188
Sheraton Sand Key Resort	256
Shorecrest Preparatory School	107
Smith & Nephew	165
SoHo South Gallery and Custom Framing	80
SouthTrust Bank	206
St. Petersburg Area Chamber of Commerce	307
St. Petersburg City Economic Development Dept.	309
St. Petersburg Junior College	112-113
St. Petersburg Museum of History	67
St. Petersburg Suncoast Association of Realtors	35
St. Petersburg Times	218-219
St. Petersburg-Clearwater International Airport	225
St. Petersburg/ClearwaterArea Convention & Visitors Bureau	236
Sterling Research Group, Inc.	83
Stetson University College of Law	118
Sun Time Enterprises	144
SunTrust Bank	208
Tampa Bay Buccaneers	128-129
Tampa Bay Devil Rays	126-127
Tampa Bay Lightning	140-141
Tampa Bay Mutiny	143
Tampa Bay Partnership	302
Tampa Bay Performing Arts Center	299
Tampa Convention Center	293
Tech Data Corporation	163
The Arts Center	86
Time Warner Communications	228
Tourtelot Bros. Realty	22
Tradewinds Island Resorts	246-247
Tyrone Square Mall	231
University of South Florida	116-117
Updegraff Lasik Vision	100
Vencor Hospital	99
Vinoy Place	58
Vintage Antiques & Emporium Antique Mall	232
Wedding, Stephenson & Ibarguen Architects, Inc.	17
West Pharmaceutical Company	164
Westin Innisbrook Resort	260
William R. Hough & Co.	72
WTSP-TV	227

Photography Contributors

Aerial Innovations
Access Stock Photography
 www.accessstock.com
Charles Alaimo
Stan Ashbrook
City of St. Petersburg
Chris Davis
Florida Photographic Collection
Ty B. Heston Photography
Jennifer Holcombe
David MacFarlane
Janie Machinchick

Joan Marcus Photographer
 (Actors Ted Reagan and Rebecca Pitcher)
Philadelphia Phillies - Al Tielemans
Pinellas County
Pinellas County Hisorical Museum
Bay Care Health Systems
Robert Rogers/Tampa Bay Devil Rays
Shay Routh
Thomas Gessler
Herb Snitzer
St. Petersburg Junior College
St. Petersburg Museum of History

St. Petersburg Times
St. Petersburg/Clearwater Area
 Convention and Visitors Bureau
Suncoast Seabird Sanctuary
Tampa Bay Buccaneers
Tampa/Hillsborough Convention and
 Visitors Association
Toronto Blue Jays
Jim Tuten
University of South Florida